OJIBWE SINGERS

OJIBWE SINGERS

Hymns, Grief, and a Native Culture in Motion

▲▲▲▲▲▲

MICHAEL D. MCNALLY

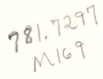

OXFORD
UNIVERSITY PRESS

2000

OXFORD
UNIVERSITY PRESS

Oxford   New York

Athens   Auckland   Bangkok   Bogotá   Buenos Aires   Calcutta
Cape Town   Chennai   Dar es Salaam   Delhi   Florence   Hong Kong   Istanbul
Karachi   Kuala Lumpur   Madrid   Melbourne   Mexico City   Mumbai
Nairobi   Paris   São Paulo   Singapore   Taipei   Tokyo   Toronto   Warsaw

and associated companies in
Berlin   Ibadan

Copyright © 2000 by Michael D. McNally

Published by Oxford University Press, Inc.
198 Madison Avenue, New York, New York 10016

Oxford is a registered trademark of Oxford University Press

Library of Congress Cataloging-in-Publication Data
McNally, Michael D.
Ojibwe singers : hymns, grief, and a native culture in motion / Michael D. McNally.
p.   cm. — (Religion in America series)
Includes bibliographical references.
ISBN 0-19-513464-8
1. Ojibwa Indians—Religion   2. Ojibwa Indians—Cultural assimilation.
3. Hymns, Ojibwa—History and criticism.   I. Title.   II. Religion in America series
(Oxford University Press)
E99.C6 M35   1999
782.27′089′973—dc21   99-039993

Portions of chapters 3 and 5 have been previously published in Michael McNally,
"The Uses of Hymn Singing at White Earth: Toward a History of Practice,"
in *Lived Religion in America*, ed. David D. Hall, pp 133–159.
Copyright © 1997 by Princeton University Press.
Reprinted by permission of Princeton University Press.

1 3 5 7 9 8 6 4 2

Printed in the United States of America
on acid-free paper

FOR MY PARENTS,
MILES W. MCNALLY AND MARJORIE GUENTHER MCNALLY

AND IN MEMORY OF
LARRY CLOUD MORGAN (1938–1999)

PREFACE

▲▲▲▲▲▲

I n public speeches, Ojibwe people often establish authority by saying how they came to know what they know. Sometimes authority is based on a teacher or some elder who entrusted them with knowledge. Other times, authority is based on life experiences. In either case, claiming authority involves pointing publicly to its limits. This study is a document of my reflections on archival research and two cumulative years of fieldwork between 1990 and 1995, with periodic visits and telephone calls made thereafter. As such, it is much more, and much less, than a faithful record of what happened. Because going to Minnesota meant returning home, as well as going into the field, the study also is a product of my own complicated relationship to that land and the people indigenous to that land, the Ojibwe, or Anishinaabe. For example, many of my field notes—indeed much of the manuscript—were written not at the White Earth Reservation but at my family's northern Minnesota summer home on Gull Lake, several hours to the southeast of the Ojibwe reservation. I had spent nearly every summer of my life at this place and had always known it was the site of the first major Episcopalian mission in the old Northwest established in 1852. The paradox is that much of this book about the dispossession and resilience of Ojibwe people was conceived and written within the safe and familiar confines of a home that my grandfather built in 1935, not sixty years after an entire Ojibwe band was removed from their fishing and sugar camps there to White Earth in what some call the Ojibwe Trail of Tears. A number of my White Earth collaborators have visited that beautiful place. They are descendants only two generations removed from its original Anishinaabe inhabitants, people who buried their relatives and who sang Ojibwe hymns within earshot of the place that is so tied up with my own identity that most of my dreams are situated there. Sometimes I chuckle nervously and sometimes I laugh aloud when one of those White Earth collaborators, Dan Kier, kids me: "Mike, tell your dad the lease is up and we're coming home."

Perhaps more than any methodological premeditations, it has been such contingencies of the human encounters in fieldwork that have given shape to my conclusions. On the basis of Anishinaabe ways of knowing, I will argue that these contingencies can be considered possibilities for the authority of my interpretation and not simply constraints upon it. More specifically, my narrative of Ojibwe hymn singing is avowedly fragmentary, local, interested, collaborative, and accountable.

First, much of what I have learned about Ojibwe singing I owe to a small group of elders at White Earth village, and, in particular, to my primary mentors, the late Larry Cloud Morgan and Erma Vizenor. My sojourn with the communities has been a brief one, amounting to two cumulative years in Minnesota, and much of that on the road in northern Minnesota at the White Earth and Leech Lake Reservations, as well as on longer trips with the singers to such places as New York City and West Virginia. Because much of the field experience was rooted in community work, my research has been less a matter of relations between "fieldworker" and "informant" than of those between fellow community organizers. Indeed, research interests have often taken a back seat. While this has proved frustrating at times, I have learned there is an advantage to the back seat. When native teachers were at the helm, I believe I was introduced to places in the life of the community where a more systematic, preconceived research program would not have taken me.

The career of my language study illustrates this well. Originally interested in research on nineteenth-century cultural encounter in missions, I set out to learn the Ojibwe language in order to provide some interpretive leverage on the documentary record as seen through missionary eyes. Before my fieldwork began, I proposed an arrangement with Larry Cloud Morgan for tutoring me in the language and raised the issue of "informant fees." He replied that because the Ojibwe language was not for sale, taking money would violate his value system. We eventually agreed that I would offer my organizing and writing skills in the service of his various political projects in exchange for language lessons in the car and at times set aside during the week. This agreement was in keeping with my desire to situate my understanding of the religious life of native communities in the fuller context of their social, economic, and political experiences.

Larry and I soon found ourselves to be liaisons between a grassroots political movement at White Earth and its legal, financial, and moral support in the Twin Cities. It involved writing press releases, securing *pro bono* legal support for three civil disobedience arrests, and, among other things, stirring stews, scrubbing pots, and stacking wood. With so much pressing work to be done, I seldom had the energy to ask questions relevant to my own language work. On our frequent five-hour drives to and from the reservation, Larry might quiz me on the Ojibwe words for animals and trees, but more commonly we were too exhausted to do any systematic language training. I remember several times when we drove for more than an hour without exchanging even one word. In such moments, physical and emotional exhaustion sharpened my awareness of what was at stake at White Earth. In the midst of these poignant silences with Larry, I perhaps learned the more valuable lessons about life at White Earth and, by extension, about the significance of hymns. I was generally comfortable with the spirit of Larry's silent pedagogy, but there were those embarrassing moments when I lost my cool and became frustrated that I was not learning enough of the language or getting it fast enough to keep up with my accustomed pace of language "acquisition." At such times, I was, in Ojibwe idiom, acting *mindawe*—discontented like a tired toddler who knows not what it wants but who is resolved no less to make its position known. Needless to say, in Ojibwe pedagogical traditions, a *mindawe* student is not in a worthy position for cultural learning. In such moments, my teachers were appropriately not forthcoming. This approach to work in the field has resulted in the collection of fewer musicological "data" and less facility with Ojibwe grammar. Yet bringing my learning more into line with the indigenous pedagogy of Anishinaabe oral traditions and rooting it in community work has brought me more in tune with Ojibwe hymns.

Second, the study is decidedly local in range and scope. I focus rather narrowly on one practice—hymn singing—in order to manage a more coherent narrative of Anishinaabe religious and cultural change. The research is situated on one reservation and primarily in one village on that reservation. This makes good sense historically, since White Earth was where the tradition began in earnest, but there are a number of singing groups on other reservations with stories that differ considerably. A localized case study comes at the cost of a more comprehensive view of how other singing groups have chosen differently from historical alternatives, but there are important benefits. Because conversations related to my research occur with people I already know, there is a greater possibility that the material gleaned from those exchanges are truer to context. Moreover, a case study is better trained on the texture of hymn singing, and on the particular reasons that particular individuals have turned to singing. Because I want to emphasize the agency of Anishinaabe actors in the ritualization of the hymns, the local does perhaps most effectively evoke the general.

Third, my narrative is interested. Contemporary sociologies of knowledge teach that because all thinking is perspectival, there is no disinterested study. This is everywhere and always a politically charged process, all the more so when one is working within native communities like White Earth, which are so divided. By virtue of an emerging friendship with Larry Cloud Morgan, from the moment I arrived at White Earth, my work has been identified closely with the people and issues of Camp Justice, a grassroots movement organized in July of 1990 to address concerns about sovereignty, land claims, and tribal governance. Given these personal and political commitments, I try to be as fair as possible to differing points of view within the reservation, perhaps to an extent that will frustrate my teachers and collaborators. Wider circles of readers will perhaps be taken aback by the tone I take at certain moments in this study because my point of view on affairs at White Earth reflects my interactions with collaborators from certain segments of the community. I nonetheless submit that what at first glance might appear to be a constraint carries the potential for a deeper, because more honestly embedded, understanding. The organizing work has certainly brought me closer to a standpoint from which at least certain White Earth people view their world and act upon it. Finally, one cannot spend a period of time as a guest in a native community without coming to feel strongly about the injustices that native peoples face on a daily basis. I would hope that this volume—as it tries to recover a fuller sense of the agency of native people—does justice to the enormity of the injustice.

The interested nature of my narrative appears most problematically at the juncture between ethnography and historical studies. Trained as a historian, I strive to suspend present interests as much as possible in order to take subjects seriously as historical actors who make choices among limited alternatives. In this respect, I read archival documents with a sympathy for the best of intentions with which missionaries dedicated themselves. At times, I even felt a sense of kinship with them, for, while I hardly share their desire to change the spiritual lives of native people, I do venture across similar cultural borders. This sympathy, becoming of a historian, rubs up against my fieldwork encounters with people who daily face the consequences of that history of dispossession. White Earth people seldom have the luxury to distinguish the missionaries' better intentions from the outcomes of the assimilation campaign. Perhaps the instincts of the historian and the commitments of an interested fieldworker can generate creative tension to illuminate both projects.

Fourth, the study is collaborative. At the expense perhaps of more systematic inquiry, I have made methodological choices to guard against what I consider the ethical and epistemological dangers of the ethnographer-"informant" relationship. Although power relationships rooted in these classic norms have surely figured in the equation, I have tried diligently to imagine my informants instead as my teachers. Ethically, my exchanges with collaborators have largely taken place while we engaged in common projects. Although I have tried to share my resources with the community as freely as their hospitality was shared with me, I do not consider the exchanges to have been matters of informant fees. Epistemologically, none of my collaborators can be considered to represent "the native point of view." Their respective views are shaped by different social locations and different agendas. In keeping with my conviction that the Ojibwe community has its own theories for how culture ought to be taught and learned, I have tried my best to make these collaborators my teachers. The insights about hymn singing they confide in me are not raw data. They are interpretations in their own right—sometimes even poetic ones—and often blur the line between the descriptive and the prescriptive. My own emplotment of hymn singing in narratives of development and meaning brings collaborators and teachers to think about this tradition from a new perspective.

Fifth, the study is embedded in a network of accountabilities. Societies that rely extensively on oral traditions and that live in closely knit communities exercise considerable control over who receives what knowledge, how it is used, and when and where it is expressed. Several different structures of accountability give shape to this research at the levels of fieldwork and writing. In terms of fieldwork, I have made a choice to record neither music nor interviews. While recordings would more reliably discipline my memory and make possible a more thorough mining of the musical data, I believe my inquiry has enjoyed a more privileged position by having observed native protocols for learning. As concerns the recording of music, there may be a point in the future when extensive recording of the hymns will be welcome, but that time has not yet come.

I imagine my audience to include people at White Earth, and thus I try to represent my experiences of life at White Earth in such a way that my collaborators and teachers might give their consent. I have shared drafts at various stages of this process with these collaborators and have tried to incorporate spoken criticisms in a manner that can contribute to a reflexive tone. Because Ojibwe people often convey their more trenchant criticisms through resistant silence, I also have tried to incorporate those silent criticisms.

Of course, each of these five points stands in tension with another set of allegiances that I have to the world of scholarship. My work is only partly collaborative in that the reflections here set forward are my own, made in conversation but not in concert with my native teachers. Indeed, they issue out of wider circles of conversation with other teachers and other scholars. My work is interested, but only partially so, in that the success of my scholarship is relatively unaffected by the outcome of contemporary politics at White Earth. The scope of my research is local, but I avowedly use the local to make more global points about how religious practices help negotiate culture change. Finally, my authority may rest on perspectival and fragmentary experience, but it also relies on the reader's judgment as to the soundness of the narrative constructed at a considerable geographical and temporal remove from those initial experiences. I invite you to entertain the current study as a tentative narrative of a classically nonnarrated ritualized practice—a rehearsal of other people's rehearsals.

Two prefatory matters are important. First is a note on my orthography for the Ojibwe language. When citing historical and secondary texts, I have used the orthographic transcriptions as they appear in the sources. In all other cases, I have relied on the currently accepted orthography found in John Nichols and Earl Nyholm, *Concise Dictionary of Minnesota Ojibwe* (Minneapolis: University of Minnesota Press, 1995). When this orthography is used, it is indicated in the text with italics. While variant spellings may seem confusing, I am reminded by my Ojibwe consultants that it helps underscore the fundamental orality of the Ojibwe language. Second, any author royalties earned from sales of this book, limited as they may be, will be donated directly to a Minnesota nonprofit organization dedicated to the ongoing vitality of Ojibwe language and culture: Ganewendan Ojibwemowin.

Ann Arbor   M. D. M.
December 1999

ACKNOWLEDGMENTS

▲▲▲▲▲▲

Publication of this book marks the culmination of a life-changing eight years of my life. The work has challenged me to integrate academic, practical, and human concerns; it has rewarded me with the company and collaboration of several circles of teachers and colleagues. I must first acknowledge the patience and teaching of the circle of elders and others at the White Earth Reservation, including Charlie Aiken, Marge and Lowell Bellanger, Josephine Degroat, Sylvia Gale, Charles Hanks Jr., Margaret Hanks, Juanita Jackson, Dan Kier, Marge MacDonald, Jack Potter, and Ethelbert Vanwert. None can know the full impact their stories and lives have made on me. In particular, I am grateful to Erma Vizenor and the late Larry Cloud Morgan. Although Larry died before seeing this book in print, his wisdom, example, and spirit animate whatever is true in it. He taught (across boundaries of language, culture, and class), that everything we have is a gift. He was a gift.

At Harvard, David Hall ably and enthusiastically directed the project as a doctoral thesis, while allowing it to develop in conversation with my teachers at White Earth. William Hutchison lent unflagging support all along the way. Lawrence Sullivan and Kay Kaufman Shelemay offered helpful criticisms and comments. I am indebted to Christopher Vecsey for originally putting me in touch with Cloud Morgan and for giving Anishinaabe people some reason to do business with nonnative academics. Inés Talamantez miraculously appeared at Harvard after my first summer at White Earth, restoring my faith in the possibility for an engaged academic study of native religious traditions. Bob Orsi and Ann Braude sharpened the focus. John Nichols graciously looked over translations of the Ojibwe hymn texts and selected portions of the manuscript. Roland Delattre, Marilyn Grunkemeyer, Stephen Marini, Joel Martin, the late William McLaughlin, James Treat, and the anonymous reviewers for Oxford University Press have been generous with comments and criticisms on drafts of chapters. Cynthia Read and others at Oxford University Press have been supportive and helpful. As the reader will appreciate in chapter 3, I am indebted to two scholars in particular, whose work appeared while the present book was yet a work in progress. Melissa Meyer's detailed study of dispossession and factionalism, *The White Earth Tragedy*, appeared in 1994, precisely when my fieldwork and archival work were maturing into a dissertation. Rebecca Kugel's examination of leadership at White Earth and elsewhere in Minnesota, *To Be the Main Leaders of*

Our People, appeared in 1998 when I was making final revisions on the manuscript, enriching my understanding of archives we mutually researched and confirming a number of conclusions. I sincerely hope this book is as helpful to these scholars as their work has been to me. Robert Ward and Heather Eisenhardt of E.M.U. were good enough to generate the three maps.

The following friends and colleagues have challenged and supported this work immeasurably: Anne Addington, Judy Avery, David Bailey, Courtney Bender, Chris Coble, Margaret Gillespie, Rebecca Gould, Marie Griffith, Joseph Harney, Steven Holmes, Larry Gross, Tom Hodge, Tracey Hucks, Nick Kurzon, David Lamberth, John McGreevy, the Morelands, John O'Keefe, Mark Severseike, Craig Townsend, Ted Trost, Stephen Young, and other members of Harvard's American Religion Colloquium. Because my fieldwork also represented a coming home of sorts, I enjoyed once again the generous hospitality and support of my parents and other members of the McNally family. Finally, I feel immeasurably grateful for my life partnership with Devon Anderson. When this project began, before we had met, I had no inkling how the project would, among other things, bring me to my wife and the Episcopal Church that she serves as a priest. Her support, trust, and keen reader's eye have carried this project through to print, and for the delights intellectual, spiritual, and otherwise, that she brought to the task, I am ever thankful.

With so many able commentators and critics, one would think I would be free of all errors of commission or omission. Needless to say, those that do remain are my own. Research and writing have been made possible by the generous support of the Lilly Endowment's Lived Religion initiative, the Louisville Institute for the Study of Protestantism and American Culture, the Mellon Foundation, the Roothbert Fund, Harvard's Committee on the Study of Religion, Graduate School of Arts and Sciences, and Longfellow Project, the T.C.U. Research and Creative Activities Fund, and the E.M.U. Office of Research and Development and Graduate Studies Research Fund.

CONTENTS

▲▲▲▲▲▲

OJIBWE SINGERS

INTRODUCTION AND
OVERVIEW

▲▲▲▲▲▲

A WAKE, 1994

A blue haze of cigarette smoke, backlit by the bare bulbs of an old ceiling light fixture, disabused me of any expectations for the exotic in this Native American ceremony. There was, though, an enormous gravity in the room, a sense of urgency that
was tangible with each sigh heard. After all, thirty or so of us had gathered in this
stark place in the city of Minneapolis to mourn the victim of a senseless murder. It
was a funeral wake, a Native American funeral wake, held in a storefront building
that served the people of Franklin Avenue as a soup kitchen by day. Shallow birchbark trays filled with free cigarettes (tobacco, *asemaa*) and candy (sugar, *ziinzibaak-
wad*) were laid out for all to enjoy, whether living or dead.

Though far from the reservation of the man's youth, his wake was held in the
heart of Minneapolis's native community. Its main artery, Franklin Avenue, had
been his home for many years, and it was to become his deathbed. In the drugstore
parking lot, just across Franklin from where we were gathered, the man had been
kicked to death. The boys who did it evidently had not realized how his internal organs were already under siege after years of drinking. Because he had grown distant
from his family over the years, it took the coroner several days to find someone to
claim the body.

The undertaker had tried to hide the contusions on the face, but they nonetheless bore silent witness to his painful death. The body was tenderly wrapped in warm,
colorful blankets, and bathed in the aromas of smoldering sage and cedar. The body
was also embraced by the prayers of a community gathered in his memory, prayers
signified with pinches of tobacco, offerings that, in turn, were gathered in a birchbark tray on the body's chest. In attendance were his street friends, family members,
and people like me, who had come to support our friend Larry Cloud Morgan, the
man's brother.

I sat down next to an older woman who looked lonely. After a pause, she described herself as the widow of a longtime friend of the deceased. "They used to
drink a lot," she said in a voice that loved them no less, "it was real hard sometimes."
Our conversation tapered off, and we sat in silence for some time. A tremor kept her
lower jaw in constant motion, but her eyes were trained straight ahead on some
pleasant or painful memory.

Wakes are important gatherings today among the Ojibwe people, also known as the Ojibwa, Chippewa, or, in their own tongue, Anishinaabe, and they have been for some time.[1] Nineteenth-century missionaries remarked on the importance their Ojibwe hosts placed on the all night watches over the body with wailing, singing, drumming, and feasting. Today, such wakes become moments when native people gather to mark deaths that are often violent, untimely, and senseless—to reflect together on how and why the old are burying the young and to generate the wherewithal to keep doing something about it.

As dusk began to settle on Franklin Avenue, more people arrived. Some visited with one another. Some stood by the body, taking pinches of tobacco and offering quiet prayers for the spirit. A number of the man's comrades from the street had arrived to pay their respects. One of them went to the body and, with wildly exaggerated gestures, raised an offering of tobacco to honor the spirit of his friend. The jarring image brought our attention to the indeterminacy of the man's death, what it could possibly mean, and whether there was, in the presence of a such a body and such a mourner, much possibility for an Anishinaabe future. Larry sat quietly, and looked on.

The still atmosphere changed upon the arrival of the Ojibwe Singers, in this case an extended family of perhaps twelve people led by a stately old woman. Some lived in the Twin Cities. Others had driven four hours from the Leech Lake Reservation to sing at the wake. They took their seats at a long table that had been reserved for them at one end of the room. In her own good time, the white-haired woman began to chant the syllables of an Ojibwe hymn set to a haunting tune. Others in her family joined in. Unaccompanied, in unison, the voices lingered so long on each syllable that more than five minutes transpired before the last verse reached its close.

> Keget na nin gi-nibotag
> Ga-nanandawiit?
> Kichi mamakadakumig,
> Nin go gi onjined.[2]

The younger ones followed phonetic translations of the hymns in well-worn little hymnbooks. Others sang largely from memory. Only a very few in the room were fluent enough in the Ojibwe language to understand the lexical meanings of the songs, but that seemed to matter little. It was more important that the singers had come and that they were singing. The singers paused between each song, creating spaces of silence. The hum of a ventilator fan and the occasional siren on Franklin Avenue heightened the sense that the silence of the occasional pauses made by older singers between songs meant something.

During one of these pauses, Larry stood to speak. With the sense of poetry, timing, and silence that had already established his reputation for eloquence, he acknowledged how the difficulty of his brother's life was a difficulty shared by many in the room and how they nonetheless needed to remember that, whatever the circumstances, they remain "a *good* people." As he took his seat again, another slow song emerged.

The singers performed some fourteen hymns in this manner. One of the hymns, set to the tune of "Jesus Loves Me," included two English verses, and some of us sang quietly along. Otherwise, the songs were entirely in the Ojibwe language. Although after some difficulty I could make out the tunes of familiar Anglo-Protestant hymnody, the songs were transformed into highly expressive laments that bore little apparent relation to the English hymns from which they ostensibly derived.

After a feast had been served and the Singers had left, Larry and I stepped outside to take in some balmy summer air. It was nearly 2:00 a.m., and Larry had wearied of being the public figure of strength. Without exchanging a word, we stood together on the sidewalk, looking out on Franklin and at the well-lit parking lot across the street. The stillness was broken by the whimpers of a delusional old native man who approached us on the sidewalk pushing a shopping cart full of his possessions, gazing out into the darkness in fear of some imagined gang of kids. Larry consoled him with tender assurances that he would be all right and that he should come inside for something to eat.

The hymn singing and other communal practices of the wake did not resolve the senselessness of this occasion. One year later, a fifteen-year-old boy was convicted of second-degree murder in the killing of Larry's brother. No motive was determined other than a capricious urge to beat up a drunk Indian. Although tried as an adult, he sobbed like a little child when the judge pronounced the sentence.

This book explores the rich tradition of singing Ojibwe language hymns in similar circumstances over the past 170 years. Although the hymns have been put to different uses and have carried different meanings since their first translation by Christian missionaries in the late 1820s, the distinctive tradition of singing them has had an abiding presence in the life of the community in such moments as this wake. Today at the White Earth Reservation, where the ritualized singing of them had gotten under way in earnest in the 1870s, the local undertaker estimates that fully thirty-five of the forty reservation funerals he oversees each year involve Ojibwe language hymn singing at the wake the night before.[3] In the span of 170 years, a historical innovation, the singing of hymns, has become, for many Ojibwe people, curiously traditional.

At first glance, the story appears to be driven by a fundamental irony. Once promoted by missionaries as a means of rooting out "Indianness," the singing of these translated hymns has, at least for many Anishinaabeg, become emblematic of who they are as a distinctive people. But if we view the story through a lens trained on the distinctive logic of religious practices, our naive sense of irony gives way to a firmer conviction that the hymns came to belong to the Ojibwe people who sang them. For Anishinaabe culture, like all cultures, is a culture in motion.[4] While some Anishinaabe hear in this music the violent history that implicates Christian missions in the disease and dispossession of land and culture, what is more surprising is how many Anishinaabe seem to hear in those Ojibwe language songs the improvisational sense of the traditional that earlier generations of Ojibwes applied, with remarkable deftness, to what few choices were available to them within the confines of the reservation and mission Christianity. The specifics of this story of hymn singing point beyond themselves to the broader cultural processes that place the resources of ritual and religion at the center of so many native struggles to negotiate community life within the constraints of poverty, racism, and the dispossession of land, language, and culture.

MAKING DO AND MAKING MEANING

The story of hymn singing suggests that the struggles of "making do" and "making meaning" are ultimately part of the same project more than is usually appreciated.[5] With respect to the role of hymn singing in negotiating colonialism, such a recognition will help account for the power of ritual practices to engender in social life what the colonized mind may find increasingly difficult to imagine. In the years of early settlement of White Earth beginning in 1868, the practice of hymn singing helped negotiate on the cultural field what would contribute to survival on the social field by those who gathered in native-led Christian communities. Hymns were legitimate music in the eyes of the mission and reservation authorities who held many of the keys to survival. Here the making of coherent meaning seems to have been subordinate to the project of making do. Still, what made hymn singing worth investing in was the spiritual value of community constituted in performances.

In more recent years at White Earth, the practice of singing at wakes helps a factionalized community recollect itself. On one level, survival in this context is a material concern, but on another level, White Earth people speak about survival as a concern of spiritual vision and solidarity. At a time when a collective future might be increasingly difficult to imagine, hymn singing can engender in sound the social unity and spiritual wherewithal that makes survival possible. Here the making do of survival seems to hinge on the making of meaning—and the integrity of both may have something important to do with the making of beauty.

The peculiar interest in native language hymnody is not exclusive to the Ojibwe. A story of similar consequence could be told about how many other native communities have similarly transformed the songs of missionaries into distinctively Kiowa or Choctaw or Cree or Comanche or Seneca traditions of music making. Although scholars have only begun to consider such cases in any detail, each story would suggest that the historical innovations of native Christianity have been fused with tradition in ways that are telling about the historicity of the traditional and the traditionality of the historical.

Thus, while this is ostensibly a book about hymns, it is as much a book about the changing historical contexts that frame the singing of them by Ojibwe people as an artful response to the colonization and dispossession of those contexts. More generally still, it is a book about how Native American religious traditions can be seen as resources that mediate the tensions between continuity and change rather than as mere bulwarks against change. Finally, it is a book that considers Christianity as, on the one hand, part of the equation of domination of native peoples and, on the other, an important religious resource in native struggles to act as agents in a history conditioned by that very domination. This marks a departure from conventional ways of thinking about both traditional Ojibwe religion and native Christianity.

LOOKING FOR "OJIBWE RELIGION"

A rather extensive body of scholarship on Ojibwe religion does much to explore the historical development and meanings of certain beliefs and practices, especially those of the Midewiwin ceremonial society. The Midewiwin, or Grand Medicine Society, is a ceremonial complex focused on healing and the restoration of cosmic balance which has endured concerted governmental efforts to stamp it out. William Hoffman's 1885 study of the Midewiwin complex set the original course for the study of Ojibwe religion.[6] Supplementing the previous writings of Henry Rowe Schoolcraft and Johann Georg Kohl, Hoffman's extensive documentation provided material for a century of studies that placed the rites of the Midewiwin at the center of what they viewed as traditional Ojibwe religion.[7] Hoffman's work also put Ojibwe ritual on the map of some consequential European studies of shamanism and so-called primitive religion.[8] Such studies focused on those traditional or archaic religious phenomena that stood in contrast to—and were assumed to proceed independent of—the modern world and its historical religions. But Hoffman's study was itself situated historically in ways that called into question the Midewiwin complex as constitutive of *traditional* Ojibwe religion in this premodern sense. His research was based on visits to the Red Lake and White Earth reservations in the 1880s, a period of volatile social change that led to such ceremonial innovations as the Drum Dance and ritualized hymn singing. Hoffman remarked that Midewiwin priests shared the esoteric ceremony with him in the first place out of their concern that native ways would not survive governmental assimilation policy.

Beginning in the 1950s, the focus of attention moved from the timelessness of the Midewiwin to the significance of culture change. Based on fieldwork with Ojibwes, A. Irving Hallowell and his students pioneered a more systematic anthropological interest in acculturation. Acculturation was said to be the process by which a unified dominant culture came to displace an indigenous culture, in turn destabilizing the social and psychological well-being thought to be a function of the organic nature of traditional societies. Because Hallowell viewed religion primarily in terms of its aspect as psychological adjustment to the world, religious beliefs figured prominently in this equation. Such changes in worldview were among the more telling indices of acculturation as Hallowell understood it. When viewed through the lens of acculturation, the ways that native people actively inflected the missionaries' religion appear simply as patinas thinly veiling the deeper processes eroding "traditional" cultures from the inside out. That said, although acculturation was a mechanism deemed so real that Hallowell believed one could begin to quantify it through Rorschach inkblot tests, he and his students brought critical attention to the very real psychological and social violence that culture change was doing to Anishinaabe people.[9]

In light of this renewed interest in change over time, Åke Hultkrantz, Harold Hickerson, Christopher Vecsey, and John Grim have reinterpreted the Midewiwin and other Ojibwe ceremonial complexes in terms of the rapid social changes and religious exchanges of postcontact history.[10] Hultkrantz argues that Christian views of heaven and hell influenced Midewiwin ideas about retribution for ethical conduct.

Following Hickerson, Vecsey and Grim pay particular attention to the role of the Midewiwin in consolidating an Ojibwe nation out of the congeries of small bands that had previously obtained. While these studies vary considerably with each other and with those explicitly taking the acculturative view, they all describe Ojibwe religion primarily in terms of its coherence as a system of belief or as a structure of religious specialists, training our eyes on a kind of traditional Ojibwe religion that is increasingly hard to find at the turn of the twenty-first century. Perhaps many Anishinaabe people would shake their heads in sad agreement.

But what does one make of the Ojibwe hymn singing described at the beginning of this chapter? Are the practices of Ojibwe Christianity best understood as "survivals" of prior Ojibwe traditions? Are they better understood as capitulations to missionary Christianity? Are they something in between—syncretistic aggregates of both religions, with an insufficient intrinsic logic of their own to last? It seems that the existing literature on Ojibwe religiousness—indeed the scholarship on most Native American traditions—provides only loose direction for interpreting the subtle processes at work in the practices of Ojibwe Christians.

COMING TO TERMS WITH NATIVE CHRISTIANITY

Either from the perspective of missions history of from the perspective of Native American religions and ethnohistory, scholarship has only very recently begun to come to terms with how native Christianity has been *both native and Christian*. The bulk of the writing on native Christianity has seen it either as an historical acculturation away from indigenous traditions, and hence no longer meaningfully "native," or as a religious ruse for other political and economic strategies, and hence not completely "Christian."

In his earlier work, Christopher Vecsey took the conversion to Christianity to be a "nominal and superficial" process through which "Ojibwas have turned from aboriginal traditions without profoundly accepting the missionaries' faith."[11] Although religion as such is not the primary concern of Anastasia Shkilnyk's ethnography of the disintegration of a Canadian Ojibwe community, she similarly observes that the absence of traditional rituals "is a measure of the extent to which certain customs and norms of behavior have become dysfunctional under fundamentally changed conditions."[12] In both views, cultures are taken to be monolithic wholes that displaced one another in a basic narrative of acculturation that leads to dysfunction.

Approaching the religious exchange from the other side, historians of missions to the Ojibwe also narrate a story of cultural collision and acculturation. A number of scholars have contributed an historian's sympathetic understanding of the good intentions of the missionaries.[13] Others have evaluated the missionary project more critically in light of its outcome. George Tinker, a native biblical scholar, theologian, and activist, distinguishes between "missionary intentions" and "missionary violence" in an important reappraisal of Christian missions to native peoples as cultural genocide.[14] Carol Devens [Green] has used gender analysis to reconfigure the narrative of missions and culture change among the Ojibwe, arguing that because they stood less to gain from religious and cultural conversion, native women "increasingly identified themselves, and were so identified by men, with traditional culture."[15]

From the anthropological tradition of Hallowell and his students, from the early work of Vecsey, and from the critical historical tradition of Tinker and Devens, important attention has been brought to the violence and coercion of Ojibwe culture change. But these studies still do not fully equip us to see how it is that religious practices have helped negotiate culture change in ways crucial to the survival of these communities. In light of the interpretive framework of acculturation, historians have tended to overestimate the ideological agency of missionaries, and consequently have either valorized them or vilified them, depending on the historian's appraisal of their intentions at the ideological level. At the same time, acculturation has eclipsed a fuller understanding of the agency of missionized communities like the Ojibwes.

In the late 1990s, a number of fresh considerations have arisen to challenge the sense that native Christianity is an outcome of a one-directional process of acculturation. The studies have crucially shifted attention away from what *missionaries intended* to appreciate what *native people made of* Christianity. In her 1998 study of nineteenth-century political leadership among Minnesota Ojibwes, Rebecca Kugel does a masterful job of showing how complicated the commitments to the Christian tradition were for those Ojibwe who came to identify with various missions, for religious affiliations were deeply implicated in political matters of strategic alliance-building and debates between civil leaders and warriors about how to negotiate a viable living in the face of American encroachment.[16] Kugel moves well beyond viewing Christian conversion as a simple consequence facing societies "too demoralized by contact to resist the alien religious message" to appreciate how native peoples opted for and molded a Christianity in the effort to "rebuild their shattered communities and reinforce select elements of their embattled traditional culture."[17]

But while close attention to political history discloses much, it also winds up cropping out the religious dimension of Ojibwe political life, for matters of community organization and decision making were distinguishable but ultimately inseparable from spiritual considerations. For example, because many Ojibwe transferred allegiance rather freely between the Episcopal and Catholic traditions, Kugel concludes that "Ojibwe commitment remained to a social ideal, not to a religious tradition as an end in itself."[18] Indeed the commitment was to a social ideal rather than to a "religion" as such or to a denominational expression of it, but that social ideal was every bit as religious as it was political, if such analytical distinctions are to be used reliably at all. More important still, spiritual engagement with the stories and practices of the Christian tradition was a seriously considered end in itself, as well as a means toward other aims and ends.[19]

Several scholars who take religion more seriously still have recently given fresh consideration to the diversity and fuller texture of native Christianity, breaking new ground in reassessing the apparent paradox of being both native and Christian. James Treat squarely addresses that apparent paradox in the introduction to his edited anthology of essays by different native Christian writers, arguing that "to disregard Indian Christians, either as Indians or as Christians, is to deny their human agency, their religious independence, and—ultimately—their very lives."[20] In another edited anthology, Jace Weaver also addresses the ways that Christianity has informed the complex identities of his circle of native contributors, choosing not to "disguise our differences" with overgeneralizations about native Christianity but to present the essays as "an ongoing dialogue"[21] In a multivolume study of native Catholics, Christopher Vecsey relates a rich array of historical vignettes, interviews, fieldnotes, and narrative about the varieties of native Christianity with little interpretive overlay. The picture of Ojibwe Catholicism that he relates enriches and complicates his earlier work on the Christian dimension of Ojibwe religion significantly.[22] Sergei Kan has drawn together, in a highly detailed book, decades of work among southeast Alaska's Tlingit people, showing the complex political, liturgical, and doctrinal reasons that many embraced Russian Orthodoxy while rejecting the Christianity preferred by Presbyterian missionaries.[23]

Vecsey's and Kan's attention to the richness of the details, Treat's and Weaver's allegiance to the irreducible variety of ways of being native and Christian, and Kugel's attunement to the political contingencies of religious affiliation all shift the attention we pay native Christianity toward what native peoples *made of* the tradition. Refreshing as it is, though, the new literature begs something of a paradigm shift of interpretation—or at least a markedly different interpretive posture—to suit it. For we have been predisposed to approach religions primarily as systems of belief, and native Christianity as a historical outcome of the collision between, in this case, Ojibwe religion and the Christian religion. What if we were to reorient our interpretations in terms of *practice* rather than *belief*? What if we were to train our eyes and ears on the religious practices of native Christians to see how Christianity came to change native traditions and how native traditions came to change the Christianity that missionaries brought to them?

If such questions have yet to be asked, it is likely because scholarship on native Christianity has absorbed unaware some key assumptions of the missionaries on whose documents it has relied for its data. Archive-bound scholarship had taken for granted a notion of *religion* that is out of step with what most native people construe as a more all-embracing way of life. Such a reductive view of religion has impoverished an understanding of Native American religious change in at least two ways.

First, like missionaries before them, scholars have drawn conventional boundaries around and between "religions" as systems—boundaries that have not always been recognized by native people. Missionaries not only considered Christianity to be a well-bounded system; they also policed those boundaries against the encroachments of syncretism or the lapses of backsliding. Of course, reflecting a wide range of theologies, missionaries differed widely in the extent to which they policed those boundaries. Some condemned native traditions; others provisionally accepted native traditions as forerunners to Christian supercession. In any event, though, most missionaries agreed that Christianity was an all-embracing system of belief, the integrity of which relied on its exclusive and universal claims to truth.

While few historians have shared the missionaries' belief in the exclusive truth of Christianity, many have nevertheless absorbed the assumption that religions in general are belief systems—coherent, self-referential wholes that provide orientation in the world because they offer singular, mutually exclusive frameworks of meaning. Small wonder, then, that missionaries and interpreters alike have looked askance at the hybridities that abound in native Christianity, for such practices transgress the putative boundaries between religious systems. Whether provisionally tolerated or flatly condemned, hybrid practices unnerved missionaries. They still baffle scholars.

Significantly, such boundary crossings were not so unnerving to native people. They recognized differences among religious traditions, of course, but for them the boundaries were often of a very different kind. For example, to affiliate with one Christian community or another was a social fact of considerable consequence, often defining one's social identity. Indeed, factionalism frequently developed along such lines of religious affiliation. But as John and Jean Comaroff point out in their studies of missions and culture change in southern Africa, such social boundaries of affiliation seldom reflected the existential complexities of religious identity among peoples who embrace what the Comaroffs describe as an "ethos of religious relativism."[24]

I contend here that native traditions have largely been relativistic in ethos—that is, concerned less with the falsehood of other traditions than with the truth that the sacred cannot be exhausted by any particular comprehension of it. In the case of the Ojibwe, the tradition has been concerned less with the precise nature of the divine than with how to access the divine powers that animate life. Indeed, for this reason, many traditions have remained remarkably open to the possibility that new truths, new visions, and new ceremonies could come to them in time. In some early encounters with Christian missionaries that were less encumbered by the dispossession of land and culture, there is considerable evidence that native people gave audience to the Christian tradition in this spirit, listening respectfully to the new stories and participating in the new ceremonies according to a familiar religious ethos of intertribal exchange.

A second, and related, way that scholarship has been impoverished by missionary assumptions concerns the relationship between the inner life and the outer life of the religious. For their part, missionaries construed the outer forms of religion as more or less reliable indicators of inner leanings. To be sure, missionaries came to appreciate how outward practices could offer effective means for cultivating that inner life, but in any case, they scrutinized those practices for evidence of inner transformation, which, in the end, mattered most. When the inner and outer did not fully correspond, as they often did not, missionaries construed the result as insincerity or backsliding. Scholars have not shared the missionaries' investment in that inner transformation, but we have often shared the perspective that religion boils down to belief. As a consequence, outward aspects of religion, especially ritual action, have been understood as symbolic expressions of inner conceptualizations and therefore derivative of them.[25] As new perspectives shift the focus away from missionaries to native Christians, then, how can we proceed to extricate our interpretive framework from these two missionary assumptions? First, I think we can take more seriously the simple, though hardly simplistic, claim that native traditions are better described as *lifeways* rather than *religions*. That, in turn, will bring us to appreciate the generativity of outward practices in native Christianity.

"WE DON'T HAVE A RELIGION, WE HAVE A WAY OF LIFE"

In travels over some eight years among Ojibwe communities in Minnesota, my inquiries as a self-described "religionist" have, quite frankly, met with some consternation. I have been reminded—on too many occasions to overlook—some version of the following: "We don't have a religion, we have a way of life." Such a claim may appear rather commonplace, perhaps even cliché. Indeed, one could say that the more devout practitioners of any religious tradition rightfully call their tradition a way of life. But the more time I spend with Ojibwe people and the more I try to interpret the dynamics of Ojibwe religiousness in scholarly language, the more convinced I am that coming to terms with such a remark is one of the key presenting problems of any inquiry into Native American religious traditions. For this is, I submit, a sophisticated, astute comment that many native people make on the conventional practices of Western theorizing. Indeed, one is hard-pressed to find a word in any native language, Ojibwe included, for "religion," at least as we conventionally use the term.[26]

Less commonplace is the suggestion that an adequate understanding of native Christianity also must take this presenting problem fully into account. Rather than looking for how something familiar—Christianity qua "religion"—has been *translated* into the vernacular languages and cultures of native communities, we ought to consider how both the form and content of the Christian tradition have been *transposed and performed* in the context of an entirely different religious idiom where religion is not a discrete segment of culture but an integrative force in the entirety of a lifeway, an idiom where multiple religious traditions can be held within view as potential resources for living. The key shift in religious idiom here, I submit, is a shift from system to bricolage, from belief to practice.

In their treatments of what distinguishes native Christianity from other forms of North American Christianity, both James Treat and Jace Weaver quote Cherokee Baptist theologian William Baldridge: "Doing theology, thinking theologically, is a decidedly non-Indian thing to do. When I talk about Native American theology to many of my Indian friends, most of them just smile and act as if I hadn't said anything. And I'm pretty sure that as far as they are concerned I truly hadn't said anything."[27] Weaver goes on to document the emergence of a postcolonial Native American literature, through which native elites inflected European-American genres of literature with the conventions of the oral tradition, especially with what Weaver calls its "communitist" pragmatic activism. Weaver, like Treat before him, offers insightful guides for reading how native Christian elites wrote about their own reconciliation of the native and the Christian in their identity.

The collections by Treat and Weaver are invaluable, but I submit that the terms of the "native and Christian" dilemma, to the extent that being both native and Christian has been a dilemma in any particular instance, have more typically been reconfigured in terms of practice rather than in terms of belief. That is, the problem of a native and Christian identity has not generally been a *theological* one in the sense that Baldridge's remark makes clear. For most native Christians, it seems to have been a *practical* problem, a problem of practice. Without question the problem has been, for some, a wrenching theological dilemma, and doubtless increasingly so as more and more native people have attended to such problems in the world of print. But if Baldridge's widely quoted remark rings true, that is because the potential contradictions of being both native and identified with the often anti-native religion of the missionaries, is something that is not sorted out *in so many words*, but rather in religious practices. This book can be construed as an attempt, parallel to those of Weaver and Treat, to appreciate how non-elite native people, who were not writing, nonetheless inflected the cultural practices of the colonizers in order to enact indigenous ways of valuing land, community, and the sacred. Putting religious practices, rather than religious beliefs, in the foreground can help make more sophisticated sense of the claim that native traditions, Christianity among them, are not religions, but ways of life.

RITUAL PRACTICE AND CULTURAL CHANGE

The task is all the more difficult as it requires a move from the familiar terrain of texts to the shifting ground of actions and behavior. Nevertheless, we have some resources to interpret these practices, especially the ritual theory rooted in the work of social theorists Pierre Bourdieu and Michel de Certeau, and amplified by Catherine Bell and John and Jean Comaroff.[28] To Bourdieu, scholarly understanding of practices does not come easily because practices proceed according to a logic all their own—a pragmatic logic that forgoes the quest for consistent, systematic meaning on which discursive endeavors like theology rely. But it is for this very reason that religious practices are equipped to do all kinds of important cultural work, especially in the highly contested spaces of the missionary encounters. For the missionary, no ordinary practice was insignificant in the task of reengineering native life. Cutting hair, observing the Sabbath, eating three meals daily, and singing evangelical hymns with neither drum nor dancing were the stuff with which missionaries exercised what Bourdieu called "symbolic power," the power of "constituting the given, confirming or transforming the vision of the world, an almost magical power that enables one to obtain the equivalent of what is obtained through force."[29]

The key insight of cultural theorist Antonio Gramsci, elaborated here by Bourdieu and others, becomes the basis for understanding the broader significance of hymn singing in Ojibwe history. The great forces of domination and resistance, Gramsci argues, are ironically seldom fleshed out by means of brute force, physical or economic. Instead, it is mostly through the subtler workings of culture that domination and resistance play off one another in the struggle to establish what is to be taken as given, real, and of value. In their study of missions and colonialism in southern Africa, John and Jean Comaroff give Gramsci's and Bourdieu's ideas a sharper edge by honing in on the practices of those missionary encounters.[30] For the Comaroffs, the social politics of domination and resistance work themselves out on a cultural field of "signifying practices," a middle ground where the deliberate, "agentive" power plays of ideology encounter the relatively "nonagentive" resistance of hegemony. In other words, the real action of domination and resistance is to be found in a field that lies somewhere between missionary intentions and the capacity of native people to both accommodate and resist.

The Comaroff's point is that interpretations of domination and resistance must immerse themselves in the murky realm of culture where domination and resistance play out somewhere between consciousness and unconsciousness. From this perspective, cultural practices like clothing, music making, body posture, and the organization of time and space take center stage and are seen to be the primary media through which domination and resistance play out, and this opposed to the whole-sale exchange of belief systems implied in *conversion*, a dualistic struggle between cultural wholes, or the unstable notion of *syncretism*.

Given their "taken-for-granted" quality, such practices were versatile weapons in the missionary campaign to remake native people, but the very same practices also could provide a subtle mechanism for successful resistance, for their taken-for-granted quality equipped them to smuggle in all sorts of alternative ways of configuring what is real and of value in the world. Missionaries could applaud the singing of their favorite hymns in the Ojibwe language as the very "sound of civilization," while at the same time Ojibwe people could articulate in the words of their own language and in their own ritualized idiom of performance an improvisation of age-old values.

In displacing the workings of power from its responsible agents, the Comaroffs do not whitewash the oppression of such encounters. Rather, they direct our inquiry away from questions that are moot in the end, such as how far missionary intentions were from their violent consequences or why so many Ojibwe people have strayed so far from a presumed baseline of resistance. Following the Comaroffs, I will take culture to be the "field of signifying practices" where structure and agency meet and where the ironies as well as the tragedies of colonial encounters are within view.

This view toward culture in motion will offer an important corrective for appreciating the agency of Anishinaabe people in their history under colonialism, but it must not eclipse due attention to the violence of cultural change in the contact era. Celebrating the creative capacity of Ojibwe people to "make do" must not overlook the obvious fact that the effects of missionization and assimilation continue to plague Ojibwe communities. James Clifford puts the issue this way: "The filth that an expansive West . . . has thrown in the face of the world's societies appears as raw material, compost for new orders of difference. It is also filth. Modern cultural contacts need not be romanticized."[31] The challenge is to hold within view both the resilience of cultures in motion and the coercive nature of cultural change. The story of Ojibwe hymns, told historically and ethnographically, will hold these two views in critical tension. Understanding that story in light of hymn singing as a ritual practice invites us squarely onto that middle ground where Protestant missionaries controlled an increasing share of political, social, and symbolic power, and where Anishinaabeg exercised considerable, if subtle, agency on the cultural field.

The category of ritual is useful even it if introduces language that Ojibwe singers do not use themselves to describe their work. Ojibwe communities have their own sense of what constitutes ritual, or ceremony. Ojibwe singing is not *ceremonial* in the sense that a pipe ceremony or the Eucharist or a sweat lodge or the singing of a dream song is. Drawing on Catherine Bell's important reworking of ritual studies, however, we can move on from the tortured question of whether a given action *is or is not* ritual to ask how and why people can be said to *ritualize* certain actions in particular contexts.

Taking ritualization instead of ritual as the matter at hand, Bell is better able to get at the strategic ways in which people take otherwise mundane activities, set them apart within frames of ritualized time, space, and formalized action such that what is established within a ritualized frame can "order, rectify or transform" the state of affairs that exists outside the frame of the ritual in order to "render them more coherent with the values" experienced within it.[32] While few of the singers would think of their performances as ceremonial, Bell's notion of ritualization opens up interpretive language to span the "more or lessness" of the hymns' ritual intensity in different contexts, and to appreciate both the continuities and changes involved in their improvisation.

In the work of ritualization, configurations of ordinary time, space, body movements, speech, and song are stylized in ways "that evoke or purport to be the way things have always been done."[33] Because actions are formalized to conform to a precedent deemed sacred or powerful, it might appear at first glance that they would be brittle to contestation and historical change. But from the perspective of practice theory, where meanings can reside in the nonnarrative "body knowledge" of the activity itself, precisely the opposite can be and usually is the case. Formalized action can absorb and thereby help defuse the contestation of meaning on the synchronic plane or radical changes in meaning over time. For this reason, communities undergoing rapid social change often call on the resources of ritual to provide the ballast and social unity that come from a sense of continuity with the past. Of course, ritual actions can and do serve as occasions for narrative meaning making. To varying degrees, there are meanings imputed to ritual action. People often reflect in their solitude or discuss together what it means to perform a given ritual gesture. Sometimes the didactic purposes of ritual even take center stage. I will show, for example, how evangelical missionaries promoted hymns as effective scripts for inculcating evangelical beliefs, values, and behaviors. But I will also show that Ojibwe performances of those hymns led to very few narratives of what it means to perform them. It is ironic, then, that I try to provide a narrative about Ojibwe singing, its meanings, and its uses—and perhaps appropriately so.

ANAMI'AAWIN: THE PRACTICE OF OJIBWE CHRISTIANITY

This shift of interpretive attention from belief to practice is not just theory for its own sake. It brings interpretive language much closer to the ground on which native communities have engaged the Christian tradition in their lifeways. Given that there is no word in their language for religion, how did Ojibwe people express the concept of Christianity when missionaries introduced it as a belief system? The answer is key to our purposes here: The word in Ojibwe is *anami'aawin*, prayer or praying, and those Ojibwes who identified as Christians called themselves by the related word *Anami'aajig*—those who pray. Actually the term is less a noun than a substantive form of the verb, and is perhaps better rendered as "that which we pray" or "how we pray." Notice here the stress on the *practice* of prayer—not on its content, its object, or the system to which it refers.

Of course, *anami'aawin* is not simply just one of many ways of praying; it implies a kind of prayer that involves many words in contrast to "liturgical" prayer or chanting in Ojibwe tradition that has relatively little denotative content. It remains difficult to ascertain whether the term *anami'aawin* had applied to other pre-Christian ritual forms of prayer prior to the coming of Christian missionaries since the earliest Ojibwe language dictionaries were authored by missionaries themselves in the nineteenth century. But *anami'aawin* was clearly no generic term for prayer in the sense of any communication with the spiritual world since it came to distinguish things Christian from things not-Christian. Hence Anami'aajig, those who pray, came to refer to those who affiliated with Christian groups; *anama'e nagamonan* referred to Christian songs, or hymns; *anama'e wiidigendiwin* referred to Christian marriage; and *anama'e giizhigad* referred to the Sabbath day. But while one cannot say that this way of praying is just like any other way of praying, what counts here is that Christianity is not marked as a system or even a body of beliefs. In Ojibwe idiom, Christianity itself is a practice, a way of praying.

The Ojibwe tradition is not unique in its practice orientation. Neither is it a novel claim here that practice is at the heart of Native American religiousness. As Sam Gill, William Powers, Gary Witherspoon, and others have shown in other contexts, indigenous traditions are fundamentally concerned with the transformative powers of performative language, art, and thought.[34] That is, when properly performed under the right conditions, ceremonies, songs, sounds, gestures, and dance steps do not merely give expression to the inner matters of feeling and meaning but are believed capable of transforming the self, the community, and the cosmos. Here, the outer is not derivative of the inner but is potentially generative in its own right. Heretofore, Gill argues, the field of religious studies has emphasized "text at the expense of context; on code at the expense of behavior; on meaning and proposition at the expense of use, relevance, and effect. . . . We have looked primarily to the authoritative basis for religious practice rather than to the immediate effects and powers of the performance of religious acts. In a sense we have denied that religious actions are of value when we have considered them principally as an encoding of some underlying system of meaning."[35] The valuable recognition of the centrality of religious action, here by Gill and elsewhere by others, needs to be carried an important step further, however. They appreciate how performative utterances and gestures can work to transform the world through the suspension of historical time, but we must also come to appreciate how ritual practices often serve as resources for negotiating culture change in the realm of historical time, especially in colonizing circumstances. Rituals have often been seen to deny history; we need to reclaim a sense of how they are at home in history.

LISTENING FOR "OJIBWE MUSIC"

As we shift attention away from the collision of "belief systems" to the middle ground where religious practices nimbly do their cultural work, it makes sense to examine music making, a practice that has proven itself supple enough to embrace cultural mixing as hybridity and in which continuity and change are equally at home. This makes it all the more surprising that much of the literature on musical change among native peoples remains fixed to the notion of acculturation. Although there are a number of important studies that place musical culture in motion, studies of Ojibwe music have made sharper distinctions between traditional and acculturative musics than native communities themselves make.[36] Frances Densmore's scholarship and wax cylinder recordings of Ojibwe song early in the twentieth century pioneered the field of ethnomusicology. But Densmore neither commented on nor recorded the hymn-singing tradition of the Minnesota Ojibwe communities she visited, presumably because she considered such music acculturative. This is revealing, for Densmore doubtless heard Ojibwe hymns sung at the White Earth Reservation and elsewhere. She wrote about her friendship with the native Episcopal clergymen Charles Wright at Leech Lake and Edward Kah-O-Sed at White Earth, and even credited the latter with having encouraged her research in the first place. Kah-O-Sed compiled the 1910 edition of the *Ojibwa Hymnal*, which remains in use to this day.[37] Thomas Vennum Jr., who revisited the sites of Densmore's field research sixty years later to document musical change over time, has contributed immeasurably to the current study. The northern Wisconsin communities where Vennum's work finds its center, however, apparently do not have a hymn-singing tradition of sufficient significance to warrant the level of analysis that Vennum brings to drum music.[38] Frederick Burton and Gertrude Kurath did pay some scholarly attention to Ojibwe hymnody in ways that are helpful to this study, but they did so in communities far to the east, and, in the case of Kurath, through the lens of acculturation theory.[39] Most considerations of other Native American hymn traditions have focused primarily on song texts.[40] More recently, Lynn Whidden, Beverley Cavanaugh, and Amy Stillman have begun to problematize and examine the hymn-singing traditions of other native societies.[41]

HEARING OJIBWE CULTURE IN MOTION: BEYOND THE SOUND OBJECT

This book takes hymn singing as a lens to view Ojibwe culture in motion, but it is not a study of the music for its own sake. Consistent with my competence, as well as with the cues of my fieldwork, my interest is directed to the social fields of power and cultural fields of meaning that surround hymn singing rather than to the structures of the music itself. If one takes music in relation to culture, however, one may find that what ethnomusicologist Thomas Turino calls "the sound object" may or may not be among the more salient features of a musical culture.[42] In some cultures, the more important aspect of musical experience may be found in the social relationships that surround the music making. This is what Turino found to be the case in Andean panpipe music. Turino contrasts the uses and meanings of this music as it is performed in different settings. In the highland villages, Turino notes, music as sound object "cannot be abstracted from the ethics, processes, and occasions of communal life." In the slums of the capital city, however, where many highlanders have relocated, Turino finds the same music performed for broader audiences to be very much a sound object, an exhibition of highland culture.

What matters most about Ojibwe hymn singing, I think, are the social relations that obtain through the singing and hearing of the music. Musicality is by no means incidental to the creation and sustenance of those relations. But the questions that most suggest themselves in light of my experiences at White Earth are not those of the inherent sacrality of music or of Ojibwe musical philosophy. They are, rather, the historian's questions (To what ends have singers set out, at particular moments in Ojibwe history, to sing?) and the anthropologist's question of ritual practice (What is the cultural work to which this tradition has been put?).

OVERVIEW: A BOOK IN TWO PARTS

The structure of this book reflects the way it brings together these two very different disciplines, based on different bodies of research and calling for different writing voices. Part I is historical in nature, telling the story of hymn singing as it is seen to develop through consideration of nineteenth-century missionary documents. Part II is ethnographic in nature, depicting the contemporary life of Ojibwe hymn singing in Minnesota and situating the practice in various social and political contexts of native life today. Although the voice of my writing changes significantly from the historian's to the ethnographer's, I want to replicate here my own process of discovery that history and ethnography can profoundly inform and sharpen one another. Archival research helped me appreciate the fuller past that shapes the contemporary experience of so many Ojibwe people. The steep learning curve I experienced in fieldwork, and the patient instruction of my collaborators, helped me ask the more pertinent questions of the archives and certainly gave me eyes and ears to discern the often subtle resonances of Ojibwe Christianity between the lines of missionary writings.

Part I: History

The first half of the book tells a story of the historical development of Ojibwe hymn singing from the conjunction of evangelical hymns, Ojibwe attitudes toward music, and the social circumstances that set the terms for the symbolic exchange between missionaries and Ojibwe people. Chapter 1 identifies the place of music in early-nineteenth-century Ojibwe culture and compares that with the place of hymnody in the culture of evangelical missionaries. Chapter 2 traces the translation and promotion of Ojibwe hymnody by those missionaries, along with the early reception of the hymns into the Ojibwe repertory. Missionaries saw to the rigorous translation and promotion of hymns, which soon took shape in the spaces between the written and the oral. In chapter 2, several close readings of the Ojibwe translations identify the nuances of Ojibwe religious thought within the Christian hymn texts themselves. Yet it was largely in the practice of singing those texts that a distinctive Ojibwe idiom of religious expression emerged. Chapter 2 proceeds, then, to document early accounts of hymn singing that suggest how performance had already begun to cast the textual message of the hymns in light of existing Ojibwe beliefs about music and social relations.

To understand what conditions brought about an even more ritualized tradition of hymnody in the reservation era, chapter 3 describes the social and material crises faced by those Ojibwes who settled on the new White Earth Reservation after its founding in 1868. Because the Episcopalian mission did much to set the terms of those social conditions, chapter 3 surveys the mission's activities and documents the emergence of a native-led community gathered within the Episcopalian fold. I proceed to show how hymn singing became a practice through which this group of Ojibwe Christians carved out a semiautonomous space within the confines of reservation life. Although hymn singing called for the conspicuous absence of drum and dance and a copious number of words, singers transformed the performance style and context of the hymns to make the music their own. Ritualized performance enabled the hymns to do more than set the tone and establish the rhythms for a new way of life at White Earth. For many, hymn singing at wakes and prayer meetings conferred a kind of spiritual integrity on that new life, making it aesthetically, morally, and spiritually desirable to be both Ojibwe and Anami'aajig.

Part II: Ethnography

The second, ethnographic, half of the book examines the different uses to which the music has been put more recently. Chapter 4 locates hymn singing in the social and material conditions of twentieth-century life at White Earth. The early twentieth century saw to the further erosion of the land base, language, and social solidarity long seen as constitutive of Ojibwe identity. At White Earth, the practice of hymn singing itself all but disappeared. A group of senior citizens, however, themselves the products of the forced forgetting of assimilation policies, took it upon themselves to bring the tradition of singing back in order to help a beleaguered community act on its circumstances by remembering an Ojibwe identity through musical performance. Sketches of their lives show how these elders' remaking of hymn singing has effectively remade them in the process. Although the conditions of the twentieth century were different, the ritualized singing of hymns was used to a similar end as it was in the nineteenth century—remembering a fragmented community in crisis and weaving a compartmentalized existence into an integrated Ojibwe way of life.

Chapter 5 introduces the work of collective memory in ritualized hymn singing today, especially as it addresses the social circumstances of life at White Earth. While hymns are performed in a variety of contexts, the primary work of the Ojibwe singers is at the funeral wakes of the community. At such moments, these social circumstances are seen in their bitterest clarity. Because so many die young and die violently at White Earth, each successive wake resonates with the dispossession of history and urges collective reflection on both social and existential matters. Gatherings around death have become crossroads where the community takes stock of history and where it resolves to act on that history. A wake creates an unstable space, one that puts on heightened display the contradictions of contemporary experience. That space calls into question the possibility of meaning on one level, and the very possibility of Ojibwe survival on another. Through the distinctive operations of music and ritualized language, however, Ojibwe singers can transform this space, creating a shared experience of Ojibwe time and structuring a process of collective remembering. This memory is socially integrative, though not unequivocally so. The operations of memory cannot resolve all contradictions and social tensions, but the practice of singing does make perseverance possible. As one singer puts it: "We sing in order to survive."

These five chapters examine hymn singing as a practice that was ritualized to different ends in different historical moments. In the Conclusion, I revisit the open questions raised by the previous five chapters in an attempt to frame a broader discussion about the work of ritual. Does hymn singing really work in the manner that I suggest? Can it really engender both accommodation *and* resistance? Can the interpretive category of "invented tradition" account for the depth of attachment Ojibwe people express about the hymns? I conclude that the contradictions that give rise to the question "does hymn singing work?" are major stumbling blocks only if one expects to find in ritual practice simply the coherent narratives of a symbolizing mind. The colonized situation in which Ojibwe people have found themselves has not always afforded the possibility of resolving such contradictions and inconsistencies. A ritualized practice of Ojibwe singing has perhaps made living within those contradictions possible precisely because its logic is one of ritualized practice and not one of a conceptualizing mind seeking order and consistency.

Before we move to the initial translation and promotion of the hymns, it is fitting to reflect on a story from my field experience that will set the right tone for the practice of studying practices. On a number of long drives in northern Minnesota, I have had a chance to visit at length with Charles "Punkin" Hanks, one of the original White Earth Singers. As I have found to be the case with other elders, he has seemed taken aback whenever I pose direct questions about hymn singing as such. Any questions I aim toward the meanings or recent history of hymn singing have been redirected to other topics—in part, no doubt, as an expression of resistance to my line of inquiry. Yet, because we speak rather frankly about my research agenda and because he seems to have taken my education under his wing, I think his measured responses are more than a matter of mistrust.

I think it has something to do with the nature of hymn singing. Talk about hymns can, at any moment, flow into talk about the high number of wakes in the past month, the young neighbor who shot herself, or the young man whose head was struck with a tire iron after a party. Talk may just as easily pass over to stories of throwing prickly wild cucumbers at other kids forty years ago or of where on the reservation the maple sap has started to run. Such connections speak to a web of life in which practices, hymn singing being but one, are inextricably related in lived experience. These connections remind those of us in the business of theorizing that our inquiries place boundaries around phenomena which are otherwise seamlessly woven into the fabric of life. As we examine the history of the practice of Ojibwe hymn singing, we cannot overlook the wild cucumbers.

PART I

HISTORY

▲▲▲▲▲▲

1

SACRED MUSICS

*Traditional Ojibwe Music
and Protestant Hymnody*

▲▲▲▲▲▲

MUSIC AND THE SACRED IN OJIBWE LIFE

The tradition of Ojibwe hymn singing emerged in the middle third of the nine-teenth century from the conjunction of evangelical hymns, Anishinaabe attitudes toward music, and the social circumstances that set the terms of symbolic exchange. To understand how hymns came into the musical life of Ojibwe communities, it is important to first illustrate the place of music generally in early-nineteenth-century Ojibwe culture and then to compare that with the place of hymnody in the evangelical culture that missionaries brought to the field. Neither Ojibwe nor evangelical culture came to this encounter as static wholes; both had been changing against the historical backdrop in their own right long before the missionary encounter.

Notwithstanding the cultural and spiritual continuities that thread through the last four hundred years, the Ojibwe nation itself had been a product and process of postcontact history. What had been a loose federation of linguistically related but highly mobile and localized bands emerged through the fur trade into a more coher-ent social network and set of political alliances. Ethnohistorians have reconsidered fur trade society in terms of culturally diverse, polyglot native villages to which the fur trading companies attached their posts. In these refugee communities, culture was produced in new ways to meet new material needs and social demands.[1] Ojibwe religious culture appears to have borne these historical changes, too. The Midewi-win rites, the ceremonial complex of the principal Ojibwe religious society, had long been viewed by scholars as synonymous with, if not the sum total of, "traditional" Ojibwe religion, as though "the traditional" was necessarily in tension with "the his-torical." But recent scholarship has shown just how thoroughly culture remained in motion in that the Midewiwin itself has evolved in the context of changing social and cultural circumstances of the fur trade.[2]

The musical life of early-nineteenth-century Ojibwe communities appears to have borne the marks of these changing circumstances as well. Thomas Vennum Jr.

has tracked historical change in repertory and function in the reservation period, noting a shift from an earlier wealth of sacred songs specific to certain ceremonial or lifeway practices to a higher proportion of more social, less overtly sacred, music.[3] While Ojibwe musical traditions bear the contingencies of historical change, it is possible to generalize a distinctive and shared conceptual framework by which Ojibwe people have made and heard music. I will return later to compare and contrast hymnody with other features of a shared Ojibwe musical repertory in motion. Here at the outset, generalizations about early-nineteenth-century Ojibwe approaches to musical life, based largely on twentieth-century ethnomusicological sources, can nonetheless place these distinctive features in heightened relief. Because music did not stand alone in an Ojibwe way of life, we will do well to begin by placing it within a larger context of Ojibwe religion and culture.[4]

When introducing their culture to outsiders, or teaching it within their own community, Ojibwe elders typically do not choose to speak in such a language of historical development and change. Instead, they often begin by identifying traditional activities associated with the recurring cycle of seasons: maple sugaring in the spring; gardening, fishing, and berrying in the summer; wild ricing and hunting ducks in the late summer/early fall; and hunting big game in the winter. Seasonality is more than a convenient outline for introducing the culture. It is the framework of time and space into which the warp and woof of a distinctly Anishinaabe way of life has been woven. While a wholly seasonal subsistence is no longer fully possible for those who want it from the diminished Ojibwe land base, the way of life has kept itself remarkably in season with historical changes. Activities of the seasonal round still capture the imagination of many Ojibwe people. Making wild rice and maple sugar, berrying, and setting out nets for fish may no longer suffice to make ends meet, but such practices continue to serve as powerful markers of identity for a people with a special relationship to a particular land.

Far more than an adaptive foodgathering strategy, this seasonal way of life has a beauty and integrity borne of its harmony with the natural movements of all that has motion. The Ojibwe term *bimaadiziwin*, often translated rather flatly as "life," encompasses these spiritual associations. *Bimaadiziwin* could be translated as "the Circle of Life," for it is derived from a verb that describes a kind of motion that sweeps by or continues along. The term in its fullness encompasses notions of well-being, balance, profound interdependence, and right relations. A. I. Hallowell, whose fieldwork with northern Manitoba's Berens River Anishinaabeg introduced him in the 1930s to the circular rhythms of the seasonal round, translated *bimaadiziwin* as the "Good Life," a rendering that encompasses the fuller scope of aesthetic, moral, and natural meanings. Here, *bimaadiziwin* is more than just "nature"; it is the ultimate goal of life. The Circle of Life was not simply a matter of "what is," but a matter of "what ought to be." As Ojibwe elder Ignatia Broker put it, "We believe in the Circle of Life."[5] In Hallowell's words, a significant part of believing in *bimaadiziwin* entailed "the obligation to preserve the equilibrium of nature." He observed that an Ojibwe person "may be aggressive, predatory, in relation to the flora and fauna of his habitat . . . but he must only take what he actually needed to provide food, clothing and warmth for himself and his family. Thus [he] was far from considering himself the lord of creation. He was only one of the 'children' of nature, a suppliant for [*bimaadiziwin*]."[6]

Perhaps it was the profound attachment to this way of life that brought a nineteenth-century Roman Catholic missionary to translate "Anishinabe-bimâdisiwin" as the "Indian life" or "pagan life." Missionaries considered the seasonality of this way of life to be among the greatest obstacles to their efforts to reduce native communities to the sedentary lives of an agrarian rhythm.[7] Missionaries would not have been far off the mark to have noticed that the Ojibwe attention to the Circle of Life went well beyond merely economic considerations, for Ojibwes understood that *bimaadiziwin* embodied the force of the sacred powers that animated it. As a consequence, to live well in light of *bimaadiziwin* was to maintain auspicious and proper ethical and ritual relations with the sacred powers that animate *bimaadiziwin*. In this state of affairs, there was no clear distinction between the natural and the supernatural, between the material and the spiritual, or between the sacred and the ordinary. The seasonal round, as part and parcel of *bimaadiziwin*, was both a sacred and an ordinary calling.

To fully understand Ojibwe music, one must see it in relation to this larger spiritual framework of the seasonal lifeway, for music was conceived as a primary mediator of the "power" that was the lifeblood of the Anishinaabe way of life. Indeed, the world of Ojibwe experience in the early nineteenth century was shot through with power—a power that could be both good and bad, give life and take it away—as evidence of the mysterious sources of life that animate the world. The term *manidoo* joins a number of other Ojibwe words that carry this meaning. John Grim notes that *manidoo*, often translated as "spirit," is not "analytically defined" but rather "springs from direct personal experience." Grim sees its "indeterminacy" to be suggestive of its "transformative power" and that the term "seems to articulate the mutuality of exchange between the experiencer and the embodiment of power." In this respect, *manidoo* is not unlike important understandings of power in other Native American traditions, such as *wakan* among the Lakota or *orenda* among the Haudenosaunee (Iroquois).[8]

As such, "power" received little elaboration in conceptual terms. Power was experienced as coursing through all life so pervasively that it did away with sharp distinctions between natural and supernatural or between sacred and profane. It was no more—and no less—*other* than that which enabled things to continue in the state of being alive. Thus does Mary Black gloss the term *bimaadiziwad* as both "those who continue in the state of being alive" and "those who have power."[9] The economy of this power was the economy of material survival, as well as the aesthetic and moral appreciation of a "Good Life" led in harmony with the nonhuman participants in the circle. Success in the hunt, the wild rice harvest, diplomacy, battle, healing, aging—all hinged on committed participation in this economy of power. Christopher Vecsey has characterized the juncture of sacred and ordinary in terms of the people's "conceptions of, and relations with, the ultimate sources of their existence." "Traditional Ojibwa religion," Vecsey has argued, "did not articulate concern for matters beyond 'existence,' beyond life. Survival in this life, this 'existence,' was the Ojibwas' ultimate concern."[10]

Collective attention was paid more to ways of accessing spiritual power than to the precise nature of the power itself. For Ojibwes, dreams represented privileged experiences of spiritual messages, conveying gifts of spiritual power as well as instructions for how to continue accessing that power. Dreams and visions involved elaborate, cultivated practices of memory and interpretation around which much religious life revolved.[11] Indeed, the "fast for a vision" associated with passage into adulthood was a central practice of Ojibwe religiousness in the nineteenth century. The ordeal leading to such visions was carefully scripted and governed by custom, as a young person's vision was viewed as critical to his or her success and health throughout life. Dreams and visions did not end with the puberty fast. Particularly during sickness or near-death experiences, visions were important sources of insight, guidance, and power for the individual and community. These practices mediated the more profound of insights into the forces at work in the world. In this spiritual world of power and dreams, music played a central role. Song was one of the principal means of access to the sources of the power that animates life.

Just as we can speak in terms of a material and spiritual economy of power, so can we speak of an economy of song, for songs provided a currency of exchange in at least three respects: spiritual, social, and historical. First, songs provided a medium for exchange between the human and spiritual worlds. While a wide range of distinctive kinds of Ojibwe songs existed, some more powerful or more sacred than others, no music could be understood as thoroughly secular.[12] Charting the repertorial sweep of Ojibwe music as she encountered it in the early twentieth century, Frances Densmore noted that most songs "are connected, either directly or indirectly, with the idea of reliance on supernatural help."[13] Identifying some of these song types will enable a better understanding of the overarching approach held by Ojibwe people toward music at the time of the earliest hymn translations.

Among the various categories of Ojibwe songs, dream songs are most illustrative of music's power to effect change in the world. These songs were, and still are, received through dreams or visions as gifts from spiritual helpers, known as *pawaganag*. Dreams were considered real experiences, often revelatory. The power associated with a dream song's origin could be brought to bear on a wide range of life pursuits. In performance, a singer reenacted the transmission of spiritual power, "renewing the original conditions of the power contract between the individual and his guardian spirit."[14] Importantly, this means of accessing power ought not be understood as a kind of mechanical incantation, where a command of ritual knowledge alone enabled one to manipulate reality at will. In an Ojibwe way of life, such ritual knowledge was embedded in a moral framework where a singer's intention and behavior in relation to the spiritual realm mattered along with his or her ritual knowledge.[15]

As a distinctive emblem of the pity extended by the *pawaganag*, a dream song was considered a valued element of one's identity. The song could be considered a personal resource of power that belonged to an individual. Ojibwe people often took on a new name as a result of their visions. Illustrating the sense of the power of song and its aspect as an elemental component of identity, an Ojibwe man who had just recorded his dream song with Densmore "bowed his head and said tremulously that he feared he would not live long, as he had given away his most sacred possession."[16]

As a powerful song could offer prestige, so too could an individual's stature contribute to the resonance of his or her songs. At death, an individual's song could be passed on to others in his or her family, shared more widely with all, or, as Densmore observed, "granted in exchange for some other fulfillment of an obligation."[17] If the person were highly esteemed, his or her songs may very well have become treasured sources of strength and identity for the community as a whole.

Songs also were key to important pursuits of life on the seasonal round. As Densmore put it, "every phase of Chippewa life is expressed in music."[18] She distinguished more than thirteen song types, each pertaining to a distinct purpose or social occasion, among them dream songs, Midewiwin songs, war songs, love songs, moccasin game songs, woman's dance songs, lullabies, begging dance songs, pipe dance songs, gifting songs, and songs for children's entertainment.[19] Applied to the variety of life pursuits, certain songs were called on for help in negotiating health and survival by means of access to life-giving powers at the heart of existence. Of course, not all songs were deep springs of spiritual power. The repertory included love songs, moccasin game songs, and lullabies. Nonetheless, each kind of song took its place on a continuum of sacred and profane.

In the early nineteenth century, Ojibwe people agreed that songs were more than aesthetic expressions of emotion, entertainment, technical virtuosity, or social solidarity. Songs fundamentally *did things* in the world of experience and survival. The distinctiveness of the place of song in Ojibwe activity is evident in the schemes of classification. Songs were labeled in terms of "ownership, origin, or use" rather than by a title or first line.[20] The substantive *nagamowin* (singing) or *nagamon* (song) applied generically to all kinds of songs, which were then further modified by reference to use. Thus Densmore identified a love song as "sagiidiwin nagumowin," a pipe song an "opwaguniniminin nagumowin," and so on.[21] Of course, this is not to say that Ojibwe music was narrowly utilitarian. Aesthetic concerns were soundly woven into the social, the economic, the biological, and the spiritual.

Moreover, songs provided the currency of social relations. Songs served to mediate relations within Anishinaabe groups, as well as between Anishinaabeg and other native peoples. Native philosophies of sound and musical performance resound with concerns of establishing proper relations among people.[22] Songs also have served as a staple currency in social exchange between different native groups, both among different Ojibwe bands and in relations with other peoples. "If an Indian visits another reservation," Densmore observed in 1910, "one of the first questions asked on his return is: what new songs did you learn?"[23] Densmore was observing Ojibwe musical practice during the reservation era, when the cessation of hostilities between Dakotas and Ojibwes led to a more formalized practice of intertribal and interreservation visiting. She even identified a distinctive genre of visiting songs appropriate to such occasions, evidence perhaps that the practice of visiting, while by no means a derivative of changing fortunes since contact with European Americans, had taken on new meanings in the contexts of the fur trade and later of U.S. Indian policy.

These musical exchanges were more than social entertainment. Music making and the symbolic actions of ceremonial speech, gifting, and pipe ceremonies were the media by which intergroup relations were negotiated among a number of native peoples. Richard White observes how the relative success or failure of European interactions with Great Lakes people often hinged less on economic reciprocity than on attention to ceremonial protocol.[24] In the context of the American Southeast,

Joel Martin notes the value of nonmaterial reciprocal exchanges of song, dance, and ritual action as the common coin of native alliance-building and resistance.[25]

Song provided a medium of exchange in a third important respect. It was a principal medium for ceremonial innovation. The exchange of songs across cultural and linguistic boundaries was key to the many ceremonial changes tied to the fur trade in the seventeenth and eighteenth centuries.[26] These innovations, in turn, have been shown to have enabled the cultural and social negotiations necessary for survival under colonialism. William Warren, a nineteenth-century Ojibwe writer, recalled the impact of Tenskwatawa, the Shawnee Prophet, whose visions gave spiritual backbone to the well-known anticolonial movement led by his brother, Tecumseh. In 1808, a messenger came to Ojibwe villages, bringing new ceremonies and the prophet's new teachings to purge communities of such impurities as liquor, lying, stealing, and intertribal violence. According to Warren, the prophet even criticized the Midewiwin leaders, bidding them to "throw away their evil and poisonous medicines, and to forget the songs and ceremonies attached thereto, and he introduced new medicines and songs in their place."[27] The prophet's songs and message, derived from visions, helped forge an intertribal movement out of separate communities in the crucible of sacred power. Such ceremonial innovations did not simply *mark* or provide the cultural trappings for the social change. Accounts like Warren's suggest that they made these changes possible in the first place.

Texts, Music, and Meaning

Because the process and meaning of Ojibwe music making was so different from European-American conventions, the function of Ojibwe song texts and their relationship to meaning invites further inquiry. Recall that Ojibwe people classified their repertory in terms of function, social context, or individual ownership. Ojibwe songs seldom if ever were entitled in reference to song texts.[28] To the extent that these schemes of classification reflect deeper valuations, musical function and context took priority over the straightforward, discursive meanings of the song texts.

Songs shared across linguistic boundaries were seldom translated, instead joining the Ojibwe repertory verbatim. In this respect, the sounds of words were at least as important as their lexical content. Even songs of Ojibwe origin often involved sounds and syllables called vocables, which, though carrying no apparent lexical meaning, were nonetheless considered essential components of a song, to be memorized and performed verbatim. Given the frequency of such seemingly meaningless texts, Densmore concluded that music was more important than words in carrying meaning or function. "The melody and the idea are the essential parts of a Midé song," Densmore wrote, "the words being forced into conformation with the melody."[29]

Both Densmore and Vennum remark on the archaic or esoteric linguistic resources that ceremonial songs often incorporated. Shamanic traditions involved with the *jiisakii,* or shaking tent tradition of divination, the *nanaandawi'iwe* doctoring tradition, and the various degrees of the Midewiwin society all relied on specialized knowledge of supernatural language. Esoteric knowledge of *manidookaazo,* translated as "to talk supernatural" or "to take on spiritual power by one's own authority,"

gave healers and diviners privileged access to the spiritual powers and was a significant element of shamanic ritual drama.[30]

These esoteric texts were consistently brief and abstruse, saying less by proposi-
tion than by allusion to the details of an empowering dream or origin myth.[31]
For example, Densmore recorded the following two dream songs by a man named
Kimiwun:

ta'minwe'we	It will resound finely
gi'jig	the sky
tci'binonda'gosinan	when I come making a noise.[32]
ka'bibabi'kwagodeg'	Great heaps
a'nakwad	of clouds
pa'ina'biyan'	in the direction I am looking.[33]

Again, to regard such esoteric texts in terms of their function as moments of access
to dream power should not preclude an appreciation for their aesthetic qualities.
Ojibwe novelist and literary critic Gerald Vizenor draws on Densmore's translations
of Ojibwe song texts to appreciate the beauty of their poetry in verbal form as "remembered shadows of the heard visions and stories of tribal survivance."[34]

Ojibwe songs were not simply poetic or esoteric. Many Midewiwin songs served
as conduits for ritual and dream power, but many also preserved the elaborate herbal
and medicinal knowledge of the community. To know the texts and melodies of
these songs gave an initiate considerable social status. While an elaborate tradition
of birchbark scroll pictography helped Midewiwin society members remember the
several hundred songs estimated by Densmore to pertain to that ceremonial complex, the right to learn and sing the songs was a privilege granted only to those
deemed worthy.[35]

Even in the case of discursively meaningful texts, a distinctive Ojibwe view of
sacred language recognized that words never simply described the world. They could,
in certain circumstances, reconstitute it. In performance, texts were stylized through
repetition, vocable, and accompanying percussion to invoke the power associated
with the song. Repetition did not indicate that a song was simplistic but, rather, that
it reflected the possibility of accentuating the presence and power of words through
redundancy. Because sung words could generate transformative power, repetition
could intensify that power. Densmore recorded the following traveling song by
Maingans at White Earth. The text of this song, associated with the journey of the
soul after death, was largely a repetition of a single line:

A ni ma dja ha ha	I am going, ha ha
A ni ma dja ha ha	
A ni ma dja ha ha	
A ni ma dja ha ha	
A ni ma dja ha ha	
A ni ma dja ha ha	
A ni ma dja	

A o da na win e he he   To the village, he he
Hin di no se he he   I am walking, he he
A ni ma dja ha ha
A ni ma dja ha ha
A ni ma dja ha ha ha
A ni ma dja ha ha
A ni ma dja[36]

The second half of the song was repeated another four times. While such texts seem flat on paper, they were richly stylized in performance to resonate with transforming power.

Finally, a song was greater than the sum of its text and music. Each had a story, an important narrative of origin, transmission, or usage. Densmore noted a custom of "prefacing a song with a brief speech concerning it."[37] Here, the relationship of singer to song, and in the case of dream songs, to the spiritual power accessed through song, was integral to its performance.

Performance and Song Structure

Since the Ojibwe lived and moved in the oral tradition, song texts and tunes had no life apart from concrete moments of performance.[38] As Densmore put it, "you do not really *hear* Indian music unless you have the atmosphere of it."[39] Like the conceptual apparatus surrounding music, performance style remained relatively constant over time despite changes in repertory. A number of these stable characteristics are worth noting.

While Ojibwe musical performance could be social and entertaining, it was no casual entertainment. Because music could do things, it also was serious business. Posture, gesture, and tonal quality made a consistent impression on observers about the ceremonious tenor of native performances. A German traveling in the region in the 1850s noted a "seriousness around singing" evidenced by a ceremonial dance performed "very solemnly and earnestly." He remarked that as six women "muttered a monotonous and melancholy chant," they kept "their eyes steadily fixed on the ground."[40] Music making was all-engrossing. Densmore noted that when Anishinaabeg gathered to perform, they would sing "almost continuously for several hours at a time, each song being repeated an indefinite number of times."[41] "When reduced to notation," Thomas Vennum writes, "most Ojibwa melodies, regardless of song types, seem to be cut from the same cloth. Contours, tonal patterns, phrase lengths, and melodic directions are basically similar from song to song." The uniformity of pattern enabled Ojibwe people in different locations to pick up new songs rather quickly and to commit a large number of variants on basic patterns. "The vitality of Ojibwa melody," Vennum adds, lay in a singer's ability to adjust tempo and delivery to convey "a variety of effects."[42]

Ojibwe music involved singing in unison, though Densmore noted that singers occasionally began on different pitches and gravitated toward unison singing. Densmore found that singers usually assumed a distinctive nasalized falsetto, and often found "a vibrato, or wavering tone . . . especially pleasing." She noted the consistent structure of a descending interval of the minor third, suggesting a uniformity of music structure which Vennum later attributed to nineteenth-century changes in Ojibwe music.

Ojibwe people evaluated the quality of performance in terms of the distinctive associations music had with power and relationality. Good singing was respectful of a song's authority, attentive to its particulars, and performed in the right spirit. Prior to the performance of certain songs, singers often told stories about the meaning or significance or told about how a song had come to them. In certain cases, good singers demonstrated their respect by deliberately keeping the texts of certain sacred songs private, even in public performances. Vennum writes, "The Ojibwa hold the general view that spiritual communication, when it occurs in public, is meant to be indistinct and unintelligible to outsiders."[43]

Importantly, Ojibwe songs were nearly always accompanied by a drum or a rattle. "Rhythm is the essential part of the Chippewa song," Densmore wrote, "the words of a song may be slightly different in rendition, or the less important melody progressions may vary, but a corresponding variation in rhythm has not been observed."[44] Frederick Burton noticed in 1909 that "dependence upon the drum for entire satisfaction is one of the features of [Ojibwe] art that differs most widely from the musical manner of civilization. The Ojibwa can sing without the drum but he misses it . . ."[45]

Drums carried such spiritual resonance in Anishinaabe thought that it cannot suffice to think of the drum as secondary accompaniment to song. In the Ojibwe language, which distinguishes grammatically between animate and inanimate things, the drum, or *dewe'igan*, is gendered animate. As such, a drum is referred to with the pronoun he/she, rather than it: A drum is not so much an object as a subject, a powerful person deserving of hospitality and care. Today, it is still the case that ceremonial drums can receive a name and are placed under the protection of a designated keeper. Drums may require regular offerings of fresh tobacco, the protective clothing of a blanket, periodic visitation, acknowledgment of gratitude, and similar gestures of respect. Some even are consulted for divination. As with personalities of human beings, there are different drums, each with its own story, sometimes associated with its origin, its discovery, or its accumulated significance for the community. As is the case with songs, Ojibwe people distinguish among a variety of kinds of drums: hand drums kept by individuals, Midewiwin drums, Drum Dance drums, and drums associated more directly with social dances.[46] Even those drums not deemed overtly ceremonial share extraordinary significance. Drums are not so much played as they are asked to speak. It may be said that certain songs achieve their purpose because of the support and sponsorship of a given drum, which carries the thoughts and prayers of the singers and listeners to the appropriate spirits.

It follows that the groups of singers who gather around drums are charged with upholding the code of respect due the drum and each other. If something is amiss in an individual singer's life or in the relationships between singers, they will typically refrain from singing until some balance is restored. This code of respect is a matter of singular importance to Ojibwe music making, again underscoring the close association between the making of music and the maintenance and restoration of right relations between persons, human and nonhuman.

Public performances of Ojibwe songs frequently involved dance. In a recent study of the instruments and musical traditions of eastern Canada's native peoples, Beverley Diamond and collaborators observe that the Ojibwe morpheme for sound, we-, which finds its way in the word for drum, dewe'igan, also refers to its "physical correlation, motion."[47] Often acknowledging the raw power of such moments, missionaries detailed how many songs were inextricably linked to body movement, especially those sung on social and ceremonial occasions. The concerted motion of communal dancing, typically moving sunwise or clockwise in a circle, worked together with the resonant motion of the drum and the sounds of language to establish social and spiritual relationships in musical performances. The power of those relationships intimidated the missionaries, who sought to replace them with social and spiritual relations of a different kind.

To appreciate the fullness and necessity of music in an early-nineteenth-century Anishinaabe worldview, it may be helpful to understand sung music in terms of prayer. While it is a category used to apply to widely divergent phenomena, the notion of prayer involves the creation, exercise, or exploration of a relationship with the divine or with others. Through voiced song, the rhythm of the drum, and the movement of the body in space, a relationship was established and renewed between human beings trying to make a living and the spiritual sources of that life.[48]

Songs governed by the Midewiwin or other ritual contexts can be seen as invocational prayers requesting or generating powers of the manidoog. Songs were also occasional, seeking supplication in moments of death, starvation, and danger. Occasional songs even existed for seeking to calm rough water for lake crossings, indeed among the more dangerous aspects of life in the region.[49]

Fusing the pharmacological and physiological aspects of medicine with the ceremonial and social, the prayers of song, dance, and drum were elemental to Ojibwe ways of healing. Missionaries wrote disparagingly that "if any one is apprehended to be dangerously sick, it is no uncommon practice for the whole band to assemble in a large lodge . . . and spend one or two days in singing, howling, drumming, dancing, and feasting."[50] A Catholic priest remarked on how deeply an Ojibwe community in Manitoba felt about the link between song, prayer, and healing:

> Their songs and the discourses they pronounced at this time were nothing more than humble supplications addressed to the CREATOR OF LIFE to RESTORE LIFE to the sick person; from time to time they would address themselves to the Patron Spirit of the infirm man with chants accompanied by the sound of drums. I have talked to them about abandoning all this, and about being content to pray to our common Master in secret without making so much noise or disturbing the sick one; I have told them that God can hear a silent prayer just as well as their endless chanting around the sick bed. After a discourse which I addressed them in the midst of a large assemblage, they replied to me that it was impossible for them to decide to give up the only thing that they considered to be good in themselves.[51]

Here as elsewhere in Ojibwe music, the melody of song joined with the rhythm of the drum and the movement of dance to produce prayer in three dimensions. These prayers were not mechanistic incantations, but woven intricately into a cosmological and moral vision of the harmony and balance of *bimaadiziwin*, the good life.

As subsequent chapters will demonstrate, the introduction of evangelical hymnody into the Ojibwe repertory would involve some measure of transformation of the hymns in terms of a standing Anishinaabe approach to song. But the Anishinaabe approach to song never stood still. It, too, was moving—and was in part moved by the very introduction of the hymn and the associations with music that missionaries brought to the encounter. Before we go on to see how this played out in the career of the translated hymns, however, we should identify more specifically the range of associations hymns had for evangelical missionaries.

HYMNODY AND PROTESTANT LIFE

Missionaries steeped in the culture of Anglo-American evangelicalism held sacred music in high regard and were caught up in the great enthusiasm for hymns in the wake of eighteenth- and nineteenth-century revivals. In this historical context, the term *evangelical* did not carry many of the same social and political connotations that it carries today, characterizing instead the broader cultural ethos in which nineteenth-century Protestant missionaries found themselves and which placed a particular emphasis on the collective singing of hymns, in contrast to other Protestant traditions. It also better reflects the religious style shared by Protestant missionaries promoting Ojibwe hymns, for they represented a rather wide range of missionary societies and denominational affiliations.

On the one hand, hymnody was so much a fixture of this shared evangelical culture that the music was often taken for granted. On the other hand, hymnody was a primary venue for theological expression, social affiliation, and cultural identity. Thus, texts, tunes, and styles of performance of hymns often became axes along which whole communities came together or divided. Should sung texts simply perform the perfection of scripture, as some argued, or should they be more effective in stirring the emotions through the sacred poetry of an Isaac Watts or a Charles Wesley? Should tunes be simple and accessible to the musically untutored, or should they carry the loftiest strains of human praise, arranged in parts for sung harmony by a trained choir? Does musical accompaniment enhance praise, or does God prefer the unalloyed human voice? In the early nineteenth century, such matters were hardly peripheral. They posed vexing theological dilemmas and did so at the heart of popular experience.[52]

I will leave more detailed discussion of hymn controversies and their relationship to social and theological differences to the discerning work of Stephen Marini and others.[53] A few generalizations will nonetheless provide context for the present story. That hymn singing could prove so controversial indicates a shared evangelical assumption about the power of hymn singing which crossed most congregational and denominational lines.[54] The music of hymns, and more importantly the practice of singing them, gave an impassioned voice to religious identity. If understood in terms of ritual and not simply as a text, the sung hymn can be seen as a locus for the condensation of individual, social, and spiritual meanings which are too various and too numerous to be elaborated otherwise, and which resonate beyond the range of meanings defined by the texts alone. Small wonder, then, that the singing of certain hymns could stimulate such powerful associations of communal identity, or make present the memory of places and people in one's past.[55]

Evangelical Conceptions and Practices of Hymn Singing

A staple of Protestant devotional and worship life since the Reformation, the singing of psalms and hymns incorporated key elements of a widely shared worldview: an affective, experiential religion of the heart, as well as of the mind, fostered in the collective life of religious communities, relatively unmediated by clerical authority, and yet concerned with some measure of theological rectitude. For Puritans in the American colonies, singing psalms was a central practice by which covenanted communities acted the part of the saints. Because the scriptures described heavenly existence in terms of unceasing praise, Puritans understood psalmody as a powerful act of participation in the life of heaven.

Eighteenth-century revivals steered enthusiasm for psalmody toward the musical settings of sacred poetry. This generated no little controversy along the way, for some considered hymn texts to be precarious assertions of human artifice compared to the godly source of psalmody. For Protestants such as John and Charles Wesley, however, hymns were best suited to plant "speculative and practical divinity" on the lips and in the minds of the people. Referring to his brother's 1779 compilation of hymns, John Wesley asked: "In what other publication have you so distinct and full an account of scriptural Christianity? such a declaration of the heights and depths of religion, speculative and practical? so strong cautions against the most plausible errors? and so clear directions for making your calling and election sure; for perfecting holiness in the fear of God?"[56] For those who favored the singing of sacred poetry, the poetic spirit brought scriptural Christianity more fully to life. "We talk common sense," wrote John Wesley, engaging both "the purity, the strength, and the elegance of the English language; and, at the same time, the utmost simplicity and plainness, suited to every capacity." Effective language was joined in the hymn with the music's affective potential. "The spirit of piety," Wesley asserted, would be found "breathing through the whole Collection," a "means of raising or quickening the spirit of devotion; of confirming . . . faith, of enlivening . . . hope, and of kindling and increasing . . . love to God and man."[57]

Among those who supported hymnody, the texts were matters of close scrutiny. Published hymnbooks drew attention to the texts, for most did not include printed music to direct their singing. The sacred poetry found within hymnbooks often was material for private devotional reading. To facilitate the setting of texts to tunes, the meter of a hymn text was encoded. In the first decades of the nineteenth century, increased writing of hymn tunes resulted in a marked proliferation of tunebooks, even supporting a growing hymn-publishing industry. A given text was not fixed to a specific hymn tune, as became the case when hymnbooks and tunebooks were joined together in print. The facility of setting hymn texts to any number of tunes had all but disappeared by the twentieth century.[58]

The importance of hymn texts in evangelical culture also can be seen in the level of concern attached to selection of hymns for worship or for compilation in printed hymnbooks. In 1843, when the interdenominational American Board of Commissioners for Foreign Missions (ABCFM) sought publishing support for an Ojibwe hymnal from the American Tract Society, the society expressed deep concerned about translations of hymns about infant baptism "that might be thought of as too sectarian in character."[59]

Controversy was not limited to texts. Evangelicals disagreed on matters of performance, especially whether hymns should be sung in unison or in harmony. Opponents to music sung in parts were either troubled by the artifice it seemed to represent or by the curbs that "regular" or ruled singing would place on the spontaneous workings of the spirit in congregational songs. Even those who, like John Wesley, were willing to admit some greater degree of musical discipline, remained wary of the dangers of excess. In a 1779 tract, Wesley praised the possibilities for carefully wrought melodies to excite the passions, but cautioned that "harmony (so-called) . . . destroys the power of music," understood as "its power to affect the hearers; to raise various passions in the human mind." Harmony applied not to the faculties of the mind responsible for joy, hope, or fear "but merely to the ear, to the imagination, or internal sense." He urged that pious music be "extremely simple and inartifical." Were it to involve harmony, Wesley thought, composers ought first attend to matters of melody.[60] Echoes of the perspective carried in well into the nineteenth century, when composers, poets, and an emerging hymnbook-publishing industry produced a proliferation of hymnbooks and tunebooks.[61]

For nineteenth-century evangelicals, sung hymnody involved more than the performed sound object of text and tune: The sound of hymnody had everything to do with the social relationships among the singers. Edmund Ely, an ABCFM schoolteacher among the Ojibwe at Fond du Lac, prayed for the choir he left behind in upstate New York: "My God! remember that Choir in mercy. Bind them to one another and to thee. Teach them the benefit and the sweetness of a forbearing forgiveness . . . so that when they shall meet together to sing the sweet songs of Zion, the spirit shall be in their midst to melt their hearts . . . In such a state of feeling, their songs would kindle up that dear Church. Incense would rise—God would be in their midst! Sinners would *melt* into contrition."[62] Hymnody was a fully participatory form of piety. Scripture passages, interpretations, and doctrinal formulations were voiced collectively by the people—men and women, lettered and unlettered, clergy and lay, in the pews of churches, in the clearings of camp meetings, and beside the hearths of evangelical homes.

Hymns often set the tone for the process of conviction of sin, conversion, and growth in grace that evangelicals fostered in their revivals. For some, the singing of hymns could induce that regeneration, or at least provide an effective mark of the regenerate life. To help make a case for the spiritual authenticity of a 1738 revival, Jonathan Edwards turned to genuine hymnody as one of the encouraging signs: "A great delight in singing praises to God and Jesus Christ, and longing that this present life may be, as it were, one continued song of praise to God; longing, as the person expressed it, to sit and sing this life away; and an overcoming pleasure in the thoughts of spending an eternity in that exercise."[63] There was no great conceptual leap for Edwards to move in the same sentence from hymn singing to other outward signs of the inner working of the Holy Spirit: "a constant and extraordinary distrust of own strength and wisdom," "filling up this life with hard labor," "feel[ing] nothing in their hearts but love and compassion to all mankind; and having freedom from all bitter zeal, censoriousness, spiritual pride, hot disputes, etc."[64]

Evangelicals of the following century differed in their opinions on the precise relationship between hymns and the workings of regeneration, but they agreed that hymns were the music appropriate to the regenerated life. Evangelicals conceived of the sung hymn as a distinctly Christian music to set the tone for a distinctly Christian way of life. In some cases, evangelical communities forbade any other kind of music completely. Hymnody thus came to accrue significance far beyond the frame of worship. Hymnody provided an occasion for socializing, artistic virtuosity, and education that cast the light of religion on all aspects of life. Even those Methodists and Baptists who tried to yoke their sacred poetry to the tunes of popular songs agreed with more genteel Protestants about a sharp distinction between the sung Christian hymn and the unregenerate music of the profane world.

Hymns and Evangelical Missions

The proselytizing spirit of evangelical culture displayed in the revivals found full institutional expression in the great nineteenth-century efforts to convert the world, and the translation and promotion of hymns remained among the more emphatic of institutional missionary endeavors, alongside the urgent task of making biblical truth readily accessible in translated form through the technology of print. Those evangelicals swept up in the fervor to convert the world took these convictions about hymnody with them to the field, where they found hymns to be exceptionally useful. Even liturgically oriented High Church Episcopalians who set out in the 1850s with missionary zeal to the native peoples of the old Northwest found compelling and useful the hymnody associated with Low Church evangelical culture.

But the story of hymnody in the region begins twenty years earlier, centered on the joint missions venture of Congregationalists, Presbyterians, and Baptists in the ABCFM.[65] Again, the translation, printing, and promotion of hymns were but parts of a larger scheme of printing and preaching the Word, and teaching the world to read the Word for themselves.

Missionary boards took delight in the number of printed pages of translated tracts that their presses were able to turn out. The ABCFM proclaimed that the "power of the press" was a "gift . . . we should probably choose in preference to that of tongues."[66] Evangelical biblicism transformed the mundane missionary work of translation and instruction into acts of piety on a par with prayer. By 1862, the ABCFM boasted that its presses alone had produced 1,841,000 pages of bibles, hymnals, and schoolbooks in the Ojibwe language.[67]

For evangelical missionaries, the ability to read was more than an isolated skill. Missionaries viewed instruction, translation, and printing as foundational to nothing short of social and cultural revolution. Even Rufus Anderson, who as General Secretary tried to steer the ABCFM away from the civilizing mission toward the unalloyed preaching of the gospel, nevertheless considered such printing figures to be among "the more important indicators of progress." Efforts aimed at "reducing languages to writing, translating the Scripture, and forming Christian schools" were the very foundations required for "awakening anxiety to learn the way of life."[68]

Missionaries thought of reading as the seed that contained the makings of an entire way of life, a Christian civilization. They could not speak of "the Book" without invoking the dramatic changes in the ordering of time, space, economy, and social relationships thought to go hand in hand with it. When an Ojibwe elder came to the ABCFM's William Boutwell for aid, his people starving on account of the depletion of game, the missionary replied: "Tell me then what makes the differe[nce] between me & an Ind[ian] since it is neither colour nor language. . . . *It is the book.* It is this that learns me how to get & how to keep something against time of need."[69] A life lived in step with the Book was to bring private property, square frame houses, fenced fields, chairs, tables, beds, short hair, and Anglo-American gender norms. "We have no doubt," wrote an ABCFM official, "that school books and large portions of Scriptures & Tracts are to have an important place in reclaiming and converting the roving Indians."[70]

Ojibwe people agreed that books came as part of a larger package. But they could not speak of "the Book" without invoking the colonial nature of that package. When asked if a mission school could be erected near the headwaters of the Mississippi, a Leech Lake leader replied: "All your letters are stained with blood. . . . The words of the long knives [*gichimookomaanag*, white people] have passed through our forests as a rushing wind, but they have been words merely."[71] Indeed, the Book appeared as an organizing metaphor for the entire cultural, social, and economic complex of the European-American invasion. An Ojibwe leader from Fond du Lac remarked to one missionary that "the white man is wise, he knows how to take the Ind[ian]s. Ever since the world was made he has been writing—counting the days ahead—& he knows what will be bye & bye."[72]

As long as the land base and its resources were sufficient to support the seasonal way of life, however, Ojibwes were relatively able to set the terms of cultural exchange with the missions. For at least the first half of the century, the Anishinaabeg of the Lake Superior and Mississippi headwaters region received missionaries into their lodges and listened respectfully, but by and large chose to remain beyond the influence of the Book. "If the Great Spirit had designed [we] should be instructed," a native leader told the ABCFM's Frederick Ayer in a characteristic interchange in 1833, "[we] would have had his word communicated to [us] before. . . . The Great Spirit designed [we] should have a different religion & customs from the Whites." And yet, Ayer noted, "they always received us kindly and though some of them refused us permission to read God's word to them in the lodges yet they conversed with us and asked & answered questions on the subject of religion more freely than we could have reasonably anticipated."[73]

Missionaries became increasingly frustrated with what they saw as a constitutional indifference to instruction. After five years of work, the head of the ABCFM's La Pointe mission found "the disposition of the Indians remains about the same. . . . They are disposed to treat us friendly, but there is no moving yet among the dry bones." Absent the influence of the Holy Spirit, he averred, "they seem as insensible as the rocks which are washed by the waves of their native lake."[74] Missionaries often growled that native people expected payment for the favor of sending their children to mission schools.

Ironically, this frustration only redoubled the missionaries' trust in the redemptive power of scripture and devotional books. For years, Sherman Hall insisted on the urgency of the work of translation. "It is in vain to attempt to introduce the English language extensively among these Indians," he argued. "They have no motive of sufficient strength to enable them to undergo the necessary labour."[75] It would be much easier to introduce the French, he thought, "but their own they would be more interested to learn than either. One important branch of missionary labor would therefore be to prepare books in the native language."[76]

The ABCFM's commission to its first missionaries in the region specified that the "acquisition of the Chippewa language and the translation of elementary books, scripture tracts, etc" ought to receive priority in the strategic task of preaching the gospel.[77] But the publication effort never seemed to bear sufficient fruit. As Sherman Hall reflected, "I do not know what opinion to form as to what will result from the introduction of books into the Chippeway language."[78]

Missionary Hymn as Affective

Herein lay the increasing strategic value of hymnbooks, for according to then-popular educational theory, hymns could be effective tools to awaken among children the passion to learn and to lead a morally upright life—and among those entire peoples that missionaries thought of as children. ABCFM missionaries looked for inspiration and direction from the manuals of the Infant School System, an educational movement promoted in England for the education of the emerging working classes by Robert Owen and others. An Infant School manual in use at the ABCFM missions celebrated the far-reaching effects of hymn singing:

> Singing is so admirably calculated to harmonize the feelings of the children, and cement attachment to each other. It seems to tranquilize and soften the more obdurate tempers. It also acts as a magnet of attraction to the volatile. It tends to soothe the impatient. By singing the hymns the infant mind is enriched with pure and important sentiments, which it is believed will not fail in some degree to direct the future conduct of all, and . . . to prepare many of them, to sing the song of Moses and the Lamb in the mansions of glory.[79]

When sacred texts were sung, the music was understood to engender an immediate connection to the sentiments expressed in words. In 1789, the Presbyterian Samuel Blair brought to bear Jonathan Edward's psychology of the affections in his view of the "intimate connection between sounds . . . and the sentiments of the heart" through which "the foundation is laid in our nature for the moral operation of external harmony."[80] Blair applied Edwards's connection between the affections and moral action to the dynamics of sacred music: "That feeling which, in its first appearance, was merely the result of musical impulses, hath now become a real, effective, and profitable sentiment."[81]

For missionaries, the singing of hymns was subordinate to the reading of scripture and the proclamation of the Word, but because hymnody was believed to do the cultural work of stirring the heart and mind to accept the preached Word, many considered it essential. An 1884 English hymnal compiled for world missions generally declared its object to have been "not so much worship, as the arousing and expressing those religious feelings which it is the function of a Mission to quicken and develop: Sorrow for sin, and the desire for pardon and a new life, have to be kindled in the heart, before there can be attended that true repentance. . . . Fervent and hearty Hymn singing is one of the most important means of that stirring up the dull and sluggish hearts on which the Mission is intended to act."[82] It is perhaps not surprising that Isaac Watts's "Come Holy Spirit, Heavenly Dove" was among the first hymns translated into the Ojibwe language:

> Come, Holy Spirit, heavenly Dove,
> With all Thy quickening powers;
> Kindle a flame of sacred love
> In these cold hearts of ours.
>
> In vain we tune our formal songs,
> In vain we strive to rise;
> Hosannas languish on our tongues,
> And our devotion dies.
>
> And shall we, Lord, for ever be
> In this poor dying state?
> Our love so faint, so cold to thee,
> And thine to us so great?
>
> Come, Holy Spirit, heavenly dove,
> With all thy quickening powers;
> Come, shed abroad a Savior's love,
> And that shall kindle ours?

Missionary Hymn as Didactic

In the preface to his brother's 1779 compilation of hymns, John Wesley wrote, "this book is in effect a little book of experimental and practical divinity."[83] It was experimental, in the sense that eighteenth-century usage of the term referred to matters of experience, because a hymn's power stemmed from an affective experience of corporate song and poetic feeling. It was practical, because evangelicals in England and North America viewed the hymn as an accessible medium through which the values of Christian living could be inculcated. Citing Paul's first letter to the Corinthians, the title page of one Ojibwe hymnbook proclaimed, "I will sing with the spirit, and I will sing with the understanding also."[84]

Taken as objects in their own right, the little hymnbooks were didactic scripts for an ordered Christian life. John Wesley was proud that his brother's 1779 compilation of hymns was "not so large as to be either cumbersome or expensive." Likewise, each nineteenth-century Ojibwe hymnbook was portable enough to accompany and inspire the Christian in any of the day's activities. Yet Wesley was quick to point out that the hymn collections were "large enough to contain such a variety of hymns" as to "contain all the important truths of our most holy religion" and "for all ordinary occasions." The hymns did not simply formulate these truths. They were to "illustrate" them, and to do so "in a regular order."[85] Ojibwe hymnbooks incorporated this concern for a methodical Christian life in their organizing of the hymns. Methodist printings of Peter Jones's Ojibwe hymnbook were organized by theme of Christian life (exhorting sinners to return to God, pleasantness of religion, Christian fellowship, etc.) and by occasion (New Year, morning, evening). Later Episcopalian hymnals organized Ojibwe hymns around the liturgical year, times of day, and occasions of the life cycle.

The content and the structure reflected this didactic purpose. While hymns were believed rich in affective possibility, they pedantically set forth each element of an evangelical life: order, punctuality, sobriety, thrift, and industry. Witness the English original of a hymn found in Peter Jones's Ojibwe hymnbook:[86]

> O for a heart to praise my God,
> A heart from sin set free!
> A heart that always feels thy blood,
> So freely spilt for me.
>
> A heart resigned, submissive, meek
> My great Redeemer's throne;
> Where only Christ is heard to speak,
> Where Jesus reigns alone.
>
> A humble, lowly, contrite heart,
> Believing, true, and clean,
> Which neither life nor death can part
> From Him that dwells within.
>
> A heart in every thought renewed
> And full of love divine
> Perfect and right and pure and good
> A copy, Lord, of Thine!
>
> Thy nature, gracious Lord, impart;
> Come quickly from above;
> Write Thy new Name upon my heart,
> Thy new, best Name of Love.

A number of scholars have examined the texts of such hymns as the coin of Victorian social control. E. P. Thompson viewed such lyrics in the culture of industrializing England as evidence of what he called the reformation of manners. According to Thompson, the genre of the hymn was mobilized to encourage England's emerging working classes to internalize values of efficiency, industry, and thrift, and to embrace the social position defined by the working-class life as godly. A conviction of the godliness of this life was significantly effected through hymn texts that made virtues of the necessities of working-class existence: behaviors of submissiveness, meekness, and quietism.[87] Susan Tamke has extended Thompson's view by examining in particular how hymns prescribed and proscribed certain behaviors and attitudes among children, reproducing such class relations.[88] Virtues of submissiveness, obedience, and earnestness were extolled, sometimes against a backdrop of threatened punishment.

Missionary societies were likewise attracted to the possibilities of systematic hymnody for training impressionable minds of the world's non-Christian majority and socializing whole peoples coded as children into evangelical life. "I can like these In[dian]s to nothing more aptly than stubborn peevish children," the ABCFM's William Boutwell declared of the Ojibwes in 1839, "who have to be gratified in all their wishes & are obstinate and refractory if refused." Boutwell concluded the natives "require therefore just the independent management that the father exercises over his little dominion. The father's will must be the child's law."[89]

Such language suggests just how strategic missionaries were in the promotion of translated hymns as affective and didactic tools of social control. But to interpret hymns solely as extensions of social control would be to miss the far more complicated politics and poetics of cultural exchange. For missionaries did not just value hymnody for its effectiveness in imparting the textual content of a civilized, Christian life. Our brief consideration of hymnody's central role in evangelical culture suggests how deeply missionaries valued hymns for the relationality that could be engendered in the collective singing of them and for the beauty created in the process.

Although Ojibwe and evangelical understandings of music making differed dramatically, each shared a deep concern for engendering social and spiritual relations in collective singing. If we attune our ears to the sparse documentation we have of such moments, we will perhaps hear a more complex dynamic than that which hindsight would assign to "acculturation" under the one-directional forces of presumed social control. This focus appreciates the more complicated politics of the exchange by shifting attention from the ideological to the cultural.[90] It is to the complex narrative of that exchange to which we now turn.

2

OJIBWES, MISSIONARIES, AND
HYMN SINGING, 1828–1867

▲▲▲▲▲▲

O ne of the earlier important narratives written at the hand of an Ojibwe fig-
ure is shot through with references to hymn texts and their significance.
Published first in 1847 and reissued in 1850 as *The Life, Letters, and
Speeches of Kah-Ge-Ga-Gah-Bowh, or G. Copway Chief Ojibway Nation*, this text offers a glimpse of how complex was the world from which Ojibwe hymns emerged.[1]
Born far to the east of Minnesota near Rice Lake, Ontario, George Kahgegagahbowh
Copway was an Ojibwe Methodist preacher who became well known on the lecture
circuit and in print in the 1840s and 1850s for his vivid descriptions of the customs
of his Ojibwe people and of their prospects for conversion and "civilization." He was
a prolific interpreter of his people's culture to a nonnative audience and a vocal advocate of native interests, at least as he saw those interests. Copway believed the survival and prosperity of Ojibwe people would best be served in the context of religious conversion to evangelical Christianity and cultural assimilation. But Copway
was a pragmatist, not an ideologue. His verbal performances of civilization in lecture
halls from Boston to Philadelphia also involved sharp criticisms of the savagery that
resulted from the oppressive circumstances that faced his people under American
rule. In some regards, Copway became what missionaries wanted him to become—a
model of that one-directional "progress" characterized by both conversion and assimilation to Anglo-American evangelical religion and culture. But a closer look re-
veals a far more complicated story that led, among other things, to a falling out with
the Methodists, short careers as a Union Army recruiter and a healer in Detroit, and
(re-)baptism into the Roman Catholic church.[2] As Ojibwe novelist and critic Gerald Vizenor observes, "tribal missionaries who base their ken on conversion, as [Cop-
way] did, cast strange shadows on familiar woodland trails," but Vizenor acknowledges that Copway's story was one of "a keen survivor, material and spiritual."[3]

Hymns were of enormous significance to Copway. But he wrote about them in
such way that Ojibwe language hymns become evidence of those complications as
much as they do evidence of a stable acculturation from heathen to "civilized convert." It was as a twelve-year-old attending a camp meeting that Copway himself

converted in 1830, but his own narration of that conversion credits the nurturing faith of his mother, who had died of tuberculosis the year before:

> Just before her death she prayed with her children; and advised us to be good Christians, to love Jesus, and meet her in heaven. She then sang her favorite hymn.
>
> Jesus ish pe ming Kah e zhod.
> Jesus, my all, to heaven is gone.
>
> This was the first hymn she heard or learned; and it is on this account that I introduce and sing this sweet hymn whenever I lecture on the origin, history, traditions, migration, and customs of the Ojebwa nation.[4]

Surely audiences marveled to hear a familiar hymn sung in such a strange tongue, but knowing how complex the lives of such figures as Copway were, we are equipped to ask more discerningly just what it was that Copway, Kahgegagahbowh, was performing when he sang these words in his language at some eastern Athenaeum. Copway was celebrated as one of the first Ojibwe Christians to articulate themselves in print in the English language, but Copway was the exception rather than rule of Ojibwe people at midcentury. Though he himself would teach these hymns at the Fond du Lac mission, it would be many years before the hymns sank deep roots in the villages of Minnesota's Anishinaabeg.

Indeed, it would be tempting to think, as I admit I did in earlier stages of research, that the story of Ojibwe hymns unfolds along the lines of the following hypothetical formula. In the meeting of Ojibwe and evangelical missionary cultures, missionary intentions to impose a Christian worldview meet the resistance of Ojibwe traditions. Hymns enjoy increasing cultural authority as missionary power waxes and Ojibwe independence wanes. But for those who have access to the original language texts, the translations themselves become documents of indigenous resistance to the entire process. So goes the anticipated formula: domination inscribed through the Christian texts; resistance of Ojibwe tradition by means of the performance of those texts. Or perhaps the native language translations themselves subverted the force of the Christian ideas they were supposed to convey.

As it happened, the story was of course far more complicated. Again, on the field of culture, the workings of domination and resistance often proceed at some remove from the conscious intentions of dominators and resisters. The task is to train our understanding of the development of Ojibwe hymn singing firmly on the tenuous spaces of culture, spaces that move *between* the oral and the written, *between* the Christian and the Ojibwe, *between* accommodation and resistance.

What can be said about the nature of such spaces is, fortunately, not so tenuous. Practices around hymn singing changed over time and were structured by changing relationships of power between missionaries and Ojibwe communities. Therefore, we can look for evidence of how historical shifts in that social field of power relationships registered in the musical practice of hymn singing. From 1828, when the first fully Ojibwe hymnbook appeared, to the 1868 founding of the White Earth Reservation, missionaries worked diligently to promote hymn translations, but their documents suggest a merely sporadic practice of native hymn singing in response. It would not be until the social transformations of concentrated reservation life after 1868 that hymn singing would take on the urgency that I explore in chapter 3. In this early period, however, we can begin to see and hear how hymn singing as a cultural practice registered mounting pressures of a collapsing fur trade, an eroding land base, and an increasingly factionalized Anishinaabe community.

The Setting

The Ojibwe people of the era of the initial introduction of the hymns lived quite differently than those of the later reservation era. In a sense, we must qualify our use of the term *Ojibwe people*, for extended families and bands never really comprised an identifiable political unit, though they were linked by language, culture, ceremony, and an overarching if weakening clan system. A defining feature of that culture, as we have seen, had been an economy and lifeway in motion with seasonal changes. The basic unit of Ojibwe social life even varied with seasonal activities: Winter found most Ojibwe people in smaller groups of extended families, dispersed widely to more effectively hunt big game; at ricing and sugaring times, larger groups congregated at rice camps and sugarbushes; summer economic activities were given to larger gatherings of people in villages along lakes. Even the social structures of Ojibwe life were calibrated to the fluid seasonal rhythms of the land. For example, Ojibwe women exercised more pronounced economic and political leadership at those times of the year when the extended family was the primary unit.[5]

When they enjoyed the relative autonomy to do so, Anishinaabe people were adept at absorbing the economic and cultural exchanges of the fur trade into their seasonal round. The trade brought together larger and larger seasonal gatherings to European-American trading posts. At certain times of the year, Sault Ste. Marie, Keweenaw Bay, La Pointe, and Fond du Lac drew large concentrations of native people. In the treaty period, annuity payments similarly brought large numbers of Ojibwe bands together at the same time, creating new constituencies and new lines of political, economic, and ceremonial exchange. The fur trade and early treaty making introduced considerable novelty to Ojibwe life, but these novelties were integrated into the fluid workings of the seasonal round. Most lived and moved within its structuring time and space.

Anishinaabe ceremonial and cultural life kept time with the changes of the seasons. The cycle of trickster myths and other powerful stories, known as *aadizookaanag*, were to be told only when snow lay on the ground. Some rites of the Midewiwin ceremonial complex were seasonal. Many songs and dances were associated with seasonal activities like ricing. Rites associated with the life passage, such as naming ceremonies, puberty fasts, and death rites, added another cycle of experience to the polyrhythms of Ojibwe life.

While most Anishinaabeg retained a seasonal life on the land, a number of Ojibwe people departed from the seasonal round to live near the posts of the fur trade. These *Métis*, so named for their often mixed French and native heritage, remained as year-round clerks and translators for the fur companies. Métis men often married women from within the communities of Anishinaabeg proper, and they played a strategic, sometimes controversial, role as social and economic go-betweens in the trade. Scholars have shown recently how the Métis emerged as a new people in their own right having distinguished themselves from—while remaining conversant with—both Anishinaabeg and Europeans. Despite the language of blood that contemporaries applied, these respective ethnicities had far more to do with non-hereditary linguistic, social, and cultural markers of identity, such as clothing, music, education, and economic commitments.[6] One marker of this identity was an affiliation with the Roman Catholicism of their French heritage. Métis congregants were seldom trusted by Protestant missionaries, even when they comprised, in some cases, the majority of active participants in the life of the mission. Although Sherman Hall considered the Métis "too ignorant and car[ing] too little about religion" to want to undermine the efforts of his American Board mission of their own accord, he cautioned that, "when put forward and directed by a priest, they can make a powerful auxiliary to the cause of Romanism."[7]

From the earliest days of the fur trade in the region, Roman Catholic missionaries, especially Jesuits, exerted a powerful influence—by far the more powerful influence up until the 1760s, when colonial authorities officially removed them from the region. Years later, Protestant missionaries came and established their mission stations and schools at the fur trade settlements.[8] Canadian Anglicans and Wesleyans made the first appreciable forays on the eastern edges of Ojibwe country in Ontario, gradually moving into the upper Mississippi region. A more pronounced effort in the region was launched at the American Fur Company's post at La Pointe, along Lake Superior's southern shore, by the ABCFM in the 1830s. The ABCFM, initially a joint venture of Presbyterians, Congregationalists, and Baptists, had already established a station and school at the busy fur trade crossroads of Mackinac Island by 1822. The La Pointe station, so influential in the production of Ojibwe texts and the promotion of Ojibwe hymns, became the headquarters for the ABCFM's extension of its mission to Fond du Lac and to the interior Ojibwe communities of Sandy Lake, Leech Lake, Pokegoma, and Yellow Lake. In the 1840s, Oberlin College–based Congregationalist missionaries who were theologically aligned with the ABCFM but at odds with its reliance on donations traceable to the slave economy, established an important presence in the Mississippi headwaters communities of Leech Lake, Red Lake, Cass Lake, and Lake Winnibigoshish. In the 1830s and 1840s, Frederic Baraga, Franz Pierz, and other priests of an Austro-Hungarian mission society restored or established a string of Roman Catholic missions on the southern and western shores of Lake Superior, and they soon moved into the Mississippi headwaters region as well. In some quarters of the region, the Roman Catholic influence far exceeded that of the Protestants.

Episcopalians gained the first foothold for their abiding presence in the region in 1852, at the Gull Lake mission established by James Lloyd Breck. Breck's vision for winning native converts where others failed wedded the emphasis on liturgy and ritual of High Church Anglicanism with the missionary fervor more characteristic of the denomination's evangelical wing. Breck had come to Gull Lake directly from Nashotah House, a monastic community that he and a circle of graduates of General Theological Seminary had established in southeast Wisconsin.[9] Breck's early efforts

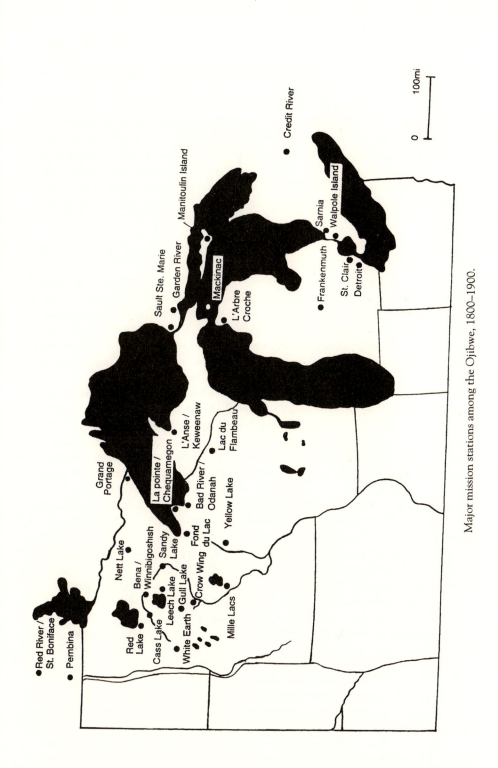

Major mission stations among the Ojibwe, 1800–1900.

100mi

0

Credit River

Manitoulin Island

Sarnia
Walpole Island

Frankenmuth

St. Clair
Detroit

Sault Ste. Marie

Garden River

Mackinac

L'Arbre
Croche

Grand
Portage

La pointe /
Chequamegon

L'Anse /
Keweenaw

Lac du
Flambeau

Bad River /
Odanah

Yellow Lake

Red River /
St. Boniface

Pembina

Nett Lake

Bena /
Winnibigoshish

Sandy
Lake

Fond
du Lac

Red
Lake

Cass Lake

Leech Lake

White Earth

Gull Lake

Crow Wing

Mille Lacs

were later expanded by Henry Benjamin Whipple, the first Episcopal Bishop of Minnesota, and John Johnson Enmegabowh, an Anishinaabe man who converted under Methodist influence in his native Ontario. With Whipple's nod of approval and Enmegabowh's hard work, Episcopalians expanded the mission in Minnesota by training and supervising a group of Anishinaabe clergy. In large part because of this level of commitment to a native-led church, the Episcopalians proved to have the more lasting of Protestant influence among Minnesota Ojibwes; this book, therefore, remains largely concerned with the Episcopalian story in the reservation period. American Methodists, Lutherans, and others also established scattered missions efforts in the region, with some peripheral contribution to traditions of hymn singing.[10]

Between the Written and the Oral: Hymnbooks and Hymn Singing

For literate Anglo-American evangelicals, hymnbooks were in effect theological texts. Hymnbooks were used in collective performance, of course, but they were also often read in as private devotional literature. In the nineteenth century, most hymnbooks did not contain music and resembled collections of sacred poetry more than they did the hymnals commonly found in church pews today. Hymnbooks gave missionaries entrée to the world of spoken Ojibwe. Absent a "suitable interpreter" or the "ability to speak the language of the Indians," one missionary found, "we are barbarians to the Indians, and they to us."[11] Especially in the early years among the Ojibwes, missionaries were completely dependent on the little Ojibwe books to command an audience. "One of the most hopeful ways of reaching the minds of this people with the truth," declared the advertisement for an ABCFM Ojibwe spelling book, "is to preach it from house to house, to read the Scriptures and religious tracts to individuals, and converse with them on religious subjects as the Missionary meets with them by the way side, in their huts, or when they visit him at his own dwelling." The dependence on native language books made missionaries vulnerable in the field. A flurry of anxious correspondence with the ABCFM headquarters in Boston erupted when three hundred copies of Jones's hymnal expected to arrive at the field stations in the winter of 1836–37 were lost en route, along with two hundred copies of *Old Testament Bible Stories/Natural History* and three hundred copies of Thomas Gallaudet's *Picture Defining and Reading Book*. The misplaced crates were recovered a year later, ironically having found their way by steamship to La Porte on Lake Michigan, rather than La Pointe on Lake Superior.[12]

Using hymnbooks as phonetic prompts for the spoken word, missionaries reported native people's intrigue at the fact that they could speak intelligibly in Ojibwe. That missionaries depended so heavily on the Ojibwe texts to navigate the oral world of the language accounts for why they spent so much energy on matters of orthography. What seem at first glance to be long and tedious debates about the merits of this or that orthography were in fact urgent matters for missionaries who lacked other resources for reaching native audiences.[13]

In a helpful study of hymn singing among the Naskapi and Innu of northern Quebec (whose language is in the same Algonkian language family as Ojibwe), Beverley Cavanaugh characterizes this tradition as situated *between* the written and oral. According to Cavanaugh, the printed hymnbooks are not so much scripts that "dictate the tradition" as they are documents that "reflect it."[14] Cavanaugh's point is that hymn singing practice is far more than a performance scripted and directed by missionaries: "Both the nomadic annual cycle of the [Innu] and the transient nature of the missions suggest that until [recently] Christian traditions had largely been sustained internally, by the Indians themselves, with only occasional direction from the clergy."[15] In her field research, Cavanaugh found that "performance practice reinforces the view that Indian hymnody was to a large extent an oral tradition in which hymnbooks functioned as mnemonic devices. The books were clearly not prerequisites for hymn singing."[16] Hymnals served as mnemonic devices and, interestingly, as iconic embodiments of the entire tradition, but they hardly functioned for native people as the textual devices of a literary culture.

Cavanaugh's findings help account for the bewildering number of variations in respective editions of Ojibwe hymnbooks. Some versions omit whole verses. Others replace them with verses that stray even further from the English. For example, six different printed versions of "Ondashan, Ondashan, Gichi Ochichag," translations of Isaac Watts's "Come, Holy Spirit, Heavenly Dove," register a number of variations. From its first printing in the ABCFM's *O-jib-ue Spelling Book* (1833) to the 1993 edition of Kah-O-Sed's *Ojibwa Hymns* (1910), one notices obvious differences in orthography, but also wholesale changes in some of the verses.[17] Table 2.1 presents the variations of this hymn.

Clearly, these variations are not to be understood as mere revisions of previous translations, corrections moving toward a closer rendition of Isaac Watts's original poem. Rather, they are to be understood as indices of wide-reaching variations in hymn-singing practice, consequences of the broad reach of the hymnbooks' geographic circulation and the highly localized, dialect-rich nature of the Ojibwe language. Moreover, like the Innu hymnals of Cavanagh's study, these variations follow from the idiosyncrasies of folk songs in an oral tradition, losing some details to the shortcomings of memory while gaining others along the way in the creativity of particular hymn-singing events.[18] Ojibwe hymnody emerged in places that were thoroughly between orality and literacy.

To better understand the impact made by these books on the oral tradition and vice versa, it will be useful to make a more self-conscious distinction between the text of the hymns and the practice of performing them collectively. We might understand *text* as the hymns of printed hymnbooks themselves, filled with Christian content, conceived and promoted by missionaries as extensions of their sphere of influence. Insofar as these texts were in the native language, they were imperfect extensions of that influence, but the texts nonetheless shaped performance. Beyond the printed books, we can assign to the category of text the set of missionary assumptions attached to hymns and the larger social field in which Ojibwe hymns were promoted and through which hymn-singing practice was disciplined.

In turn, we can take *practice* to pertain to the way that those texts became musical events in moments of hymn singing. "Practice" is more apt than "performance" here because it better conveys the *betweenness* of concrete moments of singing: between orality and literacy, between Ojibwe and evangelical culture, between con-

Table 2.1

COME, HOLY SPIRIT, HEAVENLY DOVE

O-jib-ue Spelling Book (Utica, 1833)	Ojibue Nugumouinun (Jones, Boston, 1836)	Ojibue Nugumouinun (Jones, Boston, 1844)	Fragment (n.d.)	Kah-O-Sed, Ojibwa Hymnal (Mpls., 1910)
On da shan ki ji a ji jag Pi don dosh kok in o; Ge on ji pa pi nen da ma Nin de i no pi don.	On da shan ki ji o ji jag, Pi don dush ku ki nu; Ge on ji ba pi nen du ma Nin de i na pi don.	On-da-shan, Ki-ji-o-ji-jag Pi-ton dush ku-ki-nu Ge-on-ji-pa-pi-nen-du-ma Nin-te-i-na pi-ton	On-dä-shän' Ke-che-o-'je chäg Pe'-ton dush ku-kin'-u Ga-on'-je-bä-pe-nan-däang Nin-da'-e-näng pe'-ton	Ondashan, Kichi Ochichag, Widokawishinam, Atoniu sagiiwewin Ima nindeinang.
Na got a ua bom ish in am Gi ki ti ma giz i ia; O zam ki ji pe I up la. Up a nom I a la.	Na gu ta ua bu mish in am Ki ti ma gi zi ia, O zam ki ji be ji ui ia, Ui a nu mi a ia.	Ua-bu-mi-shi-nam ni-na-uint Ke-ti-ma-gi-zi-ia O-zam su nim-pe-ji-ui-min Ish-pi-mi-ui-'zha-ia	Wa'-bum-ish-e-näm ne'-nä wint Ka-te-mä'-giz-e-yäang O-zäm' su nim-pa'-che-we-min Ish'-pe-ming we-'zhä'-'yäng.	'Na eji-gotugiziyang Oma aking ayayang; Nin kichi bejiwimin su Ishpiming wi'jayang.
Nos I nan ka gi nik no dosh Nin go zhi pe ji ui in; O zam po i sa gi o ion Ji sa gi ia dosh kin	Nos i nan ka gi nik nu dush, Nin gu i zhi be ji ui min; O zam pu i sa gi o iun Ji sa gi ia dush kin.	Ni-ni-na-ui-ta-gu-zi-min Ne-nu-gu-mo-sha-in; Ni-ma-mo-iuue-uin-in-an Non-de ko tu-ki-sin.	Ne-ne-nä-we-tä'-gö-ze-min Na-nu-gu-mo-shäng'-in Ne-mä-mo-yu-wa' win-e-nän Non-da'-ko-tu-ke-sin.	Anawi nindinend amin Nagumotagoyun; Nind anamiawinan Nonde ko takisin.
Ma no on da shan nos i nan Sha ue ni mish in am; Pi ni si na ma uish in am Ki ki ji ki ji jag.	Ma no on da shan Nos i nan Sha ue ni mish in am; Pi ni si na ma uish in am Ki ki ji ki ji jag.	No-si-nan, mi-nu a-pi-ne Ge-'zhi-pe-ji-ui-ia? O-zam pun-gi sa-gi-'go-iun Sa-gi-i-a dush kin.		
Pi na na zi ka uish in am Sha uen da gu zi iom; Ni ka ki gon o na a ton Pa pi nen dom o uin	Pi na na zi ka uish in am Sha uen da gu zi iun Ni ka ki gu na na a ton Ba pi nen du mo ouin	On-da-shan, Ki-ji-o-ji-jag, Sha-ue-ni-mi-shi-nam; Mosh-ki-nu-ton nin-te-i-na Pa-pi-nen-du-mo-uin.	On-dä-shän' Ke-che-o-'je-chäg Sha-wa'-ne-mish-e-mäm; Mosh'-ke-nu-ton nin-ta'-e-näng Pä-pe-nan'-dum-o-win.	Ondashan, Kichi Ochichag, Widokawishinam, Moshkinaton nindeinang Iu sagiiwewin.

scious and unconscious agency. The realm of practice is structured by the texts and by the spheres of missionary influence around the texts, but it allows sufficient play to maneuver within those structures to lay claim to what one student of the practices of orality calls, "utopian points of reference."[19] Moreover, the notion of practice enables us to distinguish the cultural dynamics between text and performance without presuming that the two are engaged in some clearcut standoff between the Christian content of missionary translations and the intrinsically subversive practices of Anishinaabe performance. As the details of translation unfold in the following pages, the case will be seen to have been far more complicated. Many of the more important original translations, after all, were made by bicultural native clergy. What is more, hymn-singing practice was, in this early period, decidedly a mutual affair typically involving missionaries and native people alike.

The Translation and Promotion of Ojibwe Hymns

Hymnbooks took their place alongside other scriptural and devotional tracts that were printed and promoted in the 1830s. The 1830s were years of intense translation and publication on the part of missionaries. Between 1832 and 1835, the ABCFM set its sights on publishing a spelling book, portions of Paul's epistles, and the gospels in Ojibwe. By 1837, Slovenian missionary Frederic Baraga had translated a Roman Catholic prayer book into Ojibwe, adding stories of Jesus' life on earth. In 1850, Baraga published seven hundred pages of Ojibwe meditations. By 1843, ABCFM translations of the entire New Testament were in print, along with a handful of devotional books, such as the *Life of [John] Eliot*. By 1850, Catholic presses had produced a grammar; by 1853, an initial version of Baraga's Ojibwe dictionary had appeared.[20]

The region's first printed hymns appeared as appendices to spelling books and scripture tracts, although missionaries also possessed a few precious copies of the earlier collection of hymns translated far to the east by Peter Jones. A child of an Ojibwe woman and a Welsh farmer and surveyor, Jones became a Methodist preacher and served among his mother's band on the western corner of Lake Ontario. Although Jones lived at a cultural and geographic remove from the Ojibwe communities of the Western Great Lakes, copies of his original translations of hymns, prayers, and scripture set the course later taken by ABCFM, Methodist, and Episcopalian missionaries alike. An intelligent man gifted with a remarkable dexterity in multiple cultural worlds, Jones merits our close attention, for his life is folded into the texts of many hymns sung far from his home and time. Donald B. Smith's accessible biography of Jones provides many of the details.[21]

Born Kahkewaquonaby, or Sacred Feathers, in 1802, Jones was raised by his mother and her Mississauga Ojibwe family. At fourteen, he joined his father near the Grand River and learned English and Mohawk. According to his biographer, Mohawk Christianity impressed Jones as having bridged the "division between Christianity and their old Indian faith, drawing out the similarities between the two religions."[22] Jones was moved to a conversion experience at a camp meeting in 1823. He recalled:

That very instant my burden was removed, joy unspeakable filled my heart, and I could say "Abba, Father." The love of God being now shed abroad in my heart, I loved Him intensely, and praised him in the midst of the people. Every thing now appeared in a new light. . . . The people, the trees of the woods, the gentle winds, the warbling notes of the birds, and the approaching sun, all declared the power and goodness of the Great Spirit.[23]

His talent at effecting conversions in his mother's community brought Jones to the attention of Methodist mission strategists, who were looking for a bilingual preacher to "present Christian doctrine to the Indians in intelligible terms" and to "translate hymns and Bible passages and establish Ojibwa-language equivalents for key Christian terms."[24]

Individuals like Jones were invaluable to nonnative missionaries, who often attributed any shortcomings to the language gap. Preaching through an interpreter (first in English, then in Ojibwe, English, Ojibwe, and so on) encumbered the rhythm of the spoken word and the movement of the spirit. Even "when a truth is presented with peculiar force to my mind & my soul," Edmund Ely had lamented, and "I labour to present it clearly & simply, my interpreter may not discern at what I am aiming, may not catch the spirit of it [so] the wo[rds] seem to fall powerless upon the ears of my audience."[25] In the absence of a translator, matters were worse. To preach, pray, or sing from bad translations or awkward orthographies was to be ridiculed as unintelligent or, at best, to be ignored. In a primarily oral tradition, leadership depended on the ability to command an audience.

Mission strategists saw that Peter Jones could command an audience. In 1825, Jones became an exhorter and was ordained several years later as one of Canada's two first native Methodist preachers. But he was a complicated figure. His *History of the Ojebway Indians*, published posthumously in 1861, speaks disparagingly of those who held onto Ojibwe heathenism and boastingly of those who converted. Still, Jones fought tirelessly in the halls of power on behalf of the land base and rights of his mother's Credit River community.

Jones claimed he was the first to "reduce" the Ojibwe language to a written form. After translating the Lord's Prayer, the Apostles' Creed, and the Ten Commandments, Jones recalled that he wrote a small spelling book and then "translated a few of Wesley's and Watts' hymns." His Ojibwe translations first appeared in the back pages of a Mohawk hymnal in 1827.[26] Two years later, he compiled a more extensive hymnal with thirty-four pages of alternating Ojibwe and English hymns, forty-seven pages of English hymns, and a vocabulary of some of the principal words used in the hymns.[27] Methodist presses consistently included the English hymns in subsequent versions of Jones's hymnal, "for the accommodation of our white friends who occasionally worship with us" and for "the more educated Indians" who "expressed a desire to possess the hymns in both languages."[28]

Judging from the success of their experimental efforts with printed hymns in the early spelling book, the ABCFM reissued five hundred copies of an expanded version of Jones's hymns in 1836, using what they considered a more effective orthography. "As far as I can judge," Sherman Hall wrote, the Methodist's translations were "better than any others which we can obtain at present. . . . They have some good interpreters; but they need some better acquainted with the English tongue, and better versed in the philosophy of language than themselves, to assist them to make correct translations."[29] Support for printing these Ojibwe texts came largely through donations made to the board as a whole and distributed at the direction of its Prudential Committee. But missionaries also sought public sources of support. They tried to include provisions in the administration of treaty annuities for the civilization and Christianization of native peoples. As parties negotiated the Treaty of 1835, for example, which ceded the northern half of Wisconsin, the Indian Agent Henry Rowe Schoolcraft argued that $5,000 of annuities due the Ottawa and Chippewa tribes and $1,000 of annuities from the 1826 Prairie du Chien treaty (ceding Southern Minnesota and Wisconsin) be directed to the ABCFM, Methodist, Baptist, Episcopalian, and Catholic boards having "schools or missions among them," for the "benefit of each tribe." Schoolcraft saw to the establishment of an additional thousand-dollar contingency fund annually, also funded by the treaty annuities, for the preparation of "vocabularies and grammars, spelling and reading books in the indian language, together with the Scriptures." By paying for the production of these texts, native peoples were effectively footing the bill for their own assimilation.[30]

While ABCFM missionaries never fully let go of their doctrinal rigor, Hall and Ayer seemed to overlook any theological shortcomings that they might have spied in Jones's Wesleyan hymn choices. In the mission field, expedience often tempered the principles on which theological identity stood. Jones's translations were available, and very possibly were already circulating widely in the oral tradition. By the 1870s, versions of Jones's hymns with additional translations by Sherman Hall and those natives he considered his assistants, George Copway and Henry Blatchford, had gone through another eight editions under the Methodists and the ABCFM.

In 1840, Methodist presses supplemented Jones's hymns with several translations by James Evans and Jones's relative George Henry. After an 1847 reprinting, the Jones, Evans, and Henry hymnal was issued in a second edition in 1851 and reappeared eight more times under Presbyterian, Canadian Wesleyan, American Methodist, and commercial Sunday School presses, as well as under those of the American Tract Society.[31]

Canadian Anglicans also drew on Jones's early translations in their own Ojibwe language publication effort. Frederick O'Meara's prayer book of 1853 contained twenty-five pages of hymns, a number which grew in four subsequent editions. In 1886, the O'Meara prayer book was revised by Joseph Gilfillan at the White Earth Reservation, with considerable help from John Johnson Enmegabowh and other White Earth Anishinaabe clergy. From this prayer book stemmed subsequent Minnesota Ojibwe hymnbooks, shaping and in turn shaped by the singing traditions discussed later in this book.

By 1870, roughly five thousand copies of books containing Ojibwe hymns were circulating in the region. Some translations reflected the perspectives of committed bicultural native Christians like Peter Jones and Enmegabowh. Other translations relied more on the work of nonnative missionaries like Sherman Hall and James Evans and may reflect a more didactic attempt at evangelical theology. Still other texts registered the dynamics of folk-singing practice more than they reflected the reasoned translations of schooled clergy. By 1870, the body of hymnals encompassed such a variety of translations and life experiences shaping those translations that it is difficult to distill a single textual agenda of Ojibwe hymns. Be that as it may, it is possible to shed light on the discursive meanings of the translations themselves as Ojibwe language extensions of the domain of text onto the field of practice.

"The Same Precious Words?" The Theology of Ojibwe Hymns

Ojibwe hymns were, like their English originals, oriented to the word in unprecedented ways. Hymns were texts of poetry set to music. Although traditional Ojibwe songs could relate beautiful poetic images, as we have seen, the songs were seldom simply about what they meant at the discursive or narrative level. With texts often rooted in powerful dreams and visions, many songs relied on the verbatim repetition of short phrases or syllables, repetitions which missionaries understood to be meaningless. While hymn texts translated into Ojibwe shared the poetic nature of traditional Ojibwe song, the hymn texts departed from established Ojibwe conventions in that they introduced wordiness. The style of the poetry of the Ojibwe hymns, following the style of the English originals, was didactic, going farther to delineate discursive and narrative meaning than conventional Ojibwe song texts. As such, the stories, images, and lessons of the Ojibwe language hymns provide a window into what notions shaped the belief of the increasing numbers of Anishinaabeg who heard and sang them.

On an 1872 visit to the Episcopal mission at Gull Lake, Bishop Henry B. Whipple rejoiced at his first hearing of Ojibwe people singing his favorite hymns. He recalled that they were singing the "Church battle song for missionary conquest," "From Greenland's Icy Mountains," a nineteenth-century hymn by Reginald Heber that was meant to stir up missionary zeal. Whipple wrote:

We . . . caught new inspiration from the scene before us, as those Christian Indians united with us in the familiar lines,

> Shall we, whose souls are lighted
> With wisdom from on high
> [Can we to men benighted
> The lamp of life deny?]

And now we were joined by our red brethren of the Ojibway nation, singing in their own tongue, with fervent spirit and joyful understanding, *the same precious words*.[32]

But were they really singing the same precious words in their respective languages? A closer look at these nineteenth-century hymn texts is warranted, as is equipping that closer look with insights on the Ojibwe language shared by contemporary Ojibwe speakers.

When Larry Cloud Morgan and I set out to examine the native language texts of twenty hymns from the Episcopalian *Ojibwa Hymnal*, we thought the answer would be an unequivocal no; they might have been singing precious words in each language, respectively, but they could not possibly have been the *same* precious words.[33]

While today's singers consider themselves to be Christians, and while they believe the Ojibwe hymns to bear deep witness to the truths of the Christian tradition, they emphatically do not speak of their songs in the same breath as the English-language hymns of American Protestantism, much less think of them as mere textual stand-ins for the English. It would seem, then, that culturally sensitive retranslations would disclose a wealth of ways that the nineteenth-century Ojibwe texts had subverted the message of the English. To our surprise, though, the retranslations led instead to a qualified *yes*. They were singing the "same precious words" in that the translations followed as closely as was possible the meanings of the English. But to the extent that this was so, it was in view of the fact that the Ojibwe language either could not or did not go everywhere the English did. Indeed, in his better moments, Bishop Whipple himself may have been struck by some new insight into Christian truths that his Ojibwe-speaking co-religionists had to offer.

Whipple was right in that the translated hymns were integral parts of a larger project that introduced a new story—the Christian story—and which helped inculcate new ways of imagining self, community, divinity, and the relationships among them. This was the story of a good creation with the human being established to name and have dominion over (or, more generously, have stewardship of) the non-human creation. Because of a paradigmatic act of rebellion, the first humans caused all of creation to fall. According to this view, the world remains fallen and locked as it were in a state of nature. While redemption is made possible in this world through participation in the blameless death and sacrifice of God's son, perfection and the fullness of the state of grace remain the promise of a world to come.

Ojibwe tradition, by contrast, had taught no such drastic state of fallenness or tragic struggle within the state of nature. Ojibwe traditions were not without transcendent referents, but they were resolutely this-worldly in focus. To revisit Christopher Vecsey's observation, "traditional Ojibwa religion did not articulate concern for matters beyond existence, beyond life. Survival in this life, this existence, was the Ojibwas' ultimate concern."[34] It was not simply survival that had been the Ojibwe's ultimate concern, but one of living a full life in a beautiful and proper relationship to the land and the human, natural, and spiritual communities that intersect there.

A return to the central Ojibwe term *bimaadiziwin* is warranted at this juncture, for it has associations that can help us discern the novelty of the Christian message as received. Recall that *bimaadiziwin* can be rather flatly translated as "life," or "that which lives," "nature," but that the Ojibwe term is more fully rendered as "the Good Life." In this regard, *bimaadiziwin* is not simply descriptive of natural life but also prescriptive for human life. It is, to quote A. I. Hallowell, "life in the fullest sense; life in the sense of health, longevity, and well-being, not only for one's self, but one's family." "Made possible primarily only through supernatural help," the goal of *bimaadiziwin* can be thwarted by bad conduct.[35] In this respect, the work of culture does not stand in opposition to the conditions of nature. For the Anishinaabe, what distinguished, or threatened to separate, nature from culture was a practical problem to be solved, not an ineluctable dichotomy. We would do well to render *bimaadiziwin* as that harmonious, balanced, interdependent, cycle of life to which human community at its best contributes. If something is amiss in *bimaadiziwin*, it becomes a matter of imbalance inviting restoration, not fallenness requiring redemption.

To be sure, the Christian message brought to the Ojibwe by missionaries appreciated the basic goodness of creation, but it taught the need to distrust the possibilities of the fallen world in favor of a restored world to come at the end of time. Missionaries tried to awaken their native charges to the eternal consequences of the individual soul's career in the seen world. Consider the English text of "Awake, My Soul, and with the Sun," a morning hymn that was among the first to be translated by Peter Jones:

> Awake, my soul, and with the sun
> Thy daily stage of duty run;
> Shake off dull sloth, and joyful rise
> To pay thy morning sacrifice.
>
> Redeem thy misspent moments past;
> And live this day as if thy last;
> Improve thy talent with due care;
> for the great Day thyself prepare.
>
> Let all thy converse be sincere,
> Thy conscience as the noonday clear;
> Think how all-seeing God thy ways
> And all thy secret thoughts surveys.
>
> Wake, and lift up thyself, my heart,
> And with the angels bear thy part,
> Who all night long unwearied sing,
> High praise to the eternal King.

The hymn teaches that life on this earth is best thought of as a performance on the daily stage of duty, as if each day is one's last, with a God of judgment as spectator. Life in this fallen existence is but a performance to determine one's career in the afterlife. Time runs short. Time can be misspent. Each of these ideas could be considered a novelty to an Ojibwe reckoning, which imagined time not in linear terms but in cyclical terms, and which did not take the uncertainties of mortal life as symptoms of a fallen creation but as necessary parts of *bimaadiziwin*, or, at worst, reparable imbalances in it.

Such dramatic contrasts between worldviews notwithstanding, the translations of such hymns do not appear to introduce overt resistance. One finds neither hidden messages nor the rhetorical sleight of hand often associated with peasant resistance elsewhere. Instead, one finds that the translations seem to conform, where possible, to the meanings of the original. And yet, there are many moments when Ojibwe religious thought works creatively within the constraints of the translation process to appreciate the introduced narratives and ideas of the Christian tradition in distinctive ways. Although the Ojibwe words that translators chose to carry the meaning of the English originals were accorded very different connotations in the context of the Christian story, only rarely did they introduce English words or invent radically new words within the Ojibwe language to carry the force of the Christian message. Instead, missionaries and other translators sought to strum indigenous chords in the word choices they made.

Here, we may turn fruitfully to the indigenous meanings of the Ojibwe texts to see where Bishop Whipple may have spoken too soon in thinking that his native brethren were singing the "same precious words." Consider the Ojibwe versions of "Awake, My Soul, and with the Sun" of Peter Jones and of the Episcopalian *Ojibwa Hymnal* (1910), respectively, in comparison to the (re)translation made with Larry Cloud Morgan.[36] (See Table 2.2.) The overall message of the Ojibwe versions is consistent with that of the original: Be as constant as the sun in your morning prayer. This teaching would have been familiar to those Ojibwes who were taught by tradition to be awake at sunrise and to begin each day by offering thanks. In the second verse, the Ojibwe versions do not proclaim misspent moments past in need of

Table 2.2

"AWAKE, MY SOUL, AND WITH THE SUN"

Peter Jones (1840)	Ojibwa Hymnal (1910)	(Re)Translation
Um ba o nesh kon nin je chog, Kuh ba kee zhig suh uh no keen: Wa be nun ke te me shke win, Kuhgezhaib dush nah te bun doon	Umbe koshkosin ninchichag Gizis eji-minwewizid Eji-minwewizin dush kin Kigijeb dush anamian.	Come on, wake up, my soul/spirit. How the sun is constant Be so constant. In the morning, pray!
Te besh koo go wah ne boong in Noongoom keezheguk e nain dun; Umba wuh weeng a kee zhee ton, Che be de bah ko ne goo yun.	Tibishko go wa-nibongin Nogom gijiguk anokin Man'do manikin ganwendun Ki ga-dibakonigo ma.	As if there will be death Now that it is day, work! Guard whatever god/spirit/ mystery gives. You will be judged here!
Mon oo me no Kah gee Ge doon, Ka oon je wah sa yain duh mun; Ke wah buh mig mah Mun e doo, Ewh a zhe pe mah de ze yun.		
Koshkozin, puh ze gween, nin da, Wee doo kowh egewh angel nug, Kuh baa de bik na guh mo jig, Jesus sah quah duh muh wah wod.	Koshkosin onishkan ninde, Naqueamou 'giu angenug Kabe tibik negamodjig, Wawijenimawad Man'don.	Wake up! Get up, my heart! Sing in harmony with those angels, Those who sing all through the night Those who go with the Spirit.
Mahmooyuhwuhmahdah mah buh Wainje zhuhwaindahgozeyung, Wayoosemind, Wagwese mind, Kuh ya Pah ne zid O je chog.	Mamoiwamada waau Wendji-shawendagoziyung Weosimind Wegwisimind Gaye Panizid Ochichag	Let us give thanks to him/her, for this The reason we are pitied/blessed He who is had as a father, he who is had as a son, And also the soul/spirit of he who is clean/ holy.

redemption, but they do incorporate the image of judgment. The 1910 Minnesota hymnal, however, indicates that previous translations of the fourth verse had fallen into disuse, tempering the image of the watchful God of judgment who looms above the text of the English original. Both translations are, to be sure, not inconsistent with the English, but they do lead to a different effect.

As to how intentional this effect really was, the possibility remains that the problem was simply one of fitting as much of the original content as could be carried by unwieldy Ojibwe constructions into the established meter of the English hymn stanzas. Peter Jones remarked on the mechanical difficulties of his translations: "I found it a difficult work . . . on account of the Indian words being generally much longer than the English: hence the impossibility of conveying the whole meaning of one English verse into the same measure in Indian."[37] Perhaps the Ojibwe equivalent for "shake off dull sloth" does not appear in the first verse simply because the translator exhausted the available syllables in an effort to render the full Ojibwe equivalent to "and with the sun / thy daily stage of duty run" in Ojibwe.

This appears at moments to be true. Yet the challenge was more than a mechanical one, for the language differences were more thoroughgoing than the mere length of words. The Ojibwe language produces lengthy phrases because it is a language rich in possibilities for inflecting and nuancing the root vocabulary. Moreover, the language is strikingly driven by verbs. Many substantive nouns are formed from verb stems. As a result, the possibilities for differentiating precise kinds of motion or action are rich, perhaps richer than the possibilities for differentiating among kinds of things. Substantive forms of such words, rudiments indeed of Christian theological language as it has developed in the West, appear far more frequently in the missionaries' Ojibwe-English dictionaries than they do in everyday conversation.

Plasticity of Ojibwe Texts

In light of this distinctive feature of the language, hymn translations can be seen to proceed with a considerable tolerance for ambiguity in expression. Put in more positive terms, they proceed with a remarkable plasticity of meaning. While much poetry in any human language—perhaps especially so of sacred poetry—can be said to delight in such a plasticity of meaning, I follow Larry Cloud Morgan's insight that the Ojibwe language is "refreshing" for the way it departs from the English hymns in this regard. For Cloud Morgan, the Ojibwe language is thus more effective than English in honoring the mystery of the realities to which the Christian texts bear witness. In effect, the Ojibwe texts soften the didactic edges of the English originals even while dutifully following them. For example, consider the difference in tone between the English and Ojibwe versions of "Come, Holy Spirit, Heavenly Dove." (See Table 2.3.)

The translation is hardly untrue to the original text of Isaac Watts's poem. Indeed, the Ojibwe text appeals to an Ojibwe convention of invoking spiritual help through the humbling of one's self as miserable or pitiable. To be sure, this and other Ojibwe hymns employ words to make points in ways that are without precedent in Ojibwe song. The translations consist of sentences, after all, not the repeated

Table 2.3

"COME, HOLY SPIRIT, HEAVENLY DOVE"

Isaac Watts (1707)	*Ojibwa Hymnal* (1910)	(Re)Translation
Come, Holy Spirit, heavenly Dove, With all Thy quickening powers; Kindle a flame of sacred love In these cold hearts of ours.	Ondashan, Kichi Ochichag, Widokawishinam, Atoniu sagiiwewin Ima nindeinang	Come here Great Spirit, Help us Put it there, love [to love, treasure people] There in our hearts.
In vain we tune our formal songs, In vain we strive to rise; Hosannas languish on our tongues, And our devotion dies.	'Na eji-gotugiziyang Oma aking ayayang; Nin kichi bejiwimin su Ishpiming wi-jayang.	Look how miserable we are Here as we are on earth We are very slow in our doing [to go] up there, in heaven, where we want to go.
And shall we, Lord, for ever be In this poor dying state? Our love so faint, so cold to thee, And thine to us so great?	Anawi nindinend amin Nagumotagoyun; Nind anamiawininan Nonde ko takisin.	We think vainly of that, that you are sung to; Our prayers cool too soon.[a]
Come, Holy Spirit, heavenly dove, With all thy quickening powers; Come, shed abroad a Savior's love, And that shall kindle ours?	Ondashan, Kichi Ochichag, Widokawishinam, Moshkinaton nindeinang Iu sagiiwewin.	Come here, Great Spirit help us, Fill it, our heart, With that love.

a. Larry Cloud Morgan had translated this stanza, after some difficulty, as follows:
> As we are thinking,
> As we sing,
> Our prayers
> Touch beautiful places in us.

phrases of idea fragments or strings of vocables set to music. But the Ojibwe versions are conspicuous for how few pains they take to delimit meanings of Christian notions. Instead, they seem to delight in the range of associative meanings suggested by a word image. Though far wordier than other forms of Ojibwe song, in this respect at least, the native language hymns have much in common with the conventions of other Ojibwe music.

Not surprisingly, this delight in associative meaning, whether or not it is unique to the Ojibwe language, frustrated Protestant missionaries to no end. Missionaries like Sherman Hall often thought of perceived failures in the missions enterprise as a problem of language. "The more I study the Ojibue language," he wrote, "the more convinced I am that it is a difficult language for a foreigner to acquire." It was Hall, we recall, who found it especially difficult to "give religious instruction" in Ojibwe.

"They have few or no religious ideas," he concluded, "and of course, no terms in which to express religious ideas. On this account the greatest care must be taken to explain everything or we are misunderstood, or convey no idea at all."[38]

Although Hall was clearly wrong about the lack of Ojibwe religious ideas, he was onto something about how those ideas found expression. The language's capacity to carry multiple meanings in the same utterance is quite consistent with a disinterest in making the kinds of distinctions concerning the divine that are associated with regimented, systematic theological thinking. To rephrase the point, the Ojibwe language did not deliver the kind of systematic theology that missionaries like Hall wanted, and this precisely because the language is well equipped to give voice to other modes of religious thought.

Even the term *manidoo*, commonly translated as spirit, can be translated adjectivally as "mysterious." Thus can *gichi manidoo*, Great Spirit, also be understood as "The Great Mysterious," something which is fundamentally beyond the comprehension of human language and thought. On this note, Sherman Hall called Ojibwe religiousness "scarcely less degrading and unworthy of rational beings than the religion of the Hindoo." Hall thought Ojibwe ideas of a "Supreme Being seem to be vague and indistinct. Yet they acknowledge a Great Spirit who made them. Where they imagine him to reside or what character they attach to him, I have never been able satisfactorily to ascertain."[39]

The translation gap between *manidoo* and *spirit*, between *gichi manidoo* and *Great Spirit*, is a significant one. An Anishinaabe friend familiar with an earlier draft of this study asked me about the subtle but consequential change in meaning that *gichi manidoo* came to have since the coming of missionaries. "So Mike," Dan Kier asked rhetorically, "when did *Great Mystery* become *the Great Spirit?*" His point was that the narrowing of the sovereign range of meanings encompassed by the word *manidoo* was a weighty matter with far-reaching theological ramifications.[40] The doubleness of *manidoo* here plants a fundamental mystery at the heart of the translated Christian story, a doubleness that potentially undermines the radical nature of the distinction missionaries tried to assert between the object of heathen worship and that of Christian worship. Indeed, it was a distinction on which missions projects in the early nineteenth century rested. Of course, when sung in the mission church on Sunday morning, the word *manidoo* carried a different contextual meaning than it did when sung in a Midewiwin ceremony. But appeal to the word in numerous hymn translations admitted a wide range of associations indeed. To accord respect to the *manidoog*, the powerful, incomprehensible sources of life, one did not speak directly about them or try to ascertain their nature. One spoke deferentially of them, if one spoke of them at all. And yet, as one scholar has said of the place of a similar concept in the Lakota tradition, perhaps it had been the very incomprehensibility of *manidoo* that made the quest for understanding it to be the "driving force" of Ojibwe culture.[41]

More than anything, it may have been this distinctively Anishinaabe posture toward the holy that led Sherman Hall to pronounce the Ojibwe language incapable of expressing religious ideas in ways that he sought. Contrast Hall's view with that of Peter Jones, who believed the Ojibwe language was uniquely equipped to elicit the affective response that evangelicals sought in the language of scripture and hymnody. For Jones, the enormous pull that the fundamental mystery of a term like *manidoo* could generate, and the breadth of associations it could carry, were part of the genius of his native language. "The Ojebway language," he wrote, "possesses great strength, and is full of imagery, as the words express the nature, use, or resemblance of the things spoken of. On this account it makes a deeper impression on the mind of both speaker and hearer than a language composed of arbitrary or unmeaning sounds."[42]

It would be tempting to find in Jones the character of an intellectual whose translations smuggled into the Anglo-American tunes a subversive Anishinaabe message. But from Jones's point of view, perhaps no more subversive message need have been written than a faithful translation of the original. Reflecting on his translations of scripture, Jones felt an acute "insufficiency for this important work," praying, "O Lord help me by thy Holy Spirit to understand thy Word, that I may give the true meaning in my native tongue, so that my Indian brethren may be rooted, grounded, and settled upon the true doctrines."[43]

Motifs of Ojibwe Hymn Theology

Let us consider now how the "true doctrines" Jones prayed about took root in the Ojibwe texts by tracking a number of motifs of the corpus of Ojibwe hymns. Not surprisingly, these motifs follow key contours of the Protestant theology in the English hymns: sin, salvation, grace, faith, sanctification, and life eternal. But the ways in which these ideas emerge in a language oriented to the integrity of *bimaadiziwin* mark the sometimes subtle contours of a distinctive Ojibwe theology in the hymns.

Salvation

To carry the meaning of the central concept of salvation, translators chose the Ojibwe term *bimaaji'iwewin*, a word formed from the same root as *bimaadiziwin*. Consider the translation of "A Charge to Keep I Have" in Table 2.4. To the extent that the missionaries' message of salvation concerned eternal life, this hymn provides insight into the resonances that the term *salvation* carries in Ojibwe. The hymn, in both its English and Ojibwe versions, makes a number of references to life. But in the last stanza of the Ojibwe, there is a double meaning that teaches about an Ojibwe inflection of that concept. An Ojibwe singer could understand herself here to be asking for help to pray so that she "would live" in eternity. That certainly seems to be the gist of the English original stanza. But the term "to live," if we factor in the range of associations such a term had for a fluent speaker, may also include as "I want to live well" in the here and now. Although it could be understood that the term refers to heavenly and not earthly life, the ambiguity here is theologically significant. Elsewhere in the hymn texts, *bimaadiziwin* is sometimes modified by the Ojibwe particle, *gaagige* (kagige), forever. For the many Ojibwes who still maintained that *bimaadiziwin* was the good life lived well in proper relationship to human and nonhuman persons, there was nothing in this world, per se, to be radically saved from. Ojibwe tradition values the cultivation of an awareness of one's interdepend-

Table 2.4

"A CHARGE TO KEEP I HAVE"

Charles Wesley (1762)	*Ojibwa Hymnal* (1910)	(Re)translation
A charge to keep I have,	Che anokitonan	That I will work for you,
A God to glorify,	Nose, nind ayanan,	My father, I have.
A never dying soul to save,	Che wi-gijitad ninchichag	My soul will finish at last.
And fit it for the sky.	Ishpiming wi-ijad	Heaven—my soul wants to go there.
To serve the present age,	Ki nundawenim su	You want me
My calling to fulfill;	Che anokitonan,	To thus work for you.
O may it all my powers engage	O mano anguamiishin	Let it be so. Make me hopeful
To do my Master's will!	Guayuk che anam'ayan.	That I pray in the right manner.
Arm me with jealous care,	Wawejiishin su	Dress me!
As in thy sight to live,	Che agasen'moyan,	As I feel small, humble.
And oh, thy servant, Lord, prepare	Che de-gijitayan, Nose,	So that I am completely done, Father,
A strict account to give.	Api naquesh konan.	When I meet you.
Help me to watch and pray	Widokawishin su	Help me!
And on thyself rely,	Che akawabiyan	So that I wait and watch
Assured, if I my trust betray,	Gaye che anamiayan	And also so that I pray.
I shall forever die.	Wi-bimadiziyan	I want to live.

ence in the web of life. The pervading presence of the term *bimaadiziwin* and related expressions suggests a prevalent concern with life in this broader sense in the religious thought of Ojibwe hymns.

To elaborate, consider the place of *bimaaji'iwewin* in the third verse of "From Greenland's Icy Mountains." (See Table 2.5.) Remember this is the verse that Bishop Whipple celebrated in the passage that framed the current discussion. The message of salvation is to be proclaimed by "those who have wisdom" to those in need of mercy and help. In Heber's English version, this is nothing short of salvation for those benighted who are bound in "error's chain" and who "bow down to wood and stone." But the Ojibwe text hardly promotes the necessity of a radical transformation from a state of nature to the state of grace. *Bimaaji'iwewin* here carries the same ambiguity of meaning that *bimaadiziwin* does. No modifier specifies that the life to be given in salvation is radically other than the current life. Although the term could certainly accrue that added association in the context of missionary teaching, the term itself also could mean "resuscitation"—being brought into the possibility of real life—or it could mean "restoration" to the sustaining interdependence of the Circle of Life. Two native singers in Michigan, for example translated the related term "gabimadjiiangid" as "so I can go on living," to appreciate its distinctive way of

Table 2.5

"FROM GREENLAND'S ICY MOUNTAINS"

Reginald Heber (1819)	Ojibwa Hymnal (1910)	(Re)Translation
Can we whose souls are lighted	Kinawind nebuakayung,	All us who are wise,
With wisdom from on high;	Wayaseshkagoyung,	We who are enlightened,
Can we to men benighted	Ki ga-shaguen'momin na	Will we be reluctant/
The lamp of life deny?	Che widokageyung?	discouraged
Salvation, O salvation!	O bimadjiiwewin!	To help people?
The joyful sound proclaim,	Mizi dibadjimon,	O saving/restoration of life!
Till each remotest nation	Nananj igo kakina	Tell the news everywhere,
Has learnt Messiah's Name.	Gi-minotumowad.	Until all
		Hear it with pleasure.

rendering "salvation" in the hymn "Jesus Wegwissiian."[44] Perhaps it is better to admit the possibility of both senses in the rendering—that both eternal heavenly life and restored *bimaadiziwin* in earthly life could obtain in the mind of the singer.[45]

Sin

If salvation means redemption from the consequences of a life or state of sin, then the Ojibwe term chosen to carry the meaning of *sin* is ill-equipped to convey the full opprobrium the term carries in evangelical life. *Baataaziwin* is a substantive formed from the verb "to wrong" or to transgress the natural order. In effect, the word for sin is better translated as "that which is done wrong," an expression that Larry Cloud Morgan glosses as rather benign when compared with an evangelical notion of sin. As he puts it, *baataaziwin* is "bad, but not that bad." The difficulty of rendering a sense of sin as a state in Ojibwe greatly frustrated evangelical missionaries, who considered it among their principal tasks to promote a heartfelt conviction of sin. Sherman Hall voiced the concern in the following way in 1834: "They seem to have no idea of Sin as committed against the Great Spirit. Hence they have no word to express sin in a spiritual sense. The words they use to express bad actions and bad feelings are used only in relation to external character. On this account it is extremely difficult to convey to their minds, any just idea of sin, as committed against a holy God."[46]

Baataziwin implies that one has done something really wrong, but the implication that it springs from some well of sin within that humans cannot restore to balance is not plainly evident in the Ojibwe term. Neither do the Ojibwe hymn texts reflect efforts to further qualify the meaning of *baataziwin*.[47] Consider the third verse of Wesley's "Oh, for a Thousand Tongues to Sing." (See Table 2.6.) What in Charles Wesley's original poem was the "breaking the power of reigning sin" becomes the possibility of throwing away "those things that I do wrong." The theme of cleansing,

Table 2.6

"OH, FOR A THOUSAND TONGUES TO SING"

Charles Wesley (1739)	Ojibwa Hymnal (1910)	(Re)Translation
He breaks the power of reigning sin, He sets the prisoner free; His blood can make the sinful clean, His blood availed for me.	Ogushkiton che webinunk Bataziwinishun, Piniiwemagutini Iu Jesus o-misquim.	He is able to do it, throw it [all] away The sins/things done wrong It cleanses/purifies [people] That blood of Jesus.

which follows in the third line, forms another recurring motif in the Ojibwe texts. For those schooled in Anishinaabe religious ideas, *bimaadiziwin* is a delicate balance that often requires restoration. But imbalance is a far cry from a pathology of sin said to underlie all ordinary life. Thus missionaries had their work cut out for them in trying to discipline the meanings of the Ojibwe expressions to suit their didactic purposes. While that discipline clearly found its place in the context of life around the mission, it did not find itself completely elaborated in the Ojibwe texts of the hymns themselves.

Grace

Ojibwe translations share with the English originals a conviction that no salvation from sin happens without grace. The Ojibwe term used to translate grace, *zhawenjii-gewin*, and the variety of expressions that share its root, *zhaw-*, are ubiquitous. By means of these variations, this concept recurs in nearly one third of the hymns in the Episcopalian *Ojibwa Hymnal*. *Zhaw-* is the root that indicates a relationship of pitying, also translated as having mercy or blessing. In Ojibwe, to ask for pity is emphatically to abase one's self as pitiful or poor. Indeed, this action of emptying one's self was at the core of the tradition of fasting for a vision. The simplicity of the theme ought not obscure the depth of its associations. Christopher Vecsey notes that "the pitying relationship was firmly grounded in Ojibwa life," applying to human relations as well as relations between humans and the *manidoog*, or spirits. A nineteenth-century Slovenian missionary and Ojibwe grammarian believed the relationship was "common enough to warrant a pitying conjugation of verbs, indicating an action performed in a certain manner such as to deserve pity."[48] One missionary observed that the related expression "he is poor" was among the more common statements of the Ojibwe language.[49] If the Ojibwe language posed challenges to the task of rendering precise translations of Christian concepts, such Ojibwe expressions offered translators like Jones many possibilities for rendering the fuller texture of those concepts.

Faith

In Protestant theology, it may have been grace that made all the difference, but the Christian bore responsibility for participating in that grace by means of faith. The Ojibwe term chosen to carry the meaning of this theological idea, however, casts the message in a different light. For while nineteenth-century Protestant missionaries differed on many theological matters, they did agree that the workings of salvation hinged on the individual's conviction of his/her own sinfulness and need for redemption. In Ojibwe, however, the term *debweyendamowin*, a variation on the verb *debwe-*, to speak the truth, is an inherently social statement, even in a first person formulation. This is so because *debwe-* concerns the veracity of what someone says as suggested by the mutual agreement of others on that veracity. Ojibwe writer Basil Johnston notes that *debwe*, "in its most fundamental sense," means "he (or she) explains or describes perceptions according to his (or her) command of language. In other words, there is no absolute truth, only the highest degree of accuracy of which a person is capable."[50] Truth here is socially situated and communally verified.

According to Baraga's nineteenth-century dictionary, "nindébwêendam" is to believe in one's own mind; "débwêwessin" refers to "its sound is heard at this or that place;" and "nindébwêwidam" indicates "I make myself heard from a certain distance." There appears to be a close relationship, associationally if not etymologically, between this set of ideas and expressions concerning the sound of the drum, *dewe'igan*, as Larry Cloud Morgan suggests. The sound of the drum carries a long distance. It can be felt inside one's body and can therefore bring groups of individuals into "one mind."[51] To the extent that these associations obtain, to say, "I believe it is true" is to proclaim, "I hear around that it is true." In this sense, an individual's profession of faith is at its core a social statement. This is certainly consistent with what missionaries frequently found in the nineteenth century. They were often taken aback by how reluctant native people were to act as individuals in matters of conversion and religion.

The Christian Life

Finally, the religious thought of the Ojibwe hymn texts does not assert the radical distinction made by the English hymns between sinner and saved, heathen and Christian. Returning to the translation of "A Charge to Keep I Have," the Christian life is figured as a life of "great work," that work of trying to walk in the Christian life in hopes of profound life. (See Table 2.4.) The concern of the second verse that "I pray in the right manner" is interesting. "Guayuk" (*gwayak*) is a particle that also pervades the body of Ojibwe hymn texts. It does not imply a kind of narrow doctrinal correctness. Its associations are as much with straightness as with correctness. The concern is less whether one follows "the right religion" than it is whether one "rightly follows" religion with sincerity.

Ojibwe hymn texts refer numerous times to the Christian life as a journey along a path, *mikan*. Indeed, this image would have been a powerful one for Ojibwe people whose overland travel took place on paths through dense forests, paths that might all look alike but lead to very different outcomes. Consider the Ojibwe translation of the second verse to "Jesus, My All, to Heaven Is Gone." (See Table 2.7.) Indeed, the

Table 2.7

"JESUS, MY ALL, TO HEAVEN IS GONE"

George Coles (1792-1858)	*Ojibwa Hymnal* (1910)	(Re)Translation
The way the holy prophets went, The road that leads from banishment, The King's highway of holiness, I'll go, for all His paths are peace.	Ga-'ni'jawad ga-n'buakadjig Mikans guayuk enumonig, Gaye nin ge-madadoyan Mikans kechi-shawendagwuk	The way they were going, those who were wise The little path that leads straight there I, too, will go off on it On the little path that is greatly pitied/blessed.

Ojibwe text hardly subverts the message of the English original. In using the diminutive form of path, *mikans*, the Ojibwe language underscores the difficulty of finding the little or narrow path of the wise ones that goes where Jesus had gone. But it does not specify that this path "leads from banishment," nor does the way of "those who were wise" specify the sole way of the holy prophets of the Old Testament. This path of "kechi-shawendagwuk" (*gechi-zhawendaagwak*), the path that is greatly blessed or pitied, is a path powerfully charged with traditional Ojibwe notions of the pity, compassion, or grace of the supernaturals that Hallowell noted was necessary for *bimaadiziwin*, the good life.

Indeed, as I have noted, the Ojibwe language contains no term that adequately carries the semantic freight of "religion" in the sense of the term that we share with the mid–nineteenth century: that abstraction referring to a system of beliefs and practices.[52] Instead, one finds references to "our way." When he compiled his dictionary in 1850, Frederic Baraga translated "religion" by appealing to "ijitwawin" (*izhitwawin*), a substantive formed from the verb "to do or act so." That Baraga settled on this expression discloses an Ojibwe predisposition to consider "religion" in terms of conduct or behavior rather than of assent to a set of ideas or profession of belief. Moreover, the term implies the particularity of any *izhitwawin*, since it is a term closely related to *izhichige*, "to do things in a certain way." This differs from the conventional sense of *religion* as an abstraction, like "economy" or "government."[53]

Ojibwe singers may have felt that a hymn text like "mikans guayak enumonig," "the little path that leads straight there," was distinguishing the narrow Christian path to salvation from the heathen paths which, though easier to find, lead to ruin. But because they were steeped in a language that did not structure thinking about "religions" in the way that missionaries did, these singers may indeed have felt the text was fundamentally acknowledging how difficult is the task of finding the right path of humility and grace.

Conclusion: Beyond the Text

We learn from Lamin Sanneh's research on missions in the African context that no translation of a religious text into a vernacular language, especially that of a colonized people, can be considered theologically neutral. Sanneh argues that translations authorize in the genre of the colonizers the more cherished indigenous articulations of value; the result, he says, is "tantamount to adopting indigenous cultural criteria for the message, a piece of radical indigenization far greater than the standard portrayal of mission as cultural imperialism."[54] Peter Jones and other native clergy and missionary assistants appealed to such terms to render the English ideas in language of suitable power in Ojibwe idiom; thus they set loose texts for collective singing that saw to the continuous public expression of some central values of Anishinaabe spirituality and community, even while they were viewed as performances of a cultural and spiritual revolution. The prominent example of Peter Jones suggests that translators intended their translations to be faithful to, not subversive of, the Anglo-American Christian texts. The words they chose, however, like the collective practice that gave them voice, were malleable indeed as carriers of meaning. The Christian theology of the hymns introduced novel concepts to Ojibwe religious thought: sin, salvation, grace, faith. But each was couched in an idiom that allowed for a range of meanings that appreciated familiar resonances in Christianity. The idiom was well suited to a tradition of religious thought which rested on the principle that the sacred is fundamentally a mystery beyond the grasp of human minds and ordinary human language. Again, a precedent had long been set that the sacred stories and songs of other peoples could nourish an Anishinaabe hunger for a deeper appreciation of that mystery.

Ultimately, we can only come to grips with the distinctively Anishinaabe religious thought of the hymns if we press beyond the narrative meanings of the texts themselves. But this is not because Ojibwe religious thought was inherently hostile to the novel ideas of the Christian story, as our brief consideration of hymn translations here has shown. Rather, we must press beyond the manifest thought of the hymn texts because Ojibwe religious thought itself pressed well beyond the specific uses of language that denote discursive meaning. Ojibwe religious thought was indeed elaborate and complex, but it seldom took shape in terms of doctrine or formulated systems of abstract thought. In this respect it shared a characteristic common to primarily oral traditions. Recall that the sacred songs of Anishinaabe tradition composed poetic word pictures and could contain important information, but seldom did those songs elaborate on those meanings in didactic, discursive ways. Indeed, they often represented scripts for the performance of powerful words, words made powerful by their origin as gifts from the mysterious sources of life. While hymn translations introduced a different orientation to the word in song, the more significant contribution of Ojibwe religious thought to indigenous Christianity is not to be found in the distinctive meanings of the words but in the distinctive way that those words and that Christian story were absorbed into indigenous modes of religious thought in concrete moments of ritualized practice.

In his theory about the workings of symbolic power, the French theorist of practice Pierre Bourdieu presses beyond the text to consider the social dimensions of symbolic exchanges. Bourdieu observes the peculiarity with which religious language, unlike that of mathematics or of science, can serve to mediate relationships between those with authority and those without. Religious language, he argues, contains a kind of "polysemy," a multiplicity of meanings that are simultaneously at play. Because religious language often unifies opposites, and because it often denies in ultimate terms the very distinctions that it makes in the first place, "it manages to speak to all groups and all groups speak it." Bourdieu observes that those in authority can "achieve their most successful ideological effects" by "exploiting the possibilities contained" in polysemous language.[55]

We have already seen how the Ojibwe language takes a particular delight in plasticity of meaning, but Bourdieu offers a way to consider how polysemy is already at work in the theological language of the English texts. After all, to remain viable in any social context where there are bound to be differences of interpretation, the language of even the most disciplined of theological traditions can ill afford to be brittle. Such terms as salvation and sin must have ranges of meaning broad enough to acknowledge the mysteries of faith, to speak to a variety of personal experiences, and to assemble communities of people around them. Restricting the range of acceptable meanings, then, is a social process, a contest between the centrifugal forces at work in the divergent meanings of the terms in the minds of believers and the centripetal forces at work in the discipline used by elites to rein in the range of their usage and meaning.

It may be enormously difficult, then, to identify with precision a single textual agenda at work in the body of translated hymns. But it is quite possible to observe what transpired on the field of practice. The ends to which missionaries promoted the singing of these texts was clear: They considered the genre to be a powerful signifying practice, important for its didactic and affective contribution to the project of inculcating a Christian life. If the Ojibwe translations themselves did not fully extend the theological authority of missionaries, their attempts to discipline the practice aimed to do so. Missionaries tried to extend their authority through the promotion of the practice, to fix possible meanings in contexts of worship and mission school, and to insist on the singularity of the hymn in musical repertory. What remains to be seen in the case of the religious language of Ojibwe hymns is how missionaries sought to discipline the direction that hymnody took on the field of practice, and it is to that story that we now turn.

Hymn Singing, 1828–1867

Peter Kawgodaheway Marksman recalled a day in 1832, prior to his conversion, when he and his brother were six miles out on Lake Superior and "a fog struck and a mighty easterly wind fell." Thinking themselves headed for a "watery grave," they resolved to "call on the God of Christians." "Before we prayed," Marksman recalled, "we concluded to sing first, to praise the God of the universe. The hymn we selected was as follows: A charge to keep I have, A God to glorify. And after we were through singing this beautiful hymn, we knelt down in our canoe and prayed." It would seem that the two knew such a song by heart, though still unconverted and still training in the Midewiwin tradition, as well as Christian. Interestingly, the brother asked Marksman also to call on the *manidoog* that had appeared to him in his dream fast.[56]

After his conversion, Marksman went on to become an important Methodist preacher along the southern shore of that same lake and along the northern shore of Lake Michigan, yet this particular story indicates that evangelical hymns were being absorbed into the cultural repertory of Ojibwe life in ways that prompt us to think afresh about the nature of hymns as more than what missionaries promoted them to be. While the practices of hymn singing in the 1830s, 1840s, 1850s, and even 1860s varied widely, we can recognize the early patterns of a distinctive idiom of performance, patterns that would come into even clearer focus within the native-led Christian movement later associated with the Episcopalian missions at White Earth. By construing hymnody in terms of practice—attending to who sang hymns, when they sang them, where and how—and by noting how the symbolic exchanges of mission encounters were structured in new ways by changing relations with European Americans, we will be equipped to make a few generalizations as to how Ojibwe people began to incorporate hymnody into their lifeways.

From the moment that copies of Peter Jones's hymnbook reached them, American Board missionaries were impressed with the impact it seemed to make on Ojibwe communities. In these early exchanges it was missionaries who did the singing, native people the listening. While scouting the possibilities for a mission field in the area of Sandy Lake in 1833, the ABCFM's Frederic Ayer encountered an enthusiastic–or, at least, curious—Anishinaabe assembly: "We have been reading, singing, & talking all day with Indians & Children who have been in and so monopolized our time, that we have hardly found time for anything else. There is truly a hearing ear among this people."[57] "A hearing ear" is evidently the relevant metaphor for mission exchanges in this period—more apt than "seeing the light" or "feeling the spirit." Whatever the long-term impact of the missionaries' musical performances and spoken instruction, they were seldom without an audience willing to listen. The compelling nature of shared song is clear as Ayer goes on:

> In the evening of the first day a large number assembled to hear us sing. On the evening of the 2nd day, they assembled [a house full] and requested me through their chief speaker to relate to them similar accounts to what they had heard during the day. . . . We commenced with singing; after singing till we were tired I read to them sometime from our Ojibue Spelling book some select portion of Scripture & the account of Christ's Crucifixion accompanied by remarks, after which we sung till bed time when being considerably fatigued. . . . I have never seen so many Indians together who remained silent so long as these. . . . They were all much gratified with singing in their own language. On the 2nd Evening after our meeting broke up I was met at the door by one who said to me, "Friend you might sing all day"—intimating that I had supposed them fatigued. Another [who did not hear this remark] said, "Sing sing, you go to bed early."[58]

Scripture reading and preaching in Ojibwe appeared to be less arresting for native people than singing, and missionaries came to appreciate hymns as the most effective means of instruction. In 1834, Ayer and Sherman Hall met with some chiefs and a medicine man who had earlier recommended setting fire to the mission house. Ayer recalled: "After spending an hour in conversation, we sung several hymns and explained them making application of truth as it seemed to suit their case. All listened with the most fixed attention. One remarked, 'we now know where our souls go to after our bodies die. We have not known before but have been in the dark.'"[59] On another occasion, Sherman Hall reflected in detail a story of an ill man at La Pointe, considered to be one of the few potential native converts. When he was "again attacked with raising blood," the missionary wrote, "he wanted to hear singing" and even asked for some hymns by name. Upon his death, the man's relatives seemed more eager to have hymns sung at his wake than the Bible read. When Hall asked if he and his interpreter could read the Bible in the lodge, they answered, "though not very promptly," that they were willing. "After we finished reading," Hall continued, "we sung several hymns, with which they all appeared pleased."[60]

Native people listening in these early encounters began to learn the songs themselves and on their own terms. William Boutwell brought out his copy of Jones's hymnbook to a group gathered in a wigwam on the Crow River in 1832: "[I] read several Ind[ia]n hymns, which I sung to them. After singing one the second or third time one or two young men joined & to my surprise, sung it quite well. They are *delighted* & *surprised* to hear hymns sung in their own language."[61]

Métis Hymn Singing

Missionaries soon began to report that hymns had taken root in the oral tradition, not so much among the Anishinaabeg living still according to the seasonal round, but rather among the Métis, the bicultural relatives of both fur traders and Anishinaabeg who had settled year-round at the fur posts and thus become more fully part of the life of the mission stations and schools adjacent to the fur posts. A Methodist missionary exploring the area in 1838 wrote with surprise of meeting several Métis who, though illiterate, could "sing in Chippeway . . . and to them and a few others, Stephen [Bungo] our interpreter, gave a discourse on religious subjects, sung and prayed."[62] The Bungos were an important Métis family, descendants of a former West Indies slave who was brought to Mackinac Island via Chicago and who later married two native women and settled at Leech Lake. A Methodist missionary wrote that the Bungos "have adopted civilized habits, and some of them are respectable for their literary attainments; and they all wish to settle together by our missionary establishment, thus making a village of some eight or ten families, comprising sixty or seventy souls." At a time when the region could no longer support an extensive trade in furs, the missionary noted the Bungos "say they are tired of that [fur trade] mode of living."[63]

While Métis sang hymns in sanctioned moments of public worship, the practice appeared to take place more often on occasions that were decidedly social in flavor, largely Catholic in influence, and independent of missionary direction. Because evangelicals considered hymnody to be at home in many settings outside of worship, they welcomed the Christian fellowship that sacred song fostered. Still, missionary accounts bespoke an ambivalence about the way hymns were received. In the 1830s, a Métis trader at Fond du Lac hosted crowded evening hymn sings in his house. Edmund Ely, the ABCFM teacher living nearby, would sometimes take a seat and join in, but his correspondence reflected no little uneasiness:

> This evening, I informed Mr. Cotté that I intended to Sing with those of my Scholars and others, who have come. He invited me to his house. When we entered, the room was filled. He said, he would first say Prayers; accordingly, the Catholic service was read, in [which] the Indians and Children joined. They there spent 1/2 an hour or more in Singing Catholic Hymns,—& then told me there was an opportunity for my Children to Sing. We accordingly sung several Hymns; one or two of which his congregation knew. I was entirely taken by surprise. I occasionally caught his eye piercingly fixed on me. He acted and looked rather Suspicious and jealous.[64]

Perhaps the détente that Ely reached with this strong supporter of the Catholic mission was mediated through such shared moments of music making.[65]

A distinctive trait of this Métis hymnody was its continuity with other musics in the repertory. For evangelicals like the ABCFM's William Boutwell, who wanted hymn singing to displace all non-Christian music, much less all Catholic hymnody, the manner with which his Métis guides sang hymns was shocking. On a Sabbath day in 1832, when torrents of rain and clouds of mosquitoes had "rendered it impracticable to have divine service," he sat in his tent and muttered:

> At one moment our men were singing some Ind[ian] hymn—the next a song or dancing tune—the next moment an Ind[ian] would begin to thump his drum and sing, that he might make his part of the noise, and render the scene of confusion more perfect. It was no small relief to me, that Mr. S[choolcraft] & myself . . . could have prayers and spend the day in reading the script[ure]s, tracts, and other books, though often interrupted and discomposed by every strang[e] and before unheard of noise.[66]

Similarly Edmund Ely wrote about how difficult it was to sing hymns in the trader's house at Fond du Lac in 1833: "The Frenchmen were assembled in the other part of the House, Singing Indian Airs; and conducted more heathenish than I have seen any Indians in their dances; this is the Case almost every evening; but I have not heard so much noise on the occasion as this Evening."[67] But Fond du Lac's religious diversity called for pragmatism, and Ely did what he could to participate in the larger musical life of the community. Even though his ABCFM station was eventually pushed out of Fond du Lac through the strength of the Catholic and ardently non-Christian Anishinaabeg there, the hymn singing gatherings he led in his home several evenings each week with the Catholic Métis were favorably regarded.

Hymn Singing in Mission Station Worship

Returning to Fond du Lac after an extended absence, Ely found that the "first thing that saluted my ears" was "Nibo, au Shaneminijin," one of the Protestant hymns, "echoing from a lodge, Mr. Cotté himself leading it." Ely was most surprised that Protestant hymns, toward which the Catholics had before "manifested much coldness," now "occup[ied] their full share in their worship."[68]

ABCFM missionaries spared few words in their reflections on Sabbath worship, but they did not hide their disappointment at the profile of the people in the pews. At fur trade settlements like La Pointe, Sabbath worship was regularly attended by the mission families, often the American Fur Company traders' families, the scattered orphans who comprised the non-Métis children attending school. But even when the numbers were encouraging, missionaries lamented the conspicuous absence of "uncivilized" or "full-blood" Anishinaabeg.[69] "The morning exercise which has been conducted in the Indian language, has not been fully attended," Sherman Hall observed, as "the Indians generally manifest a great reluctance to visiting our public meetings. Most of those who have usually attended are women and children."[70] The proportion of women and children may be a result of marriage to Métis employees of the fur company, who were often away on business. But it is also true that missionaries reported deeper inroads among women and children than among men. This was particularly true among women and children who, through disease or misfortune, appeared to be less anchored in stable kinship groups.

Hymns were central to worship. At La Pointe, especially on those occasions when the interpreters were away on fur trade business, missionaries gathered "the children and others who were disposed to assemble, to sing Indian hymns."[71] Although there is no evidence of an Ojibwe-language singing school at ABCFM stations, a rather unschooled Methodist missionary voiced his concern for how far the English service at La Pointe had strayed:

> I Preached, from Isa[iah]. I was not perticular to varnish what I had to say, though three Presbyterien Clurgy were present, and other big foalks. I did not like the singing. Too much *sole fah*, to sout me, and then what capted all, A *base fiddle* was played. What! to praise God with, "O yes," Well I think the braying of a *jackass*, in the house of God, would be as good, as the screaching of a fiddle. It reminded me of the Indian who sacrificed a *dog*, to please the great spiret.[72]

The fiddle music, an unlikely accompaniment for evangelical sacred song, is evidence of a strong, perhaps controlling, presence in worship of La Pointe's Métis families. The "sole fah" to which Spates refers is the practice of shape-note or *fasola* singing by which some Protestants sought to rein in the spontaneous liberties associated with "lined-out" hymnody by bringing the singing within the rule of written music. The Oberlin mission at Leech Lake opened an evening singing school where young and old native congregants met to learn "scientific" singing in parts through the use of shape-note notation.[73]

Hymnbooks did not include musical notation to direct performance in this manner, thus leaving room for the idiosyncrasy of the moment to emerge at the expense of regularity of meter. A native Methodist preacher in Michigan savored the unalloyed aesthetic of singing at a temperance meeting in the 1840s:

> Nothing gave such transports of joy to these simple hearted people as their devotional singing. None who ever heard them will say they had not charming

voices, to blend in sweetest melody. . . . Their singing was not exquisite harmony, nor operatic explosives of voice, of highest art of voice culture to the
neglect of poetic sentiment and meaning, without which singing is no more
worship than "sounding brass and a tinkling cymbal."[74]

The Roman Catholic missionary Frederic Baraga similarly appreciated the Ojibwe
singing of his Slovenian hymns as "slow, solemn, and affecting." "It is not art," he
mused, "but the heart that sings."[75] Solemnity was the term most used by missionaries to describe Ojibwe singing of hymnody. While Episcopalians did not share
Baraga's hymnody, they too prided themselves on the solemnity of native worship.
At the Gull Lake mission, begun by James L. Breck in 1852, worship took place in a
rustic log church that combined a suspended cross, open "Gothic" windows, and a
"pointed English roof" with flooring of cedar-bark and rush mats. Like its worship
space, Breck's mission combined a High Church liturgical tradition with a rather
evangelical interest in hymns and in training native leaders. John Johnson Enmegabowh, an Anishinaabe man trained for the clergy first by Methodists and then
by Breck, led Gull Lake Anishinaabeg gathered around the Episcopalian mission
there and at White Earth for fifty years.

In Breck's account of a worship service in 1857, the order and solemnity of native worship seemed important victories in the self-appointed task of "reducing" the
Ojibwes to "civility." Whatever native congregants felt inwardly about the Christian
worship and its message, for Breck it was the visible practices that counted:

> The church bell has been ringing for some time, and the natives are gathering
> in groups about the mission-house. . . . The children have assembled in their
> schoolroom, all neatly dressed in uniform. The boys' long hair has been cut off.
> . . . Their blankets have been laid aside, and nice coats substituted for them.
> . . . The girls, likewise, with their well-wadded hoods for winter and white
> bonnets for summer . . . look very pretty and neat.[76]

A procession entered the church, led by clergy, then followed by the children, who
uncovered their heads as they entered, finally followed by the adults—a "grotesque
appearance" with some civilized in part "whilst others altogether barbarous," the
men with hair hanging down in four long braids, also feathers waving above their
heads, and with faces curiously painted with the brightest colors." The church was
full of baptized and unbaptized alike, and children began to sing "very sweetly":
"Ojibwa and English hymns they commit to memory and tunes are selected for each,
which are never changed, so that both old and young soon earn them and love
them. The Prayer Book is published in their language, but the loud responses you
hear are said without a book."[77] The exchange of English and Ojibwe is interesting
in Breck's account. In school, all instruction was in English, save for "a few hymns in
their language," the creeds, and certain recited prayers. In worship, Ojibwe was the
rule. Prayers, creeds, Psalms, and hymns were performed from O'Meara's 1845 translation of the *Book of Common Prayer*. All left the church "in order, without the least
confusion or talking" to the music of a dismissal hymn. Breck was particularly proud
of the level of discipline Mrs. Welles and others of his staff were able to effect.[78]

John Johnson Enmegabowh (1807–1902), Anishinaabe Episcopalian priest, White Earth Reservation, ca. 1900. (Courtesy Becker County Historical Society)

Hymn Singing in Mission Schools

Missionary influence and control were felt strongly in public worship. They were also forcefully present in mission schools. A disciplined regimen of singing hymns was supposed to kindle indolent minds and effectively teach principles of the Christian life. One trait that distinguished the use of hymnody in schools was the practice of "singing and repeating" frequently mentioned by missionaries. Sela Wright, an Oberlin missionary at Cass Lake, wrote about his plan for Sabbath school: "Our plan is, to form them into classes, and teach them a hymn, and explain it to them, and sing it. Next we teach, or have them learn a verse from the Testament, or something that I have previously translated. This is explained. We then have another hymn repeated and sung, which closes the exercises. . . ."[79] Each evening at Gull Lake, Breck remembered, a Mrs. Welles taught "both young and old to repeat psalms and hymns orally, and then to chant and sing them, in which exercise they take great delight."[80] During the day, she had her whole school repeat English versions of the hymns they had already memorized in Ojibwa.

Welles and other missionary teachers capitalized on the mnemonic possibilities by using printed versions of hymns as points of access to the world of reading. A discussion of the practice of singing and repeating hymns with the hymnbooks led Breck seamlessly into a protracted discussion of how the schoolchildren were incorporating other practices and gender roles of "civilized" life.[81] The girls are "seated quietly about their teacher, industriously engaged with the needle" and "learning to do all kinds of housework," while the boys are "out with their male teacher learning to make gardens" and "chopping fire wood," roles typically undertaken by Ojibwe women. The boys' hair had been cut; the girls covered. In the mission, the children gather around the table three times a day, after pausing to offer grace and chant the Gloria, rather than "help[ing] themselves with wooden spoons or with their bare fingers" "on the ground and around a common platter."[82]

The impact of early mission schools should be assessed in proportion to the number of native people who would have nothing to do with them. In the second year of running a school, the La Pointe missionaries could report only twenty some scholars having attended. For Hall, the profile did not reflect inroads with the "full blood" population: "Most of the scholars are of mixed breed. A few are full Indian. They have generally attended to English and Indian studies. A few have attended to Indian only. Reading, writing, spelling, elements of arithmetic, and defining have been taught. . . . They seem to regard it in the light of a great favour done to us to permit their children to attend school."[83]

As long as a seasonal living remained viable and children followed their families to the sugaring, ricing, and fishing camps, the visible impact of missionary effort and expense on those Anishinaabe children who did attend the schools, was minimal. Even the well-behaved children at Gull Lake left the mission grounds to join their extended families at the sugarbush and ricing camps when the time came. While Breck was pleased to report that at least one child sent a friend back to the mission from the sugaring camp to get some book to read, no doubt the children who joined their families ate together not three times per day around a table, but whenever it made sense, on the ground, and around a common platter.[84]

Missions, Schools, and the New Terrain of the Treaty Period

A series of treaties beginning in 1837 punctuated the steady dispossession of land and economy along the western shores of Lake Superior and into central Minnesota and Wisconsin. Constraints on mobility made the seasonal round less feasible, and Anishinaabe people grew increasingly dependent on annuities and the resources of the missions for subsistence. Where before it had been largely Métis families that chose to live in the sedentary circles of the fur trade and missions, "full blood" communities spent more and more of their lives within the circle of influence of the mission.

There was an important connection between an emerging factionalism and an increased Ojibwe willingness to participate in the missions and their schools. Prior to the treaties and the collapse of the fur trade, missionaries complained about the irreducibly collective nature of Anishinaabe decision making. Trying to promote a voluntary religion that rested on a sinner's fundamentally individual decision proved to be enormously frustrating to missionaries among a people who were reluctant to commit as individuals without the consensus of the collective. "There is something in this nation," a Lutheran missionary wrote, "a body character, national spirit . . . above which it is impossible for a single individual to elevate himself, and whose presence absolutely obstructs the introduction of the Gospel."[85] Missionaries found that "conversions" were corporate affairs, and as a consequence they focused their efforts on the elders and children in hopes of bringing whole extended families into the Christian fold. They complained about the pressure that non-Christian natives' scorn placed on potential converts to refrain. Prior to the reservation period, missionaries even found that these larger kin networks and whole bands were often reluctant to commit without the council and consensus of allied bands. "Each band . . . stands greatly in awe of every other," wrote J. P. Bardwell at Cass Lake, "the instructed bands say—we believe your doctrine is true, and we should embrace it as a band, were it not for our neighbors of other bands—they would ridicule us, and we can't stand that."[86] While the Anishinaabeg never fully departed from a communal orientation, the collapse of the fur trade and the diminished land base brought an unprecedented division in Ojibwe communities.

The treaties themselves were negotiated between the United States and those Ojibwe leaders deemed legitimate representatives of native interests. But because there was no such political entity as "the Ojibwe nation," leaders of different bands made decisions that often impacted other Ojibwe groups not represented.[87] ABCFM missionaries spoke about the consequences for the Yellow Lake Ojibwes when leaders at Fond du Lac ceded the band's land in an 1837 treaty.[88] Exploited by nonnative interests, an increased social distance between Ojibwe groups made for a volatile state of affairs at midcentury. Missionary accounts of the 1840s and 1850s bear witness to the drinking and violence that plagued Ojibwe communities and split them apart into the competing factions of an emerging class system. "The judgements of God are abroad among them," Frederic Ayer wrote in 1848. At Red Lake, he reported: "Deaths are frequent, . . . two hundred per cent or more exceeding the number of births and this too in the absence of epidemics or prevailing fevers. Pulmonary diseases are prevalent. Bleeding at the lungs is very common." Believing that "licentious and filthy habits aggravate their disorders," Ayer concluded, "nought but the Gospel can save them and this they virtually reject and cast it behind their backs."[89] Enmegabowh reached a different diagnosis. Lamenting what he saw as the effect of whiskey at the trading settlement of Crow Wing in 1863, the preacher observed:

> Since my arrival here there are eight men killed and since my last letter . . . two more killed of Leech Lakers and one chief of Red Lake about dying inflicted upon him by Gull Lake indians during drunkenness. My greatest fear is about the Mille Lacs chiefs to whom I have entertained great hopes of their soon becoming good indians. Since last May I have counted twenty five killed among themselves—nothing else just by the effect of ishkotawahboo (firewater) and on nights since three barrels of whiskey was taken or sold to the indians on the other side of the Mississippi in one night only.[90]

Other native leaders made yet a third diagnosis of the social crisis. They identified the missions and not just the traders as the source of social breakdown and stepped up opposition to missions and literacy. Several Ojibwe bands used force and threat of force to drive away Episcopalian missionaries from Leech Lake and Gull Lake in 1862, standing squarely in a long line of organized Anishinaabe resistance to missionization and colonization that leads right through the Leech Lake Pillager uprising of 1898 to the current day.[91] Other leaders came to the conclusion that the survival of their communities required fuller participation in the life of the missions and schools and in the incorporation of agriculture into the larger way of life. In 1862, a Gull Lake leader said, "We feel as though we and our children were all going to die very soon, and our only hope is to have a teacher to show us how to live and how to follow the rules of the Great Spirit."[92] Rebecca Kugel argues persuasively that the obvious differences between the "broad accommodation" of the latter perspective and the "militant," "deeply contemptuous" posture of the former are accompanied by a mutual deep interest in bringing tradition and cultural innovation into balance for a viable way of life.[93]

An 1840 agreement signed between Hole in the Day, Strong Ground, and the superintendent of Methodist missions illustrates well how strategic was the welcome that missionaries received. The agreement stipulated that the children who "are willing to be instructed" and those "received under the exclusive control of the mission shall be considered as members of the mission family, and will be clothed and fed as such." In exchange, the native leaders granted the mission "protection of the chiefs and the people" and "privilege of as much ground, timber, stone, water, pasturage for cattle, passing over lands, navigating streams, and other things as may be necessary." Were the band to deem it no longer useful by majority vote, the mission "shall be removed from the Indian lands."[94]

When Anishinaabe opponents forced his departure from the northern missions in 1857, James L. Breck moved to Faribault in southern Minnesota and started a boarding school, where Ojibwe and Dakota children were "fitted to return to their own people as ministers of the everlasting gospel."[95] In 1860, the school had eighteen Ojibwe boys and girls and as many Dakota children, mostly orphans entrusted to the care of the mission or children of prominent leaders sent to learn to read. Removed from the rhythms of Ojibwe social and cultural life, those children who survived Faribault returned to their communities as schooled, literate spokespersons. Music formed a significant part of the pupils' routine. Most activities were conducted in English, but native Dakota and Ojibwe hymns were included and a regular Ojibwe Sabbath service was conducted from the Ojibwe prayer book.

Hymn Singing at the Periphery of Mission Influence

Beyond the disciplinary reach of the schools and public worship, there began to grow an even more distinctive singing tradition. George Copway led the Fond du Lac mission after its desertion by the ABCFM, and he noted in 1842 that both "the Indians and the half-blood Catholics" could be heard observing the Sabbath in their own way. "We hear them singing in their lodges," Copway reported, "and some praying."[96] Copway noted that they held a biweekly singing meeting in addition to two prayer meetings and two classes.

Evangelicals sang hymns on all occasions of human experience and associated certain hymns with various occasions. In the case of the Ojibwe, though, missionary accounts indicate that the repertory of hymns was applied in particular to occasions of danger, sickness, and death.

Native hymns evidently carried some abiding association with the danger of journeys. In 1849, Frederic Baraga found the "Indians very much love their prayer-books and are taking them with them on their travels so that they are able to read and sing from them at places where they stay overnight."[97] Most travel in the region was canoe travel, extremely dangerous because storms rose up from nowhere on large lakes like Superior, Leech, and Red Lake. Peter Jones even translated a hymn under the heading "Traveling by Water," which appeared in the Methodist hymnal both in English and Ojibwe.[98]

Lord, whom wind and seas obey,	Ta ba ning a, mon oo suh,
Guide us through the watery way;	Kuh nuh wa ne me she nom;
In the hollow of thy hand,	Ka uh peech pe me shkay yong
Hide, and bring us safe to land.	Nuh nonzh go che Kah bah shong.

One can picture Métis and Ojibwe sojourners raising these songs to secure safe passage through a Lake Superior storm, or if death were imminent, to sing for the soul's safe passage. Franz Pierz recalled how his Métis guides broke out in hymns during a Lake Superior gale in 1838: "We contended with powerful waves, and we slipped up and down the storm billows as if over the roof of a long city. The ice-cold water dashed above our heads in the front of our bodies from neck to heel. A European un-accustomed to such dangers would have cried with fright; my Indians sang joyous spiritual songs with good courage."[99]

In addition to its increasing association with encounters with danger, native hymn singing also took on a marked association with illness, dying, and grieving. Indeed, this association emerged from the very first days of Protestant missions in the region. As we have seen, the first forays of ABCFM missionaries into the wigwams were in response to native requests that the missionaries sing Ojibwe hymns for those about to die. But later missionaries wrote often about being summoned to deathbeds and about being deeply moved by native hymn singing, even when the performances were uneasily beyond their control. A semi-autonomous tradition of hymn singing had begun to emerge around the figures of certain elders, especially women elders, living in the shadow of their own death.

Although Frederic Ayer could not "speak with perfect confidence of any saving conversion among the Heathen" at Yellow Lake, he was encouraged about one dying woman. By the time he reached her, she was "deprived of reason," but Ayer was told that "for some time previous to her derangement and afterwards she spent much of her time in prayer, & in singing Indian hymns which she had learnt."[100] In 1859, a Lutheran missionary wrote about a blind elder named Old Sarah, who nearing death, heard "lovely sounds, such as singing and harp-playing, and asked the by-standers to bring the singers and harpists nearer."[101] In 1858, a similar experience struck the missionary Sela Wright, who wrote about a young woman at Lake Win-nibigoshish who underwent a near-death experience and later "frequently spoke of seeing the holy ones above and hearing them sing. She spent whole days in prayer and in singing hymns." Wright remembered that "one hymn in particular she sung very frequently, 'Jesus my all to heaven is gone.'"[102] This particular hymn, rendered "Jesus ishpeming Kah e zhod" in Ojibwe, by all accounts became the most popular hymn for occasions associated with death. Indeed, it had been the one that became so significant for George Copway after his consumptive mother sang it on her deathbed.

Hymns became associated with illness and dying, but even more lastingly they became associated with grieving. Missionaries were increasingly aware of how hymns were incorporated into mourning and burial practices. An Anglican missionary remembered how Ojibwes at Lake Huron's Manitoulin Island "were accustomed to sit up with their bereaved friends on the night preceding a funeral, passing the time in prayer and singing hymns. . . . About twenty hymns were sung at intervals and [the priest] filled up these intervals by reading passages from the bible."[103] In 1849, Baraga noted that he had "seen Indians, who on their deathbed have begged as a favor that after their death their prayer books might be laid on their bosom in the coffin, in order that on the Day of Judgment, they might appear before the judgment chair of Jesus with their prayer books in their hand."[104] When a "drumming over" failed to bring a sickly Anishinaabe infant at Fond du Lac back to health, Edmund Ely was asked to participate in the funeral "according to the custom of the Whites." Note the ubiquity of hymns:

> Mr. Cotté enquired if I wished a Candle (according to Cath. Custom) I left that to his own pleasure entirely & appointed 3:00 as the hour. Called my School together & proceeded with them to Mr. Cotté's. The Corpse was laid on a table in the midst of the room in its Indian wrappings & and its Coffin by its Side, and a Candle burning at its head. I commenced by Singing the 7th Hymn. Read part of Job 14 and spoke say 15 or 20 minutes—told them that the dead were out of our reach and our business was with the living—urged life as the day of salvation. Addressed a few words to the parents. Prayed and Sung Hy. 13th. The Corpse was then placed in its coffin the parents took their last look. We then proceeded to the Grave in the following order: Mr. Cotté, the Corpse borne by an Indian, Mourners, Mrs. C and A[itken]. My school, and myself at their head, then followed by several men, 25 or more in all. After depositing the Coffin in the grave we lifted up our Voices in the Hymn "Nibo au Shanem-inajin." I followed the Hymn with a short supplication and we returned.[105]

Although accounts of hymn singing increased some as the century wore on and as more Anishinaabeg were brought within the circles of mission influence, the evidence remains largely sporadic. Nonetheless, a number of trajectories that carry into the latter decades of the century had already emerged in connection with the occasional nature of Ojibwe singing outside public worship and schooling at the mission stations.

First, we notice that hymn singing made its greatest impact when and where the fabric of Anishinaabe social life was most vulnerable. Those Ojibwes who sang hymns in this early period were the "charged particles" moving in outer orbits of

Anishinaabe social life. The first Ojibwes to embrace the singing were the Métis families living near the trading posts. The mission stations were frequently entrusted with looking after widows and orphans, along with an increasing number of nonor-phaned children, as native communities were less able to provide. It is not surpris-ing, then, that it was children and elders, especially women elders, as they ap-proached death, whom missionaries heard sing hymns most frequently.

Second, instead of transforming the Ojibwe musical repertory, hymns were ab-sorbed into it. To be sure, hymn singing was a musical novelty to Ojibwe people: No drum sounded along with the voice, women sang the same songs with men, the hymns were more textually laden, and so on. But where evangelical missionaries made a sharp distinction between Christian hymnody and other musics of an unre-generate life, Métis and Anishinaabeg alike often sang hymns along with other mu-sics. Indeed, learning hymns from the missionaries took place in a long tradition of sharing music across cultural boundaries.

Third, Ojibwes in this early period appear to have distinguished singing hymns from other practices and ideas of the Christian life. For evangelical missionaries, hymnody provided a musical accent on prayer and scripture reading, but Ojibwe ea-gerness to hear, learn, and sing new songs came with an often conspicuous indiffer-ence to scripture reading, preaching, and instruction.

Fourth, sporadic singing began to be more closely associated with occasions of danger, sickness, death, and grieving. While evangelicals often associated hymnody with such moments in life experience, among Ojibwes hymns took their place in the repertory largely as a music specific to those moments.

Finally, although detailed accounts of performance in this early period are few, missionary correspondence began to remark on a strikingly uniform Anishinaabe aesthetic, described in terms of solemnity, sincerity, and unison. By the close of this period, an Episcopalian priest at White Earth observed that this musical tradition had "become indigenous."[106] The discussion now turns to these trajectories as they evolved within the structures of reservation life and assimilation policy to produce a distinctive hymn-singing tradition as part of Anishinaabe resolve to survive as a dis-tinctive people with distinctive values.

3

MUSIC AS NEGOTIATION

Uses of Hymn Singing,
1868–1934

▲▲▲▲▲▲

"No music so blinds my eyes with tears as the songs of these Christian Indians," wrote Episcopal Bishop Henry B. Whipple in 1880 as he made his rounds among the northern Minnesota missions: "Indian voices are very sweet and you could not believe that they were the same voices you have heard in the wild heathen grand medicine or the horrid scalp dances. I am sure that in the charms of song which goes up to heaven from this world they sound as sweet to Jesus as any Christian song."[1] But the soul of the music that Whipple heard in morning worship was clearly developing elsewhere, out of earshot of the mission station and beyond the ken of missionary reportage. A message dictated in broken English the next year indicated that, amid an outbreak of smallpox among the Lake Winnibigoshish Ojibwes, a group of Ojibwe men had journeyed sixty miles from their home at the White Earth Reservation to sing hymns all night long over a dying child.[2] Although the documentary record contains only sparse details of such performances, Ojibwe people placed the missionary songs in familiar social contexts of music making in ways that made them their own. By 1880, the tradition of singing hymns had become largely the province of certain groups of young men and women, respectively, who gathered around the spiritual leadership of elders and carried the music to the sick, the dying, and the grieving. In this case, the singers formed around the eldership of Shay-day-ence, or Little Pelican, a man who had been highly regarded, not coincidentally, as a spiritual leader in the Midewiwin tradition at Gull Lake before his community had been removed to the White Earth Reservation. Singing provided an occasion for the gathering of these groups of men and women, and set the tone for an improvised way of life amid the difficult circumstances on the reservation. This chapter explores this emerging musical tradition and its role in calibrating those cultural improvisations to established rhythms of the Ojibwe way of life, *anishinaabe bimaadiziwin*.

To understand what conditions brought about this more ritualized tradition of hymnody at White Earth, this chapter first describes the migration to White Earth and the social and material crises faced by Anishinaabe people there. Because the Episcopalian mission was influential in setting the terms of those social conditions at White Earth, it will be important to survey its program and sketch the contours of the native-led community gathered within the Episcopalian fold, a community that called itself the Anami'aajig, "those who pray." This chapter consequently begins with an account of the possession and subsequent dispossession of White Earth and the coordinated effort by missionaries and Indian agents to restructure Anishinaabe time and space on the reservation toward the twin goals of conversion and "civilization."

Against the backdrop of these efforts, the chapter proceeds to examine hymn singing as a practice through which the native Christians made room within the circumscriptions of the reservation for a life of integrity on Ojibwe grounds. Having ritualized it to their own ends, the Anami'aajig took their music very seriously, and rightfully so, for music making came to mean nothing short of survival for them. But survival is one thing; survival with beauty and integrity is quite another. This chapter closes with a discussion of whether the hymns were plainly a product of strategic ritualization, or whether the powerful experience of the songs rested more deeply on the integrity of the way of life they accompanied.

The Possession and Dispossession of White Earth

In an 1867 treaty with the Mississippi bands, the United States won the agreement of certain Ojibwe leaders to the emerging idea that native and nonnative interests would best be served were the Ojibwes to be concentrated on a single reservation where the possibilities for a successful agrarian life were strongest.[3] Reformers thought that if native people were to be provided with fertile land, protection from the "bad elements" of frontier society, and the benevolent cooperation of church and state in managing reservation affairs, they could then make a successful steady transition from a seasonal round to the family farm. The experiment was to take place in northwestern Minnesota, in an area of land roughly thirty miles square that straddled three distinctive ecological zones. The eastern third consisted of wide bogs and thick conifer forests. A central strip of land was characterized by lakes, hardwood groves, and rolling hills teeming with game; the western third opened the reservation onto the fertile prairie of the Great Plains.

The first wave of Ojibwe emigrants arrived one year later, calling the new land *gaa-waabaabiganikaag*, or White Earth, for the white rock that lay beneath the soil. A group of extended kin and followers of Manidowaub and Nabunashkong, two key supporters of the Episcopalian mission at Gull Lake, left the former territory reluctantly.[4] "When the government ask[ed] the indians to move into the strange country—a country that they never visit[ed] before . . . I hesitated for weeks," wrote John Johnson Enmegabowh. "I did not like the idea of leaving my native land that I loved so dearly and to think of leaving my little dear ones [buried at Crow Wing]."[5]

The settling of White Earth transpired over a considerable number of years. By 1872, 550 Anishinaabeg had come, mostly from the Gull Lake families of the Mississippi Band. By 1875, the number had grown to eight hundred, at least a third of whom were Métis relatives of prominent trader families who had won a treaty clause granting them rights to join the Anishinaabeg there. In 1876, the population nearly doubled as a large influx of Anishinaabeg of the Ottertail Pillager Band settled the village of Pine Point and a contingent of the Pembina Band settled the contemporary village of Mahnomen.[6] Respective bands either established their own villages or joined relatives already settled there.

The village structure of this early settlement pattern became an enduring feature of White Earth's social landscape, with implications for a factionalism that continues to challenge the unity of the reservation today.[7] Each settlement was placed at a considerable remove from the others, creating conditions that were especially isolating in the absence of the network of waterways that had enabled canoe travel in former territories. The Pembina Settlement near what is now Mahnomen, for instance, lay several hours by foot from the nearest settlements of the Gull Lake bands and

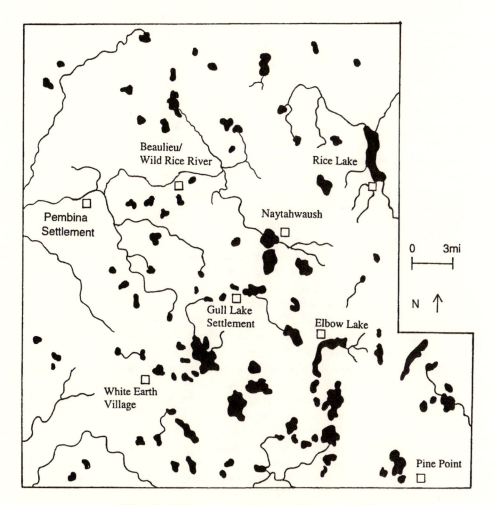

White Earth Reservation and major villages, ca. 1890.

well over thirty miles from the Pillagers' village at Pine Point. Outlying villages like Pine Point and Rice Lake had to compete with White Earth village for blacksmiths, machinery, and other scarce resources of an annuity-based economy.[8]

Separate settlements enabled each band to retain its distinctive identity and leadership pattern, such that a reservationwide political consciousness did not obtain until a series of land fraud cases emerged after the turn of the century and gave different communities a common enemy.[9] Each village band looked to its *ogimaag*, "bosses" or chiefs who rose to authority either through heredity or charisma, and who represented the band in larger councils and in meetings with the Indian Agent and missionaries. Members of the Gull Lake branch of the Mississippi Band living closer to White Earth village looked to Manidowaub, Nabunashkong, and Waubunoquod for leadership. Rabbit Lake Ojibwe, closely allied with Gull Lake, were led by Mezhukegeshig. Different waves of migrants from a third branch of the Mississippi band from Mille Lacs Lake looked to Minogezhig and later Waweyeacumig for leadership and settled at Elbow Lake and Wild Rice River. Most social activity transpired within the context of each village band, in patterns established with the seasonal ricing and sugarbush camps. A practice of visiting emerged as a significant form of social and ceremonial exchange among White Earth bands and between the Anishinaabeg and Dakota Sioux. The visiting complex involved feasting, give-aways, gaming, and the customary exchanges of songs and dances.[10]

In 1872, the United States built a government agency at White Earth village. The village soon became a kind of boomtown, where annuities were distributed and exchanged for supplies with the Métis merchant families. A thriving timber industry, nourished by the reservation's eastern pine lands, brought further cash to the town's saloons and stores. White Earth village was also the seat of mission influence. Episcopalians rebuilt Gull Lake's St. Columba mission on a hillside near the agency. On the far edge of town, Benedictines built a mission and school.

With broad support of missionaries, the treaty rights of White Earth's various bands were definitively undermined through Congress's passage of the Nelson Act in 1889. Passage of the Homestead Act in 1886, railroad expansion, and a local timber boom had brought a great deal of pressure on so-called unimproved Ojibwe lands in Minnesota. The Nelson Act sought to dissolve all Minnesota Ojibwe reservations save Red Lake and to concentrate all Ojibwe people, including the Métis, within the boundaries of White Earth. It also applied to the Ojibwe case a new assimilation paradigm for Indian policy which the United States had already applied to other tribes under the 1887 Dawes Allotment Act. Believing communal ownership of property to be the most significant obstacle to Indian assimilation, the legislation parceled communally held land into allotments of up to 160 acres to male "heads" of nuclear families. These allotments were to be held in trust for twenty-five years or until the owners were deemed competent to make sound judgments in land transactions. In the ostensible interest of exposing native people to the example of sedentary European-American farmers, the remaining reservation lands could be made available to nonnative settlement. White Earth lands rich in red and white pine were surveyed for public auction, with proceeds going to a "Chippewa in Minnesota Fund." By congressional action, Anishinaabe political and economic life was being restructured from small *ogimaa*-led bands to reservation entities to a statewide political unit later to become the Minnesota Chippewa Tribe.

Minnesota's Ojibwes were given the option to take allotments at the White Earth Reservation, or to take allotments in their home vicinity. While some did indeed relocate to White Earth, many took the latter option, undermining the resettlement intentions of the Nelson Act altogether. Those who relocated to White Earth did so gradually through the 1890s, again moving by units of extended families. By the turn of the century, another twelve hundred had relocated to White Earth, bringing the population to four thousand.[11]

The outcome of the Nelson Act was disastrous. Freed of structures of accountability, cultural misunderstanding and greed conspired to transform a well-intentioned allotment policy into the efficient vehicle for the near-complete dispossession of White Earth. As allotments were made, those uninterested in an agrarian future took lands in the eastern two thirds of the reservation, often according to a logic that would enable them to continue to live in proximity to extended kin and to the familiar resources of a seasonal round of ricing, fishing, and hunting. The families of Métis traders, however, better oriented to market agriculture and more aware of the investment value of fertile land in a rapidly developing region, took their allotments in the fertile western third of the reservation. Some members of these families, who had long lived away from the community, returned just in time at the Indian agency to receive the choicest allotments. Some simply did so for the speculative gain, having never planned to move to White Earth in the first place.

Tensions between Métis and conservative Anishinaabeg rose in 1904, when Congress yielded to pressures from the timber industry and those White Earth Métis who had become the industry's agents, to parcel out unallotted rich pine lands, circumventing the public auction safeguards established by the Nelson Act. Later investigations revealed that appraisals and public auctions for the purchase of White Earth's rich pine lands under the Nelson Act had been routinely rigged.[12] In the same year, a rider attached to a congressional appropriations bill extended the right to sell allotment timber to those deemed "competent" to deal responsibly with real estate. Under the rider, this competency was to be determined according to hereditary blood status.

Prominent Métis people had long argued that the encumbrances of the trust relationship were patronizing violations of native self-determination.[13] But what ensued was the undoing of sovereignty that accompanied the undoing of the land base. With immigrant settlers eager to till fertile native lands and timber companies eager to harvest the pines that could supply the construction of Chicago, Minneapolis, and St. Paul, White Earth enrollees ended up parting with vast amounts of their reservation. Unversed in the intricacies of real property ownership and probate, most of the conservative Anishinaabeg died intestate, leaving small tracts of land to multiple heirs. Whether by below-market purchase of land from starving families or by utter fraud, White Earth's conservative Anishinaabeg population lost its grip on the land base necessary to secure its future prosperity.

A particularly insidious aspect of White Earth's dispossession was the prominent role played in it by the nation's leading physical anthropologists. In the 1910s, Ales Hrdlicka and Albert Jenks were summoned to settle investigations of fraud in land sales by scientifically determining the blood quantum of White Earth residents. At issue was the legality of those land transactions that had been made by certain native people of questionable "competency" to circumvent the Nelson Act's trust relationship. Equipped with samples of hair and caliper measurements of skulls, the scientists dismissed half the fraud claims, determining that four hundred claimants had been of "mixed blood" after all and therefore were unprotected by the trust clause of the legislation. In many cases, these findings completely disregarded the testimony that claimants themselves made concerning their family trees. More than half the claims were dismissed on this scientific basis.[14] From the late 1880s to the mid-1930s, when the United States reversed its official policy of assimilation, native lands set apart by treaty were reduced by nearly two thirds.[15] By the 1980s, fewer than 7 percent of the White Earth land base would belong to native people.

The dispossession of the land exacerbated tensions within White Earth's native community. So, too, did the set of new U.S. Indian policies organized under the rubric of assimilation. With increased dependence on treaty annuities, different bands found that their respective treaty agreements had been subsumed under the category of the White Earth Band, a legal fiction that became the principal mechanism for administering treaty benefits. Significantly, the label "White Earth Band" pertained to no indigenous form of association or treaty-making entity, but to the amalgam of Anishinaabeg occupying the reservation. This resulted in considerable hostility among White Earth's respective band communities.

Of course, this was not the first time that social tension had arisen. Relations were long strained between Métis and conservative Anishinaabeg, between different Ojibwe bands, and even within those bands, between two customary forms of leadership: elder chiefs and warriors or young men.[16] What was without precedent at White Earth was the way that reservation conditions subverted the fundamental premises of Anishinaabe survival: a sustaining land base, autonomy to adapt to new environments, and commitment to consensus. At White Earth, a more pronounced class system emerged, as existing social distinctions of age, kin, region, and ethnicity became more consequential in the competition for survival and favor.[17] Meanwhile, the missionaries, Indian agents, and businessmen who were White Earth's power brokers capitalized on these distinctions, playing one group off another in their own competition for Anishinaabe land, timber, and souls.

Much of the dispossession was actually brokered from within Ojibwe ranks, by savvy reservation enrollees who found they could earn a living as intermediaries. A number of prominent Métis figures mediated submarket land deals and later transposed the patron-client relationships they had with the Anishinaabeg in the fur trade days into the political structures of the reservation era. Again, designations of "full blood" and "mixed blood" at White Earth rested on distinctions that were as much cultural as hereditary, and which consequently could change with new circumstance.[18] While family affiliation remained important, by the 1870s it was one's economic and cultural commitments that ultimately designated ethnic identity. These deeper value orientations were visible in the things people did, how they chose to educate their young, where they chose to live, whether they spoke English or Ojibwe, what they wore, and which songs they sang.

Differing visions for White Earth's future also generated heated conflict. The Métis distinguished themselves geographically, choosing land near White Earth village and along the new Soo Line railroad on the western edge of the reservation best

The Beaulieu's Real Estate office, which brokered much of the sale of White Earth lands previously allotted to Anishinaabe families under the Nelson Act. White Earth village, 1905. (Courtesy Minnesota Historical Society)

suited to crop-intensive market agriculture. By 1885, some 75 percent of the White Earth harvest was the work of the Métis community.[19] The Métis distinguished themselves economically from conservative Anishinaabeg, who generally chose to retain much of the seasonal hunting, fishing, and ricing that was so central to their identity.

The Métis distinguished themselves culturally. In the pages of the *Tomahawk*, Gus Beaulieu's weekly English-language newspaper, the cultural life of its primarily Métis readership was elaborated. While the *Tomahawk* was proud of the community's native culture, it spoke of myths and traditions in the past tense as a rich heritage to be appreciated rather than as a viable program to be enacted. And while its editorial viewpoint was often critical of U.S. policies, the paper celebrated a "progressive" view of an Anishinaabe future, appeared in English to an English-educated audience, and called for an end to paternalistic policies that encumbered access to the market economy. The *Tomahawk* welcomed the music and social dances that would put the tastes at White Earth in keeping with those of the wider American popular culture. It vigorously promoted and reviewed performances of White Earth's instrumental band and the many dances in the White Earth village social hall. But to those who spoke Ojibwe and tried to make a subsistence living on the seasonal round, the accumulation of wealth, improvement of land, and commodification of food implied in the *Tomahawk's* vision of market agriculture and cultural integration compromised cherished values.

Religious affiliation played a complicated role in these social affiliations. On the one hand, Catholicism had become a strong marker of Métis identity, while conservative Anishinaabeg were generally affiliated with either the Episcopalian mission or the Midewiwin society.[20] On the other hand, these religious affiliations were seldom carved in stone. A number of those identified as "full bloods" seemed to go back and forth between the missions, suggesting that religious affiliation was as much a matter of strategy as it was of identity, and therefore subject to fleeting change. It is perhaps better to say that tensions at White Earth between Episcopalians and Catholics derived as much from the deeper differences in the economic and cultural commitments of White Earth's various ethnic communities as they did from theological or liturgical preferences.

In White Earth's early years, the conservative Anishinaabe population, especially those who hailed from Gull Lake, associated themselves with the Episcopal mission. In 1870, when the bulk of White Earth's population was still Mississippi Band members with a nearly two-decade-old association with the Episcopal mission, 200 of the 370 White Earthers had accepted the terms of Christian membership. By 1880, slightly more than one in five of the eight-hundred "full bloods" on the reservation were reported as communicants by Episcopalian authorities, with many more participating in some lesser capacity in the life of the mission. But while this number indicates the significant numbers of Ojibwe Christians, it also indicates the large number of White Earthers—especially those more recent immigrants of the Pillager Band, the Pembina Band, and the Mille Lacs branch of the Mississippi Band—who did not identify themselves with the Episcopalians.

Native Episcopalians sought to distinguish themselves from the ardently non-Christian Anishinaabeg even while they distinguished themselves from Catholic Métis, distinctions that were rooted, as Rebecca Kugel shows in masterful detail, in disputes that emerged in the 1850s and 1860s between warriors and *ogimaag*.[21] But the social boundary between the Métis and conservative Anishinaabeg of either Christian or non-Christian affiliation appears to have become more consequential with the experience of fraud and dispossession. Whether one counted one's self among the Episcopalian or Midewiwin communities of the conservative Anishinaabeg, what seemed to matter in the allotment assignments, transfers, and sales that affected economic well-being was whether they were punctuated with "thumbprints" or "signatures," the terms that frame Melissa Meyer's examination of ethnicity at White Earth. This signified more than a shared preference for the Ojibwe language over and against the Métis' schooling in English: It signified a commitment shared by conservative Anishinaabeg, whether Christian or not, to a way of valuing land and life on the land that stood in contrast to the rules of real estate and the signatures that sold it.

The social boundaries between White Earth's ethnic communities were indeed significant—both between Métis and Anishinaabeg in general and among the reservation's various Anishinaabeg villages in particular. So, too, were the frequent exchanges that crossed those boundaries. Each June, a powwow celebration brought different visions for an Ojibwe future together at the White Earth agency. The parades, social dances, marching bands, and musical entertainment of Métis participants were markedly distinguished from the give-aways, moccasin games, mock battles, dancing in regalia, pipe ceremonies, and musical exchanges that the conservative Anishinaabeg staged with the visiting Dakota. Yet these distinctive cultural activities together comprised the pageantry of the event. Over shared food, both groups affirmed their rightful places at White Earth.

Though intermarriage was increasingly rare between the two communities, a continued pattern of interchange meant that the ethnic distinctions were complicated in ways that admitted considerable crossover. Since values more than heredity determined one's ethnic affiliation at White Earth, the boundary between Métis and conservative Anishinaabeg remained a porous one. Years of fur trade experience had shown that those Ojibwes living the seasonal round and their more sedentary Métis cousins needed the other for the betterment of both.

The Episcopalian mission stood in a complicit, if complicated, relationship to the dispossession of the land and people at White Earth. The mission was vocally critical of governmental fraud in the administration of treaty payments. It supported White Earth matters in Washington and helped sustain needy native people through its philanthropic network.[22] But the mission supported national policies that ultimately undermined the land and community at White Earth and used its material and social influence to put these ideas into effect on the local level.

The White Earth mission's influence extended nationally through Henry Benjamin Whipple's forty-odd years as bishop of Minnesota. From the moment he arrived in 1858 until his death in 1901, the missions to the Ojibwe and Dakota remained close to the bishop's heart. Though his public prominence involved him in numerous affairs, Whipple never seemed to lose track of the native missions. Though never a field missionary himself, Whipple relished his tours of the northern missions, embracing each opportunity to hunt, fish, and paddle a canoe. Considered to be a prominent and gifted diplomat during a contentious period in Episcopalian history, Whipple made many influential friends in the East and engaged his high office in zealous advocacy for Ojibwe causes. For example, when news of the Dakota Uprising of 1862 provoked the nation's fury and led to widespread appeals for the annihilation or removal of all Indians, Whipple took a highly public, highly unpopular stand. He argued that the uprising grew not out of innate Indian hostility but out of an understandable, if deplorable, rage among native peoples that had been fed by the fraud and deception of U.S. Indian policy. Whipple went directly to President Lincoln to secure the well-being of those native people in the region who had not participated in the rebellion. Later in the 1880s, when the Army Corps of Engineers built a series of dams on the Mississippi headwaters to make the river navigable all the way upriver to Minneapolis, the water level of the lakes of the Mississippi headwaters rose dramatically, destroying whole reservation communities and decimating the vulnerable wild rice plants at the shallow peripheries of the headwaters' lakes. Whipple lobbied aggressively for just compensation to the Ojibwe reservations reeling from the hunger, disease, and landlessness that followed the floods.[23] In part because of this resolve, in part because of the generosity and sincerity with which he behaved while touring the Northwoods, Whipple earned the Ojibwe name of

Straight Tongue. As Rebecca Kugel put it, Whipple "managed half deliberately, half by accident, to behave in a manner the Ojibwe found acceptable."[24]

All the same, Whipple had been a member of the commission that called for the Nelson Act in the first place. Whipple's intentions were complicated, since he supported allotment in order to bring native people under protection of the law as U.S. citizens.[25] But, as George Tinker argues, Whipple's call for the closing of treaty-making and the allotment of land was "intentionally designed to destroy Indian community and tribal structures by eroding their land base and converting tribal lands . . . to individually owned private property."[26] Whipple corresponded regularly with Herbert Welsh, head of the powerful Indian Rights Association that lobbied successfully for the broad shift toward assimilation in federal policy. Whipple also took part in the Lake Mohonk Conferences, where advocates gathered in genteel surroundings to "solve" what they labeled "the Indian problem."[27]

In the national assimilation policy they designed, Whipple and his cohort of reformers brought together Protestant missionary aims of conversion and civil concerns of pacification. More locally, Whipple and his St. Columba mission staff tried to work in concert with the U.S. Indian Bureau agent on the reservation to create what one historian described as a "hothouse in which the seedlings of civilization could get a protected start."[28] Episcopalian missionaries in White Earth village acted as alert watchdogs of government agency business. But the mission and the agency ultimately shared a goal of assimilation and together orchestrated land policies, annuity administration, almsgiving—even naming practices—to dismember the communal bonds and seasonal rhythms of Anishinaabe life and to engineer a new society based on the Christian faith, individual responsibility, the patriarchal family, and the family farm.

The authority of the Indian agent rested on the mechanism of the payment of treaty annuities. As resources and population reduced Anishinaabe people to a precarious reliance on treaty payments for survival, the administrative apparatus of the Indian Office viewed the payment of annuities not as an obligation to be fulfilled but as an opportunity to create incentives for assimilation goals. Agents on reservations like White Earth were given broad discretion in their administration of annuity payments. If the reservation agent were to deny payment to an Ojibwe man who chose, for example, to stay with relatives rather than relocate to his allotment, or to a woman who was not in a legal marriage, little recourse was available to air grievances. Wide latitude in the payment of annuities gave considerable control to the agent over such things as religious practice. The system was so efficient in controlling ceremonies, songs, and dances at the local level that congressional action was unnecessary to effectively prohibit the free exercise of religion.

The mission, too, could place any number of unwritten conditions on its distribution of charity and influence. While families affiliated with the Episcopalian mission for a variety of reasons, many did so simply in order to survive. When Ojibwe families needed seeds, carts, or an ox to help make ends meet, or clothes and emergency aid when in dire straits, many came to the native clergy of the Episcopalian mission, who in turn went to the archdeacon in charge of Indian missions or directly to the bishop for support. It follows that a missionary's estimation of the sincerity of a petitioner's religious commitments might have meant everything. Did they observe

Joseph A. Gilfillan, Archdeacon in charge of Episcopalian missions, in a buffalo robe, White Earth, late 1800s. (Courtesy Becker County Historical Society)

Sabbath restrictions on labor, even in the ricing or maple-sugaring season? Did they ever participate in gatherings of dancing with the drum? Had they fully abandoned Anishinaabe practices of common-law marriages and relatively easy divorce for life-long commitments to the nuclear family and its property? At White Earth, it was Archdeacon Joseph Gilfillan who functioned as the power broker who decided many such matters. He oversaw the affairs of the mission: its hospitals, its schools, and its satellite churches in the outlying villages. Although these satellite congregations were led by native deacons, Gilfillan's monthly rounds carried his oversight into every community of the White Earth mission on a regular basis.

Episcopalian missionary women were also brokers of power, although they wielded this power in distinctive ways. Pauline Colby, who served at Onigum village on the neighboring Leech Lake Reservation, was for years the only white missionary there. She worked closely with Onigum's native deacons, apparently in a power-sharing arrangement that won a considerable level of affection and respect. When Onigum was lacking a priest or deacon, Colby herself took the *Book of Common Prayer* and "accompanied those of our household of faith to their last resting place and read the beautiful service of our church over them."[29]

Sybil Carter established a vital cottage industry project of lace-making at White Earth in the 1890s. She organized groups of native women to produce fine lace products, which were later sold through networks of women's mission societies in affluent parishes in New York, Philadelphia, and Boston. "I gathered twelve Indian women of the Ojibway tribe into a log hut, and gave them a few lace lessons," Carter wrote in the summer of 1890. "I was, in a three weeks visit, amply repaid, by bringing back twelve bits of very pretty lace, thus proving two things: first they could learn; second, they wanted very much to work for their living."[30]

Carter's project began to take root, especially among the Christian women, and used lace-making as an occasion for fostering circles of native women seeking to remake themselves in light of middle-class Victorian ideals of femininity, motherhood, and domesticity. In 1892, Carter enjoined the White Earth lace-makers to make a beadwork tapestry depicting "some scenes of Indian life" for the Columbian Exposition and World's Fair in Chicago.[31] Carter's vision for the project was not simply to transform Indians but to confront racial prejudices back East. "The pretty lace goes into many homes" in the East, she averred, "plainly contradicting by its purity and beauty, two old time sayings: *Indians are so dirty!* and *Indians are lazy!*"[32] Furthermore, while the project was designed to encourage "Indian mothers" to leave the traditional activities of the seasonal round in order to make lace by the hearthside, the cash they earned actually provided these women and their families important access to an increasingly cash-based economy of survival, in effect endorsing the long-established role for Ojibwe women in the community's economic production. Missionaries like Colby and Carter stood with the vast numbers of other courageous women in the late nineteenth century who entered the mission field not as wives but as their own agents. Thus, they extended their sphere and the moral criticism associated with it far beyond the Victorian home to become public power brokers in the communities they served.[33] But they were also profoundly interested in reproducing many class and gender norms of Anglo-American Protestant society.

As they had in previous decades, missionaries often capitalized on Anishinaabe misfortune in the reservation era. Missionaries often took unpopular public stands against governmental corruption, alcohol, and other sources of native misfortune, and their language conveys a shared sense of loss with the communities to which they dedicated their lives. But missionaries hesitated no less to make religious hay on the poverty, sickness, and death that beset native communities. Missionaries may have considered native misfortune tragic, but it was, for them, tragedy with a purpose, evidence that agrarian Christian civilization was truly the only tenable alternative for an Ojibwe future.

The Structures of Reservation Time and Space

The social consequences of dislocation and concentration at White Earth, together with the dispossession and deforestation of the land, cleared the physical and social landscape for the building of what officials welcomed as a new agrarian, Christian Indian civilization. Agency and mission, church and state, conspired to survey, inscribe, and improve this new landscape of White Earth and the lives of the Anishinaabeg living on it. By 1882, the Episcopalians had extended their influence throughout the White Earth Reservation to the villages of White Earth, Wild Rice River (now Beaulieu), and the Pembina settlement (now Mahnomen), and beyond the reservation at settlements on Red Lake to the north, and on Leech Lake, Cass Lake, and Lake Winnibigoshish to the east.

The conditions established by these efforts worked powerfully to restructure the various native communities forced to settle at White Earth in close proximity. Right angles defined the reservation's perimeter, and lawful travel beyond that perimeter required passes signed by the Indian agent. Surveys and allotment of communally held land into private parcels under the Nelson Act placed even more right-angled structures on social and ecological relationships long imagined in terms of the cycles of *bimaadiziwin*.

Access to goods and services often hinged on whether the missionary or Indian agent believed a family was occupying and improving its land allotment. As we have seen, most conservative Anishinaabeg had taken allotments under the Nelson Act in order to have continued access to the lakes, woods, and rice beds of the reservation's eastern sectors, and they chose lands adjacent to one another in order to maintain the proximity of extended kin networks. For the Anishinaabeg, it was economically difficult and culturally undesirable to abandon the spatial organization, movement, and social relations of the seasonal round. But ecological setbacks resulting from the bustling timber industry, the rising Mississippi headwaters behind a series of dams in the region, and the resulting depletion of game made that choice an increasingly difficult one to live with.

The agency and mission discouraged other social, economic, and ritual practices that stood in the way of assimilation. For example, they targeted what they saw as the "excesses" of Ojibwe give-aways. To these officials, the seemingly endless circulation of property among the Anishinaabe represented a total lack of individual responsibility and respect for property. They drew new ethical lines around what constituted theft of private property and rigorously enforced encroachments. They also discouraged a number of ceremonial and social dance movements afoot in the 1880s and 1890s, when visiting Dakotas shared their Grass Dance and Ghost Dance with White Earth Anishinaabeg, and when the Ojibwes shared the Drum Dance that they had learned from the Menominee to the east. In the wake of one such movement in 1891, Archdeacon Gilfillan observed, "some communities have given themselves up almost wholly to Sioux dancing and do little else. Neither farming nor the religion of our Savior have the slightest attraction for them while their minds are filled with that."[34] Referring to this as an unceasing "dance labor," agents joined missionaries in deploying the power of the purse to discourage, even outlaw, the dances, give-aways, and feasting practices that they felt threatened their fragile presumed "successes" of assimilation.

An architectural space conducive to assimilation was vigorously promoted by the Indian agent. He offered materials for shelter designed not for the circular wigwams of the Anishinaabe past, but for square houses, log houses for those who were doing well in their farming ventures, and tarpaper shacks for the others struggling to make ends meet in more customary seasonal ways. While the tarpaper shacks were not circular like the wigwam, they did share the convenience of construction of the

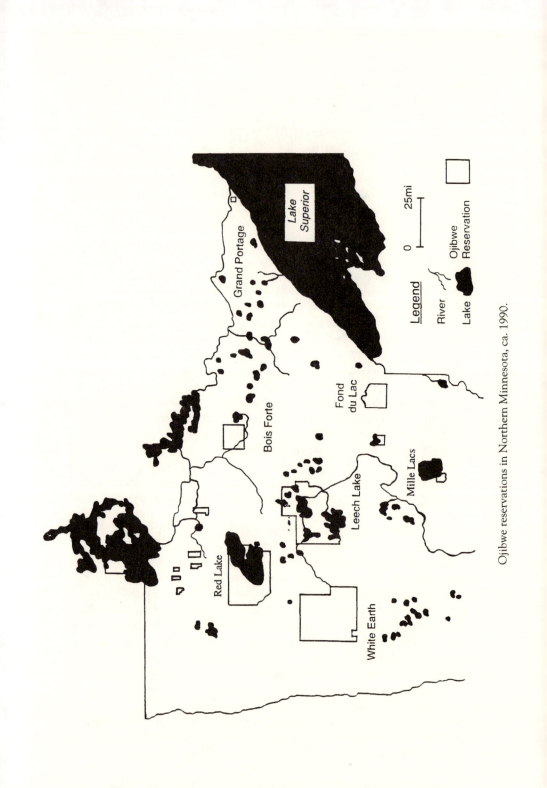

Ojibwe reservations in Northern Minnesota, ca. 1990.

traditional dwelling. Some used processed lumber for their frames. Others relied on timbers from the woods.[35]

Daunting as they may have been, the structures of assimilative time and space were never airtight. Indeed, the level of attention paid to these matters by reservation authorities indicates the level of Anishinaabe cultural resistance to assimilation. Furthermore, whatever shortcomings they saw, those authorities could not argue with the seasonal round's pivotal importance for the material survival of White Earth's native people. A lack of capital and unreliable technical resources made a successful agrarian subsistence impossible for many at White Earth. The Anishinaabeg relied on a time-tested capacity to adapt and survive—to carve out a space for some measure of autonomy in their economic, social, and spiritual lives. In turn, the seasonal activities took on an accentuated significance in contrast to the assimilated life.

The discussion now turns to look at how White Earth Anishinaabeg cleared this semiautonomous space for themselves. In a sense, they did not so much as carve out space within the controlled territory of the reservation as much as they denied its ultimate reality by asserting a continued life in relationship to the land and in rhythm with its seasons, a rhythm that did not stop for a break on Sunday. Despite powerful incentives to control and "improve" the land for intensive market-oriented agriculture, many Anishinaabeg chose to garner a subsistence off the land that stood in a more familiar ethical balance with *bimaadiziwin*. Anishinaabeg oriented quickly to their new landscape at White Earth, never fully letting go of the priorities of the seasonal round. Those native people who counted themselves among the Episcopalians embraced an expansion of their traditional horticulture to the cultivation of larger fields, livestock, and communal labor, but they frustrated the more ambitious hopes of missionaries and agents by limiting their farming to the values of subsistence rather than those of the market. "Many of them show no disposition to enlarge their farms," Gilfillan complained, "but rest satisfied with the little patches that will raise them enough to live on."[36]

When the times arose for sugaring, berrying, fishing, ricing, and hunting, many Anishinaabeg of White Earth's interior villages went off to their respective seasonal camps. Whatever the pressures introduced by the new life on the reservation, such traditional activities reaffirmed a relationship to the land that missionaries and agents underestimated. In the subtle "bush sense" of when and where to go for the harvest of ripened wild rice, in the skilled motion that knocked the right amount of rice into the canoe and that returned the right amount to the lake in gratitude, in the education of children by example in the woods, even the ardently Christian Anishinaabeg were articulating an identity that moved in relation to the land and its rhythms. Gilfillan acknowledged the depth of this way of life, even as he declared it backward: "The idleness inherited through generations, and the remembrance of their wild roving life seem to cling to them strongly. . . . When the spring comes and the sun begins to shine warm, they are impelled by an apparently irresistible impulse to leave their houses and farms and go, the women to making maple sugar, in the woods, and the men to hunt muskrats."[37] Whatever space White Earth Anishinaabeg claimed for themselves within the reservation they found through attuning themselves to the land and its rhythms. But they no longer simply lived on the land.

They lived on land that had been inscribed with reservation boundaries, surveyed and divided into allotments by a formidable regime of economic, military, and religious power. A life of integrity characterized by *bimaadiziwin* would require the wherewithal of a trickster and the endurance of a survivor.

While this book traces the choices made by certain Anishinaabeg as they further allied themselves with the Episcopalian mission and an Ojibwe Christian life, one must remember that their course was one among a number of alternatives chosen by White Earth Anishinaabeg. Moreover, what they chose departed from the Christianity that missionaries promoted in significant respects. Because Ojibwe Christians identified themselves as the Anami'aajig, those who pray, this will serve as the preferable way to designate the way that Ojibwe people articulated Christian community in their own idiom as an entire way of life based on communal ethics of subsistence. They well might have called themselves *nagumojig*, those who sing, for the singing of Ojibwe hymns accompanied almost every collective gathering.

The Anami'aajig and the Native Clergy

Although a number of circumstances led certain Ojibwe people to the Episcopalian mission, including its liturgical rather than doctrinal focus, what most set the Episcopalians apart from previous missionaries was an early commitment to developing an indigenous clergy.[38] Each satellite congregation of the White Earth mission was led by a native deacon, and although Archdeacon Gilfillan made monthly visitations to each, a surprising amount of autonomy appears to have been asserted beyond his purview. Brief biographies of the figures who led the congregations can help us understand the space that the Anami'aajig cleared for themselves.

John Johnson Enmegabowh had been the inspiration in the first place for establishing the Episcopalian mission at Gull Lake, and he maintained his position of leadership when the community moved to Crow Wing and later to White Earth. An Anishinaabe from Ontario, Enmegabowh converted under Wesleyan missionaries, who later trained him at a seminary in Illinois. He married a niece of or Hole-in-the-Day, the warrior leader at Gull Lake, giving him powerful kin in the Mississippi headwaters region.[39] Though relationships with nonnative missionaries were not always congenial, Enmegabowh developed an enduring friendship with Whipple, who knew his support was crucial to any initiative.

When James L. Breck left the mission field in 1857 to found a school in Faribault, he took a number of Gull Lake children, children of prominent *ogimaag* there, with him: Charles Wright Nashotah, the son of Waubunoquod; Fred Smith Kadawabide, the orphaned son of Hole-in-the-Day's principal warrior; and George Johnson, the son of Enmegabowh. Although still anti-Christian in the 1850s, the Gull Lake Midewiwin leader Shay-day-ence wanted his son Nabiquan to be "learned in all the learning of the Egyptians that he might have all the knowledge of the Whites, as well as of the Indian."[40] The boy was baptized Samuel Madison, brought to Faribault for two years of English instruction, and returned to Gull Lake at age twelve. In 1873, Madison moved to White Earth, where he received three years of training under Gilfillan and Enmegabowh. In 1876, he and Fred Smith Kadawabide were ordained deacons and sent to establish a mission at Red Lake.[41] Charles Wright Nashotah emerged as the powerful personality of the second wave of deacons. Wright and the other deacons did not share the English proficiency of Samuel Madison and Fred Smith, lacking the two years of English immersion at Faribault as youngsters, but Wright joined George Johnson for three years of training under Gilfillan and Enmegabowh and was ordained to the diaconate in 1877. In 1878, Fred Smith's younger brothers, George Smith and John Coleman, were ordained with two others as a third class of deacons.[42]

Using the Bible as their sole text, Gilfillan and Enmegabowh gave the deacons three hours of instruction each day. "No one affirms that these candidates were scholars," Whipple wrote, "no one thinks they were fitted by culture for our cultivated parishes; and yet I am not sure but that if all of us had more of the theology of the heart, we should help more poor souls to heaven."[43] Gilfillan found Samuel Madison Nabiquan's description of the Trinity refreshing for its simplicity. "See that lake," Nabiquan had said, "sometimes it is water, sometimes ice, sometimes snow, yet one lake."[44] The deacons were often praised for their rhetorical abilities. Kakakun, baptized George Morgan, was saluted as "a beautiful reader and a good preacher"

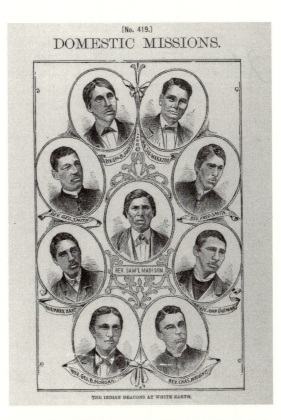

Ojibwe Deacons at White Earth, 1891. Protestant Episcopal Church, Diocese of Minnesota Papers, Box 2, MHS. (Courtesy Minnesota Historical Society)

with a "clear tenor voice" and one who spoke the Ojibwe language "with great beauty and purity."[45] The native deacons also were praised for their perseverance in refusing to "relax to the life of the people" at their respective stations.[46] If by "relax," Gilfillan meant reverting to the life of the seasonal round, the deacons were challenged indeed. Given their low cash wages, native clergy wrote often of their poverty. Clerical duties took precious time and energy away from making a subsistence for their families, and spiritual leadership among the Anishinaabe required unconditional generosity.

While the native clergy could read and write basic English, they seldom conferred in print over matters of doctrine or worship. When native deacons did put pen to paper, they did so to fight for the material needs of their communities. Whether they wrote in Ojibwe or English, these letters sought support from Whipple and the mission's philanthropic network for food, clothing, and basic supplies for people in need. Deacons often translated and transcribed requests of the *ogimaag* for Whipple's support on treaty and Indian office matters in Washington.[47]

The exchange of religious ideas, by contrast, remained resolutely a matter of oral tradition. We could justly interpret this as a strategic containment of the written word to dealings with the mission or agency. Oral exchanges concealed from nonnative superiors the operations and syncretism of the Anami'aajig and remained the native clergy's preferred mode of communication. Their sermons remained firmly rooted in the oral tradition, and we consequently know little of their theology as it might have been propositionally expressed. Of the native clergy, it was Enmegabowh whose writing involved the most scriptural citation, but his theology remains difficult to ascertain from his typical stream of consciousness style. One biblical passage that appears so frequently as to suggest its centrality to Enmegabowh's theology is Peter's admonition in Acts 10:34, which states that "God is no respecter of persons, but in every nation he that feareth him and works . . . is accepted with him."[48]

While we do not have an extensive written record of their theological views, we do know that for the deacons, as for other Anishinaabe spiritual leaders, there was little thought that was not also praxis, little spiritual leadership that was not also concerned with the basic material needs of food, shelter, and clothing. In keeping with an Anishinaabe principle that a community's leader should be its poorest, because most generous, person, they gave clothing and food away, seldom refusing what was asked of them. Enmegabowh's correspondence witnesses to the perennial need that arose from his generosity to the community. In the winter of 1873–74, when forty of the Pembina Band fled the buffalo-starved plains for White Earth, Enmegabowh wrote that he "had given all the clothing away that I could pick round my own house. I have given three pair of my old pants, three shirts of mine own two coats and my wife three of her own dresses and here are fourteen men sitting around me asking for food and clothing and here I have all my Christian Indians to come in with their old clothes."[49] Enmegabowh's generosity, consistent as it was with customary expectations of Anishinaabe leadership, was greeted by Gilfillan as imprudence.

The network of native deacons gave rise to a new structure of leadership that was important in at least two respects. Because the deacons and their families were dispersed throughout White Earth, Leech Lake, and Red Lake reservations, they did much to link Anami'aajig congregations together, garnering an interreservation consciousness that could prove significant for dealing strategically with the changing landscape of U.S. relations and the factional tensions exacerbated in the posttreaty era of assimilation policy. In the 1870s, White Earth Anami'aajig joined the non-Christian Anishinaabeg leaders at Leech Lake in their opposition to a contract for the extraction of reservation timber arranged by the agent without the consent of the Leech Lake. Through Whipple and his influence, the Anami'aajig won a review of the contract by an independent oversight board of Indian policy reformers.[50] Moreover, if Ojibwe leadership relied on an ability to command and persuade an audience, this group of clergy, conversant in the ways of dominant and Ojibwe culture alike, complemented the traditional *ogimaag* and elders with a savvy insight into the ways of the powerbrokers of dominant culture. Indeed, as Rebecca Kugel suggests, their relationship as children, nephews, or close cousins of the aging *ogimaag* may have clothed them in the "quasi-hereditary" authority of the *ogimaag*.[51] In 1889 Charles Wright wrote a letter to the editor criticizing Gus Beaulieu's newspaper for its false optimism about White Earth's success. Alongside the prosperity of crop-intensive agriculture evidently enjoyed by the Métis, a crop failure had strapped the undercapitalized cooperative farming ventures of the conservative Anishinaabeg, $140,000 in annuity payments were overdue, and compensation for the damage to the wild rice crop caused by Army Corps of Engineers' dams was still unpaid. The deacon wrote: "The Government . . . is made to understand that the Indian has plenty while the truth is he has nothing. Those who have charge of our affairs, I take, are not suffering. When their repast is over they can recline in easy chairs and smoke cigars. I know that many die from these delays in paying the annuities; children die of starvation and disease."[52] Facing starvation, Wright's father, Waubuno-quod, had told his people to kill their cattle and oxen for food. Some months later, the same paper reported an outbreak of fatal disease at Wild Rice River, which took one of Charles Wright's own children.

Native clergy proved to be effective political organizers. When additional allotments were scheduled to be assigned during the season when the conservative Anishinaabeg were known to be out in the bush at their ricing camps, Charles Wright presented a petition to the authorities testifying that "three hundred people with no rights at White Earth had received allotments; valuable pine allotments were concentrated within certain families; and more Métis had secured pine lands, while conservative Anishinaabeg found themselves in possession of cut-over lands." Wright's call for an investigation was dismissed by the Indian Commissioner as ignorant of the "rule of the world and of nature," though he later did succeed in getting a federal investigation.[53]

An orientation to communal subsistence distinguished this savvy of the native deacons from that of White Earth's other principal cultural intermediaries. Recall that in the late fur trade and treaty-making periods, it had been the Métis trader families who served as intermediaries. At White Earth, the leadership of the native deacons became important for its ability to replace the bicultural function of the Métis families without compromising long-standing Anishinaabe values of subsistence and an ethic that prioritized the needs of the collective over the gains of particular families.

The native deacons' orientation also stood in marked contrast to many of the assimilative aims of their nonnative missionary superiors. Simmering tensions between the mission and the native-led Anami'aajig came to a boil in 1882, when the deacons launched a strike. When Ojibwe from different reservation communities assembled at White Earth village to receive their annuities, Enmegabowh convened the native clergy in closed session, and Charles Wright enlisted the support of his father, Waubunoquod. The deacons agreed to refuse to hold services and in some cases even left their posts, seeking a living wage, promotion to the priesthood, and an end to the double standard by which the church meted out its discipline to native and nonnative missionaries. While native deacons John Coleman and George Johnson, Enmegabowh's son, were closely scrutinized and reprimanded by Gilfillan and Whipple for fathering children deemed illegitimate, repeated complaints by Anami'aajig women at Leech Lake about a white priest's sexual misconduct fell on deaf ears.[54] The principal aim of the strike, though, was the ouster of Gilfillan, whose paternalism had become a menacing obstacle to the Anami'aajig's self-determination. Gilfillan held Episcopal purse strings tightly against those Anami'aajig whose lives departed from his own image of what industry, family farms, and the Christian life ought to look like.[55] Moreover, as the bishop's eyes, ears, and arms among the Ojibwe, Gilfillan was the figure to whom the Anami'aajig went if they needed something from the bishop. In this role as broker, Gilfillan became increasingly mettlesome, frequently taking down the dictated appeals for support while undercutting them with his own glosses. Even Suzanna Roy, a respected elder who had brought the esteem accorded her to the Anami'aajig cause, was not beyond Gilfillan's reproach. The archdeacon wrote Whipple: "You are exceedingly kind to Mrs Roy in sending her the $10. . . . I almost fear she is imposing on your too great goodness of heart. . . . [The Roys] were better able to earn everything they want than almost any other family, [having] 2 yoke of cattle or three; and three good working men."[56]

Gilfillan found it difficult to imagine that his deacons were intelligent enough to act in such an organized and strategic manner. He thought Fred Smith was simply holding out for more cash and ascribed Smith's participation in the strike to the "natural want of perseverance and stick-to-it-iveness of the Indian." "When these poor heathen get their eyes opened," Gilfillan declared, "they do not see straight for some time."[57] Gilfillan also dismissed the grievances as the sour grapes of Enmegabowh's "unfounded jealousy. "It is a pity to see the aged Aaron," Gilfillan complained, "fashion the idol calves, to lead the people back to Egypt, but so it is."[58] Gilfillan recommended to Whipple that the deacons' request for increased salaries be denied, citing the example that Chinese clergy made one sixth the salary of the American missionaries and suggesting that to pay the deacons any more would foment envy in their communities. Gilfillan thought the deacons would soon "come to their senses after they have rested awhile and found out how they get along without their salary."[59] In the end, Whipple chose not to dismiss Gilfillan, but the deacons did succeed in tripling wages and in gaining respect as a force to be reckoned with. Still dissatisfied with Gilfillan's supervision, Enmegabowh and the native deacons issued a call three years later "to throw overboard all white people connected with the mission."[60]

While the decidedly non-Christian Anishinaabeg criticized the native deacons for accommodating to the mission life, closer analysis shows these figures, and the community they served, to have been far more complex. As Rebecca Kugel argues, the Anami'aajig were not the childlike converts that Gilfillan and other missionaries took them to be; they had taken the initiative to build a new life in a strategic alliance with the Episcopalian mission and had put Christianity into practice on Anami'aajig terms. Never able to establish an Anami'aajig community completely outside the parameters of the reservation system, the strike shows the adaptive social structures and indigenous leadership through which the Anami'aajig made room for themselves within the reservation. Though the organizing meetings of the strike remained entirely off the record, rooted firmly in the anonymity and safety of the oral tradition, it would have been very unusual indeed were the sounds of sung hymns not heard in them.

Hymn Singing and Reservation Time and Space

"Guns and pistols and the United States Army can never do it," Gilfillan exclaimed in an essay entitled, "On the Wrong Way and the Right Way to Civilize the Indians"; "there is no power on earth can do it, but the native Indian missionary, and his hymn book, and his Indian New Testament, and his words in the Indian tongue, sitting by the wigwam fire."[61] As extensions of White Earth's assimilative time and space into the everyday life of music making, hymns were no neutral matter. Neither was the practice of hymn singing, through which native people made the hymns their own. We turn now to survey the contours of mission time and space in this musical repertory and to identify ways in which the Anami'aajig arranged their own musical terrain within the genre of the hymn. The discussion of music appears to parallel the previous discussion of the Anami'aajig community as an articulation of social space. But the relationship between the two discussions, I will argue, is more than just a parallel one. Symbolic processes like music making provided the turf on which the social spaces were negotiated within the structures of mission time and reservation space. More than just a matter of strategic alliance building and political action, the distinctive way that the Anami'aajig engaged the Christian tradition in practice endowed it with meaning and integrity on Anishinaabe terms. Through the ritualization of hymn singing in performance, the Anami'aajig made room for the integrity of their fundamental values and way of life, and they intoned the fit between those values and the Christian message.

A staple offering of public worship, Ojibwe hymnody was a music that seemed to belong to Sunday morning and the buildings of the White Earth mission. "Sunday is the great day of all," Gilfillan proclaimed, when one can hear "their inspiring singing of hymns in their own musical tongue—singing, of which the writer heard a London-trained Cathedral choir boy say, that nowhere . . . had he heard such good singing."[62] As a cast iron bell rang out from St. Columba's at the appointed hour, the regular rhythm of Sabbath worship worked its way into the homes of Ojibwes living within several miles of White Earth village. Missionaries stressed Sabbath observance as an important break in the seasonal cycles of *bimaadiziwin*. It was in the public worship of the Sabbath that singing was most subject to the disciplining time and space of the mission.

Whipple described each detail of an 1872 service at which he dedicated the White Earth mission building. At 10:30, the bishop and clergy processed to Psalm 24 in English and Ojibwe, then the report for the consecration was read in both English and Ojibwe. Subsequently, a service was read in Ojibwe, including Enmegabowh's narrative of the days of "heathen darkness," and the singing of "Jesus, Saviour of My Soul" and "Nearer, My God, to Thee." "All sang," Whipple remembered, "and such singing! You will never hear the like in New York; and though it was in Ojibway I think it sounded very sweetly to our blessed Lord, seeing among these children of the forest the travail of His soul." The service concluded with a feast for the three hundred assembled, and a worship service before sundown drew another forty people for more hymns, collects, general confession, the Lord's Prayer, scripture reading, and recitation of the Nicene Creed.[63]

On the occasion of another visit to the mission church at White Earth, Whipple described the Ojibwe language service that took place on a less extraordinary occasion. "The full church service is not used, since very few can read Ojibwa," he wrote, "but nearly all joined audibly and devoutly on their knees, in the liturgical responses and afterwards in the hymns, which were sung with thrilling fervor."[64]

Many such accounts bespeak how eagerly missionaries welcomed moments of shared fellowship and true worship with native people. Such accounts also bespeak how pointedly native behavior in worship was on display. Missionaries were watching and listening intently for cues of inward transformation. In this context, sung hymns struck missionary ears as nothing less than the *sound of civilization*. "I am always deeply touched with their singing," Whipple wrote: "The *wild* Indian voice is harsh. Nothing could be more discordant than their wild yell and hideous war song. The religion of Christ softened this; their voices became plaintive, and as they sing from the heart their hymns are full of emotion."[65] Funeral practices in particular were framed for the display of native "progress." One missionary waxed enthusiastic about an Ojibwe wake he witnessed in 1860: "Instead of the drum and rattle, hear the sweet music of Indian voices joining in the sacred hymns of the Church. And instead of the wild wail of Indian lamentation, hear the solemn Ojibwa service."[66]

By 1875, Gilfillan could cite the fervor of Ojibwe singing as evidence that "the religious life planted among these Chippeway has taken root in the native soil: it is deep, sincere, [and] it has a profound hold upon their hearts."[67] Missionaries welcomed an indigenous strain of the Christian life, but an acute sense of the fragility of their gains made them nonetheless ardent in their desire to prune off its excesses and discipline its growth.

At the Episcopal mission, the disciplining of hymn singing went hand in hand with the cultivation of other traits deemed fitting to the Christian life. When Pauline Colby was stationed at White Earth's mission hospital in the 1880s, she assisted a Mrs. Wiswell, whose celebrated musical abilities enabled her to accompany Sabbath morning hymnody on the organ. During the week, Wiswell could be found "drilling" the youth choir she began. White robes donated by an Eastern congregation further patterned the youths into a disciplined unit under Wiswell's direction. "Mrs. Wiswell plays the organ and the Indians sing, and sing well," Pauline Colby recalled. "Their voices are melodious and they have an excellent ear, though they have but little training. . . . The weekly choir practice which Mrs. Wiswell conducts at the hospital is very popular with the younger people, and produces surprisingly good results."[68] In 1884, Gilfillan proudly reported that a minister from Moorhead had agreed to trek several hours to White Earth expressly to "teach the indians singing." The minister's fresh offering of new hymn tunes brought joy to old Enmegabowh, a "lover of music" himself who had grown "tired of the old tunes."[69] Clearly, missionaries relished musical accompaniment, harmony, and musical discipline for aesthetic reasons, but music discipline was part of a larger program of social discipline.[70] The organ introduced a more metrical clock time to orchestrate the voices of a choir that now was uniformly vested in white choir robes.

Because public worship put power relations on display in heightened moments, the practice of hymn singing became a likely stage for the performance of resistance as well as accommodation. Ojibwe performances gave subtle expression to a critical view of White Earth's power relations from the bottom up. Indeed, it was through such subtle practices that Ojibwe people must have gained critical purchase on the

St. Columba's Choir, White Earth, 1910. This choir's robes show the discipline of singing in Sunday morning worship at the mission church, but singing at prayer meetings and funeral wakes always involved the unison singing of elders in the Ojibwe language. (Courtesy Minnesota Historical Society)

circumstances of their subordination to affirm the dignity of their voices and the values pertaining to *bimaadiziwin*.

In marked contrast to the missionaries, neither Enmegabowh, nor Charles Wright Nashotah, nor any other native clergyman mentioned the details of worship behavior in their letters. This suggests a distinctive Anami'aajig reading of singing in public worship, or perhaps a reluctance to *read* the practice of singing altogether. Ojibwe singing at the mission was clearly more than only disingenuously Christian, but the meanings such music making held for missionaries and Anishinaabeg were worlds apart. Such wide divergences of meaning could meet in the convergence of practice on such shared occasions to negotiate the terms of a mutually acceptable world.

Making Room: The Ritualization of Hymn Singing

The soul which missionaries said they heard in Ojibwe hymn singing was no function of choir drills. What captured the imagination of missionaries was a resonance the sung hymns carried from other moments in the life of the Anami'aajig community. Because those occasions happened at the periphery of mission influence, detailed descriptions of the performances and their precise meanings for the Anami'aajig do not make their way into the written record. Nonetheless, Catherine Bell's notion of *ritualization* offers a well-trained lens to make the most of the archival material, spotting the ways in which the "where, who, and how" of hymn singing were transformed by those for whom the "what" was nonnegotiable. Bell focuses on the process by which groups differentiate or set apart certain ordinary activities in order to transform experience. Ojibwe hymn singing can be understood as a practice that the Anami'aajig differentiated from the conventional hymn singing promoted and experienced as part of the civilizing agenda of the mission and agency. Outside the time and space of mission discipline, hymns were no casual matter. Hymns became distinctly associated with particular groups of Ojibwe people who formed to sing them. In this regard, the music was incorporated into the social structures of traditional Ojibwe music making, where sacred music and the social relations that produced it were of a piece. These groups sang hymns on particular occasions, unaccompanied, and typically at night. Their performance came to be associated with a distinctive aesthetic, one that struck most missionaries who heard them as unusually rich in solemnity and spirit. We turn first to the often subtle details of ritualization, which no less transformed the genre of hymnody by making room for *bimaadiziwin*. We then return to the theoretical work of Bell and Bourdieu to make fuller sense of the details.

Singing Sodalities at White Earth

At White Earth, hymns were incorporated into a long-established idiom of Ojibwe musical performance that made strong connections between sacred music and the social matrix of its performance. The more formalized practice of hymn singing at

White Earth appears to have grown around two key elders, a woman named Suzanna Roy and a man named Shay-day-ence. As a respected Midewiwin leader, Shay-day-ence had been a keeper of medicinal knowledge, tribal history, and hundreds of songs that brought the powerful forces of life to bear on the affairs of the people. At Gull Lake, Shay-day-ence reportedly led the opposition to the mission, earning him the missionaries' derision as the erstwhile "prime minister" of Satan. Once removed to White Earth, he reportedly spent a number of years captive to drink, and later followed his son into the Anami'aajig community. In the eleven years before his death, Shay-day-ence distinguished himself as a full-time Christian holy man, called by Whipple "the real, recognized leader of the Christian community as he had before been of the heathen."[71] He was so "thoroughly saturated" with the Christian life, Gilfillan remarked, that his "whole talk and whole thought is about religion."[72]

Shay-day-ence led a group of thirty young men from "house to house," "singing Chippewa hymns, and praying and exhorting each other" in the Christian life.[73] Since they gathered to sing three or more nights each week, this Young Men's Singing and Praying Band, as missionaries called it, or just the "band" or "young men," as they were known by Ojibwe people, became a kind of sodality, extending beyond kin and traditional band lines and charged with the task of singing and praying on behalf of the people. In this respect, they very much resembled drum societies. These bands were improvisations on the old forms of religious societies, sodalities with a profound sense of purpose. They took their songs on the road to the sickbeds, deathbeds, and gravesites of surrounding communities, often singing until dawn.[74] Their sense of spiritual commitment made a deep impression on missionaries. "Sometimes I feel sick unable to make these visits," Shay-day-ence told Whipple, "but I persevere, and lo! my sickness is gone . . . so that I can carry on the meetings, take charge of them, and designate the speaker."[75]

At about the same time, a group of women gathered around the spiritual direction of Suzanna Wright Roy. Roy, whose Ojibwe name was Equay-me-do-gay, was one of the first native women baptized Episcopalian at Gull Lake. She also was clearly part of the community's leadership, being the daughter of Waubojiig, a respected leader at Gull Lake; the sister of Waubunoquod; and an aunt of deacon Charles Wright. The group of women gathered around her met weekly to "do crafts, encourage one another in good works, to watch over the young and . . . to make their homes like Christian homes."[76] Again, hymnody took its place beside other social norms and practices that the mission promoted as part of the civilized Christian life. The traditional roles of Anishinaabe women were targeted as antithetical to Christian culture, and the women's societies were clearly promoted to do the work of gendered cultural assimilation. Native women were implored to sew and cook rather than fish, rice, and gather wood. On the other hand, the societies provided women with a spiritually energizing and socially legitimate way to meet and continue to serve in more public roles as economic producers and community leaders.

By 1875, a number of these "industrial and devotional societies," as missionaries referred to the women's groups, had sprouted at White Earth and elsewhere.[77] Eventually, a number of such bands formed to meet, eat, pray, speak, sing, and make things for the community, each under the direction of a designated elder. One Anami'aajig woman, Kakabishikwe, remarked that a number of "appointed leaders of Bands have chosen one among ourselves whom we would wish to take general leadership of us, namely Susan Roy."[78] The material fruit of their collective work was as important for survival as its spiritual fruit. In the winter of 1876, Suzanna Roy's society provided White Earth with more than one hundred comforters.[79] "Our women look forward to these gatherings," observed a missionary to the neighboring Leech Lake Reservation, "as the chief social event of the week. . . . Frequently some women will rise and make an address and this always has the respectful attention of the other women." Weekly meetings concluded with a short service of worship, during which they discussed "all affairs of interest to them." Later, "the generous portions" left over after their feast were "heaped into baskets . . . to be carried around to the sick and the disabled."[80] These women's societies provided the infrastructure for Sybil Carter's lace-making project in the 1890s, which generated important cash income for native families at White Earth and Leech Lake, and began a

Ekwembis and Kakabishique, with handiwork from Sybil Carter's lace-making project, White Earth, ca. 1890s. The portrait studio pose crops out the more distinctly Anami'aajig flavor of women's leadership in the hymn-singing societies, of which Kakabishique was an active member. (Courtesy Becker County Historical Society)

pattern whereby Ojibwe women often assumed the lead role in securing a family's cash-based income.

Both the men's and women's singing societies, like the larger circle of Anami'aajig drawn around them, exhibited a broad tolerance for ways in which an Anami'aajig identity could be defined. To the extent that naming practices are telling about the way that people imagine their identity, Anami'aajig who formed these singing sodalities may have formed strong communities, but they did so without imposing a uniform baptismal identity on those affiliating with them.[81] Gilfillan's own letters admit the wide variety of names—some baptismal, some not—that carried into common parlance, even among the leaders of the women's society of whom he boasted. An 1875 list included the names "Cornelia Boardman, Mrs. Alex [Suzanna] Roy, Mrs. Maendjiwena, Kakabishikwe, and Emma Whitefisher [*Waubojiig*]," encompassing both English, Anglicized Ojibwe, and Ojibwe baptismal names.[82] Among those, Kakabishikwe is likely a name given from an Ojibwe naming ceremony. Of course, Maendjiwena indicates a given Ojibwe name as well, but in this case it is applied by marriage to Mrs. Maendjiwena, a practice uncharacteristic of Ojibwe naming traditions. Multiple identities could be carried at once, indicated by baptismal names in certain contexts, like the Reverend John Johnson, and by Ojibwe names in other contexts, like Enmegabowh, by which Johnson was more routinely addressed in Ojibwe parlance.

The varieties of naming indicate in a dramatic way that the Anami'aajig were not fully the Christian Indians of missionary desire. In the midst of profound dislocations to and on the reservations, and despite targeted assaults by U.S. Indian policy on traditional kin structures, the Anami'aajig established new versions of old social patterns emphasizing reciprocity, subsistence, and survival. The Anami'aajig and their elders charged the Young Men's Singing and Praying Bands and the Women's Industrial Societies with duties of providing mutual aid, visiting the sick, and mourning. Like baptismal names, the music promoted by missionaries on the reservation took root in ways that indicate the improvisational agency of these respective groups in their effort to make room for a life of integrity on Anishinaabe terms.

Ritualized Performance in Devotional Meetings

As was true for the young men, hymns set the tone for each of these activities. But the performances of these native sodalities stand in sharp relief to the disciplined singing that took place in morning worship and choir rehearsal. By the mid-1880s, singing in devotional meetings struck missionaries as having become noticeably uniform:

> In all these meetings the method of procedure is the same; meet about nightfall, begin with singing a Chippewa hymn, then prayer, then another hymn, then the leader names the one who is to speak after he or she sits down—another hymn, then another speaker is named and so on until nine or ten o'clock. The singers are appointed who shall select and start the hymns, generally young people. The speakers are nearly all middle aged or elderly men or women. There is never any excitement nor extravagance . . . but solemnity.[83]

When Shay-day-ence's singers toured other communities, their evening performances also took on a strophic character, alternating singing with a speech by an elder
or a clergyman, then another hymn, then the speech of another clergyman, and so
on until Shay-day-ence himself testified about his own conversion. The travels of
Shay-day-ence and his band gave rise to similar performances at Leech Lake. At
Onigum village, a devotional movement under lay leadership met every evening except Tuesday for "singing, prayer, and mutual encouragement in the Christian life."
Here both women and men assembled under the "spiritual charge" of two lay elders,
a man named Kegiosh (*kagayaashk*, Gull) and Susan Bongo, descendants of the run-
away African-American slave, George Bungo, who lived as an Anishinaabe and became a prominent trader. Kegiosh always spoke first to the gatherings, where congregants "confess[ed] sins to one another and [were] healed."[84] One visitor remarked,
"one present at their meetings would think that John Wesley or his followers had
been there."[85]

Material as well as spiritual, social as well as ceremonial, these devotional meetings were the principal gatherings of the native Christian community. Characterized
by three or more devotional meetings each week, this Anami'aajig manner of expressing and practicing faith was welcomed by missionaries, but it also seemed to
them unsettling. For such meetings reaffirmed communal values, subsistence agriculture, and frustrated efforts to develop Christian homes comprised of nuclear families.
Rebecca Kugel recognizes in these sodalities the primary engines of the larger
"process of social regeneration" that modeled agricultural and Christian forms to
give enduring shape to fundamental Anishinaabe commitments. Without them,
Kugel concludes, "the experiment with Christianization and agriculture would have
amounted to little."[86]

Edwin Benedict, the Episcopal missionary at Onigum on the Leech Lake Reservation who had been also a target of the 1882 deacon's strike, voiced concern that
nightly Ojibwe prayer meetings structured by Ojibwe hymn singing and led by native deacons and elders were eclipsing public "Prayerbook worship" in importance.
"Since we came here," Benedict wrote in 1881, we have "endeavored to make these
poor people understand the difference between the value of Public Divine worship
to almighty God and prayer meetings of a few persons. We have therefore allowed
them . . . but too many meetings of this kind in a week would to my estimation
prove rather an injury than good to them."[87]

Sickness and Death at White Earth

If hymn singing was consistently present in the regular devotional gatherings of the
Anami'aajig, it also structured the unusually charged moments in the life of the
community, as it already had begun to in the earlier period. Hymn singing now consistently set the tone for gatherings around the sick, the dying, and the recently
dead, and this became a significant work of the Young Men's Singing and Praying
Bands in their travels near and far. In May 1885, Shay-day-ence reported to the
bishop that, despite his own aging and illness, he and his band had visited and sung
more than one-hundred times since the bishop's visit the previous summer: "My

friend, I work at that which you exhorted us to do: never passing over a sick person, walking in the light. My friend, my work is over a hundred since I saw you, seeing the sick, visiting the afflicted. I think to myself, 'his spiritual work will not kill you which you carry about,' that is what I think about going around sick."[88]

In 1882, Suzanna Roy wrote of the healing significance of singing: "My son is sick. He is a son of grace. He goes with the young men. His sickness is a sore one, his flesh and skin being broken. Especially in his armpit even till that his heart seems exposed. I never have told you about how we are; that is about the health of our family. Now for the first time I tell you. I feel down spirited seeing him sick. I have invited the Christians to come tonight and sing and to pray for him."[89]

The generosity of singers extended far and wide. When a White Earth singer journeying home from Leech Lake learned that a white settler was gravely ill, he went out of his way and "sang three hymns over him loud and clear, and exhorted him to faith and patience . . . and although the sick man did not understand a word of what was said, yet its spirit made itself manifest to him."[90]

In these uncertain times, diseases often issued in death, but there was nothing "ordinary" about the many deaths that visited White Earth. While death is really never an ordinary experience in human life, the astounding numbers of premature deaths, and the violence that often caused them, posed troubling questions at White Earth about the possibility of community survival. Contrary to conventional wisdom, it was the poverty, landlessness, and violence of the late nineteenth century, not the initial microbe exchanges with Europeans of the sixteenth and seventeenth, that brought Native American population to its nadir.[91]

Sadly, White Earth proved no exception to the trend. Smallpox outbreaks in 1883 and 1901 conspired with the more consistent predation of tuberculosis and trachoma to raise White Earth's death rate in the decades surrounding the turn of the century. The unrelenting succession of untimely deaths stood in stark relief from the place of death in an Ojibwe understanding of *bimaadiziwin*. By definition, the Circle of Life had always included a natural place for the culmination of a long life lived in harmony with and contributing to the aesthetic, moral, and spiritual health of all that is. The near impossibility of this good life appears to have brought a spiritual pain so deep that ordinary words could do it no justice. A profound sadness occupies much of the correspondence from literate White Earth Anishinaabeg in this period. Enmegabowh wrote about the difficult winter of 1881: "Three more are not expected to live more than a day—yesterday one have died—to day three more have died—so you see Bishop we are fast hastening to be extinct from the face of the Earth. I feel most truly sad. I feel very lonesome."[92] Enmegabowh wrote in broken English, but he pointed to a poignant Ojibwe expression, *gashkendam*, which combines in one semantic field associations with lonesomeness, grief, affliction, dejection, homesickness, and melancholy.[93] I want to call attention to this term *gashkendam* as a historically situated emotion that points to the politics of death on reservations such as White Earth.[94] What contributed to the emotional investment in funerary hymn singing, beyond the bereavement at the loss of a loved one, was an unspeakable grief concerning the direction that history appeared to be taking the entire community and its way of life.

These circumstances led to a different order of consideration of the Christian teaching on death and resurrection, particularly as it was expressed in the missionaries' songs. The center of gravity of Ojibwe spirituality had always fallen squarely on earthly existence. But the hardships of the reservation era seemed to shift that spiritual center of gravity in the direction of the afterlife. Perhaps this in itself served to make possible fuller living in the death-ridden world they experienced. One White Earth leader related to Enmegabowh how profound sorrow had led him to consider afresh the Christian message: "Today we have been driven from our homes and from the graves of our dear little ones—today we are nearly homeless, dying like the drops of rains. While the pale faces are increasingly strong and happy . . . We are dying off very fast—it is because we have followed the wrong path and today my friend—I see plainly, too, that our people here who have embraced the new religion of the Great Spirit are happy, very happy and for this reason my friend."[95] Enmegabowh's parish records for the Saint Columba mission, though not systematically kept, suggest that Christian funerals and burials were in greater demand in cases of an infant's death, a tragedy that seemed increasingly common as the century proceeded.[96] Protestant missionaries often were taken aback when Anishinaabeg who were otherwise indifferent to their gospel invited them to participate in burial rites, notably to sing hymns. Pauline Colby, an Episcopalian missionary at Leech Lake, remarked on how "the sad, sordid and grisly predominates" in her journal. "To be sure," Colby wrote, "that side of life does come more directly under my observation. Truly, my friends here can make merry more easily without me than they can mourn without me."[97]

The predicament of *gashkendamowin* brought new forms of bereavement, but Christian Ojibwe funerary practices often proceeded according to a syncretic logic. Colby remembered that though Christian burials were in a consecrated church ground, Christian and Midewiwin graves alike were covered with wooden Ojibwe spirit houses. Rising two feet above the grave, these structures had a small hole in one end "for the escape of the spirit" and a small shelf "to hold the offerings that are brought for the refreshment of the departed." "The first fruits of the year are brought here," Colby wrote, "also tobacco . . . and the spirits are supposed to assimilate the essence of these offerings."[98] She noted that both Christians and "pagans" were careful to keep fires going through the first nights after death to warm the departed "so that the soul may suffer no hardship from cold and darkness on its three day's journey to its final resting place."[99]

Funerary Practice and the Civilizing Agenda

The clergy sought to harness the spiritual energy of Ojibwe mourning, negotiating their share of influence by conceding some measure of autonomy to the wake. Early-nineteenth-century missionaries earnestly pointed out how hymns had begun to replace Ojibwe women's custom of wailing, which the missionaries likened to the howling of dogs. In 1837 Edmund Ely called the tradition of wailing a matter of "excessive grief, improper and injurious, . . . not consistent with Christian Submission."[100] Frederick Ayer drew cosmic significance from the movement away from wailing and other burial customs toward Christian practices: "No discordant sounds

Cemetery, White Earth ca. 1910. While some of these graves are marked with crosses and even shingled, they are not located in a church yard and are sheltered with traditional Anishinaabe grave houses, with holes allowing the spirit to pass and small shelves for offerings of food and tobacco. (Courtesy Becker County Historical Society)

are heard from the noisy drums and rattles and harsh voices of the musicians employed at such seasons. No wailing rends the air. No blood flows from lacerated arms and legs. Here was witnessed a triumph of truth over error, Christianity over Paganism."[101] But other missionary accounts indicate an uneasy concern about the syncretism of their Ojibwe hosts' mourning practices. Oberlin College missionaries at Leech Lake in the 1840s found themselves complying with a bereaved father's wish to commit his child's body "not to the earth whence it was taken" but to a scaffold, "praying meanwhile, that the custom more in accordance with Christian . . . doctrines may speedily prevail."[102] After a number of these incidents, David Spencer reported that the Oberlinians had resolved "to create as wide a distinction as possible between Christian and Pagan burial."[103]

For missionaries, setting boundaries in funerary ritual was important to the larger task of staking the Christian claim to the centrality of the afterlife. Gilfillan described Ojibwe religion as a principally this-worldly matter of "calling all the gods or spirits to their aid to remove sickness or ward it off and to prolong life. Their religion has no reference to the future world, nor does it promise them anything there. What they believe is that all the Indians when they die go to a happy beautiful county, whether they have lived well or ill here; that there they hunt, feast, and dance to their heart's content; where they have a larger Indian village, see all their friends, and are attended by the souls of those whom they have killed in battle."[104] Gilfillan acknowledged that Ojibwe teachings included an ultimate accounting for one's moral life. On the third day of its four-day, three-night journey to the "village of souls," the soul must pass safely across a treacherous water. Gilfillan wrote that, if the soul "had lived well it makes the passages safely and then is soon admitted to the happy hunting grounds, but if it ill it falls into the swirling rapids below and is forever lost. This however is theoretical, and . . . does not influence their practice itself." "On this account," Gilfillan continued, Ojibwe people "look on the Christian religion as inferior, in that it promises them things only in the future world after they are dead, whereas their religion prolongs life in this world and cures disease."[105]

Thus missionaries tried to make hay of untimely deaths by turning deathbed scenes into teachable moments. Indeed, many missionaries protested the social causes of death and criticized the government's failure to deliver on treaty agreements or assumed wardship responsibilities. But they seldom hesitated to take the opportunity at any death to admonish native people of impending judgment. With more than one hundred on his sick list, Granville T. Sproat found that "much may be done . . . connected with visiting the sick. The ear is then almost always open to instruction, the sympathies are enlisted, and those will listen to the word of life who would not regard it in other circumstances."[106] A Red Lake Ojibwe man put it well: "When we come [to the mission], we are often told that we are within a step of the grave. This is not pleasant to us."[107]

Missionaries were not alone in being interested in the exceeding number of native deaths. Pauline Colby complained in 1892 about "an agent for tombstones and monuments" who came to Onigum village at annuity time and "inveigled" an elderly church member "into laying out all her money for a tombstone for a daughter long dead and half forgotten." Owenebequa became "the happy possessor of a tombstone," Colby recalled, though "she was not at all sure on which of the half obliterated graves the stone should be placed."[108]

The Ritualization of Funerary Singing

Wakes and funerals, then, were sedimented with a politics of history. But hymn singing at wakes did more than dramatize civilization. As was the case in the devotional meetings, funerary hymn singing was set apart from the civilizing agenda under which missionaries promoted the hymns. Singing was set apart to make room for the fuller expression of *gashkendamowin*, unspeakable grief. While they often conducted the funerals, missionaries and other nonnatives were seldom privy to the goings-on of the wake. What few written accounts of nineteenth-century wakes we do have warrant close reading. In 1873, for example, J. A. Gilfillan wrote of his first encounter of singing at a White Earth wake: "It was after dark. . . . The body was laid out in the whitest of linen, and they were engaged in singing their familiar Chippewa hymns of hope and faith and love in the house of death. In the intervals between hymns, silence reigned. "As the hymns arose," Gilfillan continued, "ever and anon they seemed songs of triumph over death. . . . I never saw anything more becoming in the house of mourning."[109]

Most observers who committed their experiences of Ojibwe singing to writing seldom wrote in sufficient detail about musical performance. A visitor to an Ojibwe reserve in Ontario proved to be a welcome exception. Although Frederick Burton conducted his research on native music far to the east of White Earth at the Garden River reserve near Sault Ste. Marie, Ontario, his account of a wake there at the turn of the century merits quotation at considerable length for its wealth of detail and ritual texture. The continuity with the practices of today's Ojibwe wakes suggested here is uncanny.

> At sunset came Megissun, "the singer" as he is called, a staunch Episcopalian. . . . He brought with him his . . . collection of hymns translated into Ojibway . . . and sat beside the dead. . . . No word of greeting had passed, no comment of any kind was uttered, no moan of grief escaped the lips. Upon the table at Megissun's elbow was a lamp, and beside it a saucer of lozenges and a plate of plain cakes. Shortly after Megissun's entrance three neighbors, a man and two women, drifted in, more silently, more unobtrusively than if they had been autumn leaves impelled by an idle wind. By not so much as a nod, or a glance from the eyes, did they recognize the presence of the singer or the bereaved sisters. Megissun stirred not, neither did the mourners. Presently another silent figure blotted out the doorway for an instant and joined the expectant group, and then still others, till the narrow room was full.
>
> Megissun did not wait for the room to fill. In his own good time he opened the hymnal and began to sing. Through nearly the whole of the first line his wavering voice bore the tune alone; then one and another joined in unison and sang the hymn through all its slowly toiling stanzas to the end. A pause ensued while Megissun turned the pages of the book. Presently he selected another hymn and began. As before, the assembled neighbors joined as soon as they recognized the tune. Now and again a single voice stumbled over the words of an ill remembered line, but nobody was disturbed or abashed thereby, least of all the person who committed the error. . . . Between hymns the clatter of crickets beat noisily upon the ear. . . .
>
> Some time between ten and eleven o'clock, two of the guests arose and, without word or glance of parting, drifted out into the darkness and came not again that night. By midnight others had gone, but the place of a few were filled by late comers. At rare intervals as the night wore on with its succession of hymns, Megissun relieved his throat with a lozenge, and such guests as were so minded sought the table for a piece of cake. When the sun rose, the room was no longer crowded, but a loyal handful of neighbors yet remained singing a final hymn for the comfort of their friend upon her journey through the darkness. With the full light of day Megissun closed his book and went home, and the others, with no word to him or the sisters, departed also.[110]

The Garden River Ojibwe had meaningfully absorbed Anglican worship into their lifeways as early as the late 1830s, and they had framed their performance of Protestant hymns within Anishinaabe protocols of mourning. The work of mourning befell certain people outside the immediate family, who came to sing through the night. They also ritualized the music itself, sequencing music with significant durations of silence. Burton was intrigued with the "unwitting perversion" of the tunes by Megissun and the older singers and was hard-pressed to know whether "the tunes were aboriginal, or the product of civilization." "I might have persuaded myself," Burton remembered, "that [Megissun] was singing the Christian words to an ancient Ojibway tune, so completely did he cover and disguise it with the mannerisms I had become familiar with as characteristic of ancient Ojibway song." Burton had difficulty transcribing what he heard in musical notation. He described the singing of "A Charge to Keep I Have" in Ojibwe as "so slow that it seems to be drawled rather than sung; time values are disregarded, and the voice slurs up and down from one tone to another in the most extraordinary fashion."[111]

Burton could even discern evidence of generational changes in the singing tradition. "The older people kept with the leader easily," he wrote, "for he harked them back to childhood when, perhaps, to everyone the Christian faith and its music were unknown; but the others, who had learned their hymns from the lips of a white missionary while they were young enough to receive and retain strange impressions, found the old leader's manner disconcerting."[112]

Christian wakes and funerals could involve neither dancing nor drumming. The tunes of the music were of European-American origin, and the texts of those songs pointed Ojibwe people toward a way of life promoted by missionaries with a civilizing agenda. Nonetheless, these techniques of performance and the social atmosphere of the wakes they created made room for an indigenous way of mourning and helped generate the collective resolve to persevere in the face of threatened extinction. Indeed, it was the often subtle modulations of the songs that equipped them to give voice to *gashkendam*, unspeakable grief. Burton's consultant William J. Shingwauk told him that Garden River Ojibwe "could not express their emotions freely through the white man's melody, and consequently either abandoned it altogether and adapted tunes of their own to the words of the new faith, or deliberately modified the missionary's tunes so that there resulted what Shingwauk characterized with humorous gravity as half breed music."[113]

Ritual Resources and the Negotiation of Colonialism

The "humorous gravity" with which Shingwauk delivered his remarks indicates that native people did not take their ritualized singing too seriously. But neither does it indicate that they took the songs or the manner of their performance lightly. Because such a large share of the colonial politics of domination and resistance was played out in the symbolic realm, modulations of the evangelical hymn were more than mere nuances of style. In the highly charged cultural politics of places like Garden River or White Earth, changes in performance of hymns, no matter how subtle, bespoke how the resources of ritual enriched a politically and economically impoverished people by making room within the experience of domination for something more. The Anami'aajig found music making to be a valuable resource in setting themselves apart from other spiritual alternatives. The rest of this chapter is concerned with how the Anami'aajig negotiated a middle way between the civilizing aims of the mission and alternative native religious movements.

Pierre Bourdieu has recast the study of symbolization in the context of social processes. For Bourdieu, symbolic expressions are "not only signs to be understood and deciphered; they are also signs of wealth, intended to be evaluated and appreciated, and signs of authority intended to be believed and obeyed."[114] To better understand these social politics, Bourdieu makes an analogy to the market, in which the use of symbols to convey ideas is joined by the deployment of "symbolic capital" to maximize power.

At White Earth, hymnody was the musical equivalent of what Bourdieu calls a legitimate language, one that is rendered legitimate through the exercise of a dominant culture's symbolic power. This symbolic power, which for Bourdieu is so crucial to the workings of political and economic domination, is the power of "constituting the given through utterances, of making people see and believe, of confirming or transforming the vision of the world, and thereby, action on the world and thus the world itself, an almost magical power that enables one to obtain the equivalent of what is obtained through force (whether physical or economic)."[115] What works most effectively in this regard are symbols that naturalize the arbitrary make-up of social distinctions—in this case the distinction between savage and civilization—by rooting them in the really real. To complement the insights of speech act theorists, who would locate a symbol's power primarily in its "illocutionary force," Bourdieu locates symbolic power "in and through the very structure of the [social] field in which *belief* is produced and reproduced."[116] The power of language, for Bourdieu, is the power of people that is "delegated" through language.

Bourdieu argues that practices are best equipped to shoulder the violence of symbolic power, since practices can be "transmitted without passing through language and consciousness, but through suggestions inscribed in the most apparently insignificant aspects of things, situations and practices of everyday life. Thus, . . . the ways of looking, sitting, standing, keeping silent, or even of speaking . . . are full of injunctions that are powerful and hard to resist precisely because they are silent and insidious, insistent and insinuating."[117] Hymnody here joins the other ritual gestures promoted by missionaries to distinguish "pagan" from Christian. Knelt prayer, short hair, regular bathing, and square houses were part of the same equation that assigned value to hymn singing.

Bourdieu's market analogy helps reveal much about the social function of hymn singing at White Earth. When hymns were first translated in the 1820s and 1830s, the fur trade and the viability of a seasonal subsistence guaranteed native people a measure of autonomy in their relations with missionaries. Under such terms of symbolic exchange, the appeal of Ojibwe hymn singing was casual and intermittent. In the reservation period, these terms of symbolic exchange shifted decisively. Since survival relied more urgently on the support and advocacy of missionaries, hymn singing became more valuable as symbolic capital, for it was construed as the sound of civilization. By singing hymns, the Anami'aajig bought into a devaluation of tradition associated with the civilizing agenda of the hymns' translation and promotion. Consider again the following hymn text:

> Awake my soul, and with the sun
> The daily stage of duty run,
> Shake off dull sloth, and joyful rise
> To pay thy morning sacrifice.

To perform a hymn text such as this was to impress the Mrs. Wiswells of the world on the "daily stage of duty," but to the extent that Ojibwe translations could follow the didactic meanings of the original, it was also to inscribe in one's self a view of industry and self-worth tied to Anglo-American sensibilities. Indeed, for missionaries, this was the genius of the hymn as a "civilizing" tool.

Men and women of the singing groups were committed to adapting Anishinaabe ways to new circumstances at White Earth. They brought to other native communities their message of contained social change—enough to respond to new circumstances but without compromising basic Anishinaabe values. They incorporated agriculture into small-scale, cooperative ventures to complement other subsistence activities. They also incorporated new ceremonial and cultural forms. Whipple observed that Shay-day-ence's well-dressed singers had "done much to break up old heathen dances and gambling," often timing their visits with the celebration of Midewiwin rites, in order to more directly answer their spiritual counterparts.[118] The Young Men's Singing and Praying Band took it upon itself to chart a new course for the entire community. "We would be very glad if you could tell us the ways and rules of your White Society," they asked Whipple, "write us about what we ought to do that our society may be in better order."[119]

The music of the Anami'aajig was itself a significant departure. Conspicuously absent from the hymns was the beat of the drum. Because the drum was deeply resonant with collective identity and spiritual power in Ojibwe thought, this was no merely stylistic matter. Its absence seemed to change the very nature of music making.[120] Neither did hymn singing involve dancing, which had been part and parcel of most ceremonial music making. The respective absences of drum and dance were particularly glaring omissions in the 1870s and 1880s, when Ojibwe reservations were swept with enthusiasm for the songs and dances of the so-called Dream Drum religion, a ceremonial movement shared with the Dakota peoples. Ceremonial dance steps, like songs, were often the fruit of powerful dreams. Their performance also was a prominent means of generating power, and, not surprisingly, such dances were central to the prophetic movements arising in the troubled reservation period. Although we have no access to recordings or musical notations from nineteenth-century performances, it seems that hymns sounded like no other Anishinaabe music. Melodies were European American in origin. Their slow tempo was without apparent indigenous precedent.

Perhaps most important, the shift toward hymnody as the exclusive music of the Anami'aajig repertory involved a retreat from a long-standing Anishinaabe understanding of the function and power of music. Hymns were distinguishable from dream songs and Midewiwin songs not simply because they lacked accompaniment of drum and dance, but because they did not function like other ceremonial music which, in an Anishinaabe worldview, could be called on to effect direct change in the world of experience. Indeed, this transforming capacity of song lay at the core of Ojibwe religiousness and survival.

By contrast, hymns were promoted and received as a representational symbolic practice. Hymns did not perforce bring about divination or healing; rather, they pointed beyond themselves to spiritual realities. A few exceptional uses of Christian hymns and prayers are evident in the historical record. Peter Jones remembered one

Ojibwe man in Ontario, for example, who prayed to God for deer three times prior to a hunt, in some evidently comparable fashion to the earlier Ojibwe practice.[121] Undoubtedly in a religious culture that encompassed wide variety in individual spiritual interpretation and practice, Christian symbols, like God, and symbolic actions, like prayer and hymnody, could more directly correspond to non-Christian referents. Nonetheless, Ojibwe hymnody did not entail many such instances. More frequent were accounts that contrasted the practice of hymn singing with traditional native religious practices. Two accounts depict Ojibwe crowds fervently singing hymns as they threw amulets, figurines, and medicines into a massive bonfire. In both accounts, the hymn singing went on while the objects of the former life, and the understanding that religious symbols can function in such a corporeal manner, went up in smoke.

By submitting that hymns were "just symbolic," I do not mean to suggest that Ojibwe hymns could not transform. Indeed, my entire point is that ritualized singing worked to transform the experience of White Earth's circumstances. The transformation, however, was of a different order. If certain Midewiwin songs healed, and certain dream songs instantiated the power of dreams for any number of material purposes, they did so because the melodies, sounds, and words could generate, or tap into, power. These songs often consisted of a short phrase, repeated over and again to intensify the power of the sung word and to recall the effective power of the founding vision or dream. By contrast, pronounced differences in the structure of the hymn underscored the deeper difference in their symbolic function. Ojibwe hymns were, relatively speaking, far wordier, relying on elaboration rather than repetition. While the English hymns used poetic language, and while translations drew on understatement, allusion, and other Ojibwe conventions to convey poetic power, the stanzas were long and the images were representational. With their multiple stanzas of sacred poetry, perhaps Ojibwe hymns were first to introduce a more overtly expressive function to the repertory of Ojibwe song.

The written record asserts no overt connection between any hymn and its origin in dreams. Neither did Ojibwe hymns make overt intertextual or intermelodic references to other songs in the repertory. While it is plausible that nineteenth-century Ojibwes set hymns to indigenous tunes, Minnesota missionaries made no mention of such tunes in the historical record. In fact, missionaries delighted in the sharp repertorial distinction between hymns and other Ojibwe music, since they construed hymnody to be the only music befitting the Christian life.

Hymn Singing and Other Spiritual Alternatives

At White Earth, the Christian life was hardly the sole alternative to earlier Midewiwin traditions. Other religious visions took root in the chaos and poverty of reservation life, and missionaries staked out the repertorial boundaries around the hymn to distinguish the Christian life from these movements as well. In 1880, for example, an intensely popular local prophetic movement grew around a man known as "the Pembina prophet." According to an Episcopalian missionary, a Pembina Band Ojibwe named Abita-kekek "declared himself the Son of God, come anew, complete with stigmata, to save the world." He preached that "the world would otherwise have been destroyed," save for his teachings, which centered on the "Prayer Dance." The missionary reported that Abita-kekek "desired to be approached only with Divine honors, by people on their hands and knees" and "pretended to know the thoughts of those who came to him." The prophet drained the Pembina settlement of most of its declared Episcopalians and soon drew a reservationwide following. An alternative view of the movement is offered by a Catholic missionary, who speaks of the Pembina Prophet as a Catholic proselyte and says that a Red Lake priest had blessed his "Prayer Dance" drum.[122] At any rate, Gilfillan wrote that followers gave up "all work and [did] nothing but hold councils every day with their prophet."[123] As evidence of the compelling nature of this millennial message on Ojibwe reservations, the deacons at Mahnomen reported that they were still contending with the prophet's teachings in the spring of 1884.[124]

Drawing an even larger following at White Earth was a ceremonial dance known as the Drum or Dream Dance, which Dakota visitors brought first to Red Lake, and which later spread to other Minnesota reservations through summer visiting networks. There appears to have been considerable overlap between the two movements. In the winter of 1884, the Pembina prophet and a large number of followers traveled to Red Lake, "bringing with them the big heathen drum, to dance night and day, and throw the Red Lake Indians into a fever of excitement."[125] Evidently, the message was still compelling four years after the Pembina prophet's ministry began, for Gilfillan noted the Red Lake "defection would have become almost general" had not the government overseer arrested the prophet.

An overlap of new religious visions extended into the young Anami'aajig communities as well. What missionaries fearfully considered to be backsliding appears to have been a rather commonplace spiritual eclecticism among Ojibwe Christians. In 1885, an Episcopalian official encountered the women of the Leech Lake Anami'aajig presiding at Sabbath worship, most of the men having "gone over to the other side of the lake to an Indian dance which some Red Lake heathen were holding."[126] In 1891, Gilfillan described another Sioux Dance as a "desolating wave" that swept even some of "old Christians of nearly forty years standing who had been our leaders for years." According to Gilfillan, a native deacon himself had "encouraged the dance."[127]

As we have seen, Ojibwes did not dance to drum music without spiritual implications. "The drum and the dance exercise an almost irresistible fascination over the Indians," Gilfillan remarked, "they do nothing else for days and weeks while the dance is going on night and day. . . . Sometimes even Christian men paint themselves up again like heathen savages."[128] In this context, practices like dancing and drumming must have been all the more accentuated as markers of identity. But it did not necessarily follow that the Anami'aajig who danced considered it to be mutually exclusive of the Christian life. Even those Christians who did dance, Gilfillan wrote, "recover[ed] in time from the moral downfall, but it takes time to build them up again."[129] Be that as it may, repertorial boundaries around the hymn seemed to hold.

The new scheme of power relations at White Earth was such that Ojibwe music, were it to remain legitimate, would be stripped of the drum and the dance.[130] Wittingly or not, those who sang hymns were playing into this devaluation of Ojibwe tradition. They sang dutifully, indeed beautifully, in the mission church on Sunday morning. At the same time, the Anami'aajig took the hymn outside the mission's circle of influence and transformed the genre in the autonomous spaces of their wigwams and tarpaper shacks. Ojibwe singing came to be associated with discrete groups of singers and their way of life. The singing became associated with particular occasions, each of which took place after nightfall and beyond earshot of the mission. The songs were at home in devotional meetings, wakes, and ceremonialized visits to other native communities. Ojibwe hymns came to be identified with certain sequences of singing, speaking, and silence and with particular aesthetics of performance. Anami'aajig hymns were always sung in unison, a cappella, and under the leadership of elders, not organists. If what White Earth missionaries heard as uncommonly "solemn" was consistent with the style that Frederick Burton heard among Garden River Ojibwe, the songs were sung so slowly as to undo any suggestion of the ordinary cadences of representational language.

Just as hymns stood apart from the music of the Midewiwin and the new visionary movements, singers distinguished the hymn from emerging instrumental music so important to Métis identity. The a cappella singing of hymns stood in marked contrast to the social dance tunes of Métis fiddling, and to the band music that the *Tomahawk* promoted as a sign of their embrace of the musical fashions of Anglo America. On the one hand, the distinction made by the Anami'aajig was repertorial, drawing boundaries in the musical world to correspond to the evangelical distinction between the church and "the world." On the other hand, the distinction concerned very different assumptions about the purpose of music. In the case of the fiddling and band music in vogue with White Earth's Métis families, music was primarily a medium for social entertainment. In this respect, an Anami'aajig rejection of Métis music may have been related to the discomfort with the disciplined, virtuosic approach to hymnody that took place around Mrs. Wiswell's organ.

Far from the logic of rehearsals and applause, Ojibwe hymn singing remained firmly rooted in longstanding beliefs about music making as a mode of communication with the sources of existence.[131] Though few would have asserted that sung hymns ritually restored order to the world or health to a patient, hymnody did not lie entirely outside the world of Ojibwe associations attached to the power of language and music. The Ojibwe word applied to hymns, *nagamowinan* ("that which he/she sings"), was applied equally to ceremonial songs of other Anishinaabe religious movements. Frederick Burton glossed "the deep significance of the verb" *nagamo* as nothing short of prayer, song and prayer being linguistically inseparable. "Every Ojibway to whom these words have been referred for interpretation," Burton remarked, "has indicated in one way or another that prayer is implied."[132]

To be sure, the changes brought by the Anami'aajig and the music they sang generated tensions with other White Earth Anishinaabeg. Indeed, while many at White Earth chose active, even militant, resistance against all incursions of Christian teachings, songs, and practices, the way of the Anami'aajig was clearly a middle way.[133] But the life the Anami'aajig negotiated and the music they performed also stood in tension with the civilizing agenda of the Episcopalian mission. Amidst the chaos of the 1880s, the life of the Anami'aajig can be understood as a resourceful attempt to forge a new kind of community around the more fundamental of Anishinaabe values. The hymn singing that accompanied each significant moment in the life of this collective can be understood as the musical medium through which the paradoxes and possibilities of this new life were articulated and negotiated. More than a cultural trapping of an Anishinaabe way of life, the practice of music making here ought to be understood as constitutive of that way of life. To explain, allow me to return our attention to accounts of devotional meetings. Again, the social frame of reference is as important, if not more so, as the details of performance.

Singing sodalities flourished at White Earth because they filled important gaps in the social turmoil on the reservation, extending the family of Episcopalian Ojibwes across lines of frequent social division: kin networks, villages, bands, and reservations. But such sodalities also were in keeping with a long-established social form that brought men and women together from different kin groups to serve the needs of the entire community and, in the case of drum societies, to bring the drum and its healing voice to community gatherings.

Devotional meetings brought more than spiritual nurture to bear. As the primary social gatherings of the Anami'aajig community, they also addressed the social and physical dimensions of life. One observer remarked that the Anami'aajig "seem to find most of their joy" in the devotional meetings: "They have not other parties nor meetings but only those connected with religion."[134] Those who rose to talk in the pauses between hymns had the right to speak their mind about anything. "Recit[ing] their experiences, . . . their struggles, trials, falls and risings up again," the Anami'aajig probably spoke as often about matters temporal as spiritual.[135] One might have needed to borrow the deacon's ox to plow his vegetable garden; another might have needed an elder to look after an ill child while she went off to set nets for fish. A feast during each meeting provided the entire community with at least one meal per day, and resources were pooled for the use of all. Note here that feasting and give-aways were common practices targeted by assimilation policy as pillars of communal values to be discouraged and even declared illegal. Out of scant treaty annuities, the singers raised a fund to "assist those in distress," or at least to guarantee a decent burial for those who could not endure.[136] While others at White Earth were getting ahead by adopting market values and looking out for their own, the Anami'aajig reaffirmed their commitment to collective well-being and an economy based on meeting the basic needs of all.

Singers made a pronounced effort to move beyond the factionalism that crippled White Earth. The White Earth Young Men's Singing and Praying Band, for example, told Whipple that it had tried with some success to bring feuding chiefs together in order to "have one mind."[137] If single-mindedness or consensus had underwritten Anishinaabe well-being for millennia, it was the singers who seemed most intent on making it happen. And while their ritualization of hymns could sound divisive with respect to their Métis cousins, the Anami'aajig seemed to have welcomed those members of the Métis community who wished to commit to the values of their Anishinaabe heritage.

Of course, the Anami'aajig were not free of divisions in their own ranks. But the few correspondences that document their affairs often entail collective appeals for Whipple's mediation of differences "so that we can work in harmony for the prosperity of the church."[138] And while the extensive travels of the singing groups to neighboring reservations appeared to missionaries as evidence of raw evangelical zeal, the Anami'aajig appear to have seen clearly into the mechanisms tearing their communities asunder and organized quite effectively in response. Spreading a not unfamiliar gospel of collective survival, they emphasized the Christian and Anishinaabe values of peace making, self-sacrifice, generosity, and mutual nurture. They also spread news of political matters, created interreservation networks, and, as was the case with the deacon's strike in 1882, occasionally took collective action.

As a seasonal subsistence off the land became less viable, and as disease and relocation undermined whatever social stability had been secured in the late years of the fur trade, the Anami'aajig of the evening devotional meetings and wakes were picking up the pieces and stitching together a new life at White Earth. Hymns were the music that accompanied this new life, that set its tone and established its rhythms. When hymns were raised, if the singers were of one mind, the music itself realized in sound the community values for which they struggled. As Thomas Turino observed about Andean panpipe music, "during special moments, culturally specific rhythms and forms of movement are not merely semiotic expressions of community and identity . . . they become their actual realization."[139]

Like other students of the place of art in culture, Turino has observed that music has a curious ability to communicate when other forms of expression have been exhausted. Music, he writes, "combines many signs with varied and even conflicting significance . . . into a unified whole." Where everyday speech breaks down, music is capable of articulating "the complexity and tensions of history and of life itself."[140] To return to the example of the Garden River wake, it was ritualized hymns that gave voice to *gashkendamowin* and the contradictions of living as strangers on their own land. Indeed, the music may have been so absorbing because its novel melodies and tempo carried new potential to give voice to unprecedented forms of grief.[141] Ritualized hymns also generated the resolve to continue to survive as a community in the presence of colonial contradictions. Burton noted that the atmosphere created by the singers rendered forgotten the "sectarian differences" that otherwise plagued the community.[142] For the Anami'aajig, the music of the hymns was perhaps alone capable of this semiotic work, making room for a viable new life while affirming the core values that conferred integrity on that life.

Though the terms of cultural exchange at White Earth recognized little value in Anishinaabe culture, the Anami'aajig drew on resources of ritual to make the hymns their own. As helpful as Bourdieu's analogy of the market is for thinking about the social placement of Ojibwe hymns and the change over time in their symbolic power, the market analogy cannot appreciate the fullness of symbolic power that the Anami'aajig heard in the hymns. Rooted less in Bourdieu's social valuation of symbolic capital than in a spiritual one of symbolic integrity, sung hymns nonetheless generated the social cash value necessary to survive as Anishinaabe at White Earth. Catherine Bell's notion of ritualization helps appreciate how the subtle modulations of hymn performance unleashed this power and worked to subvert, perhaps even invert, the values with which hymn singing as a staged enactment of "civilization" was laden.

By using Bell's language, I do not mean to imply that ritualization was a matter of conscious intent. No group of Christian Ojibwes gathered formally to elect the way of the hymn as the most strategic alternative. Such a line of thought would underestimate the depth of Anishinaabe religious sensibility and overlook the distinctive logic of practice with which this entire book is concerned. Following Bourdieu, Bell maintains that culture equips human beings with a more diffuse set of senses beyond the standard five, including a sense of ritual or a sense of the sacred. In a logic of practice, this sense of the sacred, like the sense of direction or the sense of timing, does not operate circuitously through the intellect. It acts more directly, seizing opportunities where they are to be had in the interest of both making meaning and making do.

For Bell, ritualization "does not resolve a social contradiction." It employs, within a ritualized frame, a differentiation, which restates and transforms "all the experienced and conventional conflicts and oppositions of social life" and continues to defer meanings into other terms such that "one is never confronted with *the meaning* to accept or reject; one is always led into a redundant, circular, and rhetorical universe of values and terms whose significance keeps flowing into other values and terms."[143]

To speak in terms of a "sense of the sacred" is especially apt concerning the expansive Anishinaabe approach to song and ceremony, and it is perhaps best to return to distinctive native attitudes toward the sacred in order to move beyond the narrower confines of Bourdieu's language about the economy of symbolic power. Missionaries were frequently surprised at the level of respect accorded them when they stood to preach their message. Even those Ojibwes who were disinclined to convert held to a principled Anishinaabe posture of respect for other religious visions. One could justly argue that this ethical priority stemmed from a fundamental Ojibwe conviction that the sacred is irreducibly mysterious. The word *manidoo* itself, usually translated as "spirit," is also an adjectival form better translated as "mysterious," not a mystery of any particular sort. It follows that one should listen for the truth in other peoples' songs and visions. Indeed, this is how Erma Vizenor understands her people's insights into the aspects of the Christian message that gave voice to cherished Anishinaabe beliefs and values.[144]

It seems to me that an acute "sense of the sacred" was what appraised the spiritual worth of the hymns and what brought the Anami'aajig over to invest themselves so deeply in this music. Imbued with Ojibwe understandings of the concept and function of music, hymn singing in the 1880s became a viable way to evoke the more deeply felt of Anishinaabe values in sound and to engender in evening hymnsings and wakes powerful feelings of solidarity. Under the strained circumstances of the early years at White Earth, survival may have depended on such spiritual boundary crossings, not only for the symbolic capital that those practices held but also for their spiritual worth or value that conferred or maintained integrity on the Anami'aajig enterprise. While this represents one among several spiritual alternatives in the Ojibwe response to colonization, for those who did embrace the hymns, the practice of singing and the practice of community—musical sound and social unity—were part and parcel of one another.

PART II

ETHNOGRAPHY

▲▲▲▲▲▲

4

TWENTIETH-CENTURY
HYMN SINGING AS
CULTURAL CRITICISM

▲▲▲▲▲▲

C hapter 3 explored how the Anami'aajig modeled hymns into a medium for negotiating a new life within the circumstances of assimilation and mission-ization while maintaining the integrity of core Anishinaabe values. We turn now to the changed landscape of hymn singing in the twentieth century and to how the meanings and uses of hymn singing changed in response. The same songs and the same ritualized practice of singing them have taken on different meanings and do different kinds of cultural work as a result of the gradual loss of language, English-only boarding school education, fuller integration into American society, relocation away from the reservations to the cities, and the ensuing contentiousness over the meaning and value of Ojibwe culture. Although hymn singing had declined in importance at White Earth by midcentury, a group of concerned senior citizens rekindled the tradition of singing in the 1980s in what could be understood as a ritual form of cultural criticism. Sketches of their lives show how the elders' remaking of hymn singing has effectively remade them in the process. Although the mode of ritualization changed with the historical situation, ritualized hymn singing was used to similar ends: the remembering of a dismembered community in crisis and the re-configuration of an existence where economics, politics, and religion had become increasingly compartmentalized into an integrated Anishinaabe way of life.

REMEMBERING HYMN SINGING IN
THE EARLY TWENTIETH CENTURY

The death of Bishop Whipple in 1901 marked the end of an era of intensive Episco-palian commitment to Indian missions in Minnesota, as missions fervor was redi-rected overseas and to the region's growing urban areas. A decline in diocesan com-mitment meant an apparent decline in oversight of the native-led congregations, and, in turn, a marked decline in historical records. If the scant written record is a reliable indicator, non-Indian church leaders knew remarkably little about the lives of Ojibwe Christians in the early twentieth century.[1]

The sources must change then, from contemporaneous archival records to the ways that Ojibwe elders remember the singing of hymns in the earlier decades of the twentieth century. As the sources change, so must the voice with which I relate them in the remaining chapters of this book. Here, for the elders who remember it, the witness of oral tradition to Ojibwe hymn singing is all the more embedded in a host of commitments, such that the story of hymn singing in the past and its meaning in the present cannot be separated and can scarcely even be distinguished. That said, the richness of the memories suggest how Ojibwe hymn singing had attained a pride of place alongside other memories of what was considered *traditional*.

Two memoirs of White Earth elders, borne of the oral tradition but committed to print later in the century, tell in their own words the story of rapid cultural change seen over the course of their lives. Each includes vivid recollections of the place of Ojibwe hymn singing in mourning. Both John Rogers and Ignatia Broker were raised at White Earth by extended families who knew the old ways before the reliance on treaty annuities, and who knew the characters mentioned in chapter 3. These elders looked back on their turn-of-the-century youth at White Earth, over the distance of space (one from California, the other from Minneapolis) and time—back beyond their boarding school educations and a life of speaking English in an American world. But both include descriptions of Ojibwe language hymn singing as something elemental to their memories of youth.

John Rogers penned *A Chippewa Speaks* at midcentury, later published posthumously under the title *Red World and White: Memories of a Chippewa Boyhood*. Rogers's story is rich in texture and details of Anishinaabe life: ricing, berrying, hunting, herbal healing, and Midewiwin ceremonies. It also tells of the challenges to that way of life posed by his impoverished conditions on the reservation and by the disruptions of his federal boarding school education far away in South Dakota. Although little is known of Rogers's life after that White Earth boyhood, his widow said he had been a self-employed interior decorator who enjoyed painting and playing golf and who had been rounding out his days in California. In her foreword to the memoir, Melissa Meyer suggests that "the narrative can be read as the elder John Rogers's ideas about what a 'genuine Chippewa' ought to be like."[2]

In Roger's memory, funerary hymn singing was indeed such a "genuine Chippewa" practice, one that was woven fully into other powerful memories of kin, land, and lifeway. When his little brother Ahmeek died, Rogers described the work of the singers in terms of "last rites": "On the next day [the deacon] Raven Feather returned to our wigwam again. At this time there was a prayer meeting and the Indians had gathered for the last rites. They sang hymns and visited till daylight. One of the songs they sang was "Lead Kindly Light," which in Chippewa tongue goes as follows: 'Man o su dush, kin Wayaseyaziyun, Sagin kenshin!'"[3] Later in the narrative, at the death of his sister Mah-ni, Rogers describes a similar prayer meeting with hymns. It is in Rogers's accounts of hymn singing that the reader finds the most sustained reference to the Ojibwe language. The hymns, sung in the language of the land, were for Rogers part of the texture of a remembered Chippewa boyhood.

Like Rogers, Ignatia Broker lived most of her adult life far from White Earth. She rounded out her days as a respected elder and activist in the Twin Cities, having moved from White Earth to Minneapolis in 1941 to work in a defense plant. She was widowed shortly thereafter when her husband was killed in action. Having lived "abroad" in the dominant society for two thirds of her life, she wrote *Night Flying Woman* out of a conviction that she was a valuable "link in a chain to the past."[4] Her book is an account of that past told through the life story of her grandmother Ni-bo-wi-se-gwe, or Oona, who had known both the unfettered life of the seasonal round and the difficult circumstances faced after the removal to White Earth. In a narrative describing how the people continued to dance, offer tobacco at sunrise and sunset, and practice the traditional ethics of *bimaadiziwin*—even after settling on the reservation—Broker remembers the work of the singing societies as an expression of those old ways: "The many changes in the Ojibway material life did not change their traditional way of sharing. There was a kindness in the people and in the help they gave to those in distress. [Oona's] Mother, On-da-g, and Sha-nood formed a little society. They sat with the sick and bereaved, and they met to help each other learn the new things that were necessary."[5]

When Oona's mother died, it was "the Christians," the Anami'aajig, who came to bury her.[6] By the time Broker herself had entered the picture, she remembers that when she was a little girl her grandmother would only leave the farm to do "what was necessary," a designation that included Ojibwe singing:

> She helped the older Ojibway with the mourning, which had become a mixture of the old and new. It was now the custom to have a wake and keep vigil with the family. These wakes were held in either the Catholic or Episcopal guild halls. The hymns of the white people were sung but the words were of the Ojibway tongue. The people still put the clothes of the dead into a bundle and gave them to a close friend to distribute among people of another do-daim [clan].[7]

In Broker's memory, the singing of the elders gave voice to the remarkable way that her forebears had incorporated the Christian tradition with their way of life. When Night Flying Woman rushes to her grandparents confused about the teachings of the missionary, they admonish her not to be "ashamed of the good that we have taught and not [to] be ashamed of the good to be learned. Our way of life is changing, and there is much we must accept. But let it be only the good. And we must always remember the old ways. We must pass them onto our children and grandchildren so they too will recognized the good in the new ways."[8] In the narratives of both John Rogers and Ignatia Broker, hymn singing is no mere inroad of missionary Christianity; it is remembered as a tradition of grieving that was seamlessly woven into the fabric of traditional life. So, too, had the evening prayer meetings become traditional for those Ojibwe who continued to identified themselves as Christian.

THE PERSISTENCE AND DECLINE OF HYMN SINGING

Minutes of occasional meetings of the native Episcopalian clergy offer no great exception to the rule of a sparse historical record, but they do make frequent mention of the need for new provisions of hymnals, particularly in connection with evening prayer meetings. Based on oral history accounts of today's singers, it was these evening "old Indian prayer meetings," conducted in Ojibwe, that became the touchstones of Christian Anishinaabe community life. Erma Vizenor recalls being summoned to prepare her grandparents' house for the meetings: sweeping, cleaning kerosene lanterns, boiling fish soup, and baking special "government cake," so named for the recipe her grandmother made as a hired cook at the government school at Pine Point. In the evening, the community would crowd into the little house, elders seated at the table and children standing along the walls. They would sing and then give long speeches in the native language, speeches that could range in content from spiritual testimony to reservation political matters.[9] The tradition of prayer meeting singing came to play an even more public role during the season of Lent. At least since the 1950s, singers from each of the three major Ojibwe reservations have gathered on successive Sundays in different communities for a "spiritual journey," in which sung hymns provide the chorus for interspersed prayers, testimonies, and speeches. Beginning at Onigum on Leech Lake, respective groups of Ojibwe singers assemble at Cass Lake, Red Lake, and on through the White Earth Reservation communities of Rice Lake, Pine Point, and the village of White Earth. Minutes of clergy meetings and oral accounts of today's elders also point to the significance of funeral wakes in the life of the community throughout the twentieth century, the singing at which will be the subject of chapter 5.

The extremely local character of Ojibwe singing in these prayer meetings and wakes makes it all the more difficult to generalize about the vitality of the practice. Prayer meetings were regularly held in homes, and singing at them continued apace. But these were in-house gatherings, and they occurred with greater frequency at Pine Point and at Leech Lake than at White Earth village. By midcentury, these practices seem to have declined both in frequency and in public significance for broader circles of the community, and although today's singers indicate no strong reasons for why this was the case, demographic factors likely contributed. In the 1950s, native clergy lamented that the incentive programs of the federal relocation policy were "draining off the most active and able group" and bringing them to the cities for employment.[10] Clergy found that once these people were in the cities, little could be done to keep them within the Episcopalian fold, since the churches in the cities were largely nonnative and unwelcoming. Their identity, it turned out, was oriented less to Episcopalianism than to the Anami'aajig tradition on the reservation within the Episcopalian fold. In the 1960s and 1970s, senior citizens' programs begun under the Office of Economic Opportunity sponsored shared meals and craft-making programs, which also may have sapped participation from hymn-singing groups, especially in White Earth village, where most programs were headquartered.

While there are only scattered recollections about the nature of hymn singing earlier in the century, there is ample evidence to examine how the tradition of singing as it was more recently revived has responded to changing context of life at White Earth. I will organize that discussion around a number of key social and cultural shifts to which contemporary hymn singing can be seen as a response.

A CHANGING SOCIAL LANDSCAPE

A series of changes in U.S. Indian policy altered the political and economic structure of White Earth dramatically from what it had been since the 1880s under official policies of assimilation. The definitive change occurred in the wake of the 1934 Indian Reorganization Act, which brought those policies of assimilation to an official close. The so-called Indian New Deal established under the act recognized distinctive native societies' right to exist, formally annulled any governmental hindrances to the practice of native languages and religious ceremonies, and saw to the creation of independent tribal governments on the model of a constitutional democracy.[11] The shift away from an overt policy of assimilation was also based on an official acknowledgment that assimilation had failed miserably.[12]

A Benedictine sociologist who conducted field research at White Earth provided a vivid picture of how acute the failures of assimilation policy had become on that reservation. By 1938, when Sister Inez Hilger visited White Earth, the reservation was largely owned by nonnatives. Farmers and lumber companies had acquired their land through the alienation of allotments and the homesteading of unallotted surplus land. The state of Minnesota acquired large tracts through the numerous tax foreclosures on the part of native owners unversed in the idea of property taxes. By 1934, it was estimated that only one in twelve White Earth enrollees held an original allotment. By 1938, fewer than four hundred of White Earth's eight thousand enrollees were believed to own any land at all.[13]

Subsistence hunting, fishing, gardening, and ricing still comprised a large share of Anishinaabe livelihood at White Earth, but extensive deforestation, fencing of privatized land, and new state regulations on hunting, fishing, trapping, and ricing made White Earth's people increasingly dependent on the cash purchase of life necessities. White Earth residents found this to be very debilitating, since wage income was difficult to come by, especially in the more remote villages of the reservation.[14] The average family income there in 1937 was slightly more than $500, and only two hundred enrollees were farming.[15] Most pieced together a living from subsistence and occasional wage labor. Men sought seasonal jobs building roads, cutting timber, or staffing Depression-era public works projects. Women contributed in large measure to family cash incomes by selling beadwork and birchbark crafts.

The need for wage labor had drawn some off the reservation for many years, but it was not until the 1950s, when the United States sponsored massive relocation efforts, that large numbers left the reservations for the cities. Incentive programs drew so many Ojibwe people to the postwar jobs in cities like Minneapolis and Chicago that well over half of White Earth's population had moved away by the 1960s. Some maintained strong connections to the reservation, returning for ricing, powwows, and wakes. Others left for good.

Significant gains in the standard of living of Native Americans were made in the 1960s and thereafter. America's War on Poverty brought dramatic improvements in housing, education, and the general standard of living at reservations like White Earth. In the 1970s, a federal policy of "Indian self-determination" began to turn over social service provision to the tribes, creating many government service jobs to be filled by White Earth native people, particularly those who were well-schooled and especially women. It also enlarged the budgets and role of tribal governments well beyond the expectations held at the time their constitutions were drafted. The shift to self-determination improved the lives of native people generally, but it also made clearer the distinction between those at White Earth who had access to the system of jobs, education, and patronage associated with the tribal government, and those who did not by reason of choice, factionalism, or both.

This new face of factionalism presented another major change in the landscape of hymn singing in the twentieth century. Although the official policies promoting independent tribal governments and self-determination were expressly designed to restore a shared tribal identity, the political structures they created effectively institutionalized existing patterns of intratribal dissent. In the late 1930s, Hilger said she found not one White Earth community, but two. For reasons related to but not corresponding with the earlier factionalism between Métis and the conservative Anishinaabeg at White Earth, Hilger built her study around the distinction between the half that lived in "frame houses" and the half that lived in one-room or two-room "tarpaper shacks." The frame house community was oriented to cultural and economic integration with wider American society. The tarpaper shack community was more concerned with maintaining boundaries around distinctive Anishinaabe cultural and economic lifeways.

Hilger acknowledged that both shack and house families had similar cash incomes, numbers of children, and boarding school educations. The principal differences were matters of chosen lifestyle. House families "followed the American standard of living more closely." Hilger found them "cleaner" and more often decorated with flowers and needlecraft. They ran up bills and paid them. In their homes, she found radios; washing machines; factory-made tables, rockers, and armchairs; pillows and sheets. She found that frame house families were far more likely to have pianos, organs, and guitars—instruments that indicated an attachment to American music. Not one of these seventy-one frame households was home to drums, rattles, or flutes—the instruments associated with Anishinaabe musical culture. Hilger found it significant that frame house families kept up with education beyond the elementary grades and tried to maintain contact "with persons other than reservation-born and reservation-bred, or who had been exposed to mental stimulation."[16]

By contrast, families in tarpaper shacks remained more closely tied to reservation circles and to Anishinaabe traditions in their material, economic, and musical culture. They were more likely to gather their own wood, wild rice, fish, and meat and to cook outdoors. She found them more resourceful, building their own oil drum stoves and tables and benches. They seldom married or divorced formally, but came into what the state recognized as common-law marriages. Hilger found no tarpaper shack family with a piano, accordion, or other large American instruments. Instead they had dance drums, Midewiwin drums, and rattles.

Ironically, Hilger found no strong correlation between religious affiliation and this bifurcation of the community. In chapter 3, we saw how religious affiliations reflected differing strategies of response to colonizing pressures in the nineteenth century. The Métis were largely Catholic; the "full blood" Anishinaabeg were either Protestant or resolutely non-Christian. But in the twentieth century, clear correlations cannot be discerned so readily. Social tensions often developed along lines of Episcopal, Catholic, and non-Christian traditionalists, but affiliation itself must be approached as a complex and shifting phenomenon at White Earth.

In 1911, Gilfillan had reported that of an estimated nine thousand Ojibwe throughout Minnesota, five thousand were baptized Roman Catholic, three thousand were baptized Protestant (mostly Episcopalian), and three thousand remained "pagan" or unbaptized.[17] At White Earth, where the share of Protestant Ojibwes was richer than in Gilfillan's estimate of the Minnesota population as a whole, Hilger found that the families living in wood frame houses were overwhelmingly Catholic. Those living in tarpaper shacks included significant numbers of Catholics as well, but were far more likely to identify as Midewiwin or Episcopalian. Among shack families, 10 percent were identified as Midewiwin, 36 percent as Protestant, and 54 percent as Catholic. Among house families, none identified as Midewiwin, 18 percent as Protestant, and 82 percent as Catholic. Although Hilger includes Methodism and Gospel Alliance under the category of Protestant, only five Protestant families in the sample of 150 families were other than Episcopalian.[18]

To complicate things even more, consider how problematic was the notion of religious affiliation in the first place. Of the four families living on the land where Pine Point's annual Midewiwin ceremonies were held, Hilger found that "only one man was a member, and he was living in common law marriage with a Catholic woman who had left her husband. Two of the four families were practicing Catholics, while the third was an Episcopal."[19] The anecdote illustrates well three reasons that twentieth-century religious affiliation has been too idiosyncratic to serve as a reliable axis for analysis. First, religious affiliation may have been an important part of identity, but it did not necessarily register one's position toward cultural and economic integration. Not all Christians, for example, were progressive. Second, religious affiliations seldom posed major barriers to intermarriage. As social tensions came to rely less on inherited ethnic distinctions between Métis and conservative Anishinaabeg, intermarriage became more prevalent. As a consequence, family religious identities came to resemble patchworks, configurations that shifted with frequent, relatively fluid, marital comings and goings. Third, Hilger's story of the four families living on the Midewiwin grounds and the confusing array of religious affiliations begs the question, "What conception of the religious obtains when such conventional notions of the boundaries between religious traditions do not occur in social life?" In such Anishinaabe spaces as the homes of the Anami'aajig, the distinctions of "religion" were negotiated with a way of life organized around the fundamental mystery of *manidoo*. Boundaries between religions—indeed, boundaries around "religion" itself as a discrete component of culture—became highly divisive social facts in the twentieth century, but these social facts stood in tension with alternative Anishinaabe ways of imagining them.

Today's seniors remember the prayer meetings and funeral wakes of their youth as gatherings where food was shared, hymns were sung, and Ojibwe prayers and speeches were made. Because these meetings were held in people's homes, not churches, and because they were led by lay elders, not clergy, the matter of religious affiliation was reconfigured as a rather fluid social affiliation rather than as a matter of creedal assent or institutional membership. And if funeral wakes today are any indicator of early twentieth-century practice, there was considerable overlap of religious affiliations among those attending hymn-singing events.

As in the nineteenth century, White Earth factionalism did not always pattern itself along the lines of two communities. Social stress could develop along lines of gender, age, family, and settlement pattern, even when groups shared political and cultural postures. For example, public assistance housing programs in the 1970s and 1980s functioned to further concentrate White Earth Anishinaabeg within particular reservation villages. Since the days of allotment, extended families had settled in compounds far enough apart to buffer social tensions. Densely settled developments of two- and three-bedroom homes in the villages of White Earth, Pine Point, Naytahwaush, and Rice Lake, however, made the villages appear like low-cost suburban developments, and families were assigned homes in ways that could fuel interfamilial strife. Many at White Earth today contend that these spatial arrangements in "the projects" foster violence and gang activity.

A CHANGING CULTURAL LANDSCAPE: LANGUAGE LOSS AND THE FOLKLORIZATION OF CULTURE

As important as these changing social contexts were, so, too, were changes in the cultural terrain of twentieth-century Ojibwe hymn singing. Most significant, of course, was the devastating level of language loss sustained by Minnesota's Ojibwe community over the course of the twentieth century. In the 1930s, Congress outlawed the overt system of rewards and punishments that discouraged the speaking of original languages in boarding schools and government day schools, but official policy did not reverse the trend away from daily use of the Ojibwe language. Indeed, larger economic, political, and cultural pressures of assimilation continued to undermine Ojibwe as a language applied to everyday life. This, in turn, has threatened the very viability of the distinctive way of construing the world structured by that language. With each passing generation, English has further replaced Ojibwe as the language of the Anishinaabe community at White Earth. In 1938, Hilger found people of all ages speaking Ojibwe. Even after forty years of assimilation efforts, more than half of the parents she interviewed spoke Ojibwe fluently. It was still the sole language spoken in twenty-two homes, 8 percent of Hilger's sample.[20] Presumably most members of the grandparents' generation spoke the language fluently. Hilger even reported that some children spoke only Ojibwe, since many were raised primarily by the grandparents.

Today, those children are White Earth's elders, and most retain some facility with the Ojibwe language. After years of disuse, many elders will not claim to speak the language, but most of them can comprehend Ojibwe when they hear it. This is due in part to the scarcity of conversation partners. It also has to do with an Anishinaabe code of respect by which English is spoken if any party to a conversation would not understand the native language. But language disuse is also a function of years of dominant society's view that Ojibwe was an obstacle to educational, financial, and social success. For many in the current generation of elders, the only way to survive while remaining Anishinaabe was to take that language, the stories, and the songs that gave it shape and to store them in places deep inside. Such an interiorization of the language and culture may account, on the one hand, for the heartfelt inner appreciation of it, and, on the other, for the frequent reluctance to speak it publicly.

According to an analysis of 1990 census data, 4 percent of Ojibwes between the ages of five and seventeen were reported to speak the original language in their home.[21] Only forty-seven of one thousand were reported to be so thoroughly schooled in Ojibwe that they had difficulty speaking English. A recent survey of fluency described a more serious loss of language facility among those in the current generation. In a 1994 study, the White Earth Land Recovery Project determined that fewer than thirty Minnesota Ojibwes aged thirty-five or younger were fluent.[22]

Fortunately, Ojibwe does remain the primary language in a considerable number of Canadian communities and in certain pockets of reservation communities in Minnesota. Though travel to these communities may be costly and difficult, the fact that such places exist makes a great deal of difference for those who live in places where they seldom hear the language spoken. Members of these communities come south to visit, and many Minnesota Ojibwes drive north to these communities for Midewiwin ceremonies, healing, and consultations with elders. Beginning in the 1970s, schools on the reservations began to teach Ojibwe, and the White Earth tribal newspaper included a section in written Ojibwe, but with few exceptions to date, efforts that situate language learning in the classroom and through the vehicle of transcription and printed materials have been surprisingly disappointing. According to one elder, it is because of efforts to "restructure our egalitarian and living grammar to fit [language scholars'] own agenda of what a language is supposed to be."[23]

It is hard to overstate the consequences or even to anticipate all the ramifications of the language loss. For Wub-e-ke-niew, a Red Lake elder, the loss of language is key to other late-twentieth-century challenges facing the Ojibwe. In what he calls "a translation of aboriginal indigenous thought, the first book ever published from an *Ahnishinahbaeotjibway* perspective," Wub-e-ke-niew underscores the necessity of the Ojibwe language to Anishinaabe identity and sovereignty. He even criticizes the approach to social change that he once embraced as treasurer of the American Indian Movement (AIM) in terms of the consequences of not thinking in terms of the Ojibwe language:

> Going about social change in the ways we could talk about it in English entrenched the problems of the community. Some of the individuals who were involved with A.I.M. moved up in the White man's social hierarchy . . . but the overall conditions in South Minneapolis are no better now than they were in 1968. The doors that were opened, opened to individuals rather than to the community. . . . The structure of the English language . . . simultaneously generates the social problems; and molds people's perceptions and ideas, which leads their thinking to prescribed solutions which maintain the overall social structure. I see the problem as being in the language.[24]

Still, the very loss of language has made its value all the more precious to elders like Wub-e-ke-niew, who has committed himself to recovering his own facility with the language after losing some of it in boarding school. The loss of the language, in turn, has created a very different niche for Ojibwe language hymnody and a variety of meanings and associations in the twentieth century that did not hitherto obtain.

Another shift of consequence for twentieth-century singing has been a rapidly expanding musical repertory, evidence of further integration of White Earth into larger circles of American culture. Hilger noted that an appreciable number of both house and shack families owned radios, illustrating how the repertory of music available to White Earth Anishinaabeg was already becoming integrated into wider American musical culture. Recall from chapter 3 how the meanings and uses of hymn singing are more clearly seen in light of alternative musics and conceptions of music available. In the context of the late nineteenth century, hymns became marks of Anishinaabe ethnicity in contrast to the way that the fiddle, cornet band, and social dance music had become associated with Métis identity.

In the early twentieth century, many at White Earth gravitated toward a popular American music valued primarily for social entertainment. Clearly popular music engaged a wide range of White Earth Anishinaabeg, not simply those in frame houses. But a significant number of White Earth enrollees, especially those who read the English-language Métis newspaper the *Tomahawk*, developed a provincial taste in their attempt to integrate White Earth's culture with that of the wider American culture. The weekly English language paper waxed enthusiastic about each piano duet, band concert, and social dance that brought the music of "culture" to White Earth. In 1904, Clement Hudson Beaulieu, brother of the *Tomahawk's* publisher, wrote:

> Twenty five years ago the blanket and the wigwam were not quite a lost sight but now one looks in vain for such sights. . . . As I listened the other day to the strains of the two brass bands I thought of the time when instrumentation above the rasp of the Pembina fiddle was an art to which no Indian thought he could attain. To him never came the vision of an Orpheus or a St. Cecilia, but now what? Most of the young people have more than a bowing acquaintance with the cultured pagan god and the patroness of Christian musical culture.[25]

Such a view as Beaulieu's sharpened the contrast between the music and dance of Anishinaabe heritage and the music of so-called culture. The *Tomahawk* never wrote of this contrast in a language of distaste, but rather articulated it with what we might call a language of folklorization.[26] In the expanding musical and cultural repertory of the twentieth century, some at White Earth were imagining their Anishinaabe heritage and its musical expression in new ways—inventing, so to speak, something called Ojibwe culture, if culture is seen to be a crystallized collection of customs. This, in turn, compelled a response from others who considered that heritage to remain viable as a way of life, and not simply a museum piece.

The folklorization of Ojibwe culture by some, and its continued practice as a viable lifeway by others, marks a final feature of the twentieth-century landscape that has reshaped the meanings and uses of hymn singing. The *Tomahawk* was resolute in asserting a shared native heritage of both Métis and "full blood" enrollees, which was put on display each June in the White Earth Powwow, an annual

White Earth's Town Band, 1908. Métis members include Bob Beaulieu (front with cornet), John B. Warren (first row, third from left), and Robert MacArthur (standing, fourth from right). (Courtesy Becker County Historical Society)

gathering begun by Enmegabowh in 1873 to commemorate the original settling of White Earth and the establishment of St. Columba's mission. The June gathering was a peculiar mix of Anishinaabe feast and county fair. Reading between the lines of the *Tomahawk*, it is clear that the powwow meant quite different things to White Earth's respective communities. Each June, Anishinaabeg from scattered villages at White Earth and neighboring reservations assembled in council, to resolve differences and establish common interests. Recall that it was here in 1882 that native Episcopalian deacons had organized their strike against the Episcopalian mission. The occasion also brought large numbers of Lakota and Dakota Sioux together with Anishinaabeg in camps outside the grounds, and thus helped forge a "Native American" identity through an emerging sense of their common lot.

These intertribal visits were solemn as well as festive, sacred as well as strategic. Pipe ceremonies reaffirmed bonds. Countless hours were spent playing the moccasin game, a small-stakes game of chance that took place to the rapid beat of a drum and moccasin game songs. New dances and songs were exchanged, some being social, others being ceremonial. Orations by Mezhakegezhig, Joseph Charette, and other aged *ogimaag* of White Earth's original band settlements must have included accounts of the "Ojibwe Trail of Tears" to White Earth and the hard-won survival of native people who were removed there.

The powwow also was a county fair. Marching bands formed a grand parade, joined by Anishinaabeg in traditional garb, and Civil War veterans both native and nonnative. A baseball tournament took place alongside an intertribal lacrosse game. The *Tomahawk* estimated that ten thousand had assembled for the thirtieth anniversary powwow in June of 1903. The affair was significant enough to draw such dignitaries as the governor of Minnesota.

Viewing the occasion as an opportunity for community promotion, the *Tomahawk* in 1904 called for a powwow committee to better organize the event. The committee succeeded in sponsoring an event that was staged for fuller effect with visiting dignitaries, people of means, and area non-Indians. Anishinaabe culture was put on display for what the paper tellingly referred to as an "amusement" of visitors. In 1903, a party of four from Detroit, having "come here to see the Indians eat dog," were reportedly amused to have seen the ceremonial feast among the Anishinaabeg and the Lakota. At the 1904 powwow, Congressman Steenerson was adopted into the tribe in reward for his advocacy against the trust regulations that the *Tomahawk* complained had blocked competent "mixed bloods" from selling their allotments. After conferring on him the name "Omahyah we gah bow," or He Who Stands in the Midst, Mezhakegezhig presented Steenerson with "Indian attire and a long stemmed pipe."[27]

Perhaps it was not Anishinaabe lifeways but a folklorized "Indian culture" that was being performed at the behest of the *Tomahawk* and the powwow committee. In 1903, for example, a costumed operatic performance of Longfellow's *Song of Hiawatha* brought cheers from a largely nonnative crowd. The performance was a staging of a popular Oberammergau-like pageant near Sault Ste. Marie, Ontario, billed by its Canadian railroad sponsor as the "Indian Passion Play." While sung in the Ojibwe language, and involving elaborate scenes of drumming and dancing, the *Song of Hiawatha* pageant itself nonetheless put native actors in a position of staging romantic caricatures of themselves. In the final two scenes, Hiawatha, a misnamed version of the Ojibwe culture hero, welcomes the "Black Robe" missionary as guests among his people, and exhorts them:

> Listen to their words of wisdom,
> Listen to the truth they tell you,
> For the Master of Life has sent them,
> From the land of light and morning.[28]

After the speech, Hiawatha mounts a canoe, which carries him, standing with arms outstretched, into the sunset. The dances, feasts, and pipe ceremonies performed earlier in the piece by the pageant's "real Indians" were safely contained on a stage and in a time now long past—and this to rounds of applause.

For those Anishinaabeg and Lakota encamped in tipis surrounding the grounds, the June event involved a performance as well, though a performance of a different kind. Complex dances to the loud beat and high-pitched voices of the drum societies must have been the heart and soul of the occasion, enactments of cultural memory, as well as integuments of intertribal alliance building. Especially in a climate of assimilation policy that still officially discouraged such practices, the condoned space of folklorized performance perhaps made room enough for the public exercise and expression of a distinctive identity.

Ojibwes, Lakota Sioux, and nonnatives alike gather in White Earth village in 1910 at the annual June 14th celebration of the founding of the reservation. Note automobiles in foreground, tipis in background, and circular dance ground with flagpole in center. The celebration continues today as the annual White Earth Powwow. (Courtesy Minnesota Historical Society)

For those White Earth Ojibwes who published and read the *Tomahawk*, the dances, the pipe ceremonies, and the regalia were viewed as entertainment. "On each afternoon," the paper reported, "the dance programs were faithfully carried out and, with the exception of the sham battle, seemed to be the most attractive feature of the proceedings strictly for amusement."[29] Like the barker hollering "step right up!" to an old sideshow, the *Tomahawk* promoted activities of the Anishinaabeg as curios of a lost way of life. In 1903, it proclaimed: "Here will be an opportunity to see Nature's red children as they were yesterday and as they are today, in a word, to see them enjoying themselves in the fun frolic and festivities, as was their happy wont in the days of long ago and ere the erect form and agile steps were bent and dulled by the trying cares of a new civilization and before assuming their share of the white man's burden."[30] With Anishinaabe music, dance, and culture safely contained within the bounds of the "long ago," White Earth's official newspaper envisioned an Anishinaabe future that valued this distinct heritage, but which looked to Anglo-America for the cultural cues of consequence. This was no minor view among White Earth enrollees in the twentieth century. The *Tomahawk* had been designated the official organ of the General Council of Minnesota Chippewas, and adopted a new masthead in 1918 that read, "Justice and Fair Dealing for Every Indian Who Desires to Become a Good Citizen."[31] This cultural perspective continued to develop through the century, and its basic contours still apply to many at White Earth.

HYMN SINGING IN THE NEW CONTEXT

Hymn singing took on new valences as it stood in heightened relief to much of the music of the expanding repertory. Today one can encounter virtually any kind of American music at White Earth, from hymnody to hip-hop, polka to powwow, country-western to rock and roll. This musical integration has resulted over time in the reduction of the distinctively Ojibwe song repertory. Economic and social integration also has reduced the number of songs specific to practices of the seasonal round.[32] That musical repertories should change so dramatically is, in itself, no surprise. What interests us are the implications that this expanding array of musics held for the meanings and uses of Ojibwe hymnody.

Whatever their posture toward cultural assimilation, White Earth people have welcomed new musics into their lives. Families of children in the boarding schools applauded the band music or theatrical musicals staged on occasion for the community by their children. Those who had radios or fed coins into jukeboxes clearly enjoyed the lonesome crying of Hank Williams. Those who worked in the munitions plants during World War II or who fought in the fields of Germany must have hummed big band tunes while they labored.

What matters is how they viewed hymn singing in light of the other musics of an expanding repertory. Ethnomusicologists have shown how broader cultural analysis is enriched through understanding the repertorial distinctions that people make among different types of music. A given piece of music can derive much of its cultural force from assertions of difference made between genres of music and music making—for example, between gospel blues and either blues or hymnody.[33]

There is a marked difference between repertories of drum music and hymnody, but the changing cultural landscape of the twentieth century has linked them in important ways. For many Ojibwes, native-language hymns, like the songs of the drum societies, continued to represent a distinctive Anishinaabe attitude about the intention, social life, and significance of music making. No guitars, pianos, or other instruments were introduced. Few songs migrated into these distinctive repertories. When they did, their texts and tunes were reconfigured in established performance styles. Drum groups perform songs such as "Yankee Doodle Dandy," but to subversive and humorous effect, since the English texts and the familiar tunes are arranged in the rhythm, repetition, and high-pitch voicings of powwow songs. A number of gospel songs, like a translation of "Remember Me," have entered the repertory of Protestant hymns and are included in the most recent reprinting of *Ojibwa Hymns*. Some of these may have entered common parlance by means of Selam Ross's "Chippewa Bible Broadcast," a weekly radio show sponsored by the Missionary Alliance Church in Cass Lake, which aired as recently as the 1970s. The program's theme music, a gospel song entitled "Jesus Ninjiminishin," can be heard with some frequency in singing groups, although the radio program's emphasis on sung harmony has not affected the preferred practice of Ojibwe singing in unison. Interestingly, the repertory of Roman Catholic hymns and chants, first translated by Frederic Baraga, did not enter the repertory of Episcopalian singing at White Earth, even though a number of today's singers hark back to the memory of those songs from their own youths.

Of course, one of the most telling markers of this boundary is that of language. In the contemporary musical culture of the Blackfoot nation in Montana studied by Bruno Nettl, a sharp repertorial boundary exists based on the uses of language in Anglo-American and Blackfoot music. "Our songs are different from white people's songs," one Blackfoot man told Nettl, "for one thing, they sound special, and they don't just have a lot of words."[34] We can profit from Nettl's attention to the way that his collaborators couch the distinctions within their repertory. We must be discerning, however, in what we make of the distinction that Nettl's consultant made between "Blackfoot music" and "white music." As shown in the previous chapters, nothing inherently *Ojibwe* or *white* is at work in the story of Ojibwe hymn singing. Through the process of ritualization, and after many years of ritualized performance, Ojibwe hymns have become, at least for many Ojibwes, Anishinaabe music.

Hymn singers distinguish sharply between their Ojibwe songs and the music of the entertainment industry and popular culture, but they do not eschew such popular music. Equipped with radios and televisions, the singers are not surprisingly fully literate in wider American cultural trends. Such rural senior citizens may, in fact, watch more television and listen to more radio than nonnative counterparts in the city. Many singers are avid fans of country-western music in particular—a music that remains popular across racial lines among people of similar economic, social, or geographic location in rural Minnesota.

That said, singers do recognize a pronounced boundary between such popular musics as country-western and Ojibwe hymns. While country music, like Ojibwe hymnody, can give voice to sadness, economic hardship, and existential pain, it does so in a far more discursive manner. Country music is many things, but it is not a uniquely native expression of the experiences of those conditions. To be sure, the vocabulary and culture of country music is also a matter of identity, a cultural medium and mark for affiliation with hard work and family values, and many native people share in this larger identity. But Ojibwe hymns mark out another space for more specifically native reflection.

In light of the Ojibwe language's diminishing role in everyday life, the prominence of the language in hymn texts sets hymnody apart from other musics. I will explore the operations of sung language and memory in greater detail in chapter 5, but we might note here that the Ojibwe hymns' value had risen dramatically as a resource of language and identity and had become recognized as culturally authoritative by wider and wider circles of the White Earth community. While some still consider hymns to be narrowly Christian or "white" music, increasing numbers of Ojibwe people experience them as Ojibwe songs. Indeed, Ojibwe singers speak of the music as "Ojibwe songs" and "Ojibwe singing" instead of "hymns" and "hymn singing." This articulates another important repertorial boundary between Ojibwe language hymns and those conventional hymns associated with Sunday morning worship in mainline Protestant churches.

Compared to the vocable-rich repertory of contemporary drum music, the very wordiness of hymn texts may set them apart as particularly rich resources of Ojibwe language and culture. Vennum found that while 89 percent of the songs Densmore recorded at the beginning of the century contained "meaningful" Ojibwe texts, fewer than 5 percent of the songs he recorded in the 1970s did.[35] The less common the experience of hearing the Ojibwe language, the more the experience of hymn singing has become principally an encounter with the language as a living entity. The language here holds something akin to the liturgical focus that Latin held in the pre-Vatican II Roman Catholic mass. Ojibwe acquires a host of associations as a sacred language. Unlike Latin, though, the Ojibwe language is not exclusively a liturgical language. Neither is Ojibwe the language of some distant, and therefore sacred, time and place, but a language closely associated with local ethnic identity and with the local landscape.

For White Earth singers, the distinction between hymn singing and other musics also hinges on the social matrix and intentions behind music making. Ojibwe singing is markedly associated with the singing groups and with the collective values to which each member commits as part of the work of singing. This kind of group commitment, while characteristic of the repertory of drum groups, is far less important in other repertories than the quality of the sound object. For example, during a large gathering of Catholic native elders, a gospel music family band from Montana performed on their electric guitars and old amplifiers. By today's conventional standards, their instruments and voices were so dreadfully out of tune and syncopation that the crowd was leaving in droves. Their lead singer interrupted a set to confront those who were leaving: "We're here to pray to God with you, not to entertain you."[36] A similar intention courses through hymn singing. "Sounding good" has more to do with the spirit in the room than with the sound object itself.

THE SOCIAL LOCATION OF OJIBWE SINGING

Some ethnomusicologists have argued that Native American communities have negotiated dramatic changes in cultural repertory by underscoring significant continuities in terms of "musical process." In other words, the kinds of music may change, but the underlying concepts about music and behaviors surrounding musical performance often remain.[37] This has been the case at White Earth too, but not because of some axiomatic process of cultural change. At White Earth, hymns came to carry important cultural freight because people acted consciously to assert differences in the practice of singing.

Musical, linguistic, political, and social changes have served to mark off the Ojibwe hymn as an expression charged with memory and value in the cultural field. But especially in light of the decline in language fluency, nothing inherent in the Ojibwe hymn gives expression to particular memories, particular values. Rather, the process of meaning-making is a complex of different Anishinaabe people making meaning in their own way. To make some sense of this protean process, we should first turn to the social field to place those people who sing hymns today in order to understand the uses to which they put their singing. I will tell a very particular story of a group of singers at White Earth village and argue that their hymn singing has constituted a cultural critical response to conditions there. Consistent with the larger argument of the book, I wish to use this specific case to show how such religious practices can be made to do certain kinds of social, cultural, and spiritual work.

DISMEMBERMENT AND REMEMBERING

As I was driving with an Anishinaabe friend back to White Earth one warm summer day after an errand in town, he pointed to a roadside ditch and told me, rather flatly, that a relative of his had been found lying there the previous winter, dead from exposure while walking home from some beer party in subzero weather. To me, it was a nondescript place of grasses and weeds cast in warm summer light. To him, it was a familiar marker in a geography of memory where his own relative breathed his last. The directness in my friend's tone may have been meant to startle me, but it also bespoke the routine facticity of violent death at White Earth. Such interchanges make it less surprising to me that young men and women of promise turn to beer and marijuana–or, cheaper still, a bottle of K-Mart nail polish remover—in order to forget. Sometimes it has seemed to me that White Earth is a culture of forgetting.

The key word here is *sometimes*, for the more powerful impression after my eight-year acquaintance is how a group of elders at White Earth have rallied to remember language, culture, and identity. On the kitchen walls of a number of Ojibwe homes I have seen displayed copies of a transcript of a message delivered by a respected spiritual leader. This man, who, even after his death, has inspired Anishinaabe people throughout Minnesota, diagnosed the social ills this way:

> We do not own the land upon which we live. We do not have the basic things of life which we are told are necessary to better ourselves. We do not have the tools to be self sufficient. But today, I want to tell you that we do not need these things. What we do need, however, is what we already have. . . . We need to realize who we are and what we stand for. . . . We need to be as one again! We need to work again for the common good of all of us! We the Anishinaabeg are the human beings of this land. . . . We are the keepers of that which the Great Spirit has given to us. . . . If it is to be destroyed, only we can do it, by turning our backs on our language, our culture, our traditional drums and our religion; then and only then do we lose because we cease to exist as Anishinaabeg. Remember what the object of the game is. Don't be enticed by their almighty dollar. Never allow them to forget the injustices. . . . And, always my friends, remember the suffering of our Anishinaabeg.[38]

Although the group of elders in White Earth village who came to be known as "the Ojibwe Singers" might view the "traditional" in slightly broader terms, they share the diagnosis: the community suffers from dismemberment understood both in social terms ("We need to be as one again!") and in spiritual terms of alienation from its true identity as Anishinaabe ("We need to realize who we are and what we stand for . . . the Anishinaabeg are the human beings of this land").

Singers also share the elder's prescription: Survival against the odds hinges on the possibility of *remembering* language, culture, and identity. The story of their formation as a singing group in the first place illustrates their commitment to help White Earth remember, for the music of the hymns has been part of the conscious cultural construction of community. After the 1980s, there are emerging signs of renewed pride in Anishinaabe identity: a growing interest in singing and dancing at powwows, in learning the language, and in understanding and practicing spiritual traditions that distinguish one as Anishinaabe and that bring one into fuller relationship with the land and the community. I wish to situate the rekindling of hymn singing at White Earth in this larger moment of cultural criticism and renewal.

THE MAKING OF THE WHITE EARTH SINGERS

Concern was growing among a loosely knit group of aging residents that White Earth village was soon to lose any leverage of cultural memory on the world. In 1983, a handful of men and women began meeting at St. Columba's on Thursday nights to sing Ojibwe hymns. With old hymnbooks, a cassette recording of a singing group from Cass Lake, and the quiet but steady direction of Charlie Aiken, a lead singer who had lived at Leech Lake, this group began to relearn (and in some cases, learn for the first time) the Ojibwe songs they had heard as younger people.

Numbers grew until seventeen, both men and women, were singing regularly on these Thursday night gatherings. Indeed, they had become some of the more vibrant gatherings in the community. Someone always brought food to the events. Anyone was welcome, and the gatherings soon included a number of Catholics, as well as the core group of Episcopalians. They began to perform as a group along with singing groups from other reservations in their Lenten journey gatherings. They began to perform at high school graduations. They began to sing at funeral wakes in the community.

On the one hand, there was nothing remarkable about the Thursday evening hymn sings. They were social affairs, opportunities to visit and share food in a place that offered few such diversions. But when we view the gatherings in light of Ojibwe approaches to music, and especially in light of how those distinctive approaches to music stood in sharper relief from other kinds of music, we can see what was at stake. The Thursday night gatherings represent value-laden choices to sing, to sing hymns, to sing hymns in the Ojibwe language, and to put into practice a belief that Ojibwe singing is appropriately a vocation—a way of life—and not simply a way of making music. The Thursday night sings represented the first step of these individuals' return to tradition to help heal a community's social and spiritual disintegration.

To appreciate more fully what this means, we must understand the singers' place in White Earth's political landscape. These seniors shared in the poverty and value system that was both responsible for and arising from their being outsiders to the official patronage network at White Earth. This shared social location, and their regular meetings around the rehearsal and performance of the music, saw to the creation of a more sustained and spirited political criticism of the status quo at White Earth. Indeed, the singers' group identity became largely tied to their leadership of a grassroots political challenge begun during the summer of 1991. The singers are not mere functions of their political affiliation, but politics does indeed shape the social constellation of, and the cultural criticism in, their music.

The singers, their families, and others in their network became increasingly politically active in the later 1980s around issues of secrecy, corruption, and accountability in the former tribal government. When Congress passed the White Earth Land Settlement Act (WELSA) in 1986, ostensibly with the endorsement of the White

Earth people, a series of extremely volatile land claims involving over one hundred thousand acres was settled for $12 million. A grassroots movement calling itself Anishinaabe Akeeng (translated variously: the people/the land, the people's land, the people of the land) challenged what its members saw as the compromising and secretive manner in which the then chairman gave the consent of the reservation to the settlement. When the tribe committed the entirety of WELSA funds to the controversial development of a casino, the movement attracted more and more followers and enlisted the support of the hymn singers, who by this time were recognized locally as something of an elders' council in White Earth village. Under their direction, and with Anishinaabe Akeeng leaders as spokespersons, several hundred White Earth enrollees organized to demand investigations into election fraud, violations of the tribal constitution in the WELSA agreement, and access to the financial and other public records of the tribe.[39] The group became known as Camp Justice, after the peaceful encampment they began on the front lawn of the tribal headquarters building in July 1991. More than sixty arrests were made that summer in a series of civil disobedience actions at the headquarters and at the casino construction site. Nearly one third of those arrested were senior citizens, most notably several of the White Earth singers.

Camp Justice was more than a protest movement. It was an experiment in putting cherished Anishinaabe values more fully into practice in the public affairs of the people. Like the Montgomery Improvement Association of the 1950s, from

The civil disobedience arrest of Marge McDonald, one of the White Earth Ojibwe Singers active in Camp Justice, a grassroots movement protesting abuses in tribal government, July 1991. (Author photo)

which its leadership drew inspiration, Camp Justice was more than a strategic coalition organized to achieve political ends. The camp was also an end in itself, a place to come for directed spiritual reflection and for experience of community. Camp Justice was something of a self-supporting village, a think tank, a language and culture project, a youth center, an entertainment complex, and a place of healing, as well as a protest camp.

At the center of the community life was a ceremonial fire, which was lit on the day of the first arrests in July and which burned continuously for over five months, well into winter. Firekeepers chosen by elders built an ironwood arbor atop the fire, and the rising heat kept animating the drying aspen boughs placed atop the arbor in a continuous rustle. When August sent its ominous thunderstorms across the Plains, the firekeepers found the hood of an old pickup truck to protect the fire from the torrents. When several camp members were visited by dreams about the fire, changes were made in the way it was kept. A coffee can of tobacco and cedar provided the community with pinches of these medicines for prayer offerings at the fire. In morning ceremonies, a pipe was lit by its coals and shared. In evening prayer circles, its coals lit the sage and sweetgrass that purified the gatherings. With the fragrance of smoldering sage still in the air, Ojibwe singers sang hymns in those evening circles around the fire.

At the height of the camp's activity in August, nightly meetings drew as many as two hundred people, and a core group of perhaps forty could be counted on to show up on a moment's notice. The camp welcomed anyone to a daily meal prior to the evening meetings. Food consistently appeared at the initiative of gracious donors, like a truckload of cantaloupe supplied by area farmers, and was prepared diligently by the women of Camp Justice. Many came simply for the meal, to listen to elders' stories or to converse in Ojibwe. Amid the smiles and laughs were more serious conversations about politics or about rethinking the tribal constitution to honor Anishinaabe decision-making structures. The camp was emphatically drug-and alcohol-free at the direction of the elders, and this boundary was broadly respected. The circle of Camp Justice worked visible transformations in a number of people's lifelong struggles with alcohol and self respect. Chronic drinkers sobered up and rose to speak publicly about matters of conscience, and re-committed themselves to serve their community. Lives were changed—some of them permanently—within that experimental community and around that ceremonial fire.

In a close community like White Earth Reservation, to take a public stand like this represents far more than anonymously attending a demonstration or a march on Washington. At that time, access to scarce jobs, educational scholarships for children, leases on tribal land, and all basic services hinged on one's relationship with White Earth's tribal government. Publicly opposing that government put all Camp Justice members and their families at considerable risk—even to the point of death threats. Indeed, people spoke of the struggles at White Earth as little short of a civil war. Ultimately, Camp Justice was challenging the United States and its systemic dishonoring of treaties, but the local faces of this system were the faces of the then federally recognized Anishinaabe leaders—some of them cousins and in-laws of the activists. Camp Justice leaders spoke of their continual struggle to subordinate personal ambitions and animosities to the interests of the community and the land.

The experimental community of Camp Justice remained encamped in protest on the grounds of White Earth Reservation Tribal Council headquarters from July through December 1991. (Author photo)

A cardinal rule of the movement was that political healing must rest on deeper social and spiritual healing. "Part of getting on track," said one organizer, "is knowing who you are." The movement tried to calibrate its political work to Anishinaabe time and Anishinaabe ways of valuing land and community. This culturally regulated process was not without its frustrations. What it gained in terms of pride of identity and resolve to take action it lost in terms of efficiency. Action plans were seldom reached when more than one hundred frustrated people would meet, having first agreed that anyone might speak their peace without interruption. Yet, more was realized in the process than would have been the case had camp leaders simply met in executive session with attorneys, since the movement maintained a conscious fidelity to Anishinaabe practices of community.[40]

The resources of ritual were integral to keeping Camp Justice on track when animosity or self-promotion threatened to prevail. Nightly circles around the fire often brought discouraging news of the day, taxing patience and stretching thin the threads that bound various families and factions together. Some even urged violent action to better command public attention to their grievances. It was at such volatile moments that hymn singing, pipe ceremonies, tobacco offerings, sweat lodges, and talking circles seemed to do their most important cultural work. Such practices carried the sharp differences and resentments that entered those evening circles to a restored sense of common purpose. What might be viewed as a narrowly political coalition of factions was constituted in such ritualized action as an Anishinaabe community.

Eight years later, people remember Camp Justice as a moment when courage prevailed and Anishinaabe community ethics were powerfully put into practice. Indeed, while federal convictions of three of the four members of the tribal council and a newly elected government better reflecting Camp Justice interests appear to be realizing many of their political aims, tensions rage today within the coalition, and many pine for the deeper sense of community engendered around that fire by song and prayer in the Ojibwe language. Memories of Camp Justice remain the yardstick by which many measure the performance of subsequent efforts at reform and the sincerity of respective commitments to the common good. Perhaps any subsequent lapses in the unity of the Camp Justice coalition only accentuate the potency of memories of the camp, its meetings, its sense of community, its prayers, and its songs.

This rather lengthy account of this movement has been necessary to fully appreciate the resonance of the singers' music today. It is as if the hours and dollars invested in Camp Justice and the way of life it sought to engender are carried along each time this group sings their songs. For those familiar with the life of struggle that culminated in the camp, the unalloyed voices of White Earth's elders singing Ojibwe hymns fans the faintly burning coals of the Camp Justice experiment.

To further place today's hymn singers in the social matrix of White Earth, I turn to the stories of their individual lives. In so doing, I hope also to extend the notion that singing performances are about so much more than the music and texts of the hymns. "I hear so much beyond what they are saying," one community leader remarked, "and that's what the elders give to our people: so much more than they are saying." The idea could be applied justly to music making as well. In light of distinctively Ojibwe approaches to song, the authority of their performance issues less from the tone, shape, and quality of their sound object than from the lives they lead. In telling about the lives of eight singers, I will attempt nothing more ambitious than to sketch details that indicate the breadth and texture of life experience that suffuses their singing with soul. This chapter will then conclude with some reflections about their life together as singers, elders, and cultural critics.

Josephine Degroat

In 1999, in her seventies, Josephine is having the time of her life—not that her life is easy, but because she finds adventure in living for others. Josephine was raised speaking Ojibwe. Her grandfather and his wife were from Gull Lake, part of the original settlement of White Earth in 1868. Josephine grew up Catholic, although her Gull Lake relatives had a strong history with the Episcopalian mission. She remembers families like the Big Bears who took on the responsibility of singing at wakes.

In late summer her family would board horse and carriage for their ricing camp on the boggy reaches of the Wild Rice River. There it was her job to gather firewood for the parching fires and "dance the rice" in barrels in order to separate the grain from the chaff. Her voice conveys the warmth of the memories as she recalls moccasin games, stories, and "singing Indian" at ricing camp. She is grateful for an interested ear. She wants young people to ask more questions about ricing camps and other traditions, and she wants elders to volunteer more knowledge of old ways.

Josephine's accent bespeaks the Ojibwe language of her early upbringing. As a girl, she attended the Catholic boarding school in White Earth village. It was here, presumably, that her original language was displaced by English, although she does not share the deep resentment for St. Benedict's felt by many others. The children who had problems with the school, she says, were those who had no discipline. Evidently for Josephine, the discipline of the school was not unlike the discipline of her home life. On the contrary, she speaks fondly of her experience with the nuns and, until recently, visited one of her elementary schoolteachers.[41] When the tribal council recently ordered the shell of the old brick building to be burned down as a monument to bad memories of missionization, Josephine was incensed. She spoke about that council's untrustworthy motives, implying the council wanted simply to glean good press coverage. For Josephine, the building was a monument to memories good as well as bad.

She married a man of Dutch and Oneida heritage. For more than thirty years, they farmed land in a community off the reservation, where she became used to all kinds of nonnative friends and neighbors. After her husband's death, Josephine took full-time care of her husband's close friend, who was suffering from Alzheimer's Disease with little support from his own family. Pitying him, she took him into her home.

His death brought an unprecedented freedom. She still takes care of several sets of grandchildren, but recent years have given her a chance to travel and indulge her curiosity for new people, places, and ideas and to nourish her spiritual life. Each August, she joins several thousand Catholic native elders who convene at a different reservation to honor the blessed Kateri Tekakwitha, a beatified seventeenth-century Mohawk woman.

For Josephine, travel with the singers of Camp Justice brings adventure and camaraderie. It also provides a structure for her reentry into the community and for the exercise of leadership. Josephine does not wear her politics on her sleeve, but she does keep close watch of where her community is going and she was demoralized by her sense of what the tribal leadership in the early 1990s was doing. On her sixty-eighth birthday, Josephine was jailed for civil disobedience along with the other women singers. She said very little the day of that arrest. In a language that her community clearly understood, she chose instead to speak through her conduct.

Josephine's old station wagon often shuttled back and forth from Camp Justice that summer, bringing large pots of wild rice soup or a "hot dish." For years thereafter, that same blue wagon was the Ojibwe singers' most precious resource. Whether or not her vehicle was running on a given day could determine whether the singers would make it to a wake. In any event, Josephine is the one often contacted when a family wants the singers to perform at a wake. Out of her basement, Josephine runs a clearinghouse for clothing donations from the Twin Cities. She scrutinizes each incoming piece and matches it up with those Camp Justice people who she thinks might best use it. Her attention can be trained on her guests as they visit over coffee and fry bread, but her hands will be busy tearing up material from old dresses and tying the scraps together for oval area rugs and quilts. She either gives them away to visitors or brings them to the senior center for fundraisers. As with her cooking, making the most out of a little is much more than a matter of necessity; it is an art.

Josephine's economy has an aesthetic and moral force that is rooted in her Anishinaabe heritage.

Josephine's spirituality observes few political boundaries. A small basin of holy water and a portrait of Pope John Paul II greet the visitor upon entry to her house. On her walls also hang portraits of Indian leaders and bundles of sage, and the famous print of a gaunt man offering pious thanks over a scrap of bread. She eagerly shows me a cable television Bible study show she watches each morning in which a man with a Southern accent explicates the end times prophesied in the Book of Revelation. For Josephine, evangelical, Catholic, Episcopalian, and Ojibwe traditions all can be put together to good use, perhaps like the various fabrics she tears and braids to make an oval rug. Josephine is not one to reduce such things as the spiritual life into propositions and words. Her eloquence resides in actions—in making quilts and foods, in giving them away, and in voting with her body when she thinks it time to take a stand. She is highly critical of what she thinks the Shooting Star Casino does to those who lose their earnings there and to those who profit thereby. On principle, Josephine does not go into the casino herself. But she does collect the plastic buckets used to hold slot machine coins. She likes to store rendered lard in them.

Josephine cherishes opportunities to sing "Ojibwe songs." Disuse, and perhaps a felt embarrassment as a result, has held her back from speaking Ojibwe regularly. Josephine nonetheless understands what she hears and is making a pronounced effort to share it with her granddaughters. When she heard Larry Cloud Morgan praying in the language, or when she hears the elders sing the hymns, Josephine says it makes her "feel just good." As part of her renewed commitment, she falls asleep each night to Ojibwe language sermon tapes that she received as a Christmas present from Larry. "Those tapes are all in Ojibwe," she tells me over the telephone, with a pride so sincere that plain language alone can convey it.

Ethelbert Vanwert

Like Josephine, Ethelbert credits faith with having brought her through a difficult life to a place where she can serve her community as an elder and singer. Born deaf, Ethelbert tells of the ridicule she endured as a child and a resulting poor sense of self-esteem. She evokes the felt imprisonment of deafness in religious terms: She would labor to get her children dressed in clean clothes and ready for church at St. Columba's each Sunday morning, and yet hear not one word of the sermon. Some years later, Ethelbert was told her hearing could be surgically restored. She relates how her second husband by thirty some years of common law drove her from the hospital straight to a place where a brook flows between two lakes. He wanted the sound of running water to be among the first sounds she would hear. Ethelbert's uncommon commitment to Ojibwe singing today perhaps stems from this fresh appreciation for the gift of sound.

Although her way of life today indicates an upbringing steeped in the subsistence and communal ethics of the Anishinaabe, Ethelbert was not raised speaking Ojibwe. In earlier years, Ethelbert drank, but now she can speak proudly of more than thirty years of sobriety. Like so many other elders at White Earth, she knows how difficult is the struggle with alcohol—or more precisely the struggle with historical forces of racism, landlessness, and poverty of which alcoholism is more symptom than cause.

Whether because of Ethelbert's hearing impairment, of her family's basic cultural orientation, or because of an earlier sense of unworthiness in her struggle with alcohol, much of what she knows about Ojibwe traditions she learned late in life. A role as an Ojibwe singer has given shape to much of this development as a traditional person, both in terms of learning language and in terms of assuming a public role as elder.

In 1994, Ethelbert was honored with a jingle dress, a woman's dancing dress decorated with 365 cones crafted from the metal lids of snuff tins, each cone marking a prayer made by its maker. At White Earth, such a gift can be a powerful expression of community confidence in the path that a particular individual is walking. The Jingle Dress dance itself is said to have come to the people long ago through a woman's vision for how to bring healing to an ailing community. Tears streamed down Ethelbert's cheeks as Josephine presented the dress on behalf of the other singers. She dances once again at powwows.

If Ethelbert's home feels stable, it is because of an enormous investment of energy and prayer on her part. Ethelbert keeps track of trouble on the reservation through a police radio scanner, constantly worried that she will find news of people she cares deeply about through this impersonal medium. Ethelbert cherishes the adventures, the travels, and the unflinching support she gets from the Ojibwe singers. She seems ever ready to rise to the occasion of community leadership. When the singers perform at wakes, it is often Ethelbert who stands on behalf of the other singers to speak words of condolence. For Ethelbert, given the years of drinking and brokenness in her past, the respect she receives today as an Ojibwe singer and as an elder come to her as something of a surprise. To realize that her opinions matter, that people stop and listen when she speaks, to know that her wisdom is worthy of attention alongside that of schooled tribal officials—this is part of the healing of Ojibwe singing.

Juanita Jackson

Though a grandmother herself, Juanita is one of the younger singers in the group and is dearly loved for the special care she shows the elders. Lulu, as she is known by friends and family, is a jovial soul. Despite the lack of employment at White Earth, she moved back to the reservation from the Twin Cities in the 1980s. Her husband worked many years during the week at a lumberyard in Minneapolis, commuting to White Earth on weekends. This has been a trying arrangement to be sure, but the partnership gives Lulu the freedom she needs to work and to serve the community, as well as her family. Lulu played an active role in the Camp Justice movement, but she was hired shortly thereafter to work security at the Shooting Star Casino. Some criticized her for it, but most sympathized that it was the only way she could make ends meet on the reservation.

Lulu was raised in a Catholic family with a strong orientation to living in an Anishinaabe way. Schooling and living in Minneapolis for many years makes her one of the more cosmopolitan singers, but she remains firmly rooted in the value system of her upbringing. With strong woods sense, she picks and applies swamp tea and other traditional medicines. Although she was not raised speaking Ojibwe fluently, Lulu does understand a good deal of the spoken language and is grateful for the chance to work closely on the songs with those elders who are fluent.

Along with Josephine's wagon, Lulu's car is the official transportation of the White Earth singers, and she has consistently spent valuable leave days to ensure that the elders could perform at wakes. Although a reliable and intelligent employee, such short notice leave-takings often aggravated casino managers, and may, along with her Camp Justice ties, have cost her the job after four years. But Lulu's priorities were clear: transporting the singers—literally with her car, figuratively with her sense of humor—is a commitment to community which Juanita takes very seriously.

Jack Potter

The oldest singer, Jack Potter, lives alone in an old blue trailer house on the edge of White Earth village. His couch, chair, and rug are well worn, but his living room is meticulously neat, and an occasional whiff of Copenhagen tobacco rounds out the atmosphere of an aging man leading a simple life in a spare room furnished more with vivid memories of life on the land than with pleasantries of middle-class homes. He keeps track of the goings-on of humans and creatures of White Earth through the two large windows that look out on the bird feeder in front of his trailer home and onto the marsh across the street. As Jack tells stories, his eyes track an occasional reservation dog trotting down the road. Screeching tires remind him of the alleged drug deals and parties that transpire across the street and trouble his rest in his own home.

Jack seldom likes to travel far from home. Unlike the others, this is not rooted in a fear of losing his home to vandalism or other forces of reservation chaos. It is rather a profound appreciation for place. A one-time logger, most of his life has been spent on the land, most of his schooling in the woods. Raised in an Ojibwe-speaking family in White Earth village, Jack attended the government school. While he joined others of his generation in speaking English, he never lost his facility with Ojibwe. He converses regularly with his friend Punkin, although he seldom speaks Ojibwe publicly. Presumably this is a gesture of respect so as not to alienate non-speakers, but it could also arise from some residual shame driven into people of his generation over the years.

A Catholic, Jack warmly recalls warm summer nights as a boy when the doors of the Catholic community hall were flung wide open and the older people would sing the Catholic hymns. "All night long," he says, "all night long they would sing—those old people long ago, they sounded just good." Jack remembers both a Catholic and a Protestant group of singers in White Earth when he was a youngster, but his descriptions of the music do not imply a sharp division between the two. Along with

Punkin and their lead singer, Jack was part of the original group of Thursday night singers. He proudly wears a black jacket on the back of which is printed "White Earth Ojibwa Singers" and carries an Ojibwe hymnbook in his back pocket wherever he travels.

In the years that I have known him, Jack has allowed his snow-white hair to grow longer and longer, a sign perhaps of an emboldened embrace of his identity as an Anishinaabe elder. Now in his eighties, Jack has taken up dancing once again and appears at powwows throughout northern Minnesota. This is no small feat, given that powwows typically involve eight or more hours of dancing each day. "I always honor the elders when I dance," Jack says as he describes a gesture he makes with his eagle feather while dancing, "yours, mine, it makes no difference, I honor them all." He says he learned to dance "in a spiritual way" from some "old people" when he was nine or ten out in South Dakota. In 1996, he was in the hospital for the first time in his life for knee surgery. A nephew discouraged him from taking the risk of surgery at his age, but Jack insisted that he wanted to continue to dance.

The circle of elders designated Jack as the keeper of a sacred staff that was made by a carver to honor the work of the White Earth Ojibwe singers and to bring spiritual strength to their singing and justice work. To be a keeper of such a piece is an honor and a responsibility. The designation implies and calls for a level of integrity in one's dealings and responsibility with how the staff is used in public. Jack carries the staff when he dances to honor the elders and to represent the work of Camp Justice. Unlike a ceremonial staff that tribal officials had previously displayed on a casino wall, the staff that Jack keeps is not visible when one walks into his house.

Punkin Hanks

Jack's best friend is a large man whose dark glasses and measured speech lend him an imposing presence. As one comes to know Punkin, though, and hears his story, one finds a gentle man who takes his role as an Anishinaabe elder very seriously. Punkin was born to a large family well known for its historic involvement with lay and clerical leadership of St. Columba's Episcopal Church. He spoke Ojibwe until he began school. Beginning in the 1950s, Punkin worked his way on the railroads to the West Coast; he tells stories of these travels with great pride, a pride that is as invested in his decision to come back to White Earth as it is in his worldly experiences. On his return to White Earth, he supported his children working seasonally in logging and the sugar beet industry. At one time, he drove a bus for the tribe and served as a leader of some reservation youth programs. Today, Punkin runs an extended household of children and grandchildren. He cherishes his role in their upbringing.

He feels that a political turnaround at White Earth must begin with the healing of the community, which, in turn, must rely on spiritual forces. Punkin had long been a member of St. Columba's vestry and for many years served the church as sexton. He was among the original singers who began to meet Thursday evenings, and has been one of the principal singers ever since. The other singers honored Punkin in the summer of 1994 by designating him keeper of a drum that was dedicated to their work. Steeped as he is in the tradition of the drum, Punkin embraced the responsibility along with the privilege. Punkin and the elders did not take their drum and staff lightly, instead looking to such symbols as the appropriate basis for renewal and political change. Punkin, too, has grown his jet-black hair longer recently and seems to wear the role of elder well. He speaks with modesty and a hint of irony that mourners will sometimes ask him to preside at wakes. A reluctance to tout himself as a spiritual leader is combined with a sense of pride in being increasingly recognized as such.

Larry Cloud Morgan

Until his death in June 1999, Larry Cloud Morgan had tried to live his life as gratefully as possible, but his life had never been an easy one. His birth mother died from complications of his birth. His mother was a Rock, an old Pine Point family with so long a history of leadership in the Episcopalian church that the community center adjacent the church is known as Rock Memorial Hall. Though Larry said her body was "waked" at the Episcopal church, his maternal grandmother, a spirited old Catholic woman, retrieved her daughter's body for burial in St. Theodore's cemetery several hundred yards away.

Larry's adoptive family lived in Minneapolis on a bricklayer's wages, but Larry spent his summers with his Ojibwe-speaking grandparents near Leech Lake. When his grandfather died, Larry remembers him being laid out on the floor in a birchbark wrap, bundled up with cedar and sage. His grandmother danced around the body all night long. When they removed his body for burial, they opened the front door, cried out in Ojibwe to capture the attention of the spirits, and snuck the body out the back window.

A love affair with books and the imagination took Larry far away through the years. On scholarship, he attended a military school for boys in Illinois. During the summers he translated for a physician who traveled by houseboat to remote native villages on the waterways of the Canadian border region. After college and graduate study, Larry settled down and worked many years at Marshall Fields in Chicago. Fluent in Spanish as well as Ojibwe and English, he lived for some years in Mexico City. Wearied by a long relationship with someone who became an alcoholic in later years, Larry returned home to Minnesota in the 1980s, earning a sufficient living with his drawings, poetry, and plays. All the while, Larry devoted most of his energy to communities in need as spokesman, activist, and counselor.

In 1984, Larry was arrested for civil disobedience—"divine obedience," he called it—after he and three other Roman Catholic peace activists broke into a nuclear missile silo that lay within earshot of an elementary school near Kansas City. After serving four years in federal prison for the action, Larry earned a reputation in Minnesota as a spiritual leader and sought-after spokesperson on native issues. His willingness and ability to build bridges with nonnative communities rendered him ever in demand.

Larry's spiritual leadership crossed many boundaries. He was not a Midewiwin priest. Neither was he known as an herbalist healer or a medicine man. Raised as a Catholic, Larry contemplated the priesthood but never took orders. Yet Larry's fundamental commitment, consistent in his mind with Anishinaabe spirituality, was to the irreducible mystery of the divine, and this commitment carried him more deeply into both Christian and Ojibwe traditions. Perhaps it was because of his flair for ritual choreography, his command of a number of traditions, and his willingness to suggest their intersections that he was increasingly called on to perform pipe ceremonies, naming ceremonies, weddings, wakes, and funerals. On Ojibwe terms, to be recognized in this way is credential enough to become a spiritual leader.

To guard his privacy, Larry no longer kept phone service at his Twin Cities apartment and his little cottage on the Leech Lake Reservation. But in nine years, I never knew him to turn down a request to pray beside a hospital bed or to ride the bus to one of the northern reservations to preside at a wake or burial. He took very seriously the responsibility to share gifts freely with others, which the community expected of him as a spiritual person. The ability to go back and forth from reservation to artist's life in the Twin Cities was something that distinguished Larry. He was as comfortable sipping boiled fish soup in a White Earth kitchen as he was dining on tarragon chicken in a Manhattan penthouse. He sang Ojibwe hymns. He also listened to Pavarotti, Mahalia Jackson, and Jimmy Buffett.

Larry's primary involvement with the White Earth singers began at Camp Justice in the summer of 1991. Since he lived in the Twin Cities, Larry did not sing with the elders at all of their wakes. When he was on hand, however, the singers made an honored space for him at the head of their table. His deep interest in the spirituality of Ojibwe hymn singing, and in the theology of the texts themselves, paralleled and

Larry Cloud Morgan, 1993. (Author photo).

nourished my own. Larry remained the practitioner, the poet. I remained the student of religion. But ours had been nonetheless a collaboration of styles. As I wrote this portion of the manuscript, Larry awaited word as to whether his leg was to be amputated, a consequence of diabetes. Something compeled him to ask on the telephone how *I was doing*.

Erma Vizenor

When she was but a young child, Erma Vizenor was given an Anishinaabe name, which translates as "Woman Who Stands up for the People." A more prescient name could hardly have been given. She is an educator and theorist on Native American educational issues and the former principal of the school in Pine Point. She was one of the three main spokespersons of Camp Justice—at once tactician, diplomat, and spiritual leader of a movement trying to unite a divided people. Erma holds a doctorate in education from Harvard. She is deeply involved in the life of the Breck Memorial parish in Pine Point and is constantly on call to help out needy families with financial assistance, advocacy, counseling, and funeral arrangements. She is a mother of two grown daughters, as well as a recent grandmother, and she

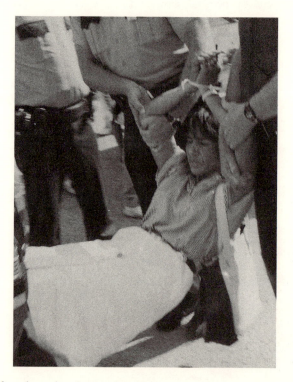

Erma Vizenor when the author first met her, being arrested for Camp Justice civil disobedience, White Earth, July 1991. (Author photo)

often looks after her aging mother. As if these responsibilities are not enough, she was elected in 1997 to join the reformers of the new White Earth Tribal Council as its secretary-treasurer. She sits on the board of the National Council of Churches and is heavily involved in Native American ministry issues with the national Episcopal church. I often wonder what holds her together. For Erma, it is no mystery: prayer, faith, fellowship, and Ojibwe hymns are sources of replenishing strength.

Like her cousin Larry Cloud Morgan, Erma Vizenor's schooling and cosmopolitan life experiences off the reservation distinguish her from many singers. But like other singers, hymn singing for her appears to be an anchor of Anishinaabe spirituality and a versatile spiritual resource in her own work for justice. Ojibwe hymns have been part of Erma's life since she was a little girl. Erma's mother came from a Pine Point family with long-established ties to both Episcopalian leadership and traditional values. Her mother was raised speaking Ojibwe, and I am told first learned English through English translations of the Ojibwe hymns. Though poor in financial terms, Erma's upbringing was rich in Anishinaabe tradition and identity.

Erma's doctoral thesis relied on in-depth, culturally informed interviews with elders who have themselves maintained a strong Anishinaabe identity in spite of the assimilative experience of the boarding schools.[42] As the tribal council's secretary-treasurer, she has similarly committed herself to incorporating the knowledge of elders more directly into tribal decision making. In both cases, it is her challenge to take the counsel of the elders seriously and to translate it into programmatic terms. Erma's ideas follow the trajectory of Ojibwe hymns and the lives of those who sing them. She aims to restore to educational institutions and programs the spirituality that has been so central to the survival of the people, an element that she finds missing in most attempts to educate native people to live successfully in two worlds. She tells her talented daughters that what they specifically choose as a career does not matter to her. She simply asks, "whatever you choose to do, do it for the people."

Erma's work as White Earth's secretary-treasurer has consumed much of her energy, as did the untimely death in 1998 of her husband, Dallas, but she draws sustenance and energy from her spiritual life and from the community of elders, children, and now grandchildren, in which that spiritual life takes shape.

WHITE EARTH SINGERS AS ELDERS

The role that Ojibwe hymns play in the making of each singer is elemental to a larger narrative of their (re)making of Ojibwe singing. Through singing, these people have become more fully Anishinaabe, assuming important roles as elders. The practice of singing, because it gives voice to their lives, has become a medium for a strong if gentle cultural critique.[43] Behind, beneath, and around the sung syllables that give voice to those hopes and fears, and which distinguish Ojibwe singers socially, is a cultural authority specific to their role as elders in the community. A newcomer to native gatherings is often impressed by how frequently (s)he hears such phrases as "honor the elders" or "respect your elders." At White Earth, such notions are organizing ideals for a marked valuation of old people and their particular kind of seasoned knowledge.

Ojibwe elders have long been the primary stewards of medicinal, spiritual, and cultural knowledge. Elders tell stories of Trickster and of the animals and of their own life experiences. Elders continue to play a lead role in the upbringing and socialization of the young. Indigenous structures of decision making also rest upon the firm footings of a community's elders. Although the authority of elders was certainly challenged and contested at times, Ojibwe tradition teaches that the wisest decisions for the community will be made by its elders and the community will be served best if authority is dispersed among circles of elders. Hard-earned life wisdom, and a fitting emphasis on spiritual reflection, ensures that decisions will be less motivated by bravado or self-interest and more respectful of nonhuman relations.

Among Ojibwe people, eldership is determined less by biological age or office than by community recognition. Among a child's first lessons is the code of etiquette stressing deference to one's elders. Elders are to speak whenever they wish and to do so without interruption. Their needs, along with those of children, are to take first priority. They are to be served first at feasts. If an immediate family is not forthcoming, others in the community are to ensure that an elder has adequate supplies of split wood for heating, a plowed driveway, and a ride to the clinic.

Although respect for elders has a long history, it does not simply issue forth as a "given" of Ojibwe heritage. The more interesting question to ask regarding the hymn singers is what it might mean to hear an elder's voice at this particular moment in history. The voice of an elder carries this extra charge in at least three ways. First, the rapid disappearance in this generation of language, medicinal lore, traditional stories, songs, and subsistence practices accentuates the role of elders as custodians of language and culture. Second, those who would navigate the treacherous waters of widespread violence and substance abuse have an acute need for moral examples of those who have survived reservation conditions to attain old age. Like other elders and the community they serve, many of the singers have known and endured real hunger, brokenness, and drinking. Violence at White Earth compels a need for stability that elders often represent. Finally, to respect elders today is to observe a code of behavior that is highly charged with Anishinaabe identity precisely because its value orientation stands in contrast to Anglo-American societal norms. Most aging Americans have been relegated to the margins of political decision making, economic production, and the socialization of children. These wider societal norms are not simply external forces: they are written into federally recognized political structures that concentrate tribal decision making in elected individuals and that organize authority hierarchically. Standards of bureaucratic efficiency and credentialed schooling often undermine any decision-making authority of elders, even while respect for elders' authority is encouraged in the private realm.

REHEARSAL AS WELL AS PERFORMANCE: BECOMING ANISHINAABEG

In Ojibwe, one does not address an assembly "Ladies and Gentleman," but as *Anishinaabedoog*—"those who *would be* the people." Implicit is the idea that to be Anishinaabe involves a lifetime of striving to become Anishinaabe. Consistent with *bimaadiziwin*, to grow old is as much a spiritual, cultural process as it is a biological one. Becoming a community elder is the culmination of a life spent learning to live in harmony with the circular movement of all that is.

This cultural process stands in marked contrast to the cultural product of the dominant American image of "the Indian." To the degree that this image carries cultural authority, the matter of "being Indian" is an essentialist one. A "real Indian" is supposedly one who lives beautifully close to nature, in harmony with it, who thinks and speaks from a precontact worldview, and so on. Perhaps most insidious about this essentializing idea of the Indian is its impossibility. Cultural critics have identified that the image is so compelling in part because it elevates Indianness so beyond reach that it denies the possibility of there being any "real Indians" anymore.[44]

The process also stands in relief to conventional views of rituals as performances of ritual competence. In her study of memory in a Melanesian culture, Deborah Battaglia appeals to Sabarl Islanders' own theories for how culture should be performed, taught, and learned. Although the Sabarl occupy an island home on the other side of the globe, there is a useful analogy to be made between White Earth elders and their singing and the Sabarl conviction about "the impossibility of fixed or stable knowledge."[45] When Sabarl elders are about to tell stories from their rich traditions, Battaglia observes, they usually begin by announcing, "we are only rehearsing," a disclaimer from any arrogance that they perform from a position of perfect cultural mastery.[46]

In the scheme of *bimaadiziwin*, cultural and ritual knowledge is accrued in the course of the life cycle. Indeed, one dictionary links the English term "knowledge" to the Ojibwe term *gikendamoozhiwewim*, "imparts knowledge to him/her as he/she grows up," stressing a socially regulated process rather than product.[47] The White Earth singers provide an excellent example of such a process. Their singing of hymns, especially because learned or relearned, is no mere eruption of deep cultural competence. Instead, each performance is, in important respects, a rehearsal, and each rehearsal a performance.

Today's singers were raised with very traditional land-oriented values of community, generosity, gratitude, humility, and respect, but requirements for survival have brought them away from the Ojibwe language and the distinctive practices of their culture. With today's ardent renewal of interest in dancing, drumming, language, and culture, more and more young people turn to this generation of elders for teaching and guidance. While thoroughly generous with the stories and wisdom they do share, some of today's elders at White Earth feel their knowledge of traditions, ceremonies, and language is incomplete or inadequate to the task.

Ojibwe singing has provided one way for these senior citizens to surmount their perceived limits of schooling, language, and community status to *become* elders. Each public appearance is another step in the singers' coming into their role as Anishinaabe elders. For some singers, this involves exercising their language skills as a means of augmenting their contribution to community healing. For others, it means learning Ojibwe in the first place. For younger singers, singing puts them in closer touch with the gentle strength of the elders who sing. For some, Ojibwe singing becomes a vehicle for getting away from the pressure of the immediate household, a forum for public speech and community leadership, and an opportunity for fellowship, travel, and, occasionally, adventure.

Audrey Jackson, Larry Cloud Morgan, Josephine DeGroat, and Marge McDonald singing in Central Park, while attending a Clergy and Laity Concerned conference in New York City, July 1992. (Author photo)

In this light, the White Earth singers are not to be understood as mere "mouth-pieces of tradition" but as agents in a ritual process through which hymnody clears a space for the work of becoming Anishinaabe elders, even while it creates the space for collective memory at charged moments in the life of the community. Here we see the circular process by which ritualization and ritual mastery constitute one another. Catherine Bell describes this process to correct our "habit of thinking about ritual as an existing entity." Instead, Bell urges us to consider how it is persons who become "ritualized," who in turn "deploy schemes of ritualization" in order to transform or nuance experience to make it "more coherent with the values of the ritualizing schemes."[48]

In light of the kind of staid, instituted roles and forms usually associated with ritual traditionalism, it is perhaps ironic that one of the celebrated singers of the White Earth group was a nonnative man in his thirties. Bruce Engebretson grew up a member of a prominent family in the area. He had become actively involved with the life of Camp Justice in the summer of 1991 and continued to support the White Earth community. An interest in the language and in helping the Ojibwe singers had brought him into a fairly regular participation in their performances at wakes. The other elders speak endearingly about Bruce's contribution to their work as singers. They see in him a genuine desire to learn the language and contribute to the life of the community. "He sings those Ojibwe songs good," smiles Josephine.

Until 1999, Bruce worked and lived in the nearby town of Detroit Lakes, but he considered himself equally if not more at home among the people of White Earth. He bought a small house on the edge of the reservation and, consistent with Anishinaabe generosity, opened his door to those who needed a place to stay. Bruce was especially helpful for the singers because he had a car and could provide the elders with reliable transportation to wakes.

At one wake, several elders inquired whether I was "that Bruce" that they had heard so many good things about, only to be disappointed that I was not. Later, in the absence of Charlie Aiken, the singers looked to Bruce as lead singer to choose the first songs and tunes, thus honoring his commitment to the way of life embodied in the music.

The warmth of the singers' acceptance of Bruce is revealing of the nature of the boundaries surrounding this ritualized performance. Unlike some essential sui generis action of ritual, Ojibwe hymn singing involves a surprisingly low barrier to entry and does not seem to hinge on cultural competence. According to the logic of hymn singing practice, because any performance is also a rehearsal, Bruce's presence is welcome as an enrichment, not a dilution, of the healing effect.

THE "TRADITIONAL" AND THE PRACTICE OF CULTURAL CRITICISM

Consistent with distinctively Anishinaabe approaches to music, the White Earth elders consider the practice of singing together to be far more than performances of sound objects. They make of the practice a vocal affirmation of a way of life that can be called a form of cultural criticism because it stands in such sharp contrast to the wider culture that surrounds their singing.

There are marked parallels here with Anishinaabe attitudes toward drum groups. Archie Mosay, an elder from the Mille Lacs community to the south, remarked on the ideal way of life surrounding a drum society's music: "Treat people good if you have a drum. Don't talk back to others. Don't retaliate when folks slap [you] up." He spoke about putting on powwows and feasts for the drum, with an emphasis on feeding everyone who comes as a way of honoring the drum.[49] According to this vision, the well-being of a drum and, in turn, the well-being of people in proximity to the drum, depends on the quality of social relations obtaining around the instrument. As Mr. Mosay put it, much of the challenge today concerns putting aside factional differences, animosities, and the impulse to retaliate against others, especially Anishinaabeg. The songs of drum groups at powwows, community gatherings, and political protests provide a shared, embodied experience of syncopation.

Though no drum helps keep time, hymn performances also help constitute community. The texture of elders' voices in unison can establish over the course of several hours a shared experience of Anishinaabe time. Since food is inevitably shared at gatherings involving hymn singing, that practice of pooling resources and meeting community needs is thick with implicit associations of Anishinaabe survival past, present, and future. So too is the seriousness with which Ojibwe singers, like drum societies, take their responsibility as stewards of a tradition. It is a point of pride that the White Earth singers do not turn down a request to sing. Punkin remembers even piling in the cars for a wake in Naytahwaush, some twenty miles away, on a night when the mercury dropped to forty-five degrees below zero. Given that the car may have logged more than two hundred thousand miles, that spells commitment.

Whether it be drum music or hymnody, music-making of this distinctively Ojibwe kind is thought to be integral and integrating to community life. If, as some prominent elders teach, survival as native people depends on whether the Anishinaabe can act as one again, with all the social, economic, political, and spiritual ramifications entailed therein, then the work of the Ojibwe singers can be understood as a vocal effort to bridge the factional tensions so present at any gathering.

In fact, social tensions at White Earth are often played out on the cultural field of defining what it means to be "traditional." Indeed, however they might choose to live their lives, few White Earth people would consider themselves to be anything but traditional. To capture the fundamental operative meaning of the term for the White Earth singers, I think one can justly focus on an economic ethic that places the needs of the many before the desires of the few, and which affirms simple, subsistence living in respectful balance with the land. This understanding ought to be seen in its rightful contrast to the more conventional sense of the term as referring to the mastery of certain fixtures of cultural content deemed in some essential sense to constitute Ojibwe belief and practice. In this sense, to be traditional would be to renounce Christianity, to know the entire cycle of Trickster stories, to master a repertory of dance steps and dream songs, and to speak the language fluently. A person may count as a traditional person on these terms, and still not be recognized as putting fully into practice that lifeway understood as essentially Ojibwe.

This way of being, or rather becoming, traditional stands in daring contrast to a folklorized conception of the traditional that is also operative for significant numbers of White Earth people. A folklorized sense of the traditional focuses less on economic ethics and commitments to community than on the trappings of Anishinaabe culture, although I ought to use the term *trappings* carefully. From the perspective of these people, of course, such markers of native identity are hardly mere trappings: They are the cultural media by which identities are negotiated in a difficult racist world. And yet, according to some Anishinaabe people, including most singers, an insistence on the precise details of a ceremony or doctrinal orthodoxy can seem overly brittle in the context of an oral tradition that allows some measure of change in response to shifting circumstances.

A story of a recent controversy can serve to illustrate. In the fall of 1995, the board of a local museum made arrangements through informal networks to return a number of human remains held in their collections for disposal by the White Earth singers as a circle of elders. For the singers, the quiet, unheralded burial of the bones seemed the most respectful way to proceed, and they planned a ceremony that would bury the remains with prayers and Ojibwe songs well out of the public limelight. The arrangement was blocked, though, by a tribal employee who claimed that, under the 1990 Native American Graves and Protection Act, tribal governments alone were responsible for repatriating human remains. A number of the singers found the motives of the council's interference suspect, seeing them as perhaps interested in turning the quiet burial of the remains into a press event. In an era when press release traditionalism seems to carry the day, understatement seems key to the singers' practice of cultural criticism. To appreciate the fuller force of their message, then, we must become better attuned to the idiom in which they articulate "the traditional" in practice. Let us look briefly to three domains in which the singers mark off "the traditional" in this way.

First, consider the domain of music. I have already discussed the accentuation of boundaries between hymn singing and other musics as one instance in a folklorization of Anishinaabe culture. Some at White Earth came to consider the hymns narrowly to be "white" or "Christian" music in stark contrast to "traditional" Ojibwe music. The lives of the White Earth singers, however, suggest no such accentuated boundary between Ojibwe hymns—remember they are usually called "Ojibwe songs"—and other Anishinaabe musics. While the singers do not consider the hymns to be like the dream songs, vision songs, traveling songs, and others performed with drums, each singer nonetheless participates fully in the musical life of these other distinctively Anishinaabe musics. Because each was raised on the reservation, each is competent in the cultural world of drum-oriented music. Some, like Larry, Punkin, and Jack, sang with drum groups as younger men.

What distinguishes this group of hymn singers from some other singing groups is its willingness to embrace both repertories—Ojibwe hymns and drum music—in the wakes, funerals, and other gatherings at which it performs. I am told that the matri

Jack Potter, Ethelbert Vanwert, Charlie Aiken, and Punkin Hanks beneath a ceremonial arbor at a feast for a traditional drum that was given the White Earth singers, Ball Club, Minnesota, August 1993. (Author photo)

arch of the family singing group that sings at wakes from Leech Lake to the Twin Cities would not enter the room of a wake until the drum had been removed. In 1993, the singers were honored with the presentation of a drum, and they selected Punkin as its keeper. The singers themselves have not played the drum. Consistent with widespread practice, younger people are asked to sing with such drums on those occasions deemed appropriate by the keeper.

So, too, with dancing: Even those White Earth singers in their seventies and eighties are among the more energetic elders dancing at community powwows. Native people today distinguish between "contest powwows," in which singers and dancers register and receive cash awards for regalia and performances, and "traditional powwows," in which all singers and dancers do so with expectations only of being fed at the late afternoon feast each day. The White Earth elders, while not eschewing contest powwows altogether, prefer to dance in the traditional ones, emphasizing that dancing is not an entertainment or money-making affair but a meaningful expression of honoring elders, peoplehood, and prayer.

A second way in which the singers inflect "the traditional" as cultural critics concerns the appropriate posture toward economic production, acquisition, and consumption. If economic success is measured by the standards of acquisitive, capitalist American culture, none of the White Earth singers is finding it—or looking for it. For the singers, economic hardship can reflect certain crucial choices made in the land of American plenty against economic, educational, and cultural assimilation. At White Earth, economic hardship can reflect value-laden choices to live outside the patronage network of the tribal council and the casino, a sign of who is paying their dues to be Anishinaabe. Many hardworking, willing, and able people choose to subsist rather than compromise what they see as their traditional values in taking such jobs or leaving the reservation for higher pay and status in the cities.

Well-being in such circumstances relies on ethics and strategies of reciprocity with food, shelter, clothing, transportation, childcare, and so on. As a result, a kind of esprit de corps obtains among people of White Earth village in their survival. To remain on the reservation, to make the most of little, to waste nothing, and to share unconditionally is to express a sincere commitment to land and people of the land that stands out from the norms of American society.

By no means do I wish to valorize poverty or suggest that the Ojibwe singers themselves do. It is a brutal, often violent, circumstance that they are committed to transcending as a community. Nor do I mean to suggest that the singers think of being Anishinaabe and participating in a modern economy as mutually exclusive. They direct their criticism instead to those who bracket Anishinaabe traditions of social equality, economy, and respect for the land from their implications for public conduct in the political and economic world.

A third domain in which the singers practice their cultural criticism is that of gender. Hymn singing has made it possible for the women singers to realize themselves as public leaders. Many were confined to home life in their younger days, lacking public voices and even lacking a share of economic decisions in their own households. Hymn singing has provided a structure and network for their emergence from confinement to become not simply matriarchs within extended families but also public community leaders.

Their stories are even more remarkable when viewed in contrast to the belittled role of women in American public life, for the White Earth singers embody a vision of strong women's leadership. While the lead singer in performance is typically a man, the women of the White Earth singing group are more likely to stand and make public addresses at wakes and community gatherings. Women were clearly more active in directing the work of Camp Justice. It was the women of the White Earth singers, and not the men, who spent several nights in jail for civil disobedience. To be sure, all took place with the full support of the elder men, but the men's support typically consisted in supporting from the sidelines.

Ever since hymn singing groups first appeared in the nineteenth century, women have played a central role. That they continue to do so is indeed a bold assertion of an Anishinaabe valuation of women as effective leaders in the political, cultural, and spiritual arenas. Implicit in the exercise of women's leadership among the White Earth singers is a critique of the way that official structures of political authority reflect American patriarchy in tribal governance.

RELIGIOUS FAULT LINES

Consistent with their broader cultural critique of a folklorized tradition, White Earth singers have been deliberate in their attempt to address divisive boundaries of religion in their lives and through their music. Among the divisive axes of social life at White Earth have been the observed boundaries between religious traditions. There are Christians and ardent non-Christians, some of whom would characterize themselves as "traditional" practitioners of Ojibwe religion. Among Christians, there are Catholics and Episcopalians. There are individuals who have departed from these historical affiliations and joined Seventh-Day Adventists, Missionary Alliance, and Pentecostal fellowships. These spiritual fault lines can run right through families. Sometimes the lines can run right through an individual's own life experiences, torn as (s)he might be between a Christian upbringing and often contentious feelings toward that Christian heritage.

To convey the volatile nature of this boundary, a metaphor of fault lines is apt, I think, because religious boundaries do not themselves appear to be the cause of the divisiveness but are rather weak spots in the solidity of the community, historical arenas of stress and strife, and areas of weakness in the face of the deeper tectonic forces of racism, land base degradation, and political and economic exploitation. While the religious identities do matter as more than the mere surface features of deeper social forces, I learned from the insights of the White Earth singers themselves that religious boundaries need not be so determinative and that, in fact, it is a distinctive spiritual resource of the Ojibwe language and tradition that the fundamental mystery surrounding the sacred sources of life admits of no such boundaries.

In the next chapter, I will carry this discussion to gatherings around death. Such moments, I will argue, place these fault lines in sharpest contrast. Deaths bring people together from respective political camps and social locations. Faced with a shared sense of loss, all present are reminded of their oneness before death and are yet equally reminded of the de facto distance in their ordinary lives. Decisions about and performances of funerary practices themselves become supercharged moments of social and psychological tension, in part because of the heightened pressure to act as one family, as one people, or as one integrated human being. Because tensions can do the most damage when they are on display, the task of social remembering in and through cultural memory becomes all the more urgent in such moments.

5

MUSIC AS MEMORY

Contemporary Hymn Singing and the
Politics of Death in Native America

▲▲▲▲▲▲

While hymns today are performed in a variety of contexts, the primary work of the Ojibwe singers takes place at the funeral wakes of the community. On these occasions, the political circumstances of life at White Earth are seen in their bitterest clarity. Because so many die young and die violently, each successive wake resonates with the dispossession of history and urges collective reflection on both social and existential matters. Gatherings around death have become crossroads where the community takes stock of history and where it musters the spiritual resources to continue to act in and on that history.

A wake creates an unstable space, one that puts on heightened display the contradictions of contemporary native experience. That space calls into question the possibility of meaning on one level and the very possibility of Anishinaabe survival on the other. The music of the Ojibwe singers, however, can carry the possibility of transforming this space. Through the distinctive operations of music and language, Ojibwe hymn singing can create a shared experience of Anishinaabe time and can structure a process of collective remembering. This memory is socially integrative, though not unequivocally so. The operations of memory cannot resolve all social tensions and contradictions of experience, but in some significant respects, the practice of singing can make perseverance possible. As Erma Vizenor has remarked: "We sing in order to survive."

THE VARIETIES OF OJIBWE HYMN SINGING

Ojibwe hymns are sung in a variety of public and private settings today. What might seem the most likely setting, Sunday worship, is ironically the least significant one at White Earth. At worship services on the reservation, Ojibwe hymns are only occasionally sung, along with more standard hymns in English, and are typically accompanied by piano or organ. Though Episcopalian, Catholic, Lutheran, Pentecostal, or

Missionary Alliance congregations are seldom filled to capacity on any given Sunday, Ojibwe hymns are part of churchgoing experience for that small segment of the Ojibwe community that does attend regularly. Nonnative people also attend churches on the reservations, and in some cases comprise the majority of the congregation. One historian who vacations in northern Minnesota remembers well a service he attended at an Episcopalian church on the Leech Lake Reservation. Though the service included both English and Ojibwe hymns, he recalled to his surprise that it was mostly the nonnative congregants who sang in either language.[1]

Singing in the context of worship is distinct from the more significant tradition of Ojibwe singing that resonates further beyond the specifically Christian circles, perhaps because it is associated more directly with the music of the Anami'aajig. It is that tradition with which this chapter is chiefly concerned. This particular tradition of singing is emphatically that of the unalloyed human voice. Erma Vizenor remarks, "We don't use piano. We don't use guitar. We don't use any kind of musical instrument. Just our voices. It makes it so beautiful, because we can sing these songs any place."[2]

Quite simply, the music of White Earth's Ojibwe singers belongs wherever and whenever they choose to perform it. They bring their music to prayer meetings and social gatherings in people's homes. They bring their music to mark moments of passages in the life cycle, including school graduations, weddings, sickbeds of the ailing, and deathbeds of those nearing life's end. They bring their music to events of cultural exchange, punctuating stories of seasonal life with Ojibwe songs. After one such performance before a college audience, they called at the home of a Twin Cities native leader who was in the late stages of her battle with cancer. In one of the most moving moments of singing that has been my privilege to hear, the singers quietly took chairs around her bed, prayed, and sang Ojibwe songs until she fell asleep an hour later. In one afternoon, the same songs were exhibits of culture for a nonnative audience and a source of profound peace for a dying woman. In the summer of 1994, the White Earth singers offered a workshop on the spirituality of their music at a national assembly of Catholic native elders. In 1991, they performed at the evening circle meetings of Camp Justice, endeavoring in this manner to anchor the political agenda to a spiritual foundation. Another of the more poignant moments of singing that I experienced took place in New York City the following summer. The White Earth singers were in New York to raise support for Camp Justice. We were driving together up Third Avenue on our way to worship at Harlem's Abyssinian Baptist Church. As the affluent high-rises of the Upper East Side gave way to the dilapidated buildings and litter-strewn blocks of East Harlem, the van became hushed as the singers took in quite another New York City than they had seen earlier at the downtown tourist sites. As if out of compassion for the neighborhood, one of the women quietly began singing a hymn. As the other voices joined in, the music seemed an apt response.

I can only point from a distance to the myriad contexts in which the music of these hymns sung and hummed have affected people at White Earth. Josephine reports that, in the final years of the elderly widower who was in her care, he listened over and over to the same cassette tape of Ojibwe songs. I have heard Erma Vizenor softly hum the slow, familiar tunes of the Ojibwe hymns to help collect herself in stressful situations. After the past nine years, I sometimes find myself doing the same.

While Ojibwe hymns can impact any nook or cranny of experience of those in hymn-singing circles, the songs are known more broadly in the Minnesota Ojibwe community as a music of mourning at funeral wakes. One bright summer day when Larry Cloud Morgan and I were inside his cabin listening to a cassette of hymns, his visiting niece opened the door and said in disbelief, "Gosh, Uncle, why are you listening to that funeral music?" The hymns are known as funeral music because it is at the funeral wakes of the community that wider circles of Ojibwe people encounter the songs, and it is in this setting that the singing of hymns has been ritualized to a far fuller effect than at other community occasions.

I turn now to the example of one wake, an example to which I will return at different points in this chapter. The wake was held for the son of a friend and conversation partner whom I had come to know at Camp Justice. The circumstances were dreadful. Dan Kier's son was the victim of a brutal gang hit, shot in the chest while at a wedding reception in the Twin Cities. To support Dan and his family, I left a weekend gathering at my family's summer home on Gull Lake. My own share in the grief at Dan's loss attuned me, I believe, to the kind of healing that Ojibwe hymns can make possible. My account recalls details of the wake, not so much because I consciously observed and noted, but because the event carried such complicated power in my own experience of it. I viewed most of the events and heard most of the hymns while sitting next to Dan. My note-taking occurred two days later, back in the quiet remove of the Gull Lake house. The even safer confines of a Harvard library are where I am now gathering these details into my own narrative witness of the event.

"THAT FUNERAL MUSIC": HYMN SINGING AT A WAKE

By the time I arrived, more than thirty old cars and trucks were parked around the Rock Memorial Guild Hall adjacent to Ponsford's Breck Memorial Episcopal Church. The warm, low-angle sunlight so characteristic of early Minnesota evenings in August cast a copper glow on the neat white chapel. The guild hall was more functional, comprised of a room crowded with folding chairs and tables arranged unceremoniously in three rows running the length of the room. Still unnerved by the typical nonchalance of greetings at White Earth, where drawing attention to one's arrival or departure is considered impolite, I by-passed the fifty people assembled in the room and delivered a lasagna I had made to the women in the kitchen who were busily arranging the potluck dishes.

The presence of the body of a dead man at once changed everything and nothing in the room. Although the casket was certainly the most conspicuous sight, it was not the obvious focus of attention. A large star quilt, symbolizing the sun and given to the deceased as a blessing, was hung behind the casket. A number of flower arrangements stood on either side. Atop the casket were bundles of sage, pictures of the man's children and their mother, a buckskin medicine bag, and birchbark baskets filled with offerings of tobacco and cedar. People sometimes peered or paused in silence as they squeezed between the casket and the end of the long table on their way for more coffee, but apart from curious children, attention was seldom directed

Fixing the bell atop Breck Memorial Episcopal Church, Pine Point. (Courtesy Nick Kurzon)

specifically to the body. The man's young children played in close proximity to their mother, who received the newly arrived guests at her place near the casket.

Time seemed suspended for those in the guild hall that night. It was a time out of time, without noticeable duration, for the many who had been awake the entire night previous or for others not yet recovered from the shock of the news. Greeting my friend, I myself felt scattered, ill-situated to offer much support. Most people had pulled chairs together in clusters, or stood along the walls in conversation. Some men were standing outside around their trucks. Some were playing cards. Some were sitting alone, sipping coffee in quiet reflection. The atmosphere changed when the singers arrived about half past seven. People hushed as the seven of them, all elders, filed in, ceremoniously, and took their places at the table reserved for them in the center of the room. Perhaps the scene was like that of a jury returning to the courtroom in a high-stakes trial. Young boys and girls were beckoned to the kitchen to carry Styrofoam cups of coffee to serve the singers at their table. The singers took their time to settle in and pull out the hymn-books from back pockets or purses. Conversation tapered off, and it felt as though some subtle threshold had been crossed and the formal grieving had begun.

The first song, like each one thereafter over the next several hours, did not so much begin as emerge. There was no change in the singers' posture, no dramatic opening of the hymnbook. At some point, the voice of the lead singer could be heard with the first phrase of the chosen hymn, and the first familiar phrase gained momentum with the other voices gradually joining in. As always is their custom, the singers had opened with "Number Twenty-Five," a loose translation of "Come Holy Spirit Heavenly Dove."

Ondashan, Kichi Ochichag,
Widokawishinam,
Atoniu sagiiwewin
Ima nindeinang.

'Na eji-gotugiziyang
Oma aking ayayang;
Nin kichi bejiwimin su
Ishpiming wi'jayang.

Anawi nindinend amin
Nagumotagoyun;
Nind anamiawinan
Nonde ko takisin.

Ondashan, Kichi Ochichag,
Widokawishinam,
Moshkinaton nindeinang
Iu sagiiwewin.

On occasion, some elders join the singers at their table. This evening, the White Earth singers alone sang. Yet theirs was no performance merely directed for the benefit of an attentive audience. Though their singing stood at the center of the wake, the singers did not draw attention to their voices or actions. Songs began and ended without drama. The singers made no eye contact with the assembly, nor did they engage in informal interaction even during the feast that followed. The fact that some voices sounded quite off-key seemed of little consequence to those gathered. These were elders, not virtuosi, and this was holy work, not the stuff of applause.

It is hopelessly difficult to convey in print the haunting, plaintive texture that this and other songs have at a gathering such as this. The reader will likely have a rather fixed idea about how Christian hymns sound to the ear. But while one could eventually, like me, make out the contours of familiar European-American hymn tunes, one would have great difficulty doing so. It is not that the scales or vocal qualities are entirely non-Western, as they would be in traditional dream songs or contemporary powwow music. Some songs, like "Number Thirty-Nine," which the lead singer set to the familiar tune of "Amazing Grace" later in the evening, sound relatively more like the hymns I had known from my Presbyterian upbringing, only slowed way down to a lugubrious tempo. But in this hymn, "Number Twenty-Five," the singers placed little emphasis on meter, following instead the texture of the sounds of particular syllables. I lost the forest of the melody for the trees of each chanted sound. Indeed, the music proceeded so smoothly, swelling and ebbing so effortlessly, that it seemed to have more to do with age-old traditions of lamentation or timeless rhythms of breath itself than it did with the conventions of hymnody.

The phrasing of the sung performance often bore little relation to the lexical meanings of the phonetic transcriptions of the *Ojibwa Hymnal*. Not only were sentences and phrases mismatched to the music, but morphemes themselves were broken up and emphasized in ways that are textually awkward. For example, in the first line of this hymn, the term Kichi (*gichi*) indicates "great," but is broken into two phrases in performance:

O—n da— sha-n Ki—
Chi—O—chi-chag-

In effect, the performance sounded more like chanted series of undifferentiated sylla-bles than the setting of a text to music. Similarly, the songs themselves flowed to-gether rather seamlessly. Although pauses existed between songs, and although each had its own melody and, presumably, text, no particular song stood apart from the others. The cumulative effect created by the slow, steady, rising and falling syllables of ten or eleven songs was for me an all-absorbing one, not wholly unlike several hours of focused breathing meditation.

The singers were at times themselves so absorbed in the music that they bowed their heads and closed their eyes as they moved through the verses. The absorption of others in the room was less consistent. Sometimes the hymns seemed like back-ground music to other important activities of a wake: friends visited quietly, some of the kids drank too much red Kool-Aid and ran around outside all wound up, people approached the body to say prayers and blessings. At other times, a particularly soul-ful hymn stilled the air and focused the meditation of all in the room on what seemed to be the same still point.

After the first three hymns, Erma Vizenor rose to speak on behalf of the singers. She acknowledged that mere words could never take the pain of such occasions away, but that the elders had come to stand with them in their grief, to sing for them even if they did not know all the gathered mourners well. It turns out that the singers had come to this particular wake even though they had not been called by the family. Perhaps it was understood they would show up to support the father, a Camp Justice activist.

The singers resumed with another eleven or twelve hymns, each punctuated with quiet pauses and some by several longer breaks. Different elders rather informally as-sumed the role of selecting each subsequent hymn. Several songs were chosen by Bruce Engebretson, the nonnative man who had provided some of the singers a ride from White Earth village. Most sang from their hymnals, a number of which were proudly encased in tooled leather covers embossed with the words *Ojibwa Hymnal*. I imagine that few in the room were fluent in Ojibwe, although the degree to which others remained attentive suggested that the sung language was making some impres-sion upon them. One gospel song, "Jesus, Remember Me," was sung in Ojibwe, and others of us were encouraged to join in the chorus, which was in English:

Re—me—mber me–
Re—me—mber me–/
Je-su–s
Re-me—mber me–.

There is neither a prescribed length for performances nor an established number of hymns to be sung. Another singing group from Leech Lake reportedly sings by custom twenty songs at each wake. The White Earth group typically sings between two and three hours. As always, they closed this wake with "Number Four," "Migwech Ni Kije Manidom." All stood for the last verse—a version of the traditional Christian Doxology:

Mamoiawamada aau	Let us be thankful to that one
Wenji shawendagoziyung,	Those of us who are pitied so
Weosimind Weguisimind	That one who is Father, That one who is Son
Gaye Panizid Ochichag.	And also the Holy Spirit.

Again, the verse is sung so slowly, with each syllable extended so far, that the performance bears very little resemblance to its appearance on the page as a coherent sentence, much less an important doctrinal formulation.

Evening activities concluded with the generous but simple spread of potluck dishes. Foods of the land—wild rice, deer meat, fry bread, swamp tea—were of course there. So, too, were the other staple foods of a White Earth budget—tuna hot dishes baked with federal commodity program cheese and macaroni, bologna sandwiches on buttered white bread, and the ubiquitous Minnesota Jell-O salad. Though plain, the food was no less significant in the scheme of the wake, food being understood as a gift for which people were demonstrably grateful. People tended to eat in relative silence, savoring the food and the chance to share it. Many in the room had known real hunger. Some had perhaps come to the wake primarily for the meal.

At the request of Larry Cloud Morgan, who had been asked to join the Episcopal priest and preside over the Anishinaabe aspects of the funeral, a small sample of each traditional food was spooned onto a paper plate and served as a spirit dish on a lamp stand adjacent to the casket, though little public attention was directed to this practice. An elder offered a spoken prayer, three or four minutes long, in Ojibwe. The singers were served at their table, followed by other elders. By the time I passed through the line, I noticed with some disappointment that the dishes involving foods of the land were all but gone. Needless to say, there remained plenty of my lasagna.

The feast concluded the directed portion of the wake for the evening. Around 12:30 a.m., the White Earth singers went home, tables were folded, blankets were spread out across the floor, children were put to sleep, and all but a dozen of those closest to the deceased left to rest before the next morning's funeral, procession, and burial. This was the third wake in Pine Point at which the singers had performed that August. Yet another was to be held in the same hall two nights hence. The undertaker who does many of the funerals at White Earth estimates that of the forty or so funerals he does on the reservation in a given year, hymn singing is a prominent part of thirty-five.[3]

THE SPACE OF THE WAKE AND THE HUMAN CONDITION

Wakes are curious events. The most usual of social activities—singing, visiting, singing, and feasting—take place in the most unusual of circumstances: in the presence of a corpse. The ostensible purpose of the wake, in addition to its function as a healing gathering for survivors, is to provide a vigil through the night, a watch of support and companionship to the deceased as the soul prepares for its journey. The music, say some, is a comfort and preparation for the spirit of the deceased, as well as a ministry of song to the bereaved. For those who mourn the loss of a family member, the wake marks the first social gesture, the first public aknowledgment that a relative has died. For wider circles of the community, wakes are welcome opportunities for socializing. Most wake activities occur with little visible interaction with the body. Yet in some sense, everything that transpires in the room happens with reference to it.

What ought we to make of that body, especially given the tangible relationship so many Native American deaths have today with the history of dispossession? Robert Orsi has suggested that a dead body in such circumstances is an "unstable sig-nifier," at once demanding interpretation and denying the possibility of any satisfy-ing one.[4] Does the corpse represent the presence or absence of the deceased? Is human being ultimately more than matter that decays? Is the social body, on display through its representation in the individual's body, also subject to decay? What can we say or do in the presence of a corpse that is meaningful?

A rich literature on the anthropology of death has concentrated on the various symbolic strategies by which human communities try to contain the flood of disorder that threatens to sweep away all socially constructed foundations of meaning and order.[5] Anthropologists and historians of religion have been drawn to funerary be-liefs and practices precisely because they train the rich diversity of culturally specific responses to death on the shared human experience of it. After all, if anything can be said to be a human condition, would it not be the facticity of death? Many studies follow the central insight made by Robert Hertz that practices performed on and around the corpse affirm that death is no "mere destruction, but a transition."[6] Over time, culturally specific processes of mourning and burial dispose of the corpse, en-able the soul to take its departure, and reincorporate the society of the living in the absence of the lost member.

Those Ojibwe wakes that I have attended, though, have involved tensions that suggest that not all symbolic actions surrounding death succeed so readily in restor-ing social order and coherent meaning. To the extent that they do, they do so in a reflexive process which, in the presence of a corpse, calls into question the very pos-sibility of meaningful symbolic action or thought. Diligent attempts to sew things up, to provide meaningful closure, are left dangling in the crosswinds.

THE SPACE OF A WAKE AND WHITE EARTH CONDITIONS

Funeral wakes at White Earth are indeed spaces of such open questions. The pres-ence of the body brings unspeakable grief to the surface and calls for an evaluation of time no less than in those traditions examined in the anthropological literature on death. To be satisfactory, however, any interpretation of a White Earth wake must ensure that the discussion of meaning-making comes fully to terms with the histori-cal experience of material and cultural dispossession that inflects Ojibwe encounters with the human condition.[7] In these respects, it is necessary to take Erma Vizenor at her word when she says, "we sing to survive." Hymn singing is not merely about the possibility of symbolic life, the survival of meaning, or the survival of society but *about survival*, period. What was true of White Earth in the nineteenth century is true today: Making meaning and making do are elements of the same project.

I turn now to that context which frames Ojibwe encounters with the human condition. Wakes are, of course, intimate occasions in which a family and close friends gather to mourn, but they also are far from private events. Along with pow-wows, wakes are the principal occasions that bring wider circles of the community together. For the many White Earth members who have moved away to the Twin Cities, Chicago, or beyond for their livelihood, wakes are key moments of home-coming. Gatherings are thus often charged with the coming and going of those who move between very different worlds. In that context, families and individuals exam-ine what it means to be Ojibwe. It is not unusual for someone to return unan-nounced to the reservation after thirty-years' absence. In some cases, the bodies of people who lived entire lives away from White Earth are brought "home" for wake and burial. If an Anishinaabe person dies in the Twin Cities, she or he often will be "waked" there and then "waked" a second night on the reservation. The Catholic Indian Ministry in Minneapolis has even begun a widely subscribed program that helps grieving families afford to bury their loved ones back on the reservations. In 1994, the Miigeweyon (I am going home) Funeral Project provided more than 120 native families with financial assistance and volunteer hearse driving to reservations within four hundred miles of the Twin Cities.

The tradition of an all-night vigil with the body has deep roots in the Anishi-naabe past. Rather than emphasizing the "timelessness" of Ojibwe wakes, though, we ought to explore how Ojibwe people rework the resources of native tradition to meet concrete needs of changing times.[8] What is it that makes this a community event, especially given its place on an American scene where death is more typically priva-tized, institutionalized, and, according to one cultural historian, "denied"?[9] I suggest the answer has to do with *a politics of death*, for, at White Earth, individual deaths pose questions not just about the human condition but also about the possibility for a community's survival. Wakes, then, are not *survivals* in the shopworn anthropo-logical sense of the term—deep oases of tradition in a desert of modernity. They are themselves survival tactics—public not because they are premodern, but because the stakes are too high to be solely of private concern.

According to the Indian Health Service, nearly one third of deaths among Na-tive Americans between 1992 and 1994 took people before they reached forty-five, compared to only 11 percent among the population as a whole.[10] This is, in part, a direct result of disproportionate violence. Native Americans were roughly twice as likely to die before their midthirties.[11] Murder rates among native people run at lev-els 40 percent higher than the national average. Teenage suicide rates ran at levels nearly three times the national average.[12] A 1999 study found that while American Indians were twice as likely than the national average to be victims of violent crime, they fell victim to interracial violence at an even more disturbingly disproportionate rate. Unlike white and black victims, 70 percent of violent crimes perpetrated against American Indians involve offenders of a different race.[13]

Sometimes the violence of native deaths is less direct, more subtle, and more insidious. According to the federal government, the rate of deaths resulting from alcoholism among Indians ran almost seven times the national average between 1992 and 1994.[14] In native communities, alcoholism is understood not simply as an individual disease, but in part as a result of a history of dispossession. Deaths by cirrhosis and other chronic liver disease run at levels more than four times the national average. Accidental deaths among American Indians, especially from automobile accidents, rise to more than three times the national average.[15] Deaths by diseases often associated with poverty, poverty-related diets, and hypertension also strike native people in disturbing proportions. Age-adjusted rates of death from tuberculosis are more than five times the national average. Death from diabetes strikes at rates three times the national average. For the region's native people, age-adjusted rates of death from heart disease run nearly twice that of the national average.[16]

In each case, statistics reveal patterns of injustice that are linked to the violence of history and that are felt viscerally to be so linked in concrete moments of grief and mourning. They can be associated with the fact that in the 1990s fewer than 7 percent of the White Earth land base belongs to native people; with the fact that, after a century's effort to stamp the language out, fewer than 10 percent speak Ojibwe fluently; with the fact that unemployment and income levels below the poverty line for Indians run at nearly three times the rates the national averages.[17] Even when the wake is for someone who lived to a ripe old age, a politics of death can be tangible. Today the passing of some Anishinaabe elders is tantamount to the loss of entire libraries of knowledge. Deaths of prominent elders can thus prompt sustained reflection on how to maintain language and culture.

Wakes are held in a variety of places: gymnasiums, community centers, church basements, and in some cases still, people's homes. Wherever the place, the space of the wake is transformed by its proximity to the body, a space that confronts those gathered with the tangible history of violence and dispossession and with the distinct possibility that the community itself may not survive. This is a space of contradiction. People speak of belonging to the land, and yet the land no longer belongs to them. They speak of a strong commitment to standing up for the land, and yet they are frustrated by a general lack of political and economic power to do so. They maintain a deep respect for life, and yet they are faced with frequent reminders of how life can be wasted. Whether caused by suicide, alcohol-related accident, or diabetes, deaths are laden with a politics of history. Indeed, we might aptly think of each case as *death by dismemberment,* since land theft, assimilation policies, subversion of indigenous social structures, brokenness of self, and the loss of a loved one are widely experienced as different faces of the same protean reality of colonization.

The politics of history pervades the space of the wake by virtue of the cause of death. It also can pervade the space by making explicit the factional tensions at White Earth believed to be the bitter fruit of that history of colonization, and precisely at those moments when expectations of community concord are at their peak. If someone had been killed in a fight or died accidentally in the presence of others, grief can be joined by feelings of anger and hostility toward parties in question. Strife can surface even within families, when unrealistic hopes for accord can heighten recurrent contention among survivors or unresolved issues between a survivor and the deceased. Long-separated parents come together to mourn the children they still share. If a family member is not present at the wake, their absence can generate tension. In some cases, so, too, can the presence of family members, especially if their attendance makes their typical absence from family life all the more conspicuous. Such stresses are seldom new to the situation. People learn to live with them. But the space of death and mourning draws people into intimate proximity, bringing anxieties into razor-sharp focus.

Tension that sometimes arises from differences in religious affiliation, perhaps tolerated under ordinary circumstances, also can become a painful reality at funeral wakes. Expectations for a peaceful and harmonious funeral often meet a barrage of difficult questions: Should a drum group be summoned? Should an outdoor fire be kindled for the lingering spirit? Do spirits linger? Should Catholic or Episcopal clergy preside? Such anxiousness surrounded the arrangements of a funeral for a well-loved member of Camp Justice who took her own life. The father of her children, a fundamentalist preacher from whom she had been separated for some years, had resolved to prohibit any extra-Christian practices. Because she had of late dedicated herself to growth in her Anishinaabe traditions, matters were all the more difficult for the singers. After the tragic death of another Camp Justice activist, funeral plans also were strained by differing religious leanings of the young woman's mother and father, who had been separated for some time. A long-time member of St. Columba's, the father wanted the native Episcopal priest to preside over arrangements at the Episcopalian church. In part to honor the young woman's own quest for traditional spirituality in her brief life, the mother and other family members wanted arrangements more in the manner of Anishinaabe custom: a wake in the home and burial on the family land. Added to the religious issues were political ones. The mourning drew together the Camp Justice circle that meant so much to the young woman, yet many of her relatives stood on the opposite side of White Earth's political divide. Several singers and surviving family members remarked on how apprehensive they had been about the wake but how healing the event had turned out to be. A medley of religious practices had resulted in a kind of dialogue between the Episcopal priest, the singers, and the non-Christian family members. A shared sense of grief and mutual concern for the future of the community brought political opponents together around sung hymns and a large feast in the home.

While gatherings in the wake of such deaths bring to the surface any number of tensions, this particular example illustrates that funerary practices can be powerful moments of healing and social integration as well. Community ideals and tensions are both on display. Singers and others allied with Camp Justice consider the troubling mortality rates to be symptoms of the need for a social and spiritual integration. Consistent with Anishinaabe understandings of illness, healing involves the restoration of balance and integration in the social and spiritual spheres as well as the bodily. As the late spiritual leader from a neighboring reservation exhorted, "we [Anishinaabe] need to realize who we are and what we stand for. . . . We need to be as one again!"[18]

Indeed, few feel the human weight of the politics of death more than Ojibwe singers. One of the White Earth singers, for example, had saved more than two hundred of the little memorial cards that are handed out at wakes. That means the

White Earth singers have brought their music to two hundred wakes in their first ten years. For those who bury someone every other week, no one wake stands alone. We return to the example of the wake already described to illustrate how their singing addresses these circumstances.

In a pause between hymns, it was Ethelbert Vanwert who stood up to offer some words of condolence. She spoke slowly, taking time to gather words befitting an occasion prompted by such absurd violence as a gangland killing at a wedding reception. Ethelbert shared the recent grief in her own life, that of a teenaged grandson who had been killed hitchhiking earlier that month. As her speech came to a close, she seemed frustrated that adequate words were not forthcoming. Somewhere between resign and resistance, she drew a deep breath and said, "Too many of our young people are dying."

It took a few moments for everyone to process her words. Silence then gave way to the voice of the lead singer with the first notes of the next hymn. Soon, nothing in the world seemed to be moving except for the chanted syllables as they rose, lingered, and fell again. As Erma Vizenor put it, "it comes to a point where all we can do is sing."

"All we can do is sing:" It is a challenge indeed to elaborate on the meaning of such a statement. Having been present myself at some wakes where attachments brought me into the circle of mourning, I begin to hear the irreducibility of Vizenor's account for how and why song emerges in response to the historical circumstances at White Earth. At least in certain consequential moments, I have felt that all I can do is listen or hum quietly along. By bringing to bear melodies and performance styles saturated with memories, and by making present the Ojibwe language, sung hymns can transform the space of the wake. They can reclaim that space from the chaos of loss and the violence of history made tangible by that loss, if only tentatively, and can synchronize the collective reflection necessary for a fresh vision of a possible communal future.

MEMORY, TIME, AND SPACE

Sung hymns can reclaim the spaces of death through the transforming work of memory. By memory, here, I mean more than the content of things recalled. I mean it in the larger sense that has been charted out by Michel de Certeau, whose social theory was informed by his years working among peasants in South America. Certeau's ideas help open up the processes of hymn singing, because he is interested in how memory and its play on time can be called on by colonized peoples to transform the confining spaces in which they consistently find themselves. Certeau juxtaposes the power relationships inscribed in the organization of social space with the alternative orderings of power that are the resources of oral traditions. He takes the stories, riposte, music, and body knowledge of oral tradition and organizes them under the larger heading of *memory*. Though having "no general and abstract formulation, no proper place" where it can be seen and pinned down by the powers that be, memory can nonetheless be brought to bear to change space.[19] Although the experience of subordinate groups is often confined to spaces circumscribed by the powers that be—

and an Indian reservation is an apt example—those subordinate groups can draw on "invisible resources of a time which obeys other laws, and which, taking it by surprise, steals something from the distribution owning the space."[20]

For Certeau, the invisibility of folk resources keeps them sufficiently agile to respond to shifting exigencies of disciplined space. "Like those birds that lay their eggs only in other species' nests, memory produces in a place that does not belong to it."[21] As it happens, a similar kind of winged opportunist, the crow, enjoys a surprising esteem in Anishinaabe stories as a clown, an opportunist, and a survivor. The fiction and criticism of Gerald Vizenor, an Ojibwe novelist and critic from White Earth, is shot through with the presence of the trickster figure as the paradigm for contemporary native survival. Most compelling for Vizenor, the trickster makes an art of keeping other characters guessing. Although the trickster is among the most sacred of figures, he defies any effort to folklorize or romanticize him into the conceptual boxes of what Vizenor labels "terminal creeds."[22]

In like manner, Certeau speaks of memory as a "sort of anti-museum."[23] Because the resources of memory and oral tradition cannot be pinpointed in space or formulated as abstractions in print, they can provide those forced to live within the constraining boundaries of colonialism a unique kind of leverage on their situation. In the past, these boundaries have been restrictive of Ojibwe autonomy through the mechanisms of forced assimilation, land loss, and structural poverty. Contemporary experience adds to this list a boundary of sorts, which I identified in the previous chapter as folklorization. This process freezes the trappings of Ojibwe culture in the amber of a colonizing (or colonized) imagination, while stripping it of the communal ethic and integrative vision which would more forcefully call into question the norms of dominant society. For those whose culture is legitimate in the mind of wider society only when it is packaged as folklore, memory's power as an "antimuseum" is rife with possibility. It follows that what Certeau means by memory "is in decay when it is no longer capable of its alteration. . . . It constructs itself from events that are independent of it, and it is limited to the expectation that something alien to the present will or must occur. Far from being the reliquary or trash can of the past, it sustains itself by *believing* in the existence of possibilities and by vigilantly awaiting them, constantly on the watch for their appearance."[24] Certeau's work sheds light on how Ojibwe singing remembers: not really by means of a content belonging to the past, but by means of a posture toward the present and future that song can bring to bear. The accrued past of Ojibwe singing provides the ballast to carry individuals and communities through the difficult spaces of grief and potential resign. Like other oral resources of memory, hymns draw their knowledge "from a multitude of events among which [they] move without possessing them." The resources of this "accumulated time," in which "ancient revolutions slumber," is mobilized to overcome the "hostile composition of place."[25]

Certeau's language here helps articulate how ritualized singing lifts the words of the texts off the page and clothes them with meanings far too numerous to elaborate in so many sentences of text. Ojibwe singing at wakes is a practice that can awaken the spiritual forces of memory. It can reimagine stolen land in sovereign terms as that which could never be owned by anyone in the first place. It can take the dispossession of history so urgently felt in the wake of a violent death and reconfigure it as merely a part of the whole story. It can refresh an exhausted gathering with the beauty of human voices and the recollection of previous generations of courageous Anami'aajig who faced similar struggles with fortitude and song. Just when the repeated experience of waking the victims of suicide or alcohol-related death or stabbing or diabetes might make the guild hall a space of despair, a space in which one might no longer believe in anything, a sung hymn can make all the difference.

Certeau's insight into the stealth of memory with respect to the gaze of theoretically oriented inquiry also helps make sense of the reticence I have encountered about hymn singing. I once met a member of an extended family that is known for singing at wakes in the Twin Cities. I was introduced to him as a Harvard graduate student interested in Ojibwe singing. The man was courteous, but replied rather flatly that "they're basically Episcopal hymns translated into Ojibwe, that's all," preempting any further conversation on the matter. The response indicated some measure of resistance on his part to my presence as perhaps just one more anthropologist interrupting community life in a search for rare cultural materials. Yet I think the resistance to my line of inquiry also had to do with the nature of hymn singing as a practice. Even the White Earth singers, with whom I have a more sustained relationship, are hardly forthcoming with commentary concerning a practice which at moments can be quite casual, but which, at other moments, can be called upon to transform experience.

Sociologist Paul Connerton's work elaborates on this aspect of memory and ritual action. Connerton asks why it is that societies tend to remember core values through ritual practices rather than through more propositional forms of expression. For Connerton, liturgical settings of texts and embodied ritual action are not simply signs—extensions of mental categories in time and space—but are, rather, expressions of a kind of body knowledge. Connerton argues that each society will "entrust to bodily automatisms the values and categories which they are most anxious to conserve. They will know how well the past can be kept in mind by a habitual memory sedimented in the body."[26] While it may seem far-fetched to speak of hymn singing as bodily action, Connerton's categories help frame Ojibwe singing as a practice rather than as a more discursive matter of simply performing texts in a musical manner. Indeed, this distinctive function of hymn language as ritualized memory is what makes an overly textual analysis of the hymns seem so clearly off the mark.

Any direct questions I have posed about discursive matters, such as "What does this hymn mean to you?" or "What are the larger resonances of this or that word?" have consistently met with indifference on the part of the singers. Their reticence is clearly not a statement of indifference toward singing but should be seen as consistent with the way Connerton notices that ritual actions "contain a measure of insurance against the process of cumulative questioning" that arise from discursive expressions. Indeed, as Connerton argues, it is this reticence that constitutes the very "source of their importance and persistence as mnemonic systems."[27]

In her study of a funerary feast cycle among the Sabarl Islanders of Melanesia, Deborah Battaglia similarly argues that it is unglossed ritual action rather than narrative which carries the social memory operative in the funeral and its music. When Battaglia asked her native consultants questions about the meanings of various parts of the ritual, as I did the Ojibwe singers, they replied, "We don't have a story of *segaiya*, because we do it all the time."[28] While Battaglia bases her interpretations on a distinctively Sabarl epistemology that places greater trust in the mnemonic value of actions than in words about actions, I find her conclusions illuminating of the role of memory in contemporary Ojibwe hymn singing. Put bluntly, the singers do not have a story of hymn singing, because they do it all the time.

WHY HYMNS?

Considered from a distance, the memories prompted by hymns would seem to have little to offer such moments as the death of a young person in a gang hit. After all, are hymns not the artifacts of a violent history of cultural dispossession and forced assimilation? Not surprisingly, for some people at White Earth hymns carry too many of these associations to be viable resources of identity. But how is it that this musical genre could become the stuff of survival for so many, and at precisely those moments when the nerves of historical experience seem most exposed? No obvious answer obtains as to how hymns address the politics of death, since they are not, textually speaking, songs of social protest. Neither do they share the history of an overt political program with some other Native American prophetic movements like the revolts of Pontiac and Tecumseh. Furthermore, Ojibwe hymn singing does not seem to represent the kind of riposte or verbal sleight of hand that first come to mind as the classic arts of peasant resistance. And yet there is something about the hymns that surely addresses the political conditions of the wake.

In earlier versions of this chapter, I found myself posing the issue rather crudely: How are hymns political? Impervious to my line of questioning, the music simply proceeded at its steady, meditative pace. Trying to squeeze an overt program of social change out of the songs is perhaps to miss the subtler operations of collective memory by which sung hymns can transform the colonized space of death and dismemberment into a space for remembering and communal vision. To begin to understand how hymns might do this cultural work, we can revisit some historical moments that show hymn singing's long association with the arts of survival in the spaces of death.[29]

Recall that it was precisely when Ojibwe survival was most at stake that missionaries began to remark on a more organized, ritualized practice of hymn singing. As more and more of the land was taken, letters from White Earth bespoke an unrelenting presence of death there. Even among Indian reservations, the place gained a reputation for its high rate of tuberculosis, trachoma, smallpox, and water-borne diseases.[30] In 1880, one missionary observed that White Earth village had buried hundreds of its own in six years while a neighboring white community had buried none. An overworked Indian Bureau doctor remarked, "there is something about the transition from the savage life to civilization that is very fatal to the Indians."[31] In this context, hymn singing was at the heart of the Anami'aajig community's response to death. A difference between the sung hymns of morning public worship and of evening wakes and prayer meetings was increasingly accentuated. The same Ojibwe songs were performed in both settings, but sources make it clear that a more indigenized tradition—the one evoked in today's singing—emerged unaccompanied from the candle-lit spaces of Anami'aajig life.

Recall also that death and funerary practices became highly contested moments in the cultural politics of missions and assimilation. The clergy's efforts to capitalize on the vital spirituality of Anami'aajig mourning practices required that they concede some measure of autonomy to the wakes. Even later in the century, when the clergy's power was at its peak, they still had to negotiate the extent of their influence on death practices. A perennial tension grew around the practice of feasting at wakes and at the traditional gathering held on the first anniversary of death. Like wailing, feasts were said to subvert the solemnity of funerals. Some of these tensions carried on into the twentieth century. In the 1950s, issues surrounding native wakes were momentous enough to command the attention of regional Episcopal clergy conferences. The clergy resolved to take more time "to instruct people on the Church's teaching and custom concerning funerals," again centering around issues of "excess." They expressed concern about the implications of open caskets and about a statute outlawing the serving of food in proximity to dead bodies. Also problematic was the continued practice of burial addresses, which the clergy agreed to condone only "if short and to the point." At the extreme, a Catholic priest serving Pine Point village in the 1960s had evidently disallowed native wakes in his parish buildings altogether.[32] Clerical tension reflected the importance of continuities in these practices.

The long history of the wake as a contested event plays itself out in spatial terms today. For example, recall that the wake I described at the outset of this chapter was held in the guild hall adjacent to Pine Point's Episcopal chapel. On the morning

Breck Memorial Church, Pine Point, and the Rock Memorial Guild Hall, left, where community wakes are held. (Author photo)

after the wake, nearly seventy people gathered again in the guild hall for the final viewing and some Ojibwe prayers. The bell rang to call the assembled next door for the funeral in the church proper, but, at best only twenty-five actually went in. Though no more than ten yards separated them—the guild hall and the church, the wake and the funeral—they might as well have been miles apart in terms of the associations they carried. Sharing the same *Ojibwa Hymnal*, the songs of the morning funeral did not carry the resonance they did when sung by the elders within the sphere of the wake the night previous. It was jarring, though ultimately not surprising, to see the father of the deceased leaning against a tree outside the church during the funeral, resolved not to enter and quietly awaiting the procession and burial.

HYMN SINGING AS RITUALIZED REMEMBERING

These spatial politics illustrate that what an individual or community remembers is never simply given, but always produced through a process of selection. In the previous chapter, I stressed the agency of today's White Earth singers in restoring the tradition of hymn singing as a strategy of memory. Like the singing sodalities of the past century, the White Earth singers have drawn on the power of this music, but they have ritualized hymn singing to different ends. In the chaotic space of death, they sing to create a shared experience of Anishinaabe time, to structure a collective process of social reflection, and to generate a field of memory.

It is curious that the singer to whom I was introduced replied so flatly that the tradition was "basically Episcopalian hymns translated into Ojibwe, that's all." A visit to a wake would persuade any newcomer that the White Earth singers do not just perform hymns translated into Ojibwe. They do so in stylized ways that are rich in references to a distinctive Anishinaabe past. They travel as a group defined in terms of its vocation of singing for the people, with little desire for applause and approval. If something is amiss in the life a member, that individual will quietly refrain from singing. They open with "Number Twenty-Five" and close with "Number Four," standing during the final verse. Their voices are unaccompanied, taking their cues from each other's voices and the spirit of the gathering rather than from the musical discipline established by a piano, an organ, or a drum. They sing to a tempo that is unique to such moments and that turns the words of the songs into extended syllables of chant. They pause between songs, sometimes giving voice to silence and other times expressing condolences in speech that are also stylized. Finally, these techniques can be said to stylize the very stylization of singing, in their reluctance to overstylize the action, to fix the singing too stiffly, to claim more for their activity than is appropriate. Perhaps this, too, was part of the strategy of the reply that "they are basically Episcopal hymns translated into Ojibwe, that's all."

What is the nature of the memory that such stylized practice awakens? The answer must be sought in two respects: first in terms of memory as recall, and, second, in terms of remembering as a social process. Erma Vizenor thinks people go to wakes not simply to mourn deaths and reflect on the past but to "become renewed" and to "rededicate themselves to the community." Taken together, renewal and rededication can illustrate the dual orientation of memory in hymn singing. On the one hand, memory looks back to the past; on the other, it serves as a socially integrative resource directed to the future.

REMEMBERING THE PAST: MEMORY AS RECALL

Remembering is a spiritual renewal oriented toward the past. To be sure, the songs set in process as many different associations as there are individuals involved. It would be absurd to try to generalize about the cumulative content of all these memories other than to acknowledge the tremendous play of associations that adhere to particular melodies and that can be released in performances. Despite the idiosyncrasy of memory in this respect, some associations nonetheless converge, and I turn now to four such convergences.

First, at White Earth today, hymn melodies, especially when voiced by the White Earth elders, carry strong associations with the work of Camp Justice, since the singers played such a major role in the movement. I might add that, for those who affiliated with Camp Justice, the music recalls the experimental community realized in that treasured summer of 1991. Today, participants look back to that first summer of the White Earth Camp Justice as an inspired period in their lives together, a time rich in social and spiritual well-being. For those who participated in the camp, the singers and the music they make can perhaps reconstitute in sound the experience of that community. For those who strongly disagreed with the movement's aims or tactics, the songs indeed may carry different valences, but I do not think such associations would carry the same force as the ingrained memories of those who heard the singers and their music in such defining moments as the gatherings of Camp Justice.

Second, regardless of one's opinion about Camp Justice, the range of memories awakened by sung hymns recollect the lives of previous generations of Anami'aajig and their capacity to endure. The orientation to the past that the hymns prompt is directed to no content in particular. It is neither a recitation of first times nor a specific reference to events or figures of the Anami'aajig. Following Certeau, we can understand the resources of oral memory here to be less a matter of localizable content than of the accrued wisdom of previous generations of survivors. Larry Cloud Morgan likens hymn singers to a chorus of Greek drama, entering the scene at watershed moments to lift onlookers above the absurdity of the moment to view the larger meanings of suffering. He also has spoken of the hymns as a shroud, tucked around the dead regardless of merit or life circumstances, and taking up the fragments of their brokenness into the enduring dignity of being Anishinaabeg, a dignity earned through the suffering and survival of the Anishinaabeg of centuries past.[33] The songs condense those lives and their dignity and make them present as resources in the reclamation of the space of death.

Third, the Christian content associated with the hymns cannot be overlooked as part of memory, especially since the teachings of the Christian tradition came to have close associations with dying and mourning. For those few in the room who are fluent in the language, or who nevertheless understand the Ojibwe Christian emphasis on the theme of sacrifice, hymn texts remember the powerful stories of Jesus' paradigmatic suffering, stories which in their own right confer a larger meaning on struggle and pain in the present day. Just as Ojibwe people made the genre of the hymn their own, they made the Jesus story their own, both investing in and drawing from the themes that addressed the joys, struggles, and contradictions of Ojibwe experience.

Ojibwe hymn translations followed closely the texts of the English originals in the depiction of the suffering passion of Jesus on the cross. In certain cases, the translations utilized Ojibwe language conventions of understatement and allusion to inflect the story with the resonances of Ojibwe idiom. Consider, for example, the fourth verse of "Number Twenty," a translation of Isaac Watts's, "Alas, and Did My Savior Bleed." (See Table 5.1.) To his translation of the first line, "I remember what they did to him," Larry Cloud Morgan adds, "somehow you know what they're say- ing. They don't have to identify who the victim was or speak about the violence in all its details." Through understatement, it retains "part of the mystery."[34] The next line also gains force in Ojibwe idiom. Cloud Morgan renders it as "and I feel so much pity," a line he glosses as suggesting, "I cannot say how bad I feel."[35]

Moreover, consistent with the original English texts of many nineteenth-century evangelical hymnody, the blood of Jesus presents a major textual theme. And yet, where English texts portray the vivid imagery of the blood of Jesus' sacrifice flowing for sinners, the Ojibwe texts trade on brevity to make the point. Consider the third verse of "Number Twenty-Two," a translation of Isaac Watts's "When I Survey the Wondrous Cross." (See Table 5.2.) Cloud Morgan maintains that today, the word *omiskwiim*, "his blood," carries powerful associations that link it to such stories of Jesus' suffering.

Finally, the strong association that these songs carry with the oral tradition is significant to the discussion of the content of memory. The oral tradition connotes an autonomous Anishinaabe discourse, an alternative way of imagining and valu- ing the past which many see as constitutive of their identity as Anishinaabe. By this, I do not claim that culture exists purely in the oral tradition: The hymns themselves are artifacts of the complex relationship between the sphere of the

---

Table 5.1

"ALAS, AND DID MY SAVIOR BLEED"

Isaac Watts (1707)	Ojibwa Hymnal (1910)	(Re)Translation
Thus might I hide my blushing face	Miquenduman ga dodawint	When I remember what they did to him,
While his dear cross appears	Nin kitimagendum;	I feel compassion/pity
Dissolve my heart in thankfulness	Ningidemagut go ninde	It melts, my heart,
And melt mine eyes to tears.	Mamoyawenduman.	I give thanks.

Table 5.2

"WHEN I SURVEY THE WONDROUS CROSS"

Isaac Watts (1707)	Ojibwa Hymnal (1910)	(Re)Translation
See, from his head, his hands, his feet,	Ki misquiwi oshtiguaning,	He bled from his head,
Sorrow and love flow mingled down!	Onijing gaye ozidang;	His hands, and his feet;
Did e'er such love and sorrow meet,	Wikana awuya o o	Does ever any
Or thorns compose so rich a crown?	Iji ki chi sagiiwe?	Love so greatly as he does?

written and the sphere of the oral. Yet to listen for the fuller resonance of Ojibwe hymns, it is crucial to recognize that, for most Anishinaabe, the oral tradition is considered the more authoritative mode of memory, a body of indigenous insight into the truths of history that have been obscured through written traditions. Both archival sources and people at White Earth today make it clear that Ojibwe singing is rooted firmly in this oral tradition. Hymnbooks provide a way into the songs for some newcomers, but for those steeped in it, the book serves more as a guide to memory than its repository. Even recent printings of the hymnbooks do not include musical notation, and thus do not fix a song with any one tune. In keeping with nineteenth-century custom, the books provide the texts and designation of meter, but leave decisions about tune settings to the creativity of lead singers. The practice relies on a singer's oral memory of the tune repertory and is cherished as an important resource of knowledge. The anonymity of this oral tradition to which songs are assigned helps explain the difficulties I have had in ascertaining the origins of texts, translations, and tunes. For the singers, the pinpointing logic that such questions represent strays too far from the logic of the songs themselves as resources of memory.

REMEMBERING THE FUTURE: MEMORY, LANGUAGE, MUSIC

While hymns remember a powerful past, they also occasion a process of re-membering that can transform relationships in the present and clear space for the envisioning of a possible collective future. To explore, we might rephrase the question of what hymns remember in terms of how they remember, for the hymns are not experienced as ordinary texts. In fact, because so few people speak Ojibwe fluently, hymn texts are beyond the lexical comprehension of most people in the room. For them, the meanings are more diffuse, emanating from the sounds of the language itself and the associations of identity that arise from those sounds. Precisely because sung hymns say nothing in particular, they are all the better equipped to prompt a host of varied, even conflicting, associations of an Anishinaabe past and to integrate divergent ways of imagining identity in a common experience of singing, listening, and re-membering. This happens through the simultaneous workings of language and music.

Language functions to help the social body remember in at least three analyti-cally distinct but interrelated aspects: the social, the semantic, and the formal. First, the Ojibwe language functions as a strong marker of social identity. One need not be fluent to have strong convictions about what values and alternative ways of envi-sioning the world are made possible by the Ojibwe language. On one level, there is an overt politics to the very fact that the language is spoken at all at this point in history. In light of the concerted effort to stamp out the language and culture, or of the more subtle effort to folklorize both, the spoken word here is nothing less than resistance. Larry Cloud Morgan observes that to think or speak in Ojibwe is to enter a wholly different way of organizing experience and valuing people and land.[36] For those who share his fluency, engaging that worldview can be subversive of modern American values. Whether or not one is fluent, a few words can evoke deep-seated allegiances that transcend civil laws and compel political action even when the odds are slim. Take, for example, the phrase *Anishinaabe akiing*, which translates roughly as "the people's land" but which implies a profound sense of mutual belonging and obligation. As one White Earth treaty rights activist put it, "We and the land are the same. What happens to the land, happens to us."[37] The implied bond between original people and land owes nothing to the "law of the land" or of land "owner-ship" and has standing prior to the history of dispossession. When the group that later would become synonymous with Camp Justice previously took the name An-ishinabe Akeeng in its effort to recover ill-gotten White Earth lands, it was more than a public relations ploy meant to sound authentically native. The term sounded the depths of the community's respect for the land of White Earth that went beyond its instrumental value for survival. Needless to say, both *Anishinaabe* and *akiing* ap-pear frequently in the texts of hymns, and the resonance of Jesus having to live and suffer on the *akiing* carries a particularly grounded Ojibwe understanding of the incarnation.

The very sounds of the Ojibwe language serve as markers of Anishinaabe iden-tity. In those charged moments in the life of the community where difference and faction threaten to carry the day, these markers become catalysts for the cementing of bonds within the social boundaries they mark. While few speak Ojibwe on a daily basis, everyday English speech is well seasoned with a number of Ojibwe terms. One frequently hears, for example, the use of *miigwech* rather than "thank you" when a heightened sincerity of gratitude is intended. This would occur in such moments as when a person is served food at a feast, when participants shake hands at the conclu-sion of a pipe ceremony, or when a grandmother receives a child's mud pie. Indeed, the term summons to mind the entire value system said to orbit around this notion of *miigwech*, for an ideal of gratitude is at once sentiment, way of knowing, aesthetic, and ethic for action.

Such a term as *miigwech* becomes a mark of identity not simply because it is some kind of linguistic survival of a once vibrant Ojibwe worldview, but rather because it is applied in a process linguists call "code-switching" to contemporary experience in marked contrast to English terms. In other words, to say *miigwech* is to mark the ab-

sence of "thank you." "Thank you" can seem from one perspective to be a mere po-
liteness, diluted by overuse. From the perspective of many at White Earth, the larger
American society which says only thank you is one characterized by waste and arrogance. To say *miigwech* is to identify with a group of people sharing an alternative
value system. "Number Four" in the *Ojibwa Hymnal* is entitled "Migwech ni Kije-
Manidom" (*miigwech*, My Great Mystery), a loose translation of "All Praise to Thee,
My God, This Night." Because the White Earth singers close each performance with
this song, one might say they want *miigwech* to be the last word. This is entirely consistent with an Ojibwe tradition of prayer and song that stresses the expression of
gratitude rather than prayer as petition.

Whether or not they are fluent in Ojibwe, most of those attending a wake bring
with them an acute hunger for the assurances that the sounds of this language offer.
Those returning to the reservation after some time away might be seeking some kind
of anchor of identity, or perhaps might be harboring a cosmopolitan resentment toward their rural roots. Many come to wakes thoroughly disoriented in the shock of
death, especially in the event of violent deaths. In those often sleepless, bewildering
first days, time and space can seem foreign and ominous. At such times, it is up to
the mechanisms of corporate ritual to begin the passage back to the world of order
and meaning. Often it is the sound of elders singing hymns in the Ojibwe language
that first invites the bereaved back into the community of the living.

When I asked one White Earth elder fluent in Ojibwe about the nature of the
language in the hymns, he replied, "the language isn't the same if you don't get it at
the beginning of life, because it is a spiritual thing."[38] Singers share such a special
feeling toward the Ojibwe words of the songs. In my work with them, I have encountered a marked reluctance to examine the song texts too closely in English
translation. Perhaps to do so is perceived as to fiddle with their integrity as Ojibwe
songs. Even with a lifetime of experience translating in and out of Ojibwe, Larry
Cloud Morgan finds it an exceedingly difficult task. As he put it, the words are "so
connected with the people." Many Ojibwe speak of their original language as a spiritual gift integrally connected with the particular land on which they were called to
live. "Tribal words have power in the oral tradition," as Gerald Vizenor puts it, "the
sounds express the spiritual energies of woodland lives. . . . The words the woodland tribes spoke were connected to the place the words were spoken."[39]

Translation and textual analysis are considered external to such workings of the
language in the oral tradition. The semantics of the Ojibwe language are closely associated with its phonetics in ways that present more than the customary barriers to
translation across languages. A distinctive Ojibwe philosophy of language privileges
the very sounds of the spoken and sung words, not simply as voicings of fixed meanings
but as the calling forth of aesthetic, moral, and spiritual meanings located in sound. In
"Languages of Sound," an illuminating chapter of their study of Ojibwe and other native musical instruments, Diamond, Cronk, and von Rosen press beyond the notion of
worldview to coin the term *world-hearing* to appreciate the way that speakers of Algonkian languages organize the world of experience in part based on the sounds of language, recognizing meaningful associations among things in the world when the
words that refer to them sound alike. The semantics of language in this kind of *world-
hearing* work in such a manner that "meaning . . . is not just in the definitions of

words but in the relationships established when they are uttered—externally by offering respect, internally through the exercise of the imagination which finds words within words and sounds within sounds."[40] For example, Larry Cloud Morgan closely associated the drum (*dewe'igan*) with the heart (*de-*) and with truth (*debwe-*) and with sound (*wewe-*), a morpheme that itself connotes particular kinds of wavelike or circular, returning motion. This would explain how my dictionary-oriented approach to finding the meanings of archaic words, while trying to (re)translate the Ojibwe hymn texts into English, contrasted markedly from Larry Cloud Morgan's approach to carefully sounding out the words and identifying the various associations carried by each meaningful unit of sound itself. At first, our being at odds frustrated me, since I considered my dictionary approach to translation more reliably tied to the original, but I came to realize that it was Larry's translation of the play of meanings resounding in the hymns, idiosyncratic as it might have been, that was probably closer to the effective meanings at play for Ojibwe speakers in concrete moments of hymn singing.

Since the semantics of the Ojibwe language are so closely associated with its sonics, the concepts, narratives, and theologies of the Ojibwe hymn texts are not fixed to the meanings specified in missionary dictionaries and missionary intentions, but to the ever-expanding concentric circles of associations created in sound. According to Wub-e-ke-niew, the distinctive workings of the Ojibwe language make it mean so much more than words:

> The *Anishinahbaeotjibway* language . . . is the totality of communication in several dimensions of reality. Our language is in living time with Grandmother Earth, rather than in a mechanical and abstract time. . . . [It] is the compiled wisdom of hundreds of thousands of generations of our people. It is a powerful tool for understanding the world, a guide for our behavior, and an interpretation of our harmonious inter-relationship with Grandmother Earth and Grandfather Midé. *Anishinahbaeotjibway* contains our eloquent oral history, the blueprints for our gift economy based on generosity, our social structure expressed in terms of *Dodems* and family, and our holistic and balanced relationship to the Universe.[41]

For Wub-e-ke-niew, the language is more than the sum of its grammatical parts. Taken as a whole, it organizes time, space, relationship, land, economy, politics, religion, and art in a manner that is necessary for Anishinaabe intellectual sovereignty and survival. This is in obvious contrast to English, but for Wub-e-ke-niew, the language is also sharply distinguished from "Chippewa," what he considers a pidgin that bears the manipulations of fur traders and missionaries. Although Wub-e-ke-niew would doubtless consider Ojibwe hymns to be "Chippewa" rather than "Anishinahbaeotjibway" in this regard, the elders who sing at wakes give voice to a language that is more than the sum of its lexical parts, one that resonates far beyond the narrower intentions of nineteenth-century missionary translators. Paul Schultz, an ordained Ojibwe Lutheran pastor and author who moved back to White Earth in 1998 to serve as a health liaison for the Reservation Tribal Council, remarked that something significant and subtle happens in Ojibwe singing, for when elders sing, they know that they are singing something very spiritual, very powerful.[42] An untrained ear may not fully appreciate it, but attuning to the subtleties of Ojibwe singing discloses a whole world of associations and meanings that are both Christian and Anishinaabe in the most subversive sense.

The singing of Ojibwe hymns, then, is in important respects a sounding out of the intellectual, aesthetic, and moral resources of the Ojibwe language. The elders who describe their singing as taking part or taking responsibility in the community, are in important respects stepping forward not to sing hymns as much as to be guardians of the living language to which the hymns give voice. The texts still matter, but they do not matter in the narrowly lexical way that those of us versed in the printed word are inclined to appreciate. The language itself is a gift, and singers are its stewards, distributing it to the people at some of the neediest times in the life of the community. The sounds it calls forth resound with associations of the land, the people, and a distinctively spiritual way of looking at the world.

At the most basic level, the sung language of the hymns creates a powerful awareness that the Ojibwe language is still alive, a rich resource still available to a community seeking new ways to imagine their circumstances. Moreover, the specific valences of certain terms like *miigwech* can claim a social space as boundary markers of identity. But the level at which language most effectively structures a social process of remembering is the formal level.

Paul Connerton argues that the language most conducive to the socially integrative function of memory is that of the performative utterance acted out in a ritualized frame of meaning. For Connerton, such speech "does not describe what . . . a community might look like, nor does it express a community constituted before and apart from it; performative utterances are as it were the place in which the community is constituted and recalls to itself the fact of its constitution."[43] Connerton adds that the more effective mnemonic language is formalized language, "systematically composed so as to restrict the range of available linguistic choices." Intoned speech—and particularly song—make use of tone and rhythm to further distance mnemonic language from that of everyday speech.[44] Perhaps this formalization of hymn language effects what James Fernandez characterized as a modus operandi of the religious thought of Africa's Fang people. In what Fernandez calls "edification by puzzlement," Fang ceremonial discourse delights in "indirection and suggestion and other kinds of puzzlements" to make meaning, while letting inconsistencies and loose ends carry the day.[45]

Unlike the Fang's language, though, the language of Ojibwe hymns today is significantly a liturgical language. Since few Minnesota Ojibwes are fluent enough to engage the lexical meaning of the hymns, Ojibwe here functions as an esoteric language—one to which they feel connected, but which nonetheless generates its meanings by virtue of its difference from ordinary language.

Even for those who are fluent, the vocabulary and perhaps the grammar of the hymn texts stand in contrast to contemporary Ojibwe usage in ways that stylize the language. John Nichols suggests that the language of the 1910 *Ojibwa Hymnal* bears idiosyncrasies of eastern Ojibwe dialects.[46] In any event, the vocabulary of the hymns includes a wealth of expressions that do not have currency in today's parlance.

Recall that performance draws hymn texts out into seemingly disconnected syllables, often lingering on the sounds of a syllable at the expense of lexically intelligible phrasing. This closely parallels the vocables so prevalent in other Ojibwe music. Performances, then, do much to supplant the specific discursive meanings of the language with imaginative possibilities that can be socially integrative precisely because they are nonspecific. Sung hymns do so much more than communicate specific propositional or informational content. For this reason, the songs are referred to by their number rather than by their first line, as in today's mainline Protestant convention. Perhaps it is for this reason as well that singers are so reticent to explain the meanings of the hymns.

Beyond their function as special texts, Ojibwe hymns can do this semiotic work because fundamentally they are *music*. A syncopated experience of musical time and a shared experience of familiar melodic sequences of sound provide the structure around which visceral feelings of power, identity, collectivity, totality, purpose, and meaning can cohere. I find it challenging to write adequately about how this music does what it does. In his "Overture" to *The Raw and the Cooked*, Claude Lévi-Strauss claims that music is "the supreme mystery of the science of man:" an art "at once intelligible and untranslatable" with "its own peculiar vehicle which does not admit of any general, extramusical use."[47] Thus chastened not to presume that analytical language can ever fully deliver, my own transforming experiences at wakes as a mourner-observer nonetheless embolden me to proceed.

First, and most important, the singing of hymns structures a shared experience of what might be called Anishinaabe time. As I have shown, the music is undisciplined by any accompanying instruments. The music proceeds at a tempo set by the singers in response to the spirit of the particular moments of singing. Because it is the elders alone who sing, the effectiveness of this shared Anishinaabe time depends on the attentiveness of those gathered, an attentiveness that I have already described as inconsistent. In most performances, though, there are at least some moments when nothing in the world seems to move except for the voices of the singers. The sound enters the bodies of all those within earshot. Whatever discord may obtain among the gathered at the level of social relations, at the level of sound, syncopation can constitute community.

The tempo of sung hymns is set apart from that of any other in the repertory, be it country-western, rap, or powwow music. Because it is widely associated with mourning, this tempo calls people out of ordinary time into a reflective, meditative time to mark their own passage through the experience of death.[48] These ways of marking Anishinaabe time, I have already suggested, are particularly welcome in the timelessness that is often experienced in the wake of death. Bewilderment, anxiety, fear, and fatigue can radically disorient the bereaved in the days following the news, especially if the death was violent. In many cases, it is the tempo of sung hymns that first brings order to that felt chaos. The tempo can refer to experiences from other wakes, reminding the bereaved that their grief, however isolating it seems, is shared by wider circles of a mourning community.

Like the bell that tolls slowly, arresting the attention of everyone within earshot and focusing their reflection on death, the silences within hymn performances are as significant as sounds, each playing off one another to make room for stillness, reflection, and acclimation in the wake of death. In my own experience, the silences that punctuate the singing of hymns create the very frame for the articulation of the un-speakable grief that the hymns are meant to address. Indeed, silence plays a particu-larly important part in Anishinaabe tradition. One Ojibwe scholar has described an Anishinaabe "culture of silence," where silence is a cultivated condition of mindful-ness and a privileged medium for social interaction.[49] Erma Vizenor recalls an elder who once came to visit her grandfather, sat with him in complete quiet for more than an hour, shared some food, and simply stood up in silence and took his leave.[50]

Suggestive of ways that the sound object of music is not necessarily of greatest import, the shared experience of time that the hymn singers structure is not simply a matter of musical time, documentable in musical notation or recording. Anishi-naabe time also is established through the collective practices at wakes that take place around the singing. Evening has fallen. Driving time has accentuated the value of the elders' presence. The singers begin their music "in their own good time" and without drawing attention to their beginning. Pauses between songs mark time as well, whether by means of silence, by speeches of condolence, or by a casual sip of coffee. The long duration of the singers' performance, typically extending into the early morning hours, indicates the level of commitment required for proper Ojibwe mourning. Lengthy performances also allow the bereaved to pass healthily through the series of emotions that grieving entails. As an ethnomusicologist found to be the case among a native South American people, lengthy songs and mourning rites can create an experience "that involves forced concentration on grief and memory" until the mourner feels "in the end, a little bored."[51]

Second, sung hymns sequence sound in melodies that can trigger experiences of individual and collective memory. One day while I was writing field notes, the full force of the memory effected through music came to me when Bob Dylan's "You're Going to Make Me Lonesome When You Go" came on the radio, arresting me with a wealth of personal associations with the song. I would be hard-pressed to delineate all the meanings the song contains for me, since the content was not present to me in such an elaborated form. It is more accurate to say that I felt as if I simply re-sounded with the many memories that seemingly have incorporated into the song it-self. The song had become, as it were, a bundle in which all those fleeting moments spread out over the years were wrapped in one. Like a place that is charged with memory, the music of a song serves as a site where temporally distinct experiences can accrue, find themselves in conversation with one another, and awaken in the lis-tener a sense of totality. We sometimes say that a song "sends us," transporting us imaginatively to other places and times, rekindling emotions or aspirations we thought had been left behind for good by our ordinary memory. The same is no less true of Ojibwe hymns.

POLITICS OF MEMORY

These distinctive operations of music and language enable hymn singing to arti-culate a workable agreement on a shared past—and this where an experience of a shared past is pivotal among people living a factionalized existence. Boundaries that distinguish Christians from ardent non-Christians, for example, can become porous at best. Of course there is a doubleness to this process, for memory is also an arena where meanings are contested. For some, the memories evoked by hymns are unequivocally those of colonization of land and mind. When one Ojibwe man heard hymns at a ceremony honoring a new drum, for instance, he whispered his opinion that such "Christian" music was disrespectful to the drum. For this man, hymn singing stood in opposition to other music of Ojibwe tradition in that the hymns do not involve a drum. The irony of this particular interchange is also instructive. The drum in question was being initiated or welcomed into the community by entrusting it to the safekeeping and discretionary use of the White Earth singers.

On the other end of the spectrum, some exclusively Christian people oppose any mingling of hymnody with non-Christian elements. In 1993, the priest and Bishop's Committee of St. Columba's Church in White Earth affirmed singing hymns in the Ojibwe language, but they ruled out any practices associated with the Midewiwin tradition at any wake using the church building. For the White Earth singers, though, the incense of smoldering sage, pipe ceremonies, and drum music are entirely consistent with if not part and parcel of the life of singing hymns. The singers' requests in 1991 to hold cold-weather meetings for the Camp Justice movement in St. Columba's also were denied, on the grounds that the church did not want to promote dissent within the community. This in itself furthered divisions within the village. A sense of alienation from the church had brought a great deal of added pain to a number of the White Earth singers long associated with St. Columba's. When her grandson was killed, Ethelbert was refused access to the church building to hold the wake there, on the grounds that too much syncretism in the wake would dishonor Christianity and Ojibwe religion alike. Although the White Earth singers got their start in the weekly meetings in St. Columba's, the elder commented that their singing seldom sounds good when they perform in the church building today. At one point, she and other singers had resolved to attend the Catholic church in White Earth village.

One axis of social tension that is articulated in moments of hymn singing is a generational one. For increasing numbers of young people at White Earth, it is not so much that hymn singing evokes highly contested memories as that it evokes no significant memories at all. Among young people, music tastes range from a firm rooting in American popular music, especially urban rap and heavy metal, to a renewed appreciation for drum songs and dancing contests associated with powwows. Especially for those who have not heard the hymns often enough in the course of their young lives to have developed another set of associations with them, hymns can seem emblematic of a symbol system and institution that many think no longer speaks to their experience.

Even with a few promising signs of exceptions to the rule, especially at Cass Lake, where singers have involved interested younger people in their music and have started a fund to raise money for the promotion of the language and values of Ojibwe hymns, no singing groups at White Earth or elsewhere involve significant numbers of young people. In part, this stems from the close association of the music with elders, but it also stems from a decreasing interest in the music. The White Earth singers often discuss strategies for reversing the trend, noting that the powwow music of interest to many young people is largely a matter of vocables and does not nourish them with a stronger sense of the language and the values it promotes. The singers acknowledge, however, that interest in Ojibwe hymns will be awakened only after youth are free from alcohol, drugs, and gangs.

As gang activity shapes the social experience of more and more White Earth young people, and as gang-related violence increases, it is possible that many will find hymn singing no longer capable of meaningfully framing the mourning of friends and comrades. A former student of mine pointed out that when he was a teenager in the housing projects of Waco, Texas, many of his fellows were finding the music, preaching, and spaces of African-American churches to be obsolete for mourning victims of gang violence. Gang members, he said, often created their own rituals to mark the passage of fallen comrades, pouring libations and vowing revenge. The young people nonetheless honored the needs of parents, grandparents, and the community at large to proceed through the mourning and burial traditions of the churches, and duly attended with no disrespect.[52] To return to the White Earth wake with which this chapter began, this Waco example may help explain why the young man's friends appeared less moved by the hymn singing than by their felt duty to avenge their fallen comrade's death. Although they did nothing overtly to disrupt the singers or other mourners, their gathering in the wake of death took place not in the guild hall but around a pickup truck in the adjacent parking lot. Whether they wanted to be out of earshot from the hymns or whether they wanted others to be out of earshot of them, their absence deeply bothered the father, whose grief over his own son's death was matched by his dread that the revenge he believed they were plotting would only extend the senseless killing. On the following morning, it was these young men who performed the final task of burial. After the funeral and procession to the burial yard, they removed their black jackets, took up six shovels, and with a crowd of quiet people watching in the warm sun, filled in the grave of their friend.

THE POLITICS OF RITUALIZED REMEMBERING

The music of hymn singing articulates boundaries even as it tries to integrate across them. But the lines of contention are complex and shifting, eluding tidy categories like Christian and Midewiwin, accommodationist and traditionalist, or young and old. Many of those Ojibwe people who stake out their identity in opposition to Christianity nonetheless strive toward a deep spiritual respect for the White Earth singers and their music. Many respect the elders' prerogative to sing what they wish.

To conclude, we might restate the presenting problem of this chapter: What is it about Ojibwe hymn singing that addresses the politics of death? Again following Michel de Certeau, we can appreciate afresh how even everyday practices like hymn singing, when performed in colonizing contexts, can carry a considerable political charge of their own. In the constricting spaces of mourning that follow in the wake of violent deaths, sung hymns can awaken, through memory, the resolve to continue to resist the violence of history and to believe in the possibility of *bimaadiziwin*. Certeau aptly observes that the capacity to transform these spaces hinges on a capacity to believe:

By a paradox that is only apparent, the discourse that makes people believe is the one that takes away what it urges them to believe in, or never delivers what it promises. . . . It opens up clearings; it allows a certain play within a system of defined places. . . . It is a crack in the system that saturates places with signification and indeed so reduces them to this signification that it is impossible to breathe in them.[53]

We might add to Certeau's insight an appreciation for the perhaps unique capacity of music to make all this happen. In a moment when community survival, much less well-being, can seem difficult to imagine, the constitution of community in sound provides the imagination with something to believe in once again. Aesthetics of performance intone the ethical priorities of the community—notably humility, balance, and the priority of community well-being over self interest. Unadorned human voices chant the syllables in common. No virtuoso voice stands out to draw the attention of the audience. Accuracy of pitch and quality of tone are less important than an appreciation for who the singers are and what value commitments are brought to their singing. The songs proceed according to a rhythm set by the spirit of the gathering rather than by the meter of an accompanying instrument.

Sung hymns can remember and constitute an idealized Anishinaabe way of life. And while politics isn't everything, everything about this way of life is politically charged in late-twentieth-century America. The memory enacted in sung hymns carries an additional charge by virtue of the history of forced forgetting. Its presence rubs against the cultural dispossession often ascribed to assimilation policies, boarding school education, and relocation programs. The need for such memory is particularly acute among a people who today find themselves at another cultural crossroads, marked not by forced assimilation but by what many elders consider to be a subtler kind of assimilation through economic individualism, acquisitiveness, and the folklorization of native culture. Indeed, it is a profoundly political act simply to endure on your own terms in a world which would see you on the Hollywood set of *Dances with Wolves* or just as soon not see you at all. Gerald Vizenor often returns to the comic affirmation of life that tribal people assert over the sentimental tragedy saddled on them. He coined the word *survivance* to more fully convey the resilience of this defiant art.[54]

For many Ojibwe people, the stylized singing of hymns can evoke, at precisely those moments that call for reassessment, the memory of the language, values, and history that spiritually renews, and that provides the cultural ballast necessary to negotiate the contemporary world. This memory recollects, reintegrates, rededicates even as it recalls a shared past. While a thirteen-year-old's suicide may be a glaring reminder of the odds stacked against Anishinaabe survival, the space of the wake is one in which other possibilities can be envisioned and other social values can be put into practice. People may know well that they will gather again to mourn a death equally distressing, but the sung hymns dare to create beauty where despair tries to reign, and that beauty of the hymns sets the tone for the spiritual renewal and rededication to community that make survival as Anishinaabe people in the modern world possible.

CONCLUSION: DOES HYMN SINGING WORK?

Notes on the Logic of Hymn-Singing Practice

▲▲▲▲▲▲

I n the preceding chapters, I have examined Ojibwe hymn singing as a practice that was ritualized to different ends in different historical moments. Rigorously promoted by missionaries as a technique of cultural revolution as well as an expression of worship, Ojibwe translations of evangelical hymns were incorporated and intermittently performed according to existing Anishinaabe beliefs about music and social relationship. Beginning in the 1870s, a significant number of people at White Earth departed from Anishinaabe precedent and embraced a new form of music making. Though hymn singing called for the conspicuous absence of drum and dance and a number of words that was copious in comparison to Ojibwe precedent, native people changed the performance style and social constellation of the music to make it their own. These changes were sometimes subtle matters of style, but they were no less consequential in the cultural politics of the reservation period. In turn, I have argued that these cultural politics were nothing less than matters of Anishinaabe survival amid the poverty, landlessness, and social chaos of those early years at White Earth. More, I argued that the ritualized performance enabled the hymns to do more than set the tone and establish the rhythms for a new way of life at White Earth. For many, hymn singing at wakes and prayer meetings conferred a kind of spiritual integrity on that new life, making it aesthetically, morally, and spiritually desirable to be both distinctively Ojibwe and distinctively Christian, to be both Anishinaabeg and Anami'aajig.

The twentieth century saw further erosion of the land base, language, and social solidarity long seen as constitutive of Anishinaabe identity. At White Earth, the practice of hymn singing itself all but disappeared. But a group of elders in White Earth village, subjected as they had been to the forced forgetting of assimilation policies, took it on themselves to bring back the tradition of singing. They did so to help a beleaguered community act on its circumstances by remembering an Anishinaabe identity through musical performance. While their singing to remember stands in some contrast to the Anami'aajig's singing to negotiate a new way of life in the late nineteenth century, in both cases, the singing was ritualized to strategic ends and spiritual effect.

OPEN QUESTIONS, ATTEMPTED ANSWERS

In previous presentations of this research, my attention to the *uses* of hymn singing has twice elicited the critical question: *Does hymn singing really work?* Did it really succeed in negotiating a viable new way of life at White Earth in the 1880s? Has hymn singing today actually done something to reduce the alarming rates of homicide, suicide, drunk-driving accidents, and diabetes? In the final analysis, does hymn singing *do anything* really?

These are probing questions indeed, and it is fitting to conclude this volume with a number of suggestions in response. Asking what one means when one says hymn singing works or fails to work will bring us face to face with a presenting problem for students of ritual and Ojibwe singers alike. As I indicated at the outset, through this volume I hope to illuminate the importance of taking ritual practice seriously in the study of religion even as I try to amplify what is moving and significant about Ojibwe hymn singing. I remain convinced that both projects can inform one another to worthy ends.

In each chapter of this book, I have kept open certain questions about the workings of ritual and about whether ritual works. These could be understood as uneasy reminders that an interpretive scheme has fallen short of accounting for all the dynamics of the subject. I am persuaded, however, that such open questions are endemic to the work of ritual and, it follows, to the work of understanding ritual. An understanding of ritual in which practice is seen as proceeding according to its own logic can shed light on the nature of these loose ends. It will be helpful to begin by orienting the discussion to several influential ways that anthropologists of religion have understood how ritual works.

A functionalist paradigm long helped anthropologists see ritual largely in its aspect as a conservative agent reining in the centrifugal forces of history and social destabilization. Because "traditional" societies were characterized by their equilibrium, a stability guaranteed by custom and tradition, rituals must have consistently achieved what they set out to accomplish. If equilibrium did not obtain, the functionalist was led to inquire not about potential ritual shortcomings but about the degree to which the cultural whole had been dissolved by the acids of acculturation.

A paradigm shift in the anthropology of religion that came to privilege *meaning* in symbolic life offered a way to interpret the significance that rituals and mythic narratives held for people, and not simply their function. However, much of this symbolic or interpretive anthropology still lacks the agility to match the deftness with which rituals do their cultural work in the rapid social change of colonial situations. This is not for lack of trying. Clifford Geertz, perhaps the most influential figure in symbolic anthropology, launched more systematic inquiry into the impact of historical change on symbolic life. In an essay entitled, "Ritual and Social Change: A Javanese Example," Geertz explores a case of what he calls "ritual failure." The case involves a funeral in a Javanese village that was undergoing rapid change and discloses, for Geertz, the distance between society and culture. As a result of modernizing influences, Geertz argues, "socially, kampong people are urbanites," whose identities are shaped more by class, ideology, occupation, and political affiliations than by village geography, "while culturally they are still folk."[1] The funeral ritual, still rooted in the traditions of folk culture, had become tangibly, painfully, obsolete for them. By opening ritual to history and to change over time, Geertz may have become the historian's cultural theorist of choice. To varying degrees, rituals can be in or out of step with historical circumstance. Rituals can even be occasions for the contestation of meaning as it is worked out in history. In this sense, the symbolic anthropology of Geertz helped redress an ahistorical analysis of religious symbols that long focused on ritual's capacity to call communities out of history into the sacred time and sacred space of first times, a province which, in Mircea Eliade's famous formulation, enabled "archaic" peoples to keep the "terror of history" at bay.[2] But as we search for ways of interpreting the story of hymn singing and its place in negotiating rapid historical change, Geertz's scheme itself warrants a more critical examination.

To say that ritual failed in the Javanese funeral begs the question what ritual looks like when it succeeds. For Geertz, the answer is that ritual begets the fuel that drives the "cultural system" of religion. In the "consecrated behavior" of ritual, Geertz argues, the "conviction that religious conceptions are veridical and that religious directives are sound is somehow generated." It is in ritual that the "general conceptions of the order of existence" meet and reinforce the "moods and motivations," effecting the wedding of worldview and ethos that makes religion work in history. In a sentence so well wrought as to have appropriately captured the imagination of scholars in years since, Geertz puts it this way: "In a ritual, the world as lived and the world as imagined, fused under the agency of a single set of symbolic forms, turns out to be the same world."[3] This latter formulation discloses Geertz's basic claim that the beliefs and practices of symbolic culture are "texts" that can be interpreted. Elsewhere in a memorable essay, "Notes on a Balinese Cockfight," Geertz writes "the culture of a people is an ensemble of texts, themselves ensembles, which the anthropologist strains to read over the shoulders of those to whom they properly belong."[4] In this view, ritual performances are narratives, stories we tell ourselves about ourselves. What rituals *do*, then, is *mean* something. They succeed when the story they tell is a coherent and persuasive one. They fail when the story no longer speaks to the social experience of the group. The Javanese funeral ritual failed because a story which it told about a small-scale, traditional, highly personalized community of *Gemeinschaft* could no longer persuade a village now characterized by *Gesellschaft*, a largely impersonal society of classes, institutions, and modern complexity.

In the essay on the Javanese funeral, Geertz masterfully addressed the stasis of the equilibrium model with which structural-functionalist anthropologists had hitherto understood society. Geertz opens up the possibility for a dynamics of history and culture where symbolic thought and action can be appreciated as creative forces in historical change. Not surprisingly, Geertz's symbolic interpretation of culture has become the coin of the realm for much recent scholarship in religious history. But while Geertz leaves open the possibility for a dynamics of history, it is likely that those taking his view will still place their money on the narrative coherence of the elements of symbolic life and of an entire cultural system as a whole.

Three criticisms are pertinent before we return, better equipped, to the matter of Ojibwe hymn singing. First, Geertz's view assumes a coherence of meaning agreed upon by various participants in a ritual. As we learn from contemporary literary studies, consideration of the meaning of a text–or, as many would have it, the textualized actions of a ritual—cannot content itself with having identified a normative "official" meaning tied to the author's intentions. Even if we were to agree that rituals could be read and interpreted like texts, there are simply too many different interpretations, from too many social locations, at play among ritual participants to settle for a tidy interpretation of ritual meaning.

Second, Geertz's view is inadequate to the task of apprehending the complex processes of cultural encounters such as those between Protestant missionaries and Ojibwe communities. Geertz has replaced the functionalist's static system of social equilibrium with a "cultural system," the coherence of which resides in meaning. In the end, both systems train the analyst's attention unduly on what Renato Rosaldo identifies as "control mechanisms," the respects in which culture maintains order against chaos, structure against change. Rosaldo calls instead for a processual perspective, one in which "change rather than structure become society's enduring state, and time rather than space becomes its most encompassing medium."[5] Of course, culture is very much involved in keeping chaos at bay, but in the end, any view that reduces culture to that project renders the messiness of cultural change anomalous, unstable, and impure. In such turbulent waters as the confluence of missionary and Anishinaabe musical traditions, the swirls and eddies of cultural process are as significant as any presumed unidirectional flow of acculturation. An undue focus on moments where the coherent fabric of culture is rent precludes a fuller view of the remarkable resilience by which ritual practices in particular help negotiate change.

A third criticism can be said to encompass the other two. A number of scholars have importantly called our attention to the whole world of embodied experience and action that is eclipsed by the reductive *textualization* of practices.[6] To consider ritual action principally as a mode of narrative expression is to miss the workings of ritual action that are the domain of bodily experiences and knowledge by making of them mere representations, or embodied confirmations, of the prior conceptualizations of the mind. This perhaps will prove the more difficult criticism to fully articulate since it basically calls for a narrative translation of a fundamentally non-narrative logic of ritual practices. In this difficult task, we benefit from the groundbreaking work of Pierre Bourdieu and Catherine Bell, but there remains much work to be done to come more fully to terms with a logic of ritual practice.

I have digressed here in order to demonstrate that the contradictions giving rise to the question "does hymn singing work?" are major stumbling blocks only if we view ritual through this Geertzian lens, if we look for the coherent narratives of a symbolizing mind. But the colonized situation in which Anishinaabe people have found themselves has not always afforded the possibility of resolving such contradictions and inconsistencies. I wish to suggest that Ojibwe singing may have made living within those contradictions possible precisely because its logic is one of ritualized practice and not one of a conceptualizing mind seeking order and consistency. What is more, such a perspective will enable us to understand how the ritualized practice of Ojibwe hymn singing has been at the heart of negotiating culture change at different moments in the struggle to survive on Anishinaabe terms.

DOES RITUALIZED HYMN SINGING WORK?

I have identified at least three moments that occasion the question whether hymn singing works. I will try to articulate those concerns in language derived from a Geertzian view of ritual success, and then reconsider them in light of a distinctive logic of ritual practice as outlined by Pierre Bourdieu and Catherine Bell.

In chapter 3, I charted the social space of the Anami'aajig, arguing that its emergence made room for a semiautonomous way of life. I also charted the cultural space cleared by the ritualized music making of hymn-singing sodalities. I argued that the latter made possible the former—that a ritualized practice of hymn singing negotiated a legitimate space for the living of *bimaadiziwin* amid the constraining expectations of reservation and mission authorities. At the same time, the choice to sing hymns was a public devaluation of certain highly charged symbolic practices, namely the dancing and singing with a drum around which so much Anishinaabe identity revolved. This negotiation involved a measure of both accommodation and resistance. *How can a ritualized practice be said to "work" if it leads simultaneously to accommodation and resistance?*

In chapter 4, I surveyed the changed social and cultural landscape of twentieth-century White Earth and the implications for hymn singing. The steady loss of language, the expansion of the musical repertory, and the accentuation of factional strife led to an even more pronounced demarcation of hymn singing as a specifically Anishinaabe cultural practice. That practice, at least in White Earth village, had all but died out until a group of people identified a need in their community and rekindled it. Through brief sketches of the singers, I tried to show how the tradition has been reinvented such that each performance is also a rehearsal. *How can an invention work as tradition? How can a rehearsal be a persuasive performance?*

In chapter 5, I explored how hymns, through the media of music and liturgical language, can function to integrate divergent ways of remembering an Ojibwe past. Yet I concluded the section by demonstrating that memory articulates social boundaries even as it functions to bring people together across them. *If memory is even nearly as divisive as it is integrative, then how can the ritualized remembering of hymns be said to work? Has it demonstrably reduced the social factionalism that continues to promote intolerable levels of violent and untimely death?*

In responding to these questions, I want to bring them together under the overarching question that has driven the study as a whole: *How is it that hymnody—a genre promoted in the first place to take the Indianness out of native peoples—has become an emblem of distinctiveness and the stuff of survival for so many Ojibwe people today?* Of course, to consider this a puzzling question in the first place is to assume a deep-seated myth that deems native peoples authentically *Indian* only to the extent that they exhibit precontact, non-Christian, *traditional* culture.[7] Nonetheless, posing the question can be illuminating if framed in terms of Bourdieu's understanding of the distinctive logic of practice. Even as we strive to make sense of a practice, we must recognize that practices are immersed in life's shifting demands and oriented toward practical concerns of survival. In practice, as Bourdieu observes, "no more logic is mobilized than is required by the needs of practice."[8]

Indeed, Bourdieu thinks this illogical logic is why practice is able to do what it does. Analysts may find their interpretations frustrated by its inconsistencies, but so many people get by in this world precisely because, to quote Bourdieu again, "practice exists on the hitherside of discourse." By eluding the discipline of discursive thought, practice remains nimble, responsive, and unnoticed. Perhaps it is appropriate that a field journal entry that I wrote at a time when I could make neither heads nor tails of why singers were so reticent about their singing tradition reads, "Long live the difficulties of my project!"

Let us explore this variety of questions by trying to characterize a logic of hymn singing practice. What distinguishes the logic of hymn singing in the 1880s from that of its revitalization in the 1980s? First, recall that the initial years at White Earth posed unprecedented social and ecological demands on those forced to settle there in close proximity. Survival had always involved making do, but the early years at White Earth pushed Anishinaabe resourcefulness to its limits. For food, clothing, shelter, and political advocacy many simply had to seek the protection of the well-connected Episcopalian mission. And at least some figures like Suzanna Equay-me-do-gay Roy or Shay-day-ence came to the conclusion that new forms, both social and spiritual, were needed to ensure that more fundamental Anishinaabe values remained viable. But the singers of the 1880s did not simply adopt the hymns as they were promoted by missionaries. In practice, the Anami'aajig transformed them. This may seem a rather commonplace observation, but it appears more fully in light of Catherine Bell's use of the term *ritualization*.

BOTH ACCOMMODATION *AND* RESISTANCE?

Bell's work on ritualization is particularly helpful for the light it sheds on how practices promoted in colonial contexts can be experienced, paradoxically, as redemptive for dominated groups even while they function to create or maintain unequal power relations. After Kenelm Burridge, Bell calls this "redemptive hegemony" in an attempt to show how structure and agency—the rules, hierarchies, and constraints of social circumstance, on the one hand, and the capacity to move somewhat freely within them, on the other—are mutually reinforcing in ritual practices.

Bell's understanding of ritualized practice here relies on the *habitus*, a concept coined by Marcel Mauss and elaborated on by Pierre Bourdieu to describe the juncture where the objective forces of history and society meet the subjective dexterity and freedom of human action.[9] What characterizes this juncture of structure and agency, for Bourdieu, is that the *habitus* is an "instance of practice, an irreducible 'unit' of culture that cannot be broken down" into the forces of structure and agency that constitute it.[10] The *habitus* is a set of dispositions or "regulated improvisation" by which a structured and structuring process occurs. "Objectively regulated and regular without being in any way the product of obedience to rules," the practices of the *habitus* can be seen as "collectively orchestrated without being the product of the organizing action of the conductor." Bourdieu also speaks of the *habitus* as "embodied history," since what appears as objective reality is the inherited field of possibilities—and limits to those possibilities—that history and social relations placed on human agency. The structures do not exist outside culture and history, but are structured in time through the dispositions of the *habitus*.[11] The *habitus* does not represent the internalization of structures that are in any real sense "out there," but rather accounts for the play within the momentum of historical and social regulation in which human agents can effectively improvise on their world. "This infinite yet strictly limited generative capacity is difficult to understand," Bourdieu continues, "only so long as one remains locked in the usual antinomies . . . of determinism and freedom, conditioning and creativity, consciousness and the unconscious, or the individual and society."[12] One could add accommodation and resistance to the list of antinomies that mingle unperturbed in the logic of practice. It is the analyst, equipped with the writing, recording, and abundant time necessary to engage in the practice of theory, who "wins the privilege of totalization" by which accommodation and resistance are seen as mutually exclusive.[13]

To return to our own case, the social conditions of the difficult early years at White Earth were such that symbolic accommodation was tantamount to survival. Amid the poverty, social chaos, and dispossession of land, missionaries and agency officials succeeded in discouraging many Anishinaabeg from the drumming, dancing, and feasting that were such central practices of communal identity. In terms of structure, upon removal to the more confining terms of existence at White Earth, the new music of hymn singing worked its way more thoroughly into Ojibwe lives than had been the case prior to the reservation period. But neither missionaries nor the Anami'aajig would have found it sufficient to infer that hymns were simply forced on a victimized people.

In terms of agency, the Anami'aajig did not simply accommodate themselves to the hymn. What might be called a "sense of the sacred" brought them to invest themselves so thoroughly in the music that hymns accompanied nearly every community gathering. This sense of the sacred was more than a derivative of missionary intentions; it was characteristic of the pragmatic impulse in Ojibwe religiousness, a practical appreciation of the sacred potential of the missionary songs. The Anami'aajig made hymns their own by stylizing their performance and by placing the singing of them in a constellation of social relationships. In the end, the missionary songs gave voice to distinctively Anishinaabe values even while they gave voice to the story and values of the Christian tradition. Viewed from above, singing hymns involved both accommodation and resistance. But at eye level, on the complex cultural field of practice, hymn singing involved neither alone.

THE INVENTION OF TRADITION?

A notion of the "invention of tradition" has animated much of cultural and historical studies since a book by that title appeared in 1983.[14] Contributors examined political rituals of modern nation states, colonial regimes, and popular social movements of the nineteenth century to show that many of the traditions dear to modern life are, in fact, "responses to novel situations which take the form of reference to old situations, or which establish their own past by quasi-obligatory repetition."[15] Invented traditions are choices among alternatives, ritualizations designed or discovered to legitimize the more or less arbitrary claims of certain figures to political authority. Eric Hobsbawm distinguishes between the invented traditions of modernity, which are characterized by "invariance," and the more fluid "custom" of "so-called traditional societies." Functioning as both "motor and fly wheel," the custom of traditional societies gives "any desired change (or resistance to innovation) the sanction of precedent, social continuity and natural law as expressed in history."[16] According to this view, we would be forced to ask whether it is "custom" or "tradition" that best characterizes the renewal of hymn singing at White Earth in the 1980s. Is the community of White Earth a modern or traditional society? The obvious answer—that White Earth is both—leaves us searching for more discerning categories than the blunt ones of custom and tradition to describe hymn singing.

Hobsbawm's idea has struck closer to home as an organizing principle for some recent scholarship on various presumed inventions of Native American traditions. In a collection of essays entitled *The Invented Indian: Cultural Fictions and Governmental Policies*, James Clifton and collaborators try to address persisting romantic cultural fictions about native peoples by disclosing how certain taken-for-granted notions of Native Americana like "Mother Earth," reverence for the land, and egalitarianism are, in fact, rooted no more deeply than in the historical encounters with European Americans, and often to suit European-American desires.[17] Vine Deloria Jr. rightly criticizes this and other efforts to expose cultural fictions in supposedly invented traditions as overconfident and underresearched, in turn generating its own dangerous cultural fictions.[18] Clearly, the invention of tradition model cannot adequately account for how deftly history and tradition work together in Native American practice.

Consider, for example, the work that the elders of White Earth village began in the 1980s to bring Ojibwe singing back to their community and its wakes. Given the cassette recordings that guided them and all the work they put in rehearsing together, this process was, in important respects, a reinvention of tradition. To thus historicize the ritual practice of hymn singing, to locate it in time rather than in timelessness, may be the best habit of thinking by which to disclose the outer dynamics of historical contingency and social power that obtain in any ritual. But, in the end, this kind of historicism may be incapable of eliciting the inner dynamics by which those contingencies become real and powerful social facts. Here the historian must rely less on the application of a positivistic view of time where linear time alone counts. While this positivistic view of time is the coin of the social scientific dimension of our trade, the historian should rely more on the coin of the humanistic side—a principled commitment to come to terms with the way our historical subjects describe their experience. If the latter is operative as well as the former, we will not content ourselves with merely exposing what we take to be the invention of tradition. Indeed, we will still try to recover the agency of historical subjects from a presumed necessity of history by disclosing the alternatives from which they choose. But we also will be prepared to accept that historical agents may choose to act in history by recourse to ritual. For it may well be that ritual offers the most strategic way to reimagine, reevaluate, and thereby act on often onerous circumstances of life in history.

When entire groups of people choose to act in history by dancing, as adherents of the Ghost Dance did, for example, in response to the devastations of the 1890s, they often leave historians puzzled. But an awareness that there is more than one way to imagine time can help the historian appreciate such ritual activities as assertions of other modes of conceptualizing time and acting in it. In his study of religions indigenous to South America, Larry Sullivan argues that the very presence of these other modes should humble any claims to the universality of a historicist view of time. "Failure to confront cognitive and existential issues while studying South American cultures must lead one to depict native concepts of time as simplistic adherence to the raw rhythms of nature or, at best, unreflexive conformity to ritual or mythic models."[19] Importantly, this need not be seen as a precarious step outside of history. Strictly speaking, no living, breathing human being ever does step out of history, even when ritual experience takes them afar.

A century after the first Anami'aajig, in the little guild halls that bear the names of White Earth's early singers, another group of White Earth elders have found power and purpose in the hymns and returned to the tradition of singing them at wakes. Again, these elders are more than mere spokespersons for some "Ojibwe Mind" and its timeless traditions. They are cultural critics equipped to diagnose community ills, and ritual agents, equipped to draw on the resources of ritual to address those ills. As elders, their presence at funeral wakes guides reflection on what another individual's death means in terms of the community's past, present, and future. As singers, their music in those same wakes creates Anishinaabe time and generates the wherewithal and beauty necessary to keep envisioning and acting on a collective future when despair might otherwise reign. According to a logic of practice, invented traditions need be neither disjunctive nor suspect. Whatever tension obtains between them in the world of theory, on the field of practice, inventions and traditions meet in a practical *sense of the traditional*. Like a sense of direction or a sense of timing, this sense of the traditional does not lend itself to abstract elaboration. But it does lend itself to tangible effects.

Perhaps the best way to appreciate how a practical sense of the traditional can both invent and maintain tradition is through the metaphor of *rekindling*. Rekindling may not seem like a particularly sophisticated concept, but those who heat with wood in northern Minnesota winters that drop routinely to forty degrees below zero can grasp both the art and necessity of starting an early morning fire from the gray ash left over from the previous night: the banking of coals, the careful venting of air through the ash, the right choice of wood at the right time (green or dry; birch, oak, or pine). To rekindle tradition is, similarly, a mix of art and necessity.

IS REMEMBERING ENOUGH?

In twentieth-century White Earth, tradition itself has become a charged ideological category in cultural politics and therefore more rigidly defined as a lens through which different Ojibwe people see their respective Anishinaabe identities. In this context, we can see the ritualized language and music of the hymns at work to bring "tradition" back within the realm of a logic of practice. In this regard, the White Earth singers can be seen as reflective actors in the cultural politics of defining tradition, as cultural critics who nonetheless appeal to the nondiscursive language of sung Ojibwe music to make their point and to subvert the very divisiveness of the cultural politics that occurs at the level of discourse. The sung hymns at funeral wakes are not elaborated commentaries on what the community at White Earth should look like. What they mean *goes without saying*. Sung hymns are musical expressions, ritualized rememberings that bring into being something more immediate, more visceral: a shared sound-vision of that idealized community. That sound-vision is both a product of recall from a shared Ojibwe past and a process of recollecting community in the present. In the space of the wake—a space that is otherwise determined solely by the presence of a lifeless body and by the threat of an end to the entire Anishinaabe project—sung hymns can transform experience from despair to vision, from factional strife to integration, from disorder to healing. The sung hymns do not ultimately resolve the contradictions and social tensions of life at White Earth any more today than they did in the 1880s. But they can be said to contain the implications of those contradictions by creating space for the remembering of *bimaadiziwin* in the twentieth century.

Only in fleeting moments does Ojibwe singing succeed in realizing this sound-vision at funeral wakes. Thus far, it has yet to be realized sufficiently in social life to reduce substantially the statistical indices of community dismemberment. In chapter 5, I acknowledged that those gathered at any given wake know they will soon assemble again to mourn another death in the community, perhaps equally violent and tragic. But to conclude on this basis that hymn singing does not work would show a failure to appreciate how hymn singing can transform the world of experience beyond the space of the wake.

HYMN SINGING AS THE RITUALIZED PRACTICE OF HOPE

How does the power to remember *bimaadiziwin* in those fleeting moments generate power beyond the wake? I have yet to meet someone who considers hymns to work like medicine songs or dream songs, as effective symbolic acts that can transform the physical realm through their proper recitation in the ritual realm. We should instead turn to the category of *hope* to understand how this music can transform social experience. Given the devastating story with which I introduced this study, it is fitting to conclude by appreciating hymn singing as the ritualized practice of hope.

In perhaps the most trenchant criticism of my work to date, Erma Vizenor took issue with what she heard to be a romanticized view of *survival* on my part.[20] She acknowledged that survival was the immediate concern of many at White Earth. But a valorization of survival on my part troubled her because, as she said, "someday, I want to move beyond survival . . . to justice." Vizenor went on to identify Ojibwe singing as a crucial part of her hopeful vision of a just future. Survival may hinge on hope, but hope does not stop at survival.

Hymn singing at wakes is a ritualized enactment of hope, a bold and beautifying assertion made in the wake of death that the story did not begin there and will not end there. The sound-vision of *bimaadiziwin* engendered by hymn singing generates the hope that inspires many Ojibwe people to keep acting in history. This hope is no mere theological abstraction; its presence is tangible at moments in the felt presence of the heard rather than the visible presence of the seen.

In a study that Anastasia Shkilnyk calls an "anatomy" of "the destruction of an Ojibwa community," she found little but despair at Ontario's Grassy Narrows Reserve, several hundred miles northeast of White Earth.[21] Documenting the "damages to community life" from alcohol, mercury poisoning, and the dispossession that underlay them, Shkilnyk tells a story of thoroughgoing despair. She does so for admirable reasons: in order to help redress the lack of compensation received by the community for its losses. The book cover graphically illustrates the relentlessly bleak view taken by the author. A photograph of an Anishinaabe extended family, each person smiling broadly, is seen as through a cracked picture frame. I have not been to Grassy Narrows, but based on my experience at White Earth, I would say with no less confidence that there is far more than despair to the story at such places.

The hope that can be renewed at White Earth by the singing of beautiful hymns hinges on no simplistic optimism about circumstances changing for the better. As cultural critic Cornel West avers, the opposite of skepticism is not optimism, but hope.[22] Hope sees what is to come with few optimistic illusions; yet hope can reorient the experience of circumstances such that oppression need not define the horizon of possibility.[23] When a White Earth singer remarks that "sometimes all we can do is sing," she gives voice not to resignation but resolve, not to despair but to hope.

Hope makes room for acting as an agent in a world that otherwise circumscribes such action. Hope also has the capacity to transform social relationships in the present so as to generate the real possibility of change. Based on my experience over the past eight years, I might add that the opposite of skepticism at White Earth is not optimism but a sense of humor. At White Earth, laughter can undermine the sense of despair and tragedy that might leave no room for agency. As I write these scholarly conclusions about hymn singing, I can still hear Larry Cloud Morgan chuckling as he introduced me as his student, an "Ojibwologist."

Given the resilience of humor and hope that one encounters at White Earth, I have taken a considerable risk in representing life there through practices performed in the presence of death. I risk invoking a powerful image of the vanishing Indian, where an overrighteous sentimentalism sets native history to the tune of hopeless tragedy. I hope enough of the music has chimed through the analysis to convince the reader that Ojibwe hymns are no such tunes of hopeless tragedy. They are neither the coping mechanisms of a dying culture nor the devalued currency of Ojibwe acculturation. Sung hymns can become an enactment of hope in a space in which the old too often bury the young. In those moments when it seems least conceivable, *bimaadiziwin* can be sung into being, if momentarily, through the logic of ritual practice and the beauty of music. Thus constituted in sound, this goal of a healthy and just Anishinaabe way of life becomes thinkable once again—and worth striving for.

NOTES

▲▲▲▲▲▲

INTRODUCTION AND OVERVIEW

1. According to the 1990 census, 106,000 Ojibwe people live in the United States. Seven Ojibwe reservations are found in the woods, lakes, bogs, and prairies of northern Minnesota, but more than half the enrolled population lives off the reservations.

2. They were singing "Number Twenty," a very loose translation of "Alas, and Did My Saviour Bleed" from Edward Coley Kah-O-Sed's *Ojibwa Hymnal* (Minneapolis: Protestant Episcopal Church, Diocese of Minnesota, 1910).

3. David Karsnia, in conversation, February 1999.

4. "Culture in motion" is an expression coined by Renato Rosaldo, *Culture and Truth: The Remaking of Social Analysis* (Boston: Beacon Press, 1989).

5. Functionalism trains our eyes on the way that religious thought and action are to fit into an organic unity with economy, polity, art, kinship,and so forth, to make a living in the world. Symbolic anthropology—and we might include much of the religious studies literature here—privileges the role of symbolic life in making a meaningful and coherent world worth living in. Taken alone, either perspective will be inadequate to understanding the cultural work and value of Ojibwe hymn singing. Taken together, the two can bring our attention to the social matrix and the experience of time and space organized by singing practice to more fully appreciate how sung hymns do what they do and mean what they mean.

6. W. J. Hoffman, *The Midé-wiwin or Grand Medicine Society of the Ojibwa*, 7th Annual Report, 1885–6 (Washington, D.C.: Bureau of American Ethnology, 1891).

7. See especially Ruth Landes, *Ojibwa Religion and the Midéwiwin* (Madison: University of Wisconsin Press, 1968); Selwyn Dewdney, *The Sacred Scrolls of the Southern Ojibway* (Toronto: University of Toronto Press, 1975). Of Schoolcraft's work, see especially *Algic Researches*, 2 vols. (New York: Harper's, 1839). Kohl's work was published originally in German in 1855, later translated as *Kitchi-Gami: Life among the Lake Superior Ojibway*, trans. Lascelles Wraxall (St. Paul: Minnesota Historical Society Press, 1985 [1855]).

8. Mircea Eliade, *Shamanism: Archaic Techniques of Ecstasy* (Princeton: Princeton University Press, 1964 [1951]); Leo Frobenius, *The Childhood of Man*, trans. A. H. Keane (New York: Meridian, 1960 [1909]).

9. See A. Irving Hallowell, *Culture and Experience* (Philadelphia: University of Pennsylvania Press, 1955); Victor Barnouw, "Acculturation and Personality among the Wisconsin Chippewa," *Memoirs of the American Anthropological Association* 72 (1950); Stephen T. Boggs,

"Culture Change and the Personality of Ojibwa Children," *American Anthropologist* 60:47–58 (1958); Bernard J. James, "Social-Psychological Dimensions of Ojibwa Acculturation," *American Anthropologist* 63:721–746 (1961). On the beginnings of acculturation studies, see Robert Redfield, Ralph Linton, and Melville Herskovits, "Memorandum for the Study of Acculturation," *American Anthropologist* 38:149–151 (1936). For a collection of viewpoints of acculturative studies, see *The Emergent Native Americans: A Reader in Cultural Contact*, ed. Deward E. Walker Jr. (Boston: Little, Brown, 1972).

10. Åke Hultkrantz, "The Problem of Christian Influence on Northern Algonkian Eschatology," in Hultkrantz, *Belief and Worship in Native North America*, ed. Christopher Vecsey (Syracuse: Syracuse University Press, 1981); Harold Hickerson, *The Chippewa and Their Neighbors: A Study in Ethnohistory*, revised and expanded by Jennifer S. H. Brown and Laura Peers (Prospect Heights, Ill.: Waveland Press, 1988 [1970]); John Grim, *The Shaman: Patterns of Religious Healing among the Ojibwa Indians* (Norman: University of Oklahoma Press, 1983); Christopher Vecsey, *Traditional Ojibwa Religion and Its Historical Changes* (Philadelphia: American Philosophical Society, 1983).

11. Vecsey, *Traditional Ojibwa Religion and Its Historical Changes*, p. 45. Vecsey's more recent volume, *The Paths of Kateri's Kin* (South Bend, Ind.: University of Notre Dame Press, 1998), takes a more sustained interest in Anishinaabe Christianity as a complex phenomenon.

12. Anastasia Shkilnyk, *A Poison Stronger Than Love: The Destruction of an Ojibwa Community* (New Haven, Conn.: Yale University Press, 1985), p. 90.

13. Carol Berg, "Climbing Learner's Hill: Benedictines at White Earth, 1878–1945" (Ph.D. diss., University of Minnesota, 1983); Henry Warner Bowden, "The Oberlin Mission to the Ojibwa," in *The Evangelical Tradition in America*, ed. Leonard Sweet (Macon, Ga.: Mercer University Press, 1984); Martin Zanger, "Straight Tongue's Heathen Wards: Bishop Whipple and the Episcopal Mission to the Chippewas," in *Churchmen and the Western Indians: 1820–1920*, ed. Clyde Milner and Floyd O'Neil (Norman: University of Oklahoma Press, 1985).

14. George Tinker, *Missionary Conquest: The Gospel and Native American Cultural Genocide* (Minneapolis: Fortress Press, 1993), especially pp. 95–111.

15. Carol Devens, *Countering Colonization: Native American Women and Great Lakes Missions, 1630–1900* (Berkeley: University of California Press, 1992), p. 119. While this work discloses the gendered nature of colonialism and, in turn, the gendered nature of "countering colonialism," I agree with Rebecca Kugel's appraisal that Devens "overstates the primacy of gender divisions" and understates how responses to colonialism often fell along axes of other social distinctions, such as kinship and age. Rebecca Kugel, *To Be the Main Leaders of Our People* (East Lansing: Michigan State University Press, 1998), note 36, p. 93.

16. Kugel, *To Be the Main Leaders of Our People*. See also Kugel, "Religion Mixed with Politics: The 1836 Conversion of Mang'osid of Fond du Lac," *Ethnohistory* 37:126–157 (Spring 1990), p. 126.

17. Kugel, *To Be the Main Leaders of Our People*, p. 122, pp. 188–189.

18. Kugel, *To Be the Main Leaders of Our People*, p. 159.

19. Kugel tellingly extracts the overall title of her book, *To Be the Main Leaders of Our People*, from a quote by a Mississippi Band civil leader who becomes Christian: "In religion and other things I ought to be the main leader of my people" (p. 125). In her gloss on the statement, Kugel implies that affiliation with the mission is to be seen primarily in its aspect as a political salvo by the civil leadership in its power struggle to define the Ojibwe future.

20. James Treat, ed., *Native and Christian* (New York: Routledge, 1995), p. 10.

21. Jace Weaver, ed., *Native American Religious Identity* (Maryknoll, N.Y.: Orbis, 1998), p. xi.

22. See especially vol. 2: Christopher Vecsey, *The Paths of Kateri's Kin* (South Bend, Ind.: University of Notre Dame Press, 1997).

23. Sergei Kan, *Memory Eternal: Tlingit Culture and Russian Orthodox Christianity through Two Centuries* (Seattle: University of Washington Press, 1999).

24. John and Jean Comaroff, *Of Revelation and Revolution: The Dialectics of Modernity on a South African Frontier,* vol. 2 (Chicago: University of Chicago Press, 1997).

25. For an insightful review of understandings of ritual, see Catherine Bell, *Ritual Theory, Ritual Practice* (New York: Oxford University Press, 1992), pp. 13–66.

26. See Wilfred Cantwell Smith's famous treatment of the emergence of the modern Western notion of religion in *The Meaning and End of Religion* (Minneapolis: Fortress Press, 1978 [1962]), pp. 15–51.

27. William Baldridge, "Toward a Native American Theology," *American Baptist Quarterly* 8, no. 4 (December 1989), p. 228, as cited in Treat, *Native and Christian,* p. 12; also cited in Jace Weaver, *That the People Might Live: Native American Literatures and Native American Community* (New York: Oxford University Press, 1997), p. 1.

28. See Pierre Bourdieu, *Outline of a Theory of Practice,* trans. Richard Nice (Cambridge: Cambridge University Press, 1987 [1972]); Michel de Certeau, *The Practice of Everyday Life,* trans. Stephen Rendall (Berkeley: University of California Press, 1984); Bell, *Ritual Theory, Ritual Practice;* Jean and John Comaroff, *Of Revelation and Revolution: Christianity, Colonialism, and Consciousness in South Africa,* vol. 1 (Chicago: University of Chicago Press, 1991); and Comaroff and Comaroff, *Of Revelation and Revolution,* vol. 2.

29. Bourdieu, *Language and Symbolic Power,* trans. Gino Raymond and Matthew Adamson (Cambridge: Harvard University Press, 1991), p. 170.

30. Comaroff and Comaroff, *Of Revelation and Revolution,* especially vol. 1, pp. 19–32.

31. James Clifford, *The Predicament of Culture* (Cambridge: Harvard University Press, 1988), p. 15.

32. Bell, *Ritual Theory, Ritual Practice,* pp. 107–108.

33. Ibid., p. 205.

34. Sam Gill, *Sacred Words: A Study of Navajo Religion and Prayer* (Westport, Conn.: Greenwood Press, 1981); Gill, *Native American Religious Action: A Performance Approach to Religion* (Columbia: University of South Carolina Press, 1987); William K. Powers, *Sacred Language: The Nature of Supernatural Discourse in Lakota* (Norman: University of Oklahoma Press, 1986); Gary Witherspoon, *Language and Art in the Navajo Universe* (Ann Arbor: University of Michigan Press, 1977).

35. Gill, *Native American Religious Action,* p. 151.

36. Among notable studies placing indigenous musical cultures in motion, see John Blacking, *Music, Culture, and Experience* (Chicago: University of Chicago Press, 1995); Thomas Turino, *Moving away from Silence* (Chicago: University of Chicago Press, 1993); Judith Vander, *Songprints: The Musical Experience of Five Shoshone Women* (Urbana: University of Illinois Press, 1988); Kay Kaufman Shelemay, *Music, Ritual, and Falasha History* (East Lansing: Michigan State University Press, 1989); and Christopher Waterman, *Juju: A Social History and Ethnography of an African Popular Music* (Chicago: University of Chicago Press, 1990).

37. Frances Densmore, "Prelude to the Study of Indian Music in Minnesota," n.d., Densmore Papers, Minnesota Historical Society (henceforth MHS). See Densmore's two-volume classic, *Chippewa Music,* Smithsonian Bureau of American Ethnology, Bulletins 45, 53 (1910, 1913). Even in "The Influence of Hymns on the Form of Indian Songs," *American Anthropologist* 40:175–176 (1938), Densmore focuses on songs of the peyote tradition and makes no mention whatsoever of Ojibwe hymns.

38. Thomas Vennum Jr., "A History of Ojibwa Song Form" in *Selected Reports in Ethnomusicology* 3:43–75 (1980); Vennum, *The Ojibwa Dance Drum* (Washington, D.C.: Smithsonian Press, 1982); Vennum, "Southwestern Ojibwa Music" (Ph.D. diss., Harvard University, 1975).

39. Frederick R. Burton, *American Primitive Music with Especial Attention to the Songs of the Ojibways* (New York: Moffat, Yard, 1909); Gertrude Kurath, "Catholic Hymns of Michigan Indians," *Anthropological Quarterly* 30:31–44 (April 1957); Kurath, "Songs and Dances of Great Lakes Indians" (annotated recordings), *Ethnic Folkways Library* Album P 1003 (1956).

40. David E. Draper, "*Abba isht tuluwa*: The Christian Hymns of the Mississippi Choctaw," *American Indian Culture and Research Journal* 6:43–61 (1982); J. Vincent Higginson, "Hymnody in the American Indian Missions," *Papers of the Hymn Society 18* (New York: Hymn Society, 1954); Thomas McElwain, "Rainbow Will Carry Me: The Language of Seneca Iroquois Christianity as Reflected in Hymns," in Christopher Vecsey, ed., *Religion in Native North America* (Moscow: University of Idaho Press, 1990), pp. 83–103; Willard Rhodes, "The Christian Hymnology of the North American Indians," in Anthony F. C. Wallace, ed., *Men and Cultures: Selected Papers of the Fifth International Congress of Anthropological and Ethnological Sciences* (Philadelphia: University of Pennsylvania Press, 1960), pp. 324–331; Marijan Smolik, "Slovenian Contributions to American Hymnody," *The Hymn* 36:14–15 (July 1985).

41. Beverley Cavanagh, "The Transmission of Algonkian Indian Hymns: Between Orality and Literacy," in *Musical Canada: Words and Music Honouring Helmut Kallmann*, ed. John Beckwith and Frederick Hall (Toronto, 1988); Richard Preston, "Transformations musicales et culturelles chez les cris de l'est," *Recherches Amérindiennes au Québec* 15:19–29 (1985); Amy Ku'uleialoha Stillman,"Himene Tahiti: Ethnoscientific and Ethnohistorical Perspectives on Choral Singing and Protestant Hymnody in the Society Islands, French Polynesia" (Ph.D. diss., Harvard University, 1991); Lynn Whidden, "Ethnic Series: Cree Hymnody as Traditional Song," *The Hymn* 40:21–25 (July 1989); Whidden, "Les hymnes, une anomalie parmi les chants traditionnels des cris du nord," *Recherches Amérindiennes au Québec* 15:29–36 (1985).

42. Turino, *Moving away from Silence*, p. 241.

CHAPTER 1

1. Gregory Evans Dowd, *A Spirited Resistance: The North American Struggle for Unity 1745–1815* (Baltimore: Johns Hopkins University Press, 1992); Hickerson, *The Chippewa and Their Neighbors*; Richard White, *The Middle Ground: Indians, Empires, and Republics in the Great Lakes Region 1650–1815* (Cambridge: Cambridge University Press, 1991).

2. Grim, *The Shaman*; Vecsey, *Traditional Ojibwa Religion and Its Historical Changes*.

3. Vennum, "Southwestern Ojibwa Music," p. 52.

4. I use the past tense in this discussion in order to give historical specificity to the observations. The reader is advised that many of these observations still apply to the experience of Ojibwe people today.

5. Ignatia Broker, *Night Flying Woman* (St. Paul: Minnesota Historical Society Press, 1983) p. 56.

6. Hallowell, Culture and Experience, p. 361. See also A. I. Hallowell, *The Ojibwa of Berens River, Manitoba: Ethnography into History*, ed. Jennifer S. H. Brown (Fort Worth: Harcourt, Brace, Jovanovich, 1992).

7. Baraga, *A Dictionary of the Ojibway Language*.

8. Grim, *The Shaman*, p. 7.

9. Mary Black, "Ojibwa Power Belief System," in *Anthropology of Power*, ed. Ray Fogelson and Richard Adams (New York: Academic Press, 1977), note 2, p. 143.

10. Vecsey, *Traditional Ojibwa Religion and Its Historical Changes*, p. 4.

11. For a rich discussion of nineteenth-century dreaming traditions in the Plains context, see Lee Irwin, *The Dream Seekers* (Norman: University of Oklahoma Press, 1994).

12. Thomas Vennum's interpretation of Ojibwe musical change relies on a distinction between sacred and secular to frame a trend from sacred to secular in musical acculturation, especially in the setting of the "secular" powwow. This scheme, however, equates the sacred with the nonacculturative tradition and does not account for ways that some Ojibwe people have refused to fix what they consider sacred to particular, especially pre-Christian, forms.

13. Densmore, *Chippewa Music*, vol. 2, p. 15.

14. Vennum, "Southwestern Ojibwa Music," p. 208.

15. John Boatman, *My Elders Taught Me: Aspects of Great Lakes American Indian Philosophy* (Lanham, Md.: University Press of America, 1992), p. 46.

16. Densmore, *Chippewa Music*, vol. 2, p. 67.

17. Vennum, "Southwestern Ojibwa Music," p. 206.

18. Densmore, *Chippewa Music*, vol. 2, p. 2.

19. Densmore also noted a variety of "unclassified" songs, including songs for intertribal dance cycles, divorce ceremonies, visiting, and recalling historical moments.

20. Vennum, "Southwestern Ojibwa Music," p. 242.

21. Densmore, *Chippewa Music*, vol. 2, p. 48. The orthography is Densmore's.

22. A group of ethnomusicologists organized their discussion of the instruments and musical life of Ojibwe and other eastern Canadian native groups around the notion of relationship. See Beverley Diamond, M. Sam Cronk, and Franziska von Rosen, *Visions of Sound: Musical Instruments of First Nations Communities in Northeastern America* (Chicago: University of Chicago Press, 1994).

23. Densmore, *Chippewa Music*, vol. 2, p. 2.

24. See White, *The Middle Ground*.

25. Joel Martin, *Sacred Revolt: The Muskogees' Struggle for a New World* (Boston: Beacon, 1991), p. 28.

26. The notion of ceremonial innovation better serves what scholarship sometimes refers to as "new religious movements" since such exchanges and innovation issue from long-standing traditions of spiritual exchange and are not exclusively derivatives of the deprivations of postcontact history. See Dowd, *A Spirited Resistance*, p. 129.

27. William W. Warren, *History of the Ojibway People* (St. Paul: Minnesota Historical Society Press, 1984 [1885]), pp. 321–322. On Tenskwatawa, see R. David Edmunds, *The Shawnee Prophet* (Lincoln: University of Nebraska Press, 1983).

28. Thomas Vennum Jr., *Ojibway Music from Minnesota: Continuity and Change* (St. Paul: Minnesota Historical Society Press, 1989), p. 9.

29. Densmore, *Chippewa Music*, vol. 1, p. 14. Vennum notes that Densmore was trying here to make a broader case that songs, especially those of the Midewiwin tradition, represented "the musical expression of religious ideas."

30. See Grim, The Shaman, pp. 120–137; William K. Powers, *Sacred Language: The Nature of Supernatural Discourse in Lakota* (Norman: University of Oklahoma Press, 1986). The translation of manidookaazo is from John D. Nichols and Earl Nyholm, *A Concise Dictionary of Minnesota Ojibwe* (Minneapolis: University of Minnesota Press, 1995).

31. Vennum, "Southwestern Ojibwa Music," p. 241.

32. Densmore, *Chippewa Music*, vol. 1, p. 270.

33. Ibid., p. 272.

34. Gerald Vizenor, ed., *Summer in the Spring: Anishinaabe Lyric Poems and Stories*, 2nd ed. (Norman: University of Oklahoma Press, 1993 [1965]).

35. See Selwyn Dewdney, *The Sacred Scrolls of the Southern Ojibway* (Toronto: University of Toronto Press, 1975).

36. Densmore, *Chippewa Music*, vol. 1, p. 108.

37. Densmore, *Chippewa Music*, vol. 2, p. 2.

38. For a fuller discussion of the implications of orality, see Walter Ong, *Orality and Literacy: The Technologizing of the Word* (London: Routledge, 1982); Jack Goody, *The Interface between the Written and the Oral* (Cambridge: Cambridge University Press, 1987).

39. Transcript, *Radio Talk*, February 23, 1932, in Densmore Papers, MHS. Emphasis is Densmore's.

40. Kohl, *Kitchi-Gami*, pp. 18–19.

41. Densmore, *Chippewa Music*, vol. 2, p. 15.

42. Vennum, "Southwestern Ojibwa Music," p. 167.

43. Ibid., p. 278.

44. Densmore, *Chippewa Music*, vol. 1, p. 7.

45. Burton, *American Primitive Music*, p. 126.

46. For discussions of Anishinaabe drums, see Thomas Vennum Jr., *The Ojibwa Dance Drum: Its History and Construction* (Washington, D.C.: Smithsonian Institution Press, 1982); Diamond, Cronk, and von Rosen, *Visions of Sound*.

47. Diamond, Cronk, and von Rosen, *Visions of Sound*, pp. 68–70.

48. In his influential phenomenology of prayer in world religions, Friedrich Heiler was constrained by his own Protestant framework to view prayer as communication with the divine, most authentic when spontaneous and "heart-felt." The term *prayer* has recently been applied more broadly in comparative religion to see the fuller social life of prayer as speech-act or even nonlinguistic action in addition to communication. See Friedrich Heiler, *Prayer*, trans. Samuel McComb (New York: Oxford University Press, 1958 [1923]); Sam Gill, *Sacred Words: A Study of Navajo Religion and Prayer* (Westport, Conn.: Greenwood Press, 1981); Riv-Ellen Prell, *Prayer and Community* (Detroit: Wayne State University Press, 1989).

49. Vennum, "Southwestern Ojibwa Music," pp. 54–56.

50. Sherman Hall and William Boutwell, Report to ABCFM, February 9, 1833, Nute Collection, box 3, MHS.

51. G. A. Belcourt to the Bishop of Quebec, July 11, 1836, Nute Collection, box 4, MHS. Emphasis his.

52. For an overview of hymn controversies in the First Great Awakening, see Stephen Marini, "Rehearsal for Revival: Sacred Singing and the Great Awakening in America," *Journal of the American Academy of Religion Thematic Studies* 50:71–93 (1983).

53. See Stephen Marini, *Sacred Song in America* (Urbana: University of Illinois Press, forthcoming).

54. See Nathan Hatch, *The Democratization of American Christianity* (New Haven, Conn.: Yale University Press, 1989), pp. 146–161.

55. Beverly Patterson demonstrates richly such resonances of hymnody among Primitive Baptists today, and particularly in terms of their communal identity. See Patterson, *The Sound of the Dove* (Urbana: University of Illinois Press, 1995).

56. John Wesley, "Preface" to *A Collection of Hymns for the Use of the People Called Methodists* (London: John Mason, 1846 [1779]).

57. Ibid.

58. For an exception, see Patterson, *The Sound of the Dove*.

59. Sherman Hall to David Green, January 10, 1843, Nute Collection, box 11, MHS. The ABCFM's Secretary persuaded Hall to "get over the difficulty about baptism" in order to secure the external financial support.

60. John Wesley, *The Power of Music* (1779), reprinted in Erik Routley, *The Musical Wesleys* (New York: Oxford University Press, 1968), pp. 15–19.

61. See Richard Crawford's introduction to *American Sacred Music Imprints 1698–1810:*

A *Bibliography*, ed. Allen Perdue Britton and Irving Lowens (Worcester, Mass.: American Antiquarian Society, 1990); see also Robert Stevenson, *Protestant Church Music in America* (New York: Norton, 1966).

62. Edmund Ely Journal, July 21, 1853, in Edmund Ely Papers, box 2, MHS.

63. Jonathan Edwards, *Some Thoughts Concerning the Present Revival of Religion in New England*, in *The Works of Jonathan Edwards*, ed. C. G. Goen (New Haven, Conn.: Yale University Press, 1972).

64. Ibid.

65. For a history of the ABCFM missions, see William R. Hutchison, *Errand to the World: American Protestant Thought and Foreign Missions* (Chicago: University of Chicago Press, 1987).

66. *ABCFM Annual Report for 1832*, p. 127.

67. Rufus Anderson, *Memorial Volume of the First Fifty Years of the American Board of Commissioners for Foreign Missions* (Boston: ABCFM, 1862), p. 344.

68. Ibid., p. 244.

69. William T. Boutwell to Henry R. Schoolcraft, June 12, 1835, Nute Collection, box 4, MHS. Emphasis his.

70. David Greene to Sherman Hall, June 17, 1834, Nute Collection, box 3, MHS.

71. Journal of William T. Boutwell, 1832, p. 49, Nute Collection, box 1, MHS.

72. "Fragment of a Dialogue between Ely and an Ojibway," 1839, Nute Collection, box 6, MHS.

73. Frederic Ayer to David Green, December 1, 1833, Nute Collection, box 3, MHS.

74. Sherman Hall to David Greene, January 2, 1837, Nute Collection, box 5, MHS.

75. Sherman Hall to Aaron Hall, Jr., Aug. 28, 1833, Nute Collection, box 3, MHS.

76. Sherman Hall and William Boutwell to ABCFM, Feb. 7, 1833, Nute Collection, box 3, MHS.

77. ABCFM Commission to Sherman Hall and William T. Boutwell, Summer, 1831, Nute Collection, box 2, MHS.

78. Sherman Hall to David Greene, ABCFM, June 14, 1832, Nute Collection, box 2, MHS.

79. Mrs. Howland, *The Infant School Manual*, 8th ed. (Worcester, Mass., 1835), p. 25.

80. Samuel Blair, *Discourse on Psalmody* (Philadelphia, 1789), pp. 11–12, as cited in Stephen Marini, "Rehearsal for Revival," p. 86.

81. Ibid.

82. A. G. Jackson, *The Missioner's Hymnal with Accompanying Tunes* (London: Rivingtons, 1884).

83. Wesley, "Preface."

84. Peter Jones, *A Collection of Chippeway and English Hymns* (Cincinnati: Walden and Stowe, 1847). The passage cited is I Corinthians 14.

85. John Wesley, "Preface."

86. Peter Jones, James Evans, and George Henry, *Ojebway Nuhguhmonun* (Cincinatti: Walden and Stowe, 188? [1840]), *Nuhguhmowin* 53.

87. E. P. Thompson, *The Making of the English Working Class* (New York: Vintage, 1966 [1963]).

88. Susan Tamke, *Make a Joyful Noise unto the Lord: Hymns as a Reflection of Victorian Social Attitudes* (Athens: Ohio University Press, 1978).

89. William Boutwell to Samuel Pond, March 22, 1839, Nute Collection, box 6, MHS.

90. Again, I am indebted to John and Jean Comaroff's theoretical framework laid out in their introduction to *Of Revelation and Revolution: Christianity, Colonialism, and Consciousness in South Africa*, vol.1.

CHAPTER 2

1. See especially George Copway (Kahgegagahbowh), *Life, Letters, and Speeches*, ed. A. LaVonne Brown Ruoff and Donald B. Smith (Lincoln: University of Nebraska Press, 1997 [1850]).

2. See Donald Smith's biographical introduction to Copway, *Life, Letters, and Speeches*, pp. 48–49.

3. Vizenor, *The People Named the Chippewa*, p. 61.

4. Copway, *Life, Letters, and Speeches*, p. 99; also cited in Vizenor, *The People Named the Chippewa*, p. 60.

5. Priscilla K. Buffalohead, "Farmers, Warriors, Traders: A Fresh Look at Ojibway Women," in *The American Indian Past and Present*, 3rd ed., ed. Roger L. Nichols (New York: Knopf, 1986), pp. 28–38.

6. On the emergence and history of Métis ethnic identity, see *The New Peoples: Being and Becoming Métis in North America*, ed. Jacqueline Peterson and Jennifer S. H. Brown (Lincoln: University of Nebraska Press, 1985).

7. Sherman Hall to David Greene, August 9, 1836, Nute Collection, box 4, MHS.

8. On the impact of earlier Jesuit missions, see Hickerson, *The Chippewa and Their Neighbors*; Devens, *Countering Colonialism*; Vecsey, *Traditional Ojibwa Religion and Its Historical Changes*; and John Webster Grant, *The Moon in Wintertime: Missionaries and the Indians of Canada in Encounter since 1534* (Toronto: University of Toronto Press, 1984).

9. On the relationship between the evangelical and High Church wings of nineteenth-century Episcopalianism, see Robert Bruce Mullin, *Episcopal Vision/American Reality: High Church Theology and Social Thought in Evangelical America* (New Haven, Conn.: Yale University Press, 1986); Diana Hochstedt Butler, *Standing against the Whirlwind: Evangelical Episcopalians in Nineteenth-Century America* (New York: Oxford University Press, 1995).

10. For a concise chronicle of missions among the Ojibwe, see Vecsey, *Traditional Ojibwa Religion and Its Historical Changes*, pp. 26–44.

11. Sherman Hall to Lydia Hall, Dec. 25, 1832, in Nute Collection, box 2, MHS.

12. *Iu Pitabun; Gema Gaie Okikinoamaguziuiniua Idiu Abinojiug. The Peep of Day; or, A Series of the Earliest Religious Instruction the Infant Mind Is Capable of Receiving* (Boston: Crocker and Brewster, 1844).

13. Sherman Hall to David Green, October 1, 1837, Nute Collection, box 5, MHS.

14. Beverley Cavanagh, "The Transmission of Algonkian Indian Hymns: Between Orality and Literacy," in *Musical Canada*, ed. John Beckwith and Frederick Hall (Toronto: University of Toronto Press, 1988).

15. Cavanagh, "Transmission of Algonkian Indian Hymns," p. 7.

16. Ibid., p. 27.

17. *Ojib-ue Spelling Book Designed for the Use of Native Learners* (Utica, N.Y.: G. Tracy, 1833); Peter Jones, *Ojibue Nugumouinun Gaaiouajin igiu Anishinabeg Enumiajig* (Boston: Crocker and Brewster, 1836); a subsequent edition of Jones, *Ojibue Nugumouinun Gaaiouajin igiu Anishinabeg Enumiajig* (Boston: Crocker and Brewster, 1844); unidentified fragment found in Grace Lee Nute Collection of Documents Relating to Northwest Missions, Box 3, MHS (n.d.); Edward C. Kah-O-Sed, compiler, *Ojibwa Hymnal* (Minneapolis: Protestant Episcopal Church, Diocese of Minnesota, 1910).

18. Cavanagh, "Transmission of Algonkian Indian Hymns," p. 21.

19. Michel de Certeau, *The Practice of Everyday Life*, trans. Steven Rendall (Berkeley: University of California Press, 1984), p. 18.

20. For the history of nineteenth-century Ojibwe language publications, see James C. Pilling, *Bibliography of the Algonkian Languages* (Washington, D.C.: G.P.O., 1891).

21. Donald B. Smith, *Sacred Feathers: The Reverend Peter Jones Kahkewaquonaby and the Mississauga Indians* (Toronto: University of Toronto Press, 1987). See also Homer Noley, *First White Frost* (Nashville: Abingdon Press, 1991); Jace Weaver, *That the People Might Live* (New York: Oxford University Press, 1997), pp. 59–65.

22. As cited in Smith, *Sacred Feathers*, p. 53.

23. Ibid., p. 60.

24. Ibid., p. 64.

25. Edmund Ely to David Greene, September 3, 1839, Nute Collection, box 7, MHS.

26. Peter Jones, *History of the Ojebway Indians with Especial Reference to Their Conversion to Christianity* (London: A.W. Bennett, 1861), pp. 188–189.

27. Peter Jones, *Nahkahmoonun kanahnahkahmoowaudt ekewh ahnueshenahpaigk anah-meahchik* (New York: J. Collord, 1829).

28. Peter Jones, "Preface" to Peter Jones, James Evans, and George Henry, *A Collection of Chippeway and English Hymns* (New York: Phillips and Hunt, 1847).

29. Sherman Hall to David Greene, August 9, 1836, Nute Collection, box 4, MHS.

30. Henry Rowe Schoolcraft to the Commissioner of Indian Affairs, November 9, 1836, Nute Collection, box 9, MHS.

31. Pilling, *Bibliography of the Algonquian Languages*.

32. H. B. Whipple in *Spirit of Missions* 37 (October, 1872), p. 616, emphasis mine.

33. Our translations were from a 1993 reprint of the 1910 *The Ojibwa Hymnal*, compiled by Edward C. Kah-O-Sed. Because of Larry's poor eyesight and frequent discrepancies in the hymnal's orthography, the translations were limited in certain cases by my own pronunciation as I read them to Larry. I am deeply indebted to John Nichols for scrutinizing these translations and providing helpful glosses and many corrections—corrections of my own liberties rather than of Larry's translations per se.

34. Vecsey, *Traditional Ojibwa Religion and Its Historical Changes*, p. 4.

35. Hallowell, *Culture and Experience*, p. 294.

36. Peter Jones, James Evans, and George Henry, *Ojebway Nuguhmonun* (Cincinnati: Walden and Stowe, 188? [1840]); Kah-O-Sed, *Ojibwa Hymnal*. In this instance, the 1910 hymnal from which Cloud Morgan and I rendered our translations happens to follow the Jones translation quite closely, though in a different orthography. In other songs, there are a considerable number of variant Ojibwe usages in the 1910 hymnal. As with the other translations, I am grateful for the generous assistance of John Nichols.

37. Peter Jones, *Life and Journals of Kah-ke-wa-quo-na-by (Rev. Peter Jones), Wesleyan Missionary* (Toronto: Anson Green, 1860), p. 187.

38. Sherman Hall to David Greene, October 17, 1834, Nute Collection, box 3, MHS.

39. Sherman Hall to Richards and Tracy, July 10, 1834, Nute Collection, box 3, MHS.

40. Dan Kier, in conversation, May 1997.

41. Raymond DeMallie was speaking of the Lakota concept of *wakan*, roughly similar to *manidoo* in terms of its fundamental incomprehensibility. See Raymond DeMallie Jr., "Lakota Belief and Ritual," in *Sioux Indian Religion*, ed. Raymond DeMallie Jr. and Douglas Parks (Norman: University of Oklahoma Press, 1987), p. 32.

42. Jones, *History of the Ojebway Indians*, p. 179.

43. Jones, *Life and Journals*, p. 188.

44. Fred Ettewageshik and Thomas Shalifoe, translations of *Jesus Wegwissiian*, in Gertrude Kurath and Jane Ettawageshik, *Religious Customs of Modern Michigan Algonqians*, unpublished typescript (1959), chapter 8, p. 6.

45. Again, the Ojibwe language here is not necessarily undermining the Christian message, since the implications of salvation for earthly existence were hardly unappreciated in Christian thought. Nevertheless, it is useful to point out that nineteenth-century Protestant

missionaries frequently fought to replace an Ojibwe focus on this-worldly life with an overriding concern for its eternal consequences.

46. Sherman Hall to Richards and Tracy, July 10, 1834, Nute Collection, box 3, MHS.

47. John Nichols has never heard an Ojibwe person use this expression. He indicates that the form of "bataziwinishun," *bataaziwinishan*, though appearing as a plural, involves a stative verb final, a pejorative suffix (*-ish*), and a nominalizing suffix (*-win*), and thus would be "considered to mean sin by missionaries." John Nichols, correspondence with author, June, 1999.

48. Chrysostom Verwyst, "Some Peculiarities of the Chippewa Language," Smithsonian Institution, Bureau of American Ethnology Archives, Chippewa Manuscripts, n.d., p. 1, as cited in Vecsey, *Traditional Ojibwa Religion and Its Historical Changes*, p. 134.

49. Edward E. Hale, "Eliot's Bible and the Ojibway Language," *Proceedings of the American Antiquarian Society* 9:317, as cited in Vecsey, *Traditional Ojibwa Religion and Its Historical Changes*, p. 134.

50. Basil Johnston, *The Manitous: The Supernatural World of the Ojibway* (New York: Harper, 1995), p. 241.

51. See the discussion of the close link between motion, community, and Ojibwe ideas of sound in Diamond et al., *Visions of Sound*.

52. For an insightful discussion of the historical career of the term's meaning, see Wilfred Cantwell Smith, *The Meaning and End of Religion* (Minneapolis: Fortress Press, 1991 [1962]), pp. 15–50.

53. Nichols and Nyholm translate *izhitwaa* as "to have a certain custom, practice a certain religion." See *A Concise Dictionary of Minnesota Ojibwe*; Frederic Baraga, *A Dictionary of the Ojibway Language* (St. Paul: Minnesota Historical Society Press, 1992 [1878]).

54. Lamin Sanneh, *Translating the Message: The Missionary Impact on Culture* (Maryknoll, N.Y.: Orbis Press, 1989), p. 3.

55. Pierre Bourdieu, *Language and Symbolic Power*, pp. 39–40.

56. Pitezel, *Life of Rev. Peter Marksman: An Ojibwa Missionary* (Cincinnati: Western Methodist Book Concern, 1901), p. 41.

57. Frederic Ayer to David Greene, October 4, 1833, Nute Collection, box 3, MHS.

58. Frederic Ayer to David Greene, October 4, 1833, Nute Collection, box 3, MHS.

59. Frederic Ayer to David Greene, May 15, 1834, Nute Collection, box 3, MHS.

60. Sherman Hall Diary, May 18, 1832, Nute Collection, box 2, MHS.

61. Journal of W. T. Boutwell, August 5, 1832, Nute Collection, box 1, MHS.

62. Alfred Brunson to the Secretary of the Missionary Society of the Methodist Episcopal Church, September 4, 1838, in *Western Christian Advocate* November 9, 1838, Nute Collection, box 6, MHS.

63. Alfred Brunson to the Secretary of the Missionary Society of the Methodist Episcopal Church, *Western Christian Advocate*, November 9, 1838, Nute Collection, box 6, MHS.

64. Edmund Ely Journal, June 8, 1834, Edmund Ely Papers, box 1, MHS.

65. Attending one of Cotté's hymn sings, Frederic Baraga was puzzled to hear how his own translations of Slovenian hymns had been set to French folktunes. As cited in Marijan Smolik, "Slovenian Contributions to American Hymnody," *The Hymn* 36 (July 1985), p. 14.

66. Journal of W. T. Boutwell, July 1, 1832, Nute Collection, box 1, MHS.

67. Edmund Ely Journal, December 22, 1833, Edmund Ely Papers, box 1, MHS.

68. Edmund Ely Journal, May 24, 1835, Edmund Ely Papers, box 1, MHS.

69. Sherman Hall and William Boutwell, Report to ABCFM, Feb. 7, 1833, Nute Collection, box 3, MHS.

70. Sherman Hall to David Greene, October 17, 1834, Nute Collection, box 3, MHS.

71. Sherman Hall and William Boutwell, Report to ABCFM, February 7, 1833, Nute Collection, box 2, MHS.

72. Diary of Samuel Spates, October 31, 1841, Nute Collection, box 9, MHS.

73. Alonzo Barnard, "Events of the Years 1844–5 at Leech Lake," *North and West*, Nute Collection, box 11, MHS.

74. Pitezel, *Life of Rev. Peter Marksman*, pp. 157–159.

75. Frederic Baraga, as cited in Marijan Smolik, "Slovenian Contributions to American Hymnody," *The Hymn* 36 (July 1985), p. 14.

76. James L. Breck, "Chippewa Pictures" (1857), in *Early Days in Minnesota: The Church in Story and Pageant* (Hartford: Church Missions Publishing, 1929), p. 16.

77. Ibid.

78. Ibid., pp. 22-29.

79. Sela Wright Journal, October 26, in *American Missionary* (n.d.), Nute Collection, box 14, MHS.

80. James L. Breck, *Spirit of Missions* 18 (March 14, 1853), p. 265.

81. As more and more schoolchildren had gone through this process, hymnbooks were beginning to function more fully as texts that were read by numbers of Ojibwe people in their schooling and worship. In the 1840s and 1850s, as increasing numbers of Anishinaabe and Métis children attended school, learned to read, and brought books back to their families, demand for hymnbooks rose dramatically. "We must have a new edition of our hymnbook soon," wrote L.H. Wheeler in 1862, "we have not a half dozen for our Indian meetings." L. H. Wheeler to Edmund Ely, March 20, 1862, Nute Collection, box 20, MHS.

82. Breck, "Chippewa Pictures," p. 27.

83. Sherman Hall to David Greene, October 17, 1834, Nute Collection, box 3, MHS.

84. Breck, "Chippewa Pictures," p. 29.

85. Ottmar Clöter, untitled letter, May 22, 1859, in *Lutheraner*, n.d., Nute Collection, box 19, MHS.

86. J. P. Bardwell, "Second Annual Report of American Missionary Association," September 26, 1848, Nute Collection, box 14, MHS.

87. What is more, sharp differences existed within each band in terms of the appropriate posture toward the United States and its encroachments. Rebecca Kugel argues persuasively that in the 1850s and 1860s, warrior leaders and civil leaders, or *ogimaag*, alike challenged many agreements made with the other party on behalf of a band. See Kugel, *To Be the Main Leaders of Our People*, pp. 56–88.

88. See Kugel, "Factional Alignment among the Minnesota Ojibwe, 1850–1880."

89. Frederic Ayer to S. B. Treat, October 5, 1848, Nute Collection, box 14, MHS. Ayer reported two deaths per month in a community of roughly six hundred people—"Second Annual Report of American Missionary Association," September 1848, Nute Collection, box 14, MHS.

90. Enmegabowh to H. B. Whipple, July 20, 1863, Whipple Papers, box 3, MHS.

91. For a brief overview of Ojibwe resistance to Christianity, see Vecsey, *Traditional Ojibwa Religion and Its Historical Changes*, pp. 45-50.

92. As cited in E. Steele Peake to Domestic Committee of Board of Missions of the Protestant Episcopal Church, April, 1862, Nute Collection, box 20, MHS.

93. Kugel, *To Be the Main Leaders of Our People*, p. 4.

94. "An Agreement between B. T. Kavanaugh, superintendent of the Indian Mission District of the Illinois Conference and Hole in the Day, Wahboojeeg, Moosah kah oos, and Soon gan ko mig," 1840, Nute Collection, box 8, MHS.

95. Missionary Paper no. 5 at the Associate Mission for Minnesota (Faribault, Minn.: 1860), in Protestant Episcopal Church, Diocese of Minnesota Papers, box 1, MHS.

96. George Copway to Kavanaugh, February 22, 1842, Nute Collection, box 9, MHS.

97. Frederic Baraga, as cited in Marijan Smolik, "Slovenian Contributions to American Hymnody," *The Hymn* 36 (July 1985), p. 14.

98. Jones et al., *A Collection of Chippeway and English Hymns*.

99. Franz Pierz to *Leopoldinen Stiftung*, November 5, 1838, Nute Collection, box 6, MHS.

100. Frederic Ayer to David Greene, n.d. [1835?], Nute Collection, box 3, MHS.

101. Report of Pastor Miessler from Bethany Mission, April 17, 1859, in *Lutheraner*, n.d., Nute Collection, box 19, MHS.

102. Sela Wright to American Missionary Association, February 1858, in *American Missionary*, n.d., Nute Collection, box 19, MHS. Other missionary documents similarly point to this particular hymn, which was often associated with death, as the most popular Ojibwe hymn.

103. H. N. B., *Manitoulin, or Five Years of Church Work among Ojibwa Indians* (London, 1895), 132.

104. Frederic Baraga to *Leopoldine Stiftung*, August 25, 1849, Nute Collection, box 14, MHS.

105. Edmund Ely Journal, March 3, 1835, Edmund Ely Papers, box 1, MHS.

106. J. A. Gilfillan, *Spirit of Missions* 40 (July 1875), p. 501.

CHAPTER 3

1. H. B. Whipple to *Evening Dispatch*, July 28, 1880, in Whipple Papers, box 14, MHS.

2. "Indian Notes," *Minnesota Missionary* 4, no. 9 (June 1881).

3. Kugel, *To Be the Main Leaders of Our People*, pp. 101–126.

4. On the complexity of the respective support of Manidowab, Nabunashkong, and other chiefs, see Kugel, *To Be the Main Leaders of Our People* pp. 109–113.

5. Enmegabowh to S. Hollingsworth, December 6, 1873, John Johnson Enmegabowh Papers, MHS.

6. Melissa Meyer, *The White Earth Tragedy* (Lincoln: University of Nebraska Press, 1994), p. 48. I am grateful throughout this section for Melissa Meyer's detailed treatment of the settlement of White Earth and its future implications.

7. See Meyer, *The White Earth Tragedy*, pp. 49–67.

8. Ibid., p. 94.

9. Ibid.

10. Ibid., pp. 128–129

11. Compiled from Bureau of Indian Affairs censuses and cited in Meyer, *The White Earth Tragedy*, p. 223.

12. See Meyer, *The White Earth Tragedy*, pp. 138–140.

13. Ibid., p. 151.

14. See ibid., pp. 167–171, and David Beaulieu, "Curly Hair and Big Feet: Physical Anthropology and the Implementation of Land Allotment on the White Earth Chippewa Reservation," *American Indian Quarterly* 8:281–314 (1984).

15. Allotment policy had reduced native land holdings from 138 million acres in 1887 to 48 million in 1934. John Collier, *Memorandum, Hearings on H.R. 7902 before the House Committee on Indian Affairs*, 73rd Congress, 2nd Session (1934), p. 16, as cited in Vine Deloria Jr. and Clifford Lytle, *American Indians, American Justice* (Austin: University of Texas Press, 1983), p. 10.

16. A powerful leader of Gull Lake warriors, Bugonegezhig, or Hole-in-the-Day, threatened that he would kill anyone agreeing to leave for White Earth before the United States honored his demand that it build houses for the emigrants. He also added the Métis trader families to the treaty annuity rolls and later secured a place at White Earth for them. But in 1868, feeling the traders had crossed his people, Bugonegezhig publicly reversed his support. He was assassinated shortly thereafter in what many White Earth people today believe to have been a plot by the traders to ensure their lucrative place at White Earth.

17. For insights on these social processes as they developed in the American Southeast, see Martin, *Sacred Revolt*.

18. Meyer, *The White Earth Tragedy*, p. 122.

19. Ibid., p. 75.

20. Ibid., p. 70.

21. Kugel, *To Be the Main Leaders of Our People*, p. 101–160.

22. See ibid., pp. 117ff.

23. See Whipple's memoir, *Lights and Shadows of a Long Episcopate* (New York: Macmillan, 1899).

24. Kugel, *To Be the Main Leaders of Our People*, p. 117.

25. Meyer, *The White Earth Tragedy*, p. 50.

26. Tinker, *Missionary Conquest*, p. 108.

27. See Frederick Hoxie, *A Final Promise: The Campaign to Assimilate the Indians, 1880–1920* (Lincoln: University of Nebraska Press, 1984), and Robert Mardock, *The Reformers and the American Indian* (Columbia: University of Missouri Press, 1971).

28. Francis Paul Prucha, *American Indian Policy in Crisis* (Norman: University of Oklahoma Press, 1976), p. 193.

29. Pauline Colby, *Reminiscences* (1981), MHS.

30. Sybil Carter, *Indian Mothers and Their Work*, n.d., Whipple Papers, box 21, MHS.

31. Sybil Carter to H. B. Whipple, September 2, 1892, in Whipple Papers, box 22, MHS.

32. Carter, *Indian Mothers and Their Work*.

33. See Devens, *Countering Colonization*. On the distinctive ways that women missionaries used their power, see also Jane Hunter, *The Gospel of Gentility: American Women Missionaries in Turn-of-the-Century China* (New Haven, Conn.: Yale University Press, 1984), and Patricia Hill, *The World Their Household* (Ann Arbor: University of Michigan Press, 1984).

34. J. A. Gilfillan to H. B. Whipple, n.d., 1891, Whipple Papers, box 1, MHS.

35. Inez Hilger, *A Social Study of One Hundred Fifty Chippewa Indian Families of the White Earth Reservation of Minnesota* (Washington, D.C.: Catholic University Press, 1939).

36. J. A. Gilfillan, fragment entitled "The Field" (1882), in Gilfillan Papers, MHS.

37. Ibid.

38. Kugel adds that the Episcopalian missionaries demonstrated a commitment to gift giving and advocacy that restored confidence that the Episcopalians were worthy of an alliance on Anishinaabe terms. See Kugel, *To Be the Main Leaders of Our People*, p. 118.

39. Ibid., p. 108.

40. J. A. Gilfillan, "Some Indians I Have Known," *The Red Man* (December 1913), pp. 152–155.

41. J. A. Gilfillan to H. B. Whipple, November 1873, in *Spirit of Missions* (January 1874); Gilfillan, "The Indian Deacons at White Earth," Protestant Episcopal Church, Diocese of Minnesota Papers, box 3, MHS.

42. Gilfillan, "Indian Deacons of White Earth." After several more years at White Earth village, Wright spent a year at Seabury Divinity School in Faribault.

43. H. B. Whipple, *The Churchman* (September 2, 1876).

44. Gilfillan, "Some Indians I Have Known," p. 155.

45. Gilfillan, in *Detroit Record* (October 25, 1895).

46. Gilfillan, "The Field" (1882), Gilfillan Papers, MHS.

47. Gilfillan saved a handful of Ojibwe language correspondence that he had received from the deacons in the 1890s, and later transcribed them in an interlinear fashion as a contribution to the documentation of the Ojibwe language. The correspondence is found in the microfilmed portion of the Gilfillan Papers at the MHS.

48. See, for example, Enmegabowh to Samuel Hollingsworth, August 23, 1870, John Johnson Enmegabowh Papers, MHS.

49. Enmegabowh to Samuel Hollingsworth, December 6, 1873, John Johnson Enmegabowh Papers, MHS.

50. Kugel, *To Be the Main Leaders of Our People*, pp. 179–181.

51. Ibid., p. 142.

52. Charles Wright, Letter to the Editor, *The Progress* 12 (February 15, 1889).

53. Meyer, *The White Earth Tragedy*, p. 149.

54. Kugel, *To Be the Main Leaders of Our People*, p. 149.

55. Ibid., p. 146.

56. J. A. Gilfillan to H. B. Whipple, January 30, 1883, Whipple Papers, box 16, MHS; also cited in Kugel, *To Be the Main Leaders of Our People*, p. 147.

57. J. A. Gilfillan to H. B. Whipple, January 4, 1883, Whipple Papers, box 16, MHS.

58. J. A. Gilfillan to H. B. Whipple, January 10, 1883, Whipple Papers, box 16, MHS.

59. J. A. Gilfillan to H. B. Whipple, January 4, 1883, Whipple Papers, box 16, MHS.

60. J. A. Gilfillan to H. B. Whipple, July 19, 1886, Whipple Papers, box 15, MHS.

61. J. A. Gilfillan, "On the Wrong Way and the Right Way to Civilize the Indians," October 14, 1911, Gilfillan Papers, MHS.

62. Ibid.

63. H. B. Whipple, *Spirit of Missions* 37 (October 1872).

64. Ibid., p. 616.

65. H. B. Whipple, *Minnesota Missionary* 4, no. 10, (July 1881); emphasis his.

66. "Missionary Paper no. 5," Associate Mission for Minnesota, 1860, Protestant Episcopal Church, Diocese of Minnesota Papers, box 1, MHS.

67. J. A. Gilfillan, *Spirit of Missions* 40 (July 1875), p. 501.

68. Pauline Colby, *Reminiscences*.

69. "Indian Notes," *Minnesota Missionary* 7, no. 3 (April 1884).

70. For an elaboration on this theme, see Katherine Bergeron's "Prologue: Disciplining Music," in *Disciplining Music*, ed. Katherine Bergeron and Philip Bohlman (Chicago: University of Chicago Press, 1992).

71. H. B. Whipple, "Indian Notes," *Minnesota Missionary* 10, no. 1 (January 1886).

72. J. A. Gilfillan to H. B. Whipple, n.d., Whipple Papers, box 1, MHS.

73. Shay-day-ence via J. A. Gilfillan to H. B. Whipple, November 23, 1875, Whipple Papers, box 11, MHS.

74. "Indian Notes," *Minnesota Missionary* 3, no. 7 (April 1880), p. 2; "Indian Notes," *Minnesota Missionary* 4, no. 9 (June 1881).

75. J. A. Gilfillan to H. B. Whipple, February 15, 1876, Whipple Papers, box 11, MHS.

76. H. B. Whipple, in *Minnesota Missionary* 4, no. 10 (July 1881), p. 5.

77. J. A. Gilfillan to H. B. Whipple, December 3, 1875, Whipple Papers, box 11, MHS.

78. Kakabishique via J. A. Gilfillan to H. B. Whipple, July 25, 1876, Whipple Papers, box 11, MHS.

79. J. A. Gilfillan to H. B. Whipple, February 15, 1876, Whipple Papers, box 11, MHS.

80. Pauline Colby, *Reminiscences*.

81. On the struggle within the "linguistic colonialism" of naming practices, see Comaroff and Comaroff, *Of Revelation and Revolution*, vol. 1, p. 219.

82. J. A. Gilfillan to H. B. Whipple, December 3, 1875, Whipple Papers, box 11, MHS.

83. J. A. Gilfillan, "Indian Notes," *Minnesota Missionary* 10, no. 5 (May 1886).

84. "Notes from the Indian Field," *Minnesota Missionary* 4, no. 6 (March 1881).

85. Ibid.

86. Kugel, *To Be the Main Leaders of Our People*, p. 123.

87. Edwin Benedict to H. B. Whipple, September 26, 1881, Whipple Papers, box 15, MHS.

88. Shay-day-ence via J. A. Gilfillan to H. B. Whipple, June 6, 1885 [dictated May 6, 1885], Whipple Papers, box 18, MHS.

89. Suzanna Roy via J. A. Gilfillan to H. B. Whipple, April 13, 1882, Whipple Papers, box 16, MHS.

90. "Indian Notes," *Minnesota Missionary* 5, no. 6 (March 1882).

91. See Russell Thornton, *American Indian Holocaust and Survival: A Population History since 1492* (Norman: University of Oklahoma Press, 1987).

92. Enmegabowh to H. B. Whipple, September 20, 1881, Whipple Papers, box 15, MHS.

93. Enmegabowh's English appears to have become increasingly broken as he aged, evidence perhaps of a shift toward his native language and culture in the mature years of a life lived in perennial tension with nonnative Episcopalian superiors and non-Christian Anishinaabeg.

94. On the cultural practices of emotion, see Steven Feld, *Sound and Sentiment: Birds, Weeping, Poetics, and Song in Kaluli Expression*, 2nd ed. (Philadelphia: University of Pennsylvania Press, 1990 [1982]). On the historical situation of emotion, see Robert Orsi, *Thank You Saint Jude: Women's Devotion to the Patron Saint of Hopeless Causes* (New Haven, Conn.: Yale University Press, 1996).

95. Enmegabowh to Samuel Hollingsworth, March 20, 1872, John Johnson Enmegabowh Letters, MHS..

96. Parish Record of the Saint Columba Parish, White Earth, Minn., Diocese of Minnesota 1853–1905, 1930–1933.

97. Colby, *Reminiscences*.

98. In a coda, Colby adds, "although the substantial part is devoured by the birds and other denizens of the wilds, and sometimes by the children who are always roaming about in search of some toothsome edible." Colby, *Reminiscences*.

99. Ibid. The persistence of Anami'aajig belief in the journey of the spirit seemed to Colby to have been part of the allure of hymn singing. Upon a visit to a dying woman, whose husband had laid out so much food near her deathbed that "the mice dug in," Colby recalled, "it was but a matter of a few hours when the poor dying creature would be beyond all wants and so through the brief prayers and hymns, which helped her passing soul on its flight, the mice's banquet continued undisturbed."

100. Edmund Ely Journal, January 7, 1837, Edmund Ely Papers, box 1, MHS.

101. Frederick Ayer to David Greene, January 2, 1846, Nute Collection, box 12, MHS.

102. Alonzo Barnard, *Diary* (Summer 1846) in *North and West* 11, Nute Collection, box 16, MHS. The practice of committing a body to a scaffold was not prevalent among Ojibwes but appears to have been appropriate in certain circumstances, especially when the ground was frozen.

103. David Spencer to American Missionary Association, September 6, 1851, *American Missionary* 6 (1851), MHS

104. J. A. Gilfillan, "The Religion of the Indians" (March 1896?), Whipple Papers, box 23, MHS.

105. Ibid.

106. G. T. Sproat to David Greene, January 18, 1840, Nute Collection, box 7, MHS.

107. Sela Wright to American Missionary Association, March 6, 1854, in *American Missionary* 8:59, Nute Collection, box 18, MHS. The native man continues, "We do a great deal to secure the favor of Him who gives us all life, that we *may live long*, and we always avoid talking about death, hoping that it may be far from us."

108. Colby, *Reminiscences*.

109. J. A. Gilfillan to H. B. Whipple, November 1873, *Spirit of Missions* (January 1874).

110. Burton, *American Primitive Music*, pp. 133–137. The reference to his old age in Burton's account suggests that this Megissun is the son-in-law of Shingwaukonse, or Little Pine, the famous leader of the Garden River Ojibwe, who converted to Anglicanism in the late 1830s. See Janet Chute, *The Legacy of Shingwaukonse* (Toronto: University of Toronto Press, 1998), p. 56.

111. Burton, *American Primitive Music*, p. 279. Certain hymns took on associations with particular individuals. Burton remarks that a Chief Bukujjinini had a favorite hymn that, in keeping with an Anishinaabe convention of a "death song" pertaining to an individual "was sung at [his] bedside by the members of his family while he lay dying." "Every Indian has his death song," Burton added, "one that he will sing himself, if possible, at the very moment of dissolution; and if voice fails him, his friends sing it for him."

112. Ibid., pp. 135–136.

113. Ibid., p. 137. Burton also reports having made several wax cylinder recordings of this William J. Shingwauk singing Ojibwe hymns "in the manner of a bygone age." Unfortunately, these recordings appear to have been lost.

114. Bourdieu, *Language and Symbolic Power*, p. 66.

115. Ibid., p. 170. On speech act theory, see J. L. Austin, *How to Do Things with Words*, 2nd ed. (Cambridge: Harvard University Press, 1981 [1962]).

116. Ibid.

117. Bourdieu, *Language and Symbolic Power*, pp. 52–53.

118. Gilfillan spoke of the struggle that the Singing and Praying Bands waged against the Drum Dance that spread like wildfire in 1882. "As if in a poetical sort of revenge," he wrote, the White Earth mission sends the Indian laymen of the young Men's Singing and Praying Band to Red Lake, to preach the Gospel there, and to go singing their Christian hymns."—"Indian Notes," *Minnesota Missionary* 5, no. 6 (March 1882).

119. Committee of Majigizhig via Henry Selkrig to H. B. Whipple, August 14, 1881, Whipple Papers, box 15, MHS.

120. See Vennum, *Ojibwa Dance Drum*; Diamond et al., *Visions of Sound*.

121. Jones, *History of Ojebway Indians*, pp. 228–229.

122. Alban Fruth, *A Century of Missionary Work among the Red Lake Chippewa Indians 1858–1958* (Red Lake, Minn.: St. Mary's, 1958), pp. 15–16.

123. J. A. Gilfillan, "Indian Deacons at White Earth," Protestant Episcopal Church, Diocese of Minnesota Papers, box 3, MHS. See also *Minnesota Missionary* 4, no. 7 (April 1881).

124. "Indian Notes," *Minnesota Missionary* 7, no. 3 (April 1884).

125. Ibid.

126. "Indian Notes," *Minnesota Missionary* 9, no. 4 (April 1885).

127. J. A. Gilfillan to H. B. Whipple (n.d., 1891), Whipple Papers, box 1, MHS.

128. "Indian Notes," *Minnesota Missionary* 7, no. 3 (April 1884).

129. Ibid.

130. That it took some years for missionaries to persuade Ojibwe Christians of the urgency of this repertorial distinction only added to the political charge of the songs.

131. Indeed, because missionaries also heard the hymn as a privileged form of social and spiritual communication, they found common ground with this Anami'aajig practice.

132. Burton, *American Primitive Music*, pp. 237, 106. Burton also related *nagamo* to poetry. "Whatever departs from plain prose is nogamon," Burton observed, "which means that [an Ojibwe's] poetry is not only inseparable but indistinguishable from music. Even in his oratory the voice is modulated to a manner of utterance that is beyond the pale of declamation, and a long step toward singing."

133. For a survey of Ojibwe resistance to Christianity, see Vecsey, *Traditional Ojibwa Reli-*

gion and Its Historical Changes, pp. 45–50. Taking resistance as the baseline, Vecsey attributes the growth of an Ojibwe Christian community entirely to the fact that White Earth was "controlled territory, subject to the autocratic rule of missionaries." "The Ojibwas," continues Vecsey, "were a defeated, captive audience to the Christian message" (p. 50).

134. J. A. Gilfillan, "Indian Notes," *Minnesota Missionary* 10, no. 5 (May 1886).

135. "Notes from the Indian Field," *Minnesota Missionary* 4, no. 6 (March 1881).

136. Taycumigizhig via J. A. Gilfillan to H. B. Whipple, June 23, 1884, Whipple Papers, box 16, MHS.

137. "What We Did in This Year," unsigned fragment, June 6, 1881, Whipple Papers, box 15, MHS.

138. Majigizhig "for and by desire of the young men's association" to H. B. Whipple, Whipple Papers, box 16, MHS.

139. Turino, *Moving away from Silence*, p. 111.

140. Ibid., p. 99.

141. I am indebted to Steve Holmes for this insight.

142. Burton, *American Primitive Music*, p. 134.

143. Bell, *Ritual Theory, Ritual Practice*, p. 106. I find there to be an interesting tension here in Bourdieu's thought. Bourdieu's "sense of the sacred," existing as it does on the "hitherside of discourse" appears—like Durkheim's effervescence, Weber's charisma, and Freud's unconscious—to be a generative principle in society and history for which social analysis cannot fully account.

144. Erma Vizenor, Symposium Comments, "Crossing Boundaries: New Perspectives on Ojibwa Religion," Burlington, Vt., November 1995.

CHAPTER 4

1. The principal written documents are to be found in the Protestant Episcopal Church, Diocese of Minnesota, Papers, MHS. This collection includes documents of the former Diocese of Duluth, which oversaw Ojibwe missions from 1896 to 1938.

2. Melissa Meyer, "Foreword" to John Rogers, *Red World and White* (Norman: University of Oklahoma Press, 1996 [1974]), pp. iv, xxi.

3. Rogers, *Red World and White*, pp. 48–49.

4. Ignatia Broker, *Night Flying Woman: An Ojibway Narrative* (St. Paul: Minnesota Historical Society Press, 1983), p. 3.

5. Ibid., p. 97.

6. Ibid., p. 103.

7. Ibid., p. 116.

8. Ibid., p. 94.

9. Erma Vizenor, in conversation, August 1994.

10. "Annual Report on Indian Mission Work for 1956," Protestant Episcopal Church, Diocese of Minnesota, Papers, box 70, MHS.

11. For more on the Indian Reorganization Act, see Graham Taylor, *The New Deal and American Indian Tribalism: 1934–1945* (Lincoln: University of Nebraska Press, 1980).

12. See Brookings Institution [Lewis Meriam], *The Problem of Indian Administration* (Baltimore: Johns Hopkins Press, 1928).

13. Inez Hilger, *A Social Study of 150 Chippewa Indian Families of the White Earth Reservation of Minnesota* (Washington, D.C.: Catholic University of America Press, 1939), pp. 5–7.

14. Ibid., p. 10.

15. 1937 BIA report, as cited in Hilger, *A Social Study of 150 Chippewa Indian Families*, p. 28.

16. Hilger, *A Social Study of 150 Chippewa Indian Families*, pp. 196–205.

17. J. A. Gilfillan, untitled fragment, 1911, Gilfillan Papers, MHS.

18. Hilger, *A Social Study of 150 Chippewa Indian Families*, p. 112.

19. Ibid.,

20. Ibid., p. 99.

21. Marlita Reddy, *Statistical Records of Native North Americans* (Detroit: Gale Research, 1993), p. 387. Reddy's survey included 23,686 Ojibwes between ages 5 and 17, of which 1,059 reported speaking Ojibwe at home. The same study finds more than 70 percent of Navajo children aged 5–17 speak their native language at home. Among Lakota Sioux children of the same age, the figure is 15 percent.

22. White Earth Land Recovery Project, Occasional Report (1994).

23. Wub-e-ke-niew, *We Have the Right to Exist* (New York: Black Thistle Press, 1995), p. 223.

24. Ibid.

25. C. H. Beaulieu, "Letter to the Editor," *Tomahawk*, June 30, 1904. Adding further complexity to the issue of twentieth-century religious affiliation, Beaulieu had broken with his family's Catholicism and become an Episcopalian clergyman.

26. Here I am grateful for Thomas Turino's understanding of the "folklorization" of cultural forms as he compares performances of panpipe music in Andean villages, ensconced as they are in indigenous conceptions of community and sound, with performances of the same repertory in the concerts and contests of Lima, Peru, which represent attempts to capture the essence of the highland music. See Turino, *Moving away from Silence*.

27. *Tomahawk*, June 11, 1903.

28. Although performed in Ojibwe, the libretto includes the original language of Longfellow's poem.—Louis Olivier Armstrong, *Hiawatha, or Nanabozho: An Ojibway Indian Play: Descriptive Notes and Excerpts to Be Used as a Libretto for "Hiawatha or Nanabozho"* (1901).

29. *Tomahawk*, June 23, 1904.

30. *Tomahawk*, May 21, 1903.

31. The prior masthead had read, "Truth before Favor."

32. See Vennum, "Southwestern Ojibwa Music."

33. See Michael W. Harris, *The Rise of Gospel Blues: The Music of Thomas Andrew Dorsey in the Urban Church* (New York: Oxford University Press, 1992). The assertion of sacred over profane music here would seem the most obvious, though I follow Jonathan Z. Smith's attention to the human assertion of difference rather than to the givenness of either sacred or profane. See Smith, *To Take Place: Toward Theory in Ritual* (Chicago: University of Chicago Press, 1987).

34. Bruno Nettl, *Blackfoot Musical Thought: Comparative Perspectives* (Kent, Oh.: Kent State University Press, 1989), p. 171.

35. Vennum, "Southwestern Ojibwa Music," p. 200. The songs Vennum recorded contained more vocables, a process he found commensurable to the "loss of the native religion and the gradual disuse of the Ojibwa language." Vennum acknowledges that his figure may be skewed by having recorded fewer "sacred" songs than Densmore, but a significant distinction remains.

36. Kateri Tekakwitha Conference, Bemidji, Minn., August 3, 1994.

37. See Vander, *Songprints: The Musical Experience of Five Shoshone Women*; Nettl, *Blackfoot Musical Thought*.

38. George Aubid, *Words of Wisdom*, widely circulated typescript, ca. 1985.

39. Later, in 1996, the Tribal Chair and two of the Reservation Tribal Council members began serving prison terms for convictions on election fraud and embezzlement.

40. On the importance of culturally relevant processes of political action in the context of Gandhian resistance, see Ashis Nandy, *The Intimate Enemy: Loss and Recovery of Self under Colonialism* (Delhi: Oxford University Press, 1983).

41. For a history of St. Benedict's, see Carol Berg, "Climbing Learner's Hill: Benedictines at White Earth, 1878–1945" (Ph.D. diss., University of Minnesota, 1983).

42. Erma J. Vizenor, "Tribal Identity and Cultural Triumph in Traditional Anishinabe Indian Elders" (Ed.D. diss., Harvard University Graduate School of Education, 1996).

43. The compound of gentleness and strength appears to be of some significance in the native community. A cardboard sign proclaiming "In gentleness is strength" hung prominently in the small trailer that served as Camp Justice's winter headquarters.

44. See Philip Deloria, *Playing Indian* (New Haven, Conn.: Yale University Press, 1999); Robert Berkhofer Jr., *The White Man's Indian: Images of the Indian from Columbus to the Present* (New York: Vintage, 1978).

45. Deborah Battaglia, *On the Bones of the Serpent* (Chicago: University of Chicago Press, 1990), p. 4.

46. Ibid., p. 11.

47. John Nichols and Earl Nyholm, *Ojibwewi-Ikidowinan: An Ojibwe Word Resource Book* (St. Paul: Minnesota Archeological Society, 1979).

48. Bell, *Ritual Theory, Ritual Practice*, pp. 107–108.

49. Archie Mosay, interviewed by Jerry Martin (1968), "The Drum Society," *American Indian Oral History Collection*, ed., Joseph Cash, in the library of Bemidji State University.

CHAPTER 5

1. John Sommerville, in conversation, September 1994.

2. Erma Vizenor, Workshop on Ojibwe Singing, Kateri Tekakwitha Conference, Bemidji, Minn., August, 1994.

3. David Karsnia of David-Dauenhower, in conversation, February 1999.

4. Robert Orsi, comment on panel "Death and Ritual in American Religion," American Academy of Religion, Annual Meeting (November 1994), at which I presented an earlier version of this chapter. Orsi here is extending Elaine Scarry's work on the symbolization of pain. See Scarry, *The Body in Pain* (New York: Oxford University Press, 1985); see also Gary Laderman, "A History of Death in Antebellum, Anglo-Protestant Communities," *Journal of the American Academy of Religion* 63:27–52 (Spring, 1995).

5. Peter Berger's notion of "world maintenance" here brings together those studies oriented around the preservation of social equilibrium, as emphasized by Emile Durkheim, Robert Hertz, and others, and the preservation of coherent cultural meaning, as stressed by symbolic anthropologists. See Peter Berger, *The Sacred Canopy* (New York: Anchor Books, 1969), pp. 3–28; Loring M. Danforth, "The Anthropology of Death," in Danforth, *The Death Rituals of Rural Greece* (Princeton, N.J.: Princeton University Press, 1982).

6. Robert Hertz, "A Contribution to the Study of the Collective Representation of Death," trans. Rodney and Claudia Needham, in Hertz, *Death and the Right Hand* (Aberdeen: Cohen and West, 1960 [1907]), p. 48.

7. In another context, Richard Kalish and David Reynolds conclude that African-American responses to death "cannot be adequately understood without reference to the accompanying persistent historical presence of violent death." They continue: "To be black in America is to be part of a history told in terms of contact with death and coping with death." See Kalish and Reynolds, *Death and Ethnicity: A Psychohistorical Study* (Los Angeles: University of Southern California Press, 1976), p. 94. See also Orsi's social history of hopelessness among Catholic women during the depression in *Thank You, St. Jude*, pp. 48–69.

8. On earlier funerary practices, see Frances Densmore, *Chippewa Customs* (St. Paul: Minnesota Historical Society Press, 1979 [1929]), pp. 73–78; Johann G. Kohl, *Kitchi Gami: Life among the Lake Superior Ojibway*, pp. 105–106, 249–251; Jones, *History of the Ojebway Indians*, pp. 98–100.

9. Phillippe Ariès, *The Hour of Our Death*, trans. Helen Weaver (New York: Oxford University Press, 1981). For Ariès, the denial of death can be understood as a principal symptom of modernity.

10. *Trends in Indian Health, 1997* (Washington, D.C.,: U.S. Indian Health Service, 1997).

11. Ibid. For ages 1–4, the ratio is 2.2 times the national average; for ages 5–15, the ratio is 1.7 times; for ages 15–34, the ratio is 2.1 times.

12. Ibid. The "teenage suicide rate" refers to the figures for ages 5–14 and 15–24, both of which sustained suicide rates nearly three times the national average between 1992 and 1994. See also Ronet Bachman, *Death and Violence on the Reservation: Homicide, Family Violence, and Suicide in American Indian Populations* (New York: Auburn House, 1992).

13. U.S. Department of Justice, Bureau of Justice Statistics, *American Indians and Crime*, NCJ 173386 (Washington, D.C.: U.S.G.P.O., February 1999)

14. *Trends in Indian Health, 1997*.

15. Ibid.

16. Ibid. Data for 1992–1994 in Minnesota, Indiana, Michigan, and Wisconsin.

17. Unemployment data from the 1990 census disclosed that in 1989, American Indians in Minnesota, Wisconsin, Michigan, and Indiana experienced a 16 percent unemployment rate, compared to slightly more than 6 percent for Americans as a whole. In the same region, 33 percent of Indians fell below the poverty line, compared to 13 percent of the American population as a whole. *Trends in Indian Health, 1997*.

18. George Aubid, *Words of Wisdom*, unpublished typescript, ca. 1985.

19. Certeau, *The Practice of Everyday Life*, p. 82.

20. Ibid., p. 89.

21. Ibid., p. 86.

22. See, for example, Gerald Vizenor, *Bearheart: The Heirship Chronicles* (Minneapolis: University of Minnesota Press, 1990 [1978]); and Vizenor, *A People Named the Chippewa*, pp. 139–153.

23. Certeau, *The Practice of Everyday Life*, p. 108.

24. Ibid., p. 87.

25. Ibid., p. 82.

26. Paul Connerton, *How Societies Remember* (Cambridge: Cambridge University Press, 1991), p. 102.

27. Ibid., p. 102.

28. Battaglia, *On the Bones of the Serpent*, p. 197.

29. For an important discussion of the space of death, see Michael Taussig, *Shamanism, Colonialism, and the Wild Man* (Chicago: University of Chicago Press, 1987), especially pp. 3–50.

30. Meyer, *The White Earth Tragedy*, p. 220.

31. J.A. Gilfillan, untitled typescript, 1880, Gilfillan Papers, MHS.

32. "Digests of Indian Field Staff Meetings," July 20, 1953, September 23, 1958, Tuesday, February. 16, 1960, Protestant Episcopal Church, Diocese of Minnesota Papers, box 70, folder entitled "Deaneries—NW and Cass Lake 1953–1965," MHS.

33. Larry Cloud Morgan, in conversation, December 1991.

34. Once again, I am grateful to John Nichols for clarifications on Larry Cloud Morgan's translation.

35. Larry Cloud Morgan, Workshop on Ojibwe Singing, Kateri Tekakwitha Conference, Bemidji, Minn., August 1994.

36. Larry Cloud Morgan, in conversation, December 1991.

37. Marvin Manypenny, address to Camp Justice assembly, August 1991.

38. George Earth, in conversation, March 1999.

39. Vizenor, *The People Named the Chippewa*, p. 24.

40. Diamond et al., *Visions of Sound*, p. 65.

41. Wub-e-ke-niew, *We Have the Right to Exist*, pp. 215–216.

42. Paul Schultz, in conversation, March 1999. See also Paul Schultz and George Tinker, *Rivers of Life: Native Spirituality for Native Churches* (Minneapolis: Augsburg Press, 1988).

43. Connerton, *How Societies Remember*, p. 59.

44. Ibid., pp. 60–61.

45. James Fernandez, *Bwiti: An Ethnography of the Religious Imagination in Africa* (Princeton, N.J.: Princeton University Press, 1982), p. 572.

46. John Nichols, in conversation, April 1995.

47. Claude Lévi-Strauss, *The Raw and the Cooked: Introduction to a Science of Mythology,* Vol. 1, trans. John and Doreen Weightman (Chicago: University of Chicago Press, 1969 [1964]), p. 18.

48. For a discussion of music's role in structuring the ritual time of Native American rites of passage, see Anne Dhu Shapiro and Inés Talamantez, "Mescalero Apache Girls Puberty Ceremony: The Role of Music in Structuring Ritual Time," *Yearbook for Traditional Music* (1986), pp. 77–90.

49. Lawrence Gross, "Making the World Sacred, Quietly, Carefully: Silence, Concentration, and the Sacred in the Soto Zen and Ojibwa Indian Experience," unpublished paper, April 1996.

50. Erma Vizenor, in conversation, October 1995.

51. Ellen Basso, *A Musical View of the Universe: Kalapalo Myth and Ritual Performance* (Philadelphia: University of Pennsylvania Press), p. 107.

52. Nester Clark, in conversation, March 1996.

53. Certeau, *The Practice of Everyday Life*, p. 106.

54. Gerald Vizenor, "Crossblood Survivance," in *Crossbloods: Bone Courts, Bingo, and Other Reports* (Minneapolis: University of Minnesota Press, 1990 [1976]).

CONCLUSION

1. Clifford Geertz, "Ritual and Social Change: A Javanese Example," in Geertz, *The Interpretation of Cultures* (New York: Basic Books, 1973), p. 164.

2. See Mircea Eliade, *The Myth of the Eternal Return or, Cosmos and History*, trans. Willard Trask (Princeton: Princeton University Press, 1974 [1949]).

3. Geertz, "Ritual as a Cultural System," in Geertz, *The Interpretation of Cultures*, p. 112.

4. Geertz, "Notes on a Balinese Cockfight," in Geertz, *The Interpretation of Cultures*, p. 452.

5. Rosaldo, *Culture and Truth*, p. 103.

6. See Talal Asad, "The Concept of Ritual," in Asad, *Genealogies of Religion* (Baltimore: Johns Hopkins University Press, 1993), pp. 55–79; Bell, *Ritual Theory, Ritual Practice*, especially pp. 19–29; Connerton, *How Societies Remember*; Rosaldo, *Culture and Truth*.

7. In regard to this issue of the "authenticity" as it relates to native Christians, see James Treat's introduction to *Native and Christian*.

8. Bourdieu, *Outline of a Theory of Practice*, p. 109.

9. Bourdieu elaborates on the *habitus* in several books. See Bourdieu, *The Logic of Practice*, trans. by Richard Nice (Palo Alto, Calif.: Stanford University Press, 1990 [1980]), pp. 52-65; Bourdieu, *Outline of a Theory of Practice*, pp. 78–95.

10. Bell, *Ritual Theory, Ritual Practice*, p. 79.

11. Bourdieu, *The Logic of Practice*, p. 53.

12. Ibid., p. 55.

13. Bourdieu, *Outline of a Theory of Practice*, p. 106.

14. Eric Hobsbawm and Terence Ranger, eds., *The Invention of Tradition* (Cambridge: Cambridge University Press, 1994 [1983]).

15. Hobsbawm, "Introduction: Inventing Traditions," in Hobsbawm and Ranger, *The Invention of Tradition*, p. 2.

16. Ibid.

17. James Clifton, ed., *The Invented Indian: Cultural Fictions and Government Policies* (New Brunswick, N.J.: Transaction Publishers, 1990); see also Sam Gill, *Mother Earth* (Chicago: University of Chicago Press, 1987); Fergus Bordewich, *Killing the White Man's Indian: Reinventing Native Americans at the End of the Twentieth Century* (New York: Doubleday, 1996).

18. Vine Deloria Jr., "Comfortable Fictions and the Struggle for Turf: An Essay Review of *The Invented Indian: Cultural Fictions and Government Policies*," in *Natives and Academics*, ed. Devon Mihesuah (Lincoln: University of Nebraska Press, 1998) pp. 63–83.

19. Sullivan himself says he follows the work of Kenelm Burridge in this regard. See Sullivan, *Icanchu's Drum*, p. 154 and section entitled "Eschatology," pp. 549–614. For an excellent discussion of this issue in anthropological method, see Johannes Fabian's *Time and the Other: How Anthropology Makes Its Object* (New York: Columbia University Press, 1983).

20. Erma Vizenor, Symposium Comment, "Crossing Boundaries: New Perspectives on Ojibwe Religion," Burlington, Vt., November, 1995.

21. Shkilnyk, *A Poison Stronger Than Love*.

22. Cornel West, Convocation Address, Harvard Divinity School (September 1995), Cambridge, Mass.

23. This is not unlike the case described by Robert Orsi in his study of the devotional life of twentieth-century Catholic women oriented to St. Jude, the patron saint of hopeless causes and things despaired of. The practice of telling religious stories through the devotional network by women otherwise isolated in their despair gave the women tangible leverage over their circumstances. It did "to time what religious ritual is to space. It organized the otherwise disorderly field of human experience into a coherent sequence and situated this within a broader frame of meaning opening out toward purposefulness. The hopeless moment had actually become the middle section of a larger plot rather than what it had been before, the suffocating entirety of the story." Orsi, *Thank You, St. Jude*, p. 133.

GLOSSARY

▲▲▲▲▲▲

Anishinaabe (plural: *Anishinaabeg*)	the people, humans; typically refers as an ethnonym more specifically to native people, and frequently more specifically to the Ojibwe people and other relatives of the Three Fires speaking similar languages, namely the Potawatomi and Odawa
Anami'aajig	"those who pray," Christians
Anami'aawin	"prayer," Christianity
Anishinaabe akiing	Anishinaabe land, the land to which the Anishinaabeg belong
Anishinaabedoog	"those who would be people, human," a term of formal address
bimaadiziwin	that which lives, nature, culture, the Good Life
Chippewa	Anglicization of Ojibwe, official term for Ojibwes in U.S. law
dewe'igan	drum
gashkendam	to be lonesome, grieved, afflicted, homesick, melancholy
gichi manidoo	great spirit, great mystery, great mysterious, great holy
manidoo (plural: *manidoog*)	spirit, mystery, mysterious, holy
Métis	"mixed-blood," a cultural identity, not necessarily hereditary, that emerges from fur trade and other interactions between native and European peoples. Typically, Métis were descendants of Anishinaabe women and European or European-American traders
Midewiwin	Grand Medicine Society, a ceremonial society identified with "traditional" Ojibwe religion, in which men and women are inducted into various levels of honor and sacred/herbal knowledge
miigwech	thank you

nagamowin/nagamonan   "what we sing," song, songs

ogimaa (plural: boss, leader
  ogimaag)

Ojibwe (variously: ethnonym for peoples speaking the Ojibwe language
  Ojibway, Ojibwa,
  Otchipwe)

BIBLIOGRAPHY

▲▲▲▲▲▲

ARCHIVAL RESOURCES

Boston Athenaeum, Boston, Mass. Henry Rowe Schoolcraft Collection An Indian Agent and folklorist in the 1840s and 1850s, Schoolcraft assembled a broad collection of hymnbooks, prayer books, scripture and catechetical materials translated into Ojibwe and other Algonkian languages.

Houghton Library, Harvard University, *American Board of Commissioners for Foreign Missions* This is a vast collection of journals, correspondences, and reports of this large coordinated Protestant missions effort, including documents related to Ojibwe missions at La Pointe, Leech Lake, and Fond du Lac. Grace Lee Nute identified most of the documents relevant to Ojibwe missions and stored chronologically ordered copies of these documents in the Minnesota Historical Society.

Minnesota Historical Society, St. Paul, Minn. The Historical Society has rich and well-organized collections of primary materials concerning missions among the Ojibwe, including the following:

> Grace Lee Nute Collection of Northwest Missions (twenty-one boxes) (includes 21,000 card index of documents concerning area missions)
> Protestant Episcopal Church, Diocese of Minnesota Papers (ninety-seven boxes)
> Papers of Edmund Ely
> Papers of Joseph Alexander Gilfillan
> Papers of John Johnson Enmegabowh
> Henry Benjamin Whipple Papers (forty-five boxes)

Pilling, James Constantine. *Bibliography of the Algonkian Languages* (Washington, D.C.: Government Printing Office, 1891).

Schoolcraft, Henry Rowe. *A Bibliographical Catalogue of Books, Translations of the Scriptures, and Other Publications in the Indian Tongues of the United States with Brief Critical Notices* (Washington, D.C.: C. Alexander, 1849).

PUBLISHED SOURCES

Alexiou, Margaret. *The Ritual Lament in Greek Tradition*. Cambridge: Cambridge University Press, 1974.

Anderson, Owanah. *Four Hundred Years: Anglican/Episcopal Mission among American Indians*. Cincinnati: Forward Movement Publications, 1997.

Anderson, Rufus. *Memorial Volume of the First Fifty Years of the American Board of Commissioners for Foreign Missions*. Boston: ABCFM, 1862.

Ariès, Phillippe. *The Hour of Our Death*. New York: Oxford University Press, 1981.

Baierlein, E. R. *In the Wilderness with the Red Indians: German Missionary to the Michigan Indians, 1847–1853*. Trans. Anita Z. Boldt; ed. Harold Moll. Detroit: Wayne State University Press, 1996.

Balmer, Randall. *Mine Eyes Have Seen the Glory: A Journey into the Evangelical Subculture in America*. New York: Oxford University Press, 1989.

Baraga, Friedrich. *A Dictionary of the Ojibway Language*. St. Paul: Minnesota Historical Society Press, 1992 [1878].

Barnouw, Victor. "Acculturation and Personality among the Wisconsin Chippewa." *Memoirs of the American Anthropological Association* 72. Menasha, Wisc., 1950.

Barth, Fredrick, ed. *Ethnic Groups and Boundaries*. Bergen: Universitetsforlaget, 1969.

Barthes, Roland. *Image-Music-Text*. Trans. Stephen Heath. New York: Hill and Wang, 1977.

Basso, Ellen B. *A Musical View of the Universe: Kalapalo Myth and Ritual Performance*. Philadelphia: University of Pennsylvania Press, 1985.

Basso, Keith H. *Wisdom Sits in Places: Landscape and Language among the Western Apache*. Albuquerque: University of New Mexico Press, 1996.

Battaglia, Deborah. *On the Bones of the Serpent: Person, Memory, and Mortality in Sabarl Island Society*. Chicago: University of Chicago Press, 1990.

Bauman, Richard. *Verbal Art as Performance*. Prospect Heights, Ill.: Waveland Press, 1977.

Bell, Catherine. *Ritual: Perspectives and Dimensions*. New York: Oxford University Press, 1997.

———. *Ritual Theory, Ritual Practice*. New York: Oxford University Press, 1992.

Benton-Banai, Edward. *The Mishomis Book: The Voice of the Ojibwa*. St. Paul, Minn.: Red School House, 1988.

Berg, Carol. "Climbing Learner's Hill: Benedictines at White Earth. 1878–1945." Ph.D. diss., University of Minnesota, 1983.

Bergeron, Katherine and Philip Bohlman, eds. *Disciplining Music: Musicology and Its Canons*. Chicago: University of Chicago Press, 1992.

Berkhofer, Robert, Jr. *Salvation and the Savage: An Analysis of Protestant Missions and American Indian Response 1797–1862*. Lexington: University of Kentucky Press, 1965.

———. *The White Man's Indian: Images of the Indian from Columbus to the Present*. New York: Vintage, 1978.

Bishop, Charles. *Northern Ojibwa and the Fur Trade: An Historical and Ecological Study*. Toronto: Holt, Rinehart and Winston, 1974.

Black, Mary. "Ojibwa Power Belief System," in *The Anthropology of Power*, ed. Raymond Fogelson and Richard Adams. New York: Academic Press, 1977.

Blacking, John. *Music, Culture, and Experience*. Chicago: University of Chicago Press, 1995.

Bloch, Maurice and Jonathan Parry, eds. *Death and the Regeneration of Life*. Cambridge: Cambridge University Press, 1982.

Blum, Stephen, Philip V. Bohlman, and Daniel M. Neuman. eds. *Ethnomusicology and Modern Music History*. Urbana: University of Illinois Press, 1991.

Boatman, John. *My Elders Taught Me: Aspects of Great Lakes American Indian Philosophy*. Lanham, Md.: University Press of America, 1992.

Boggs, Stephen. "Culture Change and the Personality of Ojibwa Children," *American Anthropologist* 60:47–58, 1958.

Bourdieu, Pierre. *Outline of a Theory of Practice*. Trans. Richard Nice. Cambridge: Cambridge University Press, 1987 [1972].

———. *Language and Symbolic Power*. Trans. Gino Raymond and Matthew Adamson. Cambridge: Harvard University Press, 1991.

————. *The Logic of Practice*. Trans. Richard Nice. Stanford, Calif.: Stanford University Press, 1990 [1980].

Bowden, Henry Warner. *American Indians and Christian Missions: Studies in Cultural Conflict*. Chicago: University of Chicago Press, 1981.

————. "The Oberlin Mission to the Ojibwa." In *The Evangelical Tradition in America*, ed. Leonard Sweet. Macon, Ga.: Mercer University Press, 1984.

Breck, Charles, ed. *The Life of the Reverend James Lloyd Breck, D.D., Chiefly from Letters Written by Himself*. New York: E and J. B. Young, 1883.

Briggs, Charles. *Competence in Performance: The Creativity of Tradition in Mexicano Verbal Art*. Philadelphia: University of Pennsylvania Press, 1988.

Brightman, Robert A. "Toward a History of Indian Religion: Religious Changes in Native Societies." In *New Directions in American Indian History*, ed. Colin Galloway. Norman: University of Oklahoma Press, 1987.

Broker, Ignatia. *Night Flying Woman*. St. Paul: Minnesota Historical Society Press, 1983.

Brown, Jennifer S. H. and Robert Brightman. *The Orders of the Dreamed: George Nelson on Cree and Northern Ojibwa Religion and Myth, 1823*. St. Paul: Minnesota Historical Society Press, 1988.

Brown, Jennifer S. H. and Maureen Matthews. "Fair Wind: Medicine and Consolation on the Berens River," *Journal of the Canadian Historical Association* 4:55–74, 1994.

Brown, Jennifer S. H. and Elizabeth Vibert, eds. *Reading beyond Words: Contexts for Native History*. Peterborough, Ont.: Broadview Press, 1996.

Brown, Karen McCarthy. *Mama Lola: A Vodou Priestess in Brooklyn*. Berkeley: University of California Press, 1991.

Buffalohead, Priscilla K. "Farmers, Warriors, Traders: A Fresh Look at Ojibway Women." In *The American Indian: Past and Present*, ed. Roger L. Nichols, 3rd ed. New York: Knopf, 1986.

Burton, Frederick R. *American Primitive Music with Especial Attention to the Songs of the Ojibways*. New York: Moffat, Yard, 1909.

Butler, Diana Hochstedt. *Standing against the Whirlwind: Evangelical Episcopalians in Nineteenth-Century America*. New York: Oxford University Press, 1995.

Casey Edward S. *Remembering: A Phenomenological Study*. Bloomington: Indiana University Press, 1987.

Cavanaugh, Beverley [Diamond]. "The Performance of Hymns in Eastern Woodland Indian Communities." In *Sing out the Glad News: Hymn Tunes in Canada*, ed. John Beckwith. Canadian Musical Documents 1, Toronto: Institute for Canadian Music, pp. 45–56.

————. "The Transmission of Algonkian Indian Hymns: Between Orality and Literacy." In *Musical Canada: Words and Music Honouring Helmut Kallmann*, ed. J. Beckwith and F. Hall. Toronto: University of Toronto Press, 1988.

de Certeau, Michel. *The Practice of Everyday Life*. Trans. Stephen Rendall. Berkeley: University of California Press, 1984.

Chute, Janet. *The Legacy of Shingwaukonse: A Century of Native Leadership*. Toronto: University of Toronto Press, 1998.

Clifford, James. *The Predicament of Culture*. Cambridge: Harvard University Press, 1988.

———— and George Marcus, eds. *Writing Culture: The Poetics and Politics of Ethnography*. Berkeley: University of California Press, 1986.

Coleman, Sr. Bernard. "The Religion of the Ojibwa of Northern Minnesota," *Primitive Man* 10:33–57, 1937.

Comaroff, Jean, and John Comaroff. *Of Revelation and Revolution: Christianity, Colonialism, and Consciousness in South Africa*. Chicago: University of Chicago Press, 1991.

————. *Of Revelation and Revolution: The Dialectics of Modernity on a South African Frontier*. Chicago: University of Chicago Press, 1997.

Connerton, Paul. *How Societies Remember*. Cambridge: Cambridge University Press, 1989.

Copway, George (Kah-ge-ga-gah-bowh). *The Life, Letters, and Speeches of George Copway*. New York, 1850.

Crissman, James. *Death and Dying in Central Appalachia*. Urbana: University of Illinois Press, 1994.

Danforth, Loring M. *The Death Rituals of Rural Greece*. Princeton: Princeton University Press, 1982.

Danziger, Edmund, Jr. *The Chippewas of Lake Superior*. Norman: University of Oklahoma Press, 1979.

DeMallie, Ray and Douglas Parks, eds. *Sioux Indian Religion*. Norman: University of Oklahoma Press, 1987.

Densmore, Frances. *Chippewa Customs*. St. Paul: Minnesota Historical Society Press, 1979 [1929].

———. *Chippewa Music*. Smithsonian Bureau of American Ethnology, 2 vols., Bulletins 45, 53, 1910, 1913.

———. "The Influence of Hymns on the Form of Indian Songs," *American Anthropologist* 40: 175–176, 1938.

Devens, Carol. *Countering Colonization: Native American Women and Great Lakes Missions 1630–1900*. Berkeley: University of California Press, 1992.

Dewdney, Selwyn. *The Sacred Scrolls of the Southern Ojibway*. Toronto: University of Toronto Press, 1975.

Diamond, Beverley, M. Sam Cronk, and Franziska von Rosen. *Visions of Sound: Musical Instruments of First Nations Communities in Northeastern America*. Chicago: University of Chicago Press, 1994.

Diamond Cavanaugh, Beverley. "Christian Hymns in Eastern Woodlands Communities: Performance Contexts." In *Musical Repercussions of 1492: Explorations, Encounters, and Identities*, ed. Carol E. Robertson. Washington D.C.: Smithsonian Institution, 1992, pp. 381–394.

——— "Music and Gender in the Sub-Arctic Algonkian Area." In *Women in North American Indian Music: Six Essays*, ed. R. Keeling. SEM Special Series No. 6. Bloomington, Ind.: Society for Ethnomusicology.

Dowd, Gregory. *A Spirited Resistance: The North American Struggle for Unity 1745–1815*. Baltimore: Johns Hopkins University Press, 1992.

Draper, David E. "*Abba isht tuluwa*: The Christian Hymns of the Mississippi Choctaw," *American Indian Culture and Research Journal* 6:43–61, 1982.

Ebbott, Elizabeth. *Indians in Minnesota*. 4th ed. Minneapolis: University of Minnesota Press, 1985 [1971].

Eliade, Mircea. *The Myth of the Eternal Return or Cosmos and History*. Trans. Willard Trask. Princeton: Princeton University Press, 1974 [1949].

———. *Shamanism: Archaic Techniques of Ecstasy*. Trans. Willard Trask. Princeton: Princeton University Press, 1964 [1951].

Erdrich, Louise. *Tracks*. New York: Henry Holt, 1988.

Fabian, Johannes. *Time and the Other: How Anthropology Makes Its Object*. New York: Columbia University Press, 1983.

———. *Language and Colonial Power*. Berkeley: University of California Press, 1986.

Farrell, James. *Inventing the American Way of Death 1830–1920* . Philadelphia: Temple University Press, 1980.

Feld, Steven. *Sound and Sentiment: Birds, Weeping, Poetics, and Song in Kaluli Expression*. Philadelphia: University of Pennsylvania Press, 1990.

Fernandez, James. *Bwiti: An Ethnography of the Religious Imagination in Africa*. Princeton: Princeton University Press, 1982.

Flam, Gila. *Singing for Survival: Songs of the Lodz Ghetto, 1940–1945.* Urbana: University of Illinois Press, 1992.

Foucault, Michel. *Discipline and Punish: The Birth of the Prison.* Trans. Alan Sheridan. New York: Vintage, 1979 [1975].

Geertz, Armin. *The Invention of Prophecy: Continuity and Meaning in Hopi Indian Religion.* Berkeley: University of California Press, 1994.

Geertz, Clifford. *The Interpretation of Cultures.* New York: Basic, 1973.

Giglio, Virginia. *Southern Cheyenne Women's Songs.* Norman: University of Oklahoma Press, 1995.

Gill, Sam. *Native American Religious Action: A Performative Approach to Religion.* Columbia: University of South Carolina Press, 1987.

Goffman, Erving. *The Presentation of Self in Everyday Life.* Garden City, N.Y.: Doubleday, 1959.

Goody, Jack. *The Interface between the Written and the Oral.* Cambridge: Cambridge University Press, 1987.

Grant, John Webster. *Moon of Wintertime: Missionaries and the Indians of Canada in Encounter since 1534.* Toronto: University of Toronto Press, 1984.

Griffith, R. Marie. *God's Daughters.* Berkeley: University of California Press, 1997.

Grim, John. *The Shaman: Patterns of Religious Healing among the Ojibwa Indians.* Norman: University of Oklahoma Press, 1983.

Guilbault, Jocelyne. "Fitness and Flexibility: Funeral Wakes in St. Lucia, West Indies," *Ethnomusicology.* Spring/Summer 1987, pp. 273–299.

Halbwachs, Maurice. *Les cadres sociaux de la mémoire.* Paris: Mouton 1976 [1925].

———. *On Collective Memory.* Ed. and trans. Lewis Coser. Chicago: University of Chicago Press, 1992.

———. *La topographie légendaire des évangiles en terre sainte: étude du mémoire collective.* Paris: Presses Universitaires de France, 1941.

Hallowell, A. Irving. *Culture and Experience.* Philadelphia: University of Pennsylvania Press, 1955.

———. "Ojibwa Ontology, Behavior, and World View." In *Culture in History: Essays in Honor of Paul Radin,* ed. Stanley Diamond. New York: Columbia University Press, 1960.

———. *The Ojibwa of Berens River, Manitoba: Ethnography into History.* Ed. Jennifer S. H. Brown. Fort Worth: Harcourt, Brace, Jovanovich, 1992.

Harris, Michael W. *The Rise of Gospel Blues: The Music of Thomas Andrew Dorsey in the Urban Church.* New York: Oxford University Press, 1987.

Heth, Charlotte. "Update on Indian Music: Contemporary Trends." In idem, *Sharing a Heritage.* Los Angeles: U.C.L.A. American Indian Studies Center, 1984, pp. 89–103.

Hickerson, Harold. *The Chippewa and Their Neighbors: A Study in Ethnohistory.* Revised and enlarged by Jennifer S. H. Brown and Laura Peers. Prospect Heights, Ill.: Waveland Press, 1988 [1970].

Higginson, J. Vincent. "Hymnody in the American Indian Missions." *Papers of the Hymn Society XVIII.* New York, 1954.

Hilger, M. Inez. *A Social Study of One Hundred Fifty Chippewa Indian Families of the White Earth Reservation of Minnesota.* Washington, D.C.: Catholic University of America Press, 1939.

Hobsbawm, Eric, and Terence Ranger, eds. *The Invention of Tradition.* Cambridge: Cambridge University Press, 1983.

Hoffman, Walter. *The Midéwiwin or Grand Medicine Society of the Ojibwa.* Bureau of American Ethnology Seventh Annual Report 1885–86, pp. 143-300.

Hultkrantz, Åke. *Belief and Worship in Native North America.* Ed. Christopher Vecsey. Syracuse, N.Y.: Syracuse University Press, 1981.

————. *The Religions of the American Indians*. Trans. Monica Setterwall. Berkeley: University of California Press, 1979 [1967].

Huntington, Richard and Peter Metcalf. *Celebrations of Death: The Anthropology of Mortuary Ritual*. Cambridge: Cambridge University Press, 1979.

Hutchison, William R. *Errand to the World*. Chicago: University of Chicago Press, 1987.

Hymes, Dell. *Foundations in Sociolinguistics: An Ethnographic Perspective*. Philadelphia: University of Pennsylvania Press, 1974.

Irwin, Lee. *The Dream Seekers*. Norman: University of Oklahoma Press, 1994.

Jacobs, Peter. *Journal of the Rev. Peter Jacobs, Indian Wesleyan Missionary, from Rice Lake to the Hudson's Bay Territory and Returning, Commencing May, 1852*. Toronto: Anson Green, 1853.

James, Bernard J. "Social-Psychological Dimensions of Ojibwa Acculturation," *American Anthropologist* 63:721–746, 1961.

James, C. L. R. *Beyond a Boundary*. Durham, N.C.: Duke University Press, 1983 [1963].

Johnson, Basil. *The Manitous: The Supernatural World of the Ojibway*. New York: Harper, 1995.

————. *Ojibway Ceremonies*. Lincoln: University of Nebraska Press, 1982.

————. *Ojibway Heritage*. Lincoln: University of Nebraska Press, 1976.

Jones, Peter. *History of the Ojebway Indians with Especial Reference to their Conversion to Christianity*. London: A. W. Bennett, 1861.

————. *Life and Journals of Kah-ke-wa-quo-na-by (Rev. Peter Jones), Wesleyan Missionary*. Toronto: Anson Green, 1860.

Jorgenson, Joseph. *The Sun Dance Religion: Power for the Powerless*. Chicago: University of Chicago Press, 1972.

Kalish, Richard A. and David K. Reynolds. *Death and Ethnicity: A Psychocultural Study*. Los Angeles: University of Southern California Press, 1976.

Kan, Sergei. "Memory Eternal: Orthodox Christianity and the Tlingit Mortuary Complex," *Arctic Anthropology* 24:32–55, 1987.

————. *Memory Eternal: Tlingit Culture and Russian Orthodox Christianity through Two Centuries*. Seattle: University of Washington Press, 1999.

————. *Symbolic Immortality: The Tlingit Potlatch of the Nineteenth Century*. Washington, D.C.: Smithsonian Institution Press, 1989.

Keeling, Richard. *Cry for Luck: Sacred Song and Speech among the Yurok, Hupa, and Karok Indians of Northwestern California*. Berkeley: University of California Press, 1992.

Kohl, Johann G. *Kitchi-Gami: Life among the Lake Superior Ojibway*. Trans. Lascelles Wraxall. St. Paul: Minnesota Historical Society Press, 1985 [1855].

Kugel, Rebecca. *To Be the Main Leaders of Our People: A History of Minnesota Ojibwe Politics, 1825–1898*. East Lansing: Michigan State University Press, 1998.

————. "Factional Alignment among the Minnesota Ojibwe, 1850–1880," *American Indian Culture and Research Journal* 9:23–47, 1985.

————. "Of Missionaries and Their Cattle: Ojibwa Perceptions of a Missionary as Evil Shaman," *Ethnohistory* 41:227–245, Spring 1994.

————. "Religion Mixed with Politics: The 1836 Conversion of Mang'osid of Fond du Lac," *Ethnohistory* 37:126–157, Spring 1990.

Kurath, Gertrude. "Catholic Hymns of Michigan Indians," *Anthropological Quarterly* 30:31–44, April 1957.

————. *Michigan Indian Festivals*. Ann Arbor: Ann Arbor Publishers, 1966.

Kurath, Gertrude, and Jane Ettawageshik. "Religious Customs of Modern Michigan Algonquins." Unpublished manuscript in American Philosophical Society. 1959.

————. "Songs and Dances of Great Lakes Indians" (annotated recordings). *Ethnic Folkways Library*. Album P 1003, 1956.

Landes, Ruth. *Ojibwa Religion and the Midéwiwin*. Madison: University of Wisconsin Press, 1968.

———. *Ojibwa Sociology*. New York: Columbia University Press, 1937.

———. *The Ojibwa Woman*. New York: W. W. Norton, 1971 [1938].

Lanternari, Vittorio. *The Religions of the Oppressed: A Study of Modern Messianic Cults*. Trans. Lisa Sergio. New York: Knopf, 1963 [1960].

Lévi-Strauss, Claude. *The Raw and the Cooked*. Trans. John and Doreen Weightman. Chicago: University of Chicago Press, 1969 [1964].

Marcus, George, and Michael Fischer, eds. *Anthropology as Cultural Critique*. Chicago: University of Chicago Press, 1986.

Marini, Stephen. "Rehearsal for Revival: Sacred Singing and the Great Awakening in America," *Journal of the American Academy of Religion Thematic Studies* 50:71–93, 1983.

Martin, Calvin, ed. *The American Indian and the Problem of History*. New York: Oxford University Press, 1987.

Martin, Joel. "Before and Beyond the Sioux Ghost Dance: Native American Prophetic Movements and the Study of Religion," *Journal of the American Academy of Religion* 59:677–702, 1991.

———. *Sacred Revolt: The Muskogees' Struggle for a New World*. Boston: Beacon Press, 1991.

McElwain, Thomas. "Rainbow Will Carry Me: The Language of Seneca Iroquois Christianity as Reflected in Hymns." In *Religion in Native North America*, ed. Christopher Vecsey. Moscow: University of Idaho Press, 1990, pp. 83–103.

McLoughlin, William G. *Cherokees and Missionaries 1789–1839*. New Haven: Yale University Press, 1984.

———. *Cherokees and Christianity 1794–1870: Essays on Acculturation and Cultural Persistence*. Ed. Walter Conser, Jr. Athens: University of Georgia Press, 1994.

McNally, Michael D. "Religion and Culture Change in Native North America." In *Perspectives on American Religion and Culture*, ed. Peter Williams. New York: Blackwell Press, 1999.

———. "The Uses of Hymn-Singing at White Earth, 1868–1988: Towards a History of Practice." In *Lived Religion in America*, ed. David D. Hall. Princeton: Princeton University Press, 1997.

Meyer, Melissa. *The White Earth Tragedy: Ethnicity and Dispossession at a Minnesota Anishinaabe Reservation 1889–1920*. Lincoln: University of Nebraska Press, 1994.

Mihesuah, Devon, ed. *Natives and Academics: Researching and Writing about American Indians*. Lincoln: University of Nebraska Press, 1998.

Morrison, Kenneth. "Baptism and Alliance: The Symbolic Mediations of Religious Syncretism," *Ethnohistory* 37:416–437, Fall 1990.

———. "Discourse and the Accommodation of Values: Toward a Revision of Mission History," *Journal of the American Academy of Religion* 59:365–382, Fall 1985.

———. *The Embattled Northeast: The Elusive Ideal of Alliance in Abenaki-Euroamerican Relations*. Berkeley: University of California Press, 1984.

Müller, Werner. *Die Blaue Hütte: Zum Sinnbild der Perle bei Nordamerikanishen Indianern*. Studien zur Kulturkunde 12. Wiesbaden, 1954.

———. *Die Religionen der Waldlandindianer Nordamerikas*. Berlin, 1956.

Nelson, George. *Orders of the Dreamed: George Nelson on Cree and Northern Ojibwe Religion and Myth*. Winnipeg: University of Manitoba Press, 1988 [1823].

Nelson, Richard. *Make Prayers to the Raven*. Chicago: University of Chicago Press, 1983.

Nettl, Bruno. *Blackfoot Musical Thought: Comparative Perspectives*. Kent, Oh.: Kent State University Press, 1989.

Nichols, John, and Earl Nyholm. *A Concise Dictionary of Minnesota Ojibwe*. Minneapolis: University of Minnesota Press, 1995.

————. *Ojibwewi-Ikidowinan: An Ojibwe Word Resource Book*. St. Paul: Minnesota Archeological Society, 1979.

Noley, Homer. *First White Frost: Native Americans and United Methodism*. Nashville: Abingdon Press, 1992.

Ong, Walter. *Orality and Literacy: The Technologizing of the Word*. London: Routledge, 1982.

Orsi, Robert. *The Madonna of 115th Street*. New Haven: Yale University Press, 1985.

————. *Thank You, Saint Jude: Women's Devotion to the Patron Saint of Hopeless Causes*. New Haven: Yale University Press, 1996.

Osgood, Phillips Endecott. *Straight Tongue: A Story of Henry Benjamin Whipple, First Episcopal Bishop of Minnesota*. Minneapolis: T. S. Denison, 1958.

Overholt, Thomas W. and J. Baird Callicott. *Clothed in Fur and Other Tales: An Introduction to an Ojibwa World View*. Lanham, Md.: University Press of America, 1982.

Paredes, J. Anthony, ed. *Anishinabe: Six Studies of Modern Chippewa*. Tallahassee: University Presses of Florida, 1980.

Patterson, Beverly. *The Sound of the Dove*. Urbana: University of Illinois Press, 1995.

Peelman, Achiel. *Christ Is a Native American*. Ottawa: Novalis, 1995.

Peers, Laura. *The Ojibwa of Western Canada, 1780–1870*. Winnipeg: University of Manitoba Press, 1994.

Peterson, Jacqueline, and Jennifer S. H. Brown. *The New Peoples: Being and Becoming Métis in North America*. Lincoln: University of Nebraska Press, 1985.

Pflüg, Melissa. *Ritual and Myth in Odawa Revitalization: Reclaiming a Sovereign Place*. Norman: University of Oklahoma Press, 1998.

Pitezel, John H. *The Life of Rev. Peter Marksman, An Ojibwa Missionary*. Cincinnati: Western Methodist Book Concern, 1901.

Powers, William K. *Sacred Language: The Nature of Supernatural Discourse in Lakota*. Norman: University of Oklahoma Press, 1986.

Preston, Richard J. "*Transformations musicales et culturelles chez les cris de l'est,*" *Recherches Amérindiennes au Québec* 15:19–29, 1985.

Prucha, Francis Paul. *American Indian Policy in Crisis: Christian Reformers and the Indian, 1865–1900*. Norman: University of Oklahoma Press, 1976.

Rogers, John. *Red World and White: Memories of a Chippewa Boyhood*. Norman: University of Oklahoma Press, 1974 [1957].

Rohrl, Vivian. *Change for Continuity: The People of a Thousand Lakes*. Lanham, Md.: University Press of America, 1981.

Rosaldo, Renato. *Culture and Truth: The Remaking of Social Analysis*. Boston: Beacon Press, 1989.

Rouget, Gilbert. *Music and Trance: A Theory of the Relations between Music and Possession*. Chicago: University of Chicago Press, 1985.

Routley, Eric. *Hymns and Human Life*. London: Murray, 1959.

Sahlins, Marshall. *Islands of History*. Chicago: University of Chicago Press, 1985.

Sanneh, Lamin. *Translating the Message: The Missionary Impact on Culture*. Maryknoll, N.Y.: Orbis Press, 1989.

Scarry, Elaine. *The Body in Pain: The Making and Unmaking of the World*. New York: Oxford University Press, 1985.

Schmalz, Peter S. *The Ojibwa of Southern Ontario*. Toronto: University of Toronto Press, 1991.

Schoolcraft, Henry Rowe. *Algic Researches*. 2 vols. New York: Harper's, 1839.

————. *Narrative Journal of Travels*. Ed. Mentor L. Williams. E. Lansing: Michigan State University Press, 1953.

Scott, James C. *Domination and the Arts of Resistance*. New Haven: Yale University Press, 1990.

Shelemay, Kay Kaufman. *Falasha Music, Ritual, and History.* E. Lansing: Michigan State University Press, 1989.

———. "The Musician and Transmission of Religious Tradition: The Multiple Roles of the Ethiopian *Däbtära*," *Journal of Religion in Africa* 22:242–260, 1992.

Shils, Edward. *Tradition.* Chicago: University of Chicago Press, 1981.

Shkilnyk, Anastasia M. *A Poison Stronger Than Love: The Destruction of an Ojibwa Community.* New Haven, Conn.: Yale University Press, 1985.

Slough, Rebecca J. "Let Every Tongue, by Art Refined, Mingle Its Softest Notes with Mine." In *Religious and Social Ritual: Interdisciplinary Explorations,* ed. Michael Aune and Valerie DeMarinis. Albany: State University of New York Press, 1996, pp. 175–205.

Smith, Donald B. *Sacred Feathers: The Reverend Peter Jones Kahkewaquonaby and the Mississauga Indians.* Toronto: University of Toronto Press, 1987.

Smith, Jonathan Z. *To Take Place: Toward Theory in Ritual.* Chicago: University of Chicago Press, 1987.

Smith, Theresa. *The Island of the Anishnaabeg: Thunderers and Water Monsters in the Traditional Ojibwe Life-World.* Moscow: University of Idaho Press, 1995.

Smith, Wilfred Cantwell. *The Meaning and End of Religion.* Minneapolis: Fortress Press, 1985.

Smolik, Marijan. "Slovenian Contributions to American Hymnody," *The Hymn* 36:14–15, July 1985.

Spencer, Jon Michael. *Protest and Praise: Sacred Music of Black Religion.* Minneapolis: Fortress Press, 1990.

———. *Sing a New Song: Liberating Black Hymnody.* Minneapolis: Fortress Press, 1995.

Stillman, Amy Ku'uleialoha. "Himene Tahiti: Ethnoscientific and Ethnohistorical Perspectives on Choral Singing and Protestant Hymnody in the Society Islands, French Polynesia." Ph.D. diss., Harvard University, 1991.

Steinmetz, Paul. *Bible, Pipe, and Peyote.* Syracuse, N.Y.: Syracuse University Press, 1998 [1980].

Sullivan, Lawrence. *Icanchu's Drum: An Orientation to Meaning in South American Religions.* New York: Macmillan, 1988.

Sullivan, Lawrence, ed. *Death, Afterlife, and the Soul.* New York: Macmillan, 1989.

Tamke, Susan. *Make a Joyful Noise unto the Lord: Hymns as a Reflection of Victorian Social Attitudes.* Athens: Ohio University Press, 1978.

Tanner, Helen Hornbeck. *The Ojibwas: A Critical Bibliography.* Bloomington: Indiana University Press, 1976.

Taussig, Michael. *Shamanism, Colonialism, and the Wild Man: A Study in Terror and Healing.* Chicago: University of Chicago Press, 1987.

Thwaites, Reuben, trans. and ed. *Jesuit Relations and Allied Documents: Travels and Explorations of the Jesuit Missionaries in New France 1610–1791.* Cleveland: Burrows Brothers Co., 1896–1901, 73 vols.

Tinker, George. *Missionary Conquest: The Gospel and Native American Cultural Genocide.* Minneapolis: Fortress Press, 1993.

Treat, James B., ed. *Native and Christian.* New York: Routledge, 1995.

Turino, Thomas. *Moving away from Silence.* Chicago: University of Chicago Press, 1993.

Tweed, Thomas. *Our Lady of the Exile.* New York: Oxford University Press, 1998.

Vander, Judith. *Songprints: The Musical Experience of Five Shoshone Women.* Urbana: University of Illinois Press, 1988.

Vecsey, Christopher. *Imagine Ourselves Richly: Mythic Narratives of North American Indians.* New York: Crossroad, 1988.

———. *The Paths of Kateri's Kin.* South Bend: University of Notre Dame Press, 1997.

———. *Traditional Ojibwa Religion and Its Historical Changes.* Philadelphia: American Philosophical Society, 1983.

Vennum, Thomas. "A History of Ojibwa Song Form." In *Selected Reports in Ethnomusicology* III, no. 2. Ed. Charlotte Heth. 1980, pp. 43–75.

———. *The Ojibwa Dance Drum*. Washington, D.C.: Smithsonian Institution Press, 1982.

———. "Southwestern Ojibwa Music." Ph.D. diss., Harvard University, 1975.

———. *Wild Rice and the Ojibwa People*. St. Paul: Minnesota History Society Press, 1988.

Vizenor, Gerald. *Crossbloods: Bone Courts, Bingo, and Other Reports*. Minneapolis: University of Minnesota Press, 1990 [1976].

———. *The People Named the Chippewa: Narrative Histories*. Minneapolis: University of Minnesota Press, 1984.

Warren, William Whipple. *History of the Ojibway People*. St. Paul: Minnesota Historical Society Press, 1984 [1885].

Waterman, Christopher. *Juju: A Social History and Ethnography of an African Popular Music*. Chicago: University of Chicago Press, 1990.

———. "Juju History: Toward a Theory of Sociomusical Practice." In *Ethnomusicology and Modern Music History*, ed. Stephen Blum, Philip Bohlman, and Daniel Neuman. Urbana: University of Illinois Press, 1991, pp. 49–67.

Weaver, Jace, ed. *Native American Religious Identity: Unforgotten Gods*. Maryknoll, N.Y.: Orbis, 1998.

———. *That the People Might Live: Native American Literatures and Native American Community*. New York: Oxford University Press, 1997.

Whidden, Lynn. "Ethnic Series: Cree Hymnody as Traditional Song," *The Hymn* 40:21–25, July 1989.

———. "Les hymnes, une anomalie parmi les chants traditionnels des cris du nord," *Recherches Amérindiennes au Québec* 15:29–36, 1985.

Whipple, Henry Benjamin. *Lights and Shadows of a Long Episcopate*. New York: Macmillan, 1912.

White, Richard. *The Middle Ground: Indians, Empires, and Republics in the Great Lakes Region 1650–1815*. Cambridge: Cambridge University Press, 1991.

Zanger, Martin. "Straight Tongue's Heathen Wards:' Bishop Whipple and the Episcopal Mission to the Chippewas." In *Churchmen and the Western Indians: 1820–1920*, ed. Clyde Milner and Floyd O'Neil. Norman: University of Oklahoma Press, 1985.

Zuckerkandl, Victor. *Man the Musician*. Princeton: Princeton University Press, 1973.

INDEX

▲▲▲▲▲▲